1970

GREEK MYTHS AND MESOPOTAMIA

GREEK MYTHS AND MESOPOTAMIA

Parallels and Influence in the Homeric Hymns and Hesiod

Charles Penglase

London and New York

First published 1994
by Routledge
11 New Fetter Lane, London EC4P 4EE

Simultaneously published in the USA and Canada
by Routledge
29 West 35th Street, New York, NY 10001

First published in paperback 1997

Typeset in Garamond by
Ponting–Green Publishing Services,
Chesham, Buckinghamshire
Printed and bound in Great Britain by
T.J. International Ltd, Padstow, Cornwall

British Library Cataloguing in Publication Data
Penglase, Charles
Greek Myths and Mesopotamia: Parallels and Influence
in the Homeric Hymns and Hesiod
I. Title
883.01

Library of Congress Cataloguing in Publication Data
Penglase, Charles
Greek Myths and Mesopotamia: Parallels and Influence
in the Homeric Hymns and Hesiod / Charles Penglase.
p.   cm.
Includes bibliographical references and index.
1. Mythology, Greek.   2. Mythology, Assyro-Babylonian.
3. Homeric hymns.   4. Hesiod. Theogony.   5. Hesiod.
Works and Days.
I. Title.
BL785.P46   1994
292.1'3dc20   93–14611

ISBN 0–415–08371–0 (hbk)
ISBN 0–415–15706–4 (pbk)

CONTENTS

ACKNOWLEDGEMENTS

John Donne's immortal phrase 'no man is an island, entire of itself' applies nicely to an author of an academic book, and this author is no exception. I am pleased to be able to thank here the many who have given their assistance and support over the period of composition of this book.

Thanks go first to the Australian Research Council for a three-year Large Grant and a Fellowship to enable this research to be undertaken. A debt of gratitude is also owed to the German government for a grant from the Deutscher Akademischer Austauschdienst to allow me to conduct my research in Heidelberg and Munich. I would like to express my thanks to several persons who have lent me assistance in this work and given encouragement in many different ways. Grateful thanks and appreciation are due to Dr Jeremy Black of the Oriental Institute, Oxford University, for reading much of the material, for his helpful criticism, and correction of errors in Sumerian and Akkadian, and especially for his wide-ranging and penetrating discussions. I wish to express my appreciation to Professor Walter Burkert of the Department of Classics, University of Zurich, for reading my work and offering many helpful comments, and for his support. Much gratitude is also owed to my German colleagues for their kindness and hospitality during my visits to their universities: Professors Karlheinz Deller and Hartmut Waetzoldt of the Seminar für Sprachen und Kulturen des Vorderen Orients in Heidelberg, and Professors Dietz Otto Edzard and Claus Wilcke in the Institut für Assyriologie und Hethitologie in Munich. To Dr Robert Parker of Oriel College, Oxford, Dr Robin Osborne of Corpus Christi College, Oxford, and to Mr Hugh Lindsay of the Department of Classics, University of Newcastle, Australia, who have offered their comments on the work, I wish to express my sincere gratitude. Last but far from least, I should like to thank my mother, Dr Bethia Penglase, of the Department of Community Programmes, University of Newcastle, Australia, for her help in matters of expression and scholarship, and for her unflagging support.

Charles Penglase

ABBREVIATIONS

ARV – J.D. Beazley, *Attic Red-Figure Vase Painters*, 2nd edition, volumes 1 and 2, Clarendon Press, Oxford, 1963
AV – *Ishtar's Descent to the Netherworld*
ID – *Inanna's Descent to the Netherworld*

Periods: see the following chronological chart
NS – Neo-Sumerian
OB – Old Babylonian
MB – Middle Babylonian
NB – Neo-Babylonian
LB – Late Babylonian
SB – Standard Babylonian
OA – Old Assyrian
MA – Middle Assyrian
NA – Neo-Assyrian

For the abbreviations of journal titles, see for instance, Leland G. Alkire, Jnr, ed., *Periodical Title Abbreviations: By Abbreviation*, 4th edition, Gale Research Company, Detroit, 1983.

CHRONOLOGICAL CHART

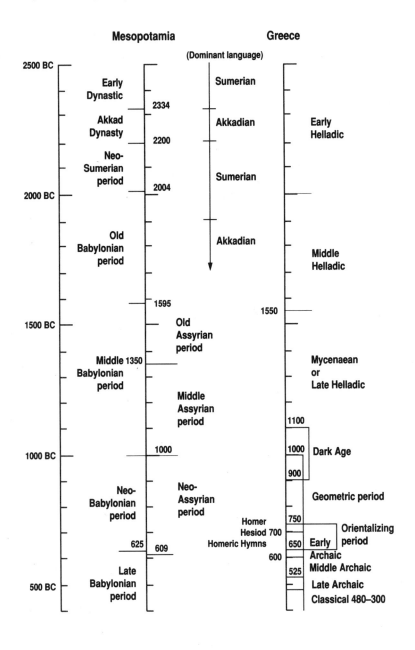

Mesopotamia

Greece

(Dominant language)

2500 BC	Early Dynastic	Sumerian
	2334	
	Akkad Dynasty	Akkadian
	2200	
	Neo-Sumerian period	Sumerian
2000 BC	2004	
	Old Babylonian period	Akkadian
	1595	
1500 BC	Old Assyrian period	1550
	Middle Babylonian period 1350	
	Middle Assyrian period	
1000 BC	1000	1100
	Neo-Babylonian period	Neo-Assyrian period
	625	609
500 BC	Late Babylonian period	

Early Helladic

Middle Helladic

Mycenaean or Late Helladic

1100
1000 — Dark Age
900

Geometric period

Homer
Hesiod 700
Homeric Hymns

750
650 — Early | Orientalizing period
600 — Archaic
525 — Middle Archaic
— Late Archaic
Classical 480–300

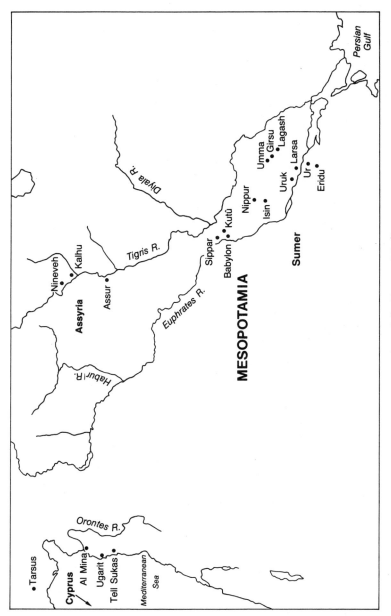

Map 1 Mesopotamia and the Eastern Mediterranean

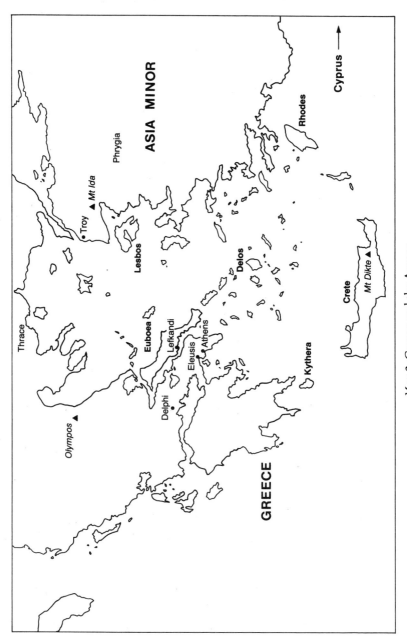

Map 2 Greece and the Aegean

1

FOUNDATIONS

Apollo strides through the halls of Olympos bending his radiant bow, and the gods spring up from their seats in alarm at the sight of the young god. His mother Leto comes forward and takes the bow and quiver from her impetuous son and hangs them on a golden peg. She bids him sit and presents him to the supreme god Zeus, his father, who offers him nectar and ambrosia.

The scene is found at the beginning of the *Homeric Hymn to Apollo*, in which it is one of the descriptions of the first arrival of the young god in the Assembly of the supreme god. The scene is typically Greek but, like the whole hymn to Apollo, it is full of motifs and ideas which are central features in Mesopotamian myths. In fact, the profound significance and purpose of these motifs and ideas in the hymn become clear only in the light of the mythology of Mesopotamia, where they are found in texts dating from the end of the third millennium BC to the middle of the first millennium BC.

The *Homeric Hymn to Apollo* is not alone. There are several other Greek myths of the early archaic period which display a similar number and range of parallels and the same awareness of the significance of the ideas underlying the activities of the gods which are presented in the myths. These ideas are of central importance to the myths analysed in this study, which, in the discussion of Greek myths, confines itself to literary works of the early archaic era or slightly later. The main works are the longer Homeric hymns, which were composed for the most part in the seventh century BC, and the poems of Hesiod, the *Theogony* and *Works and Days*, which slightly preceded the Homeric hymns. Almost all of the Mesopotamian and Greek myths analysed in this investigation of parallels and influence involve journeys, and one of the major ideas which is followed through them is the idea of the god's acquisition and demonstration of power in the journey.

Parallels between Near Eastern and Greek myths, and the question of influence have been pursued for a long time with varying degrees of success. Some Near Eastern, including Mesopotamian, origins and influence have long been generally accepted in certain areas of Greek religion and mythology. Possibly the most famous parallels with Near Eastern material are found in Hesiod's *Theogony*. Close parallels in the succession myth which forms the backbone of the plot in the work have been found with Hurrian/Hittite and Mesopotamian, specifically Babylonian, cosmological myths, and these have been discussed at length since the discovery and reconstruction of the Near Eastern texts.[1] The difficulty in the comparison in many cases is just what kind of connection is involved. Near Eastern influence is generally accepted in the case of aspects of Hesiod's *Theogony*.

1 Hans Gustav Güterbock, 'The Hittite Version of the Hurrian Kumarbi Myths: Oriental Forerunners of Hesiod', AJA 52 (1948) 123–34; W.G. Lambert and P. Walcot, 'A New Babylonian Theogony and Hesiod', *Kadmos* 4 (1965) 64–72; P. Walcot, *Hesiod and the Near East*, University of Wales Press, Cardiff, 1966, *passim*; M.L. West, ed., *Hesiod Theogony*, Clarendon Press, Oxford, 1966, pp.19ff.; G. Komoróczy, 'The Separation of Sky and Earth', AAntHung 21 (1973) 21ff.; G.S. Kirk, *The Nature of Greek Myths*, Penguin Books, Harmondsworth, 1974, pp.26–7, 116ff.; Jacqueline Duchemin, *Prométhée: Histoire du mythe, de ses origines orientales à ses incarnations modernes*, Société d'édition «Les belles lettres», Paris, 1974, pp.33ff.; Jacqueline Duchemin, 'Les mythes de la Théogonie hésiodique. Origines orientales: Essai d'interpretation', in Jean Hani, ed., *Problèmes du mythe et de son interprétation*, Actes du Colloque de Chantilly (24–25 avril 1976), Société d'édition «Les belles lettres», Paris, 1979, pp.51–67; Albert I. Baumgarten, *The Phoenician History of Philo of Byblos: A Commentary*, E.J. Brill, Leiden, 1981, pp.94–139; Henry Podbielski, 'Le mythe cosmogonique dans la *Théogonie* d'Hésiode et les rites orientaux', LEC 52 (1984) 207–16; Robert Mondi, 'The Ascension of Zeus and the Composition of Hesiod's *Theogony*', GRBS 25 (1984) 342ff.; M.L. West, 'Hesiod's Titans', JHS 105 (1985) 174–5; Gérard Naddaf, 'Hésiode, précurseur des cosmogonies grecques de type «évolutioniste»', RHR 203 (1986) 339–64; Friedrich Solmsen, 'The Two Near Eastern Sources of Hesiod', *Hermes* 117 (1989) 413–22; Robert Mondi, 'Greek Mythic Thought in the Light of the Near East', in Lowell Edmunds, ed., *Approaches to Greek Myth*, Johns Hopkins University Press, Baltimore and London, 1990, pp.151ff. and *passim*; Christoph Auffarth, *Der drohende Untergang: 'Schöpfung' in Mythos und Ritual im Alten Orient und in Griechenland am Beispiel der Odyssee und des Ezechielbuches*, Walter de Gruyter, Berlin and New York, 1991, pp.129–30.

An example of religious and perhaps even cultic influence rather than just mythological influence is found in the case of the goddess Aphrodite. The general view of classicists is that many aspects of the goddess that the Greeks worshipped in historical times appear to have come ultimately from the major Mesopotamian goddess Ishtar. Even those who look for Indo-European origins of Greek myth and religion are apt to concede that Aphrodite seems to have received aspects from the Mesopotamian goddess or her derivatives.[2]

A remarkable case of Mesopotamian influence in Hesiod's poems was pointed out by Jacqueline Duchemin in the 1970s and early 1980s. The parallels in role and function of the god Prometheus in the myth of Pandora and Prometheus with those of the god Enki in some of his myths were discussed by Duchemin and by other scholars.[3]

While the correspondences which have been discussed are striking, there are, in fact, a phenomenal number of parallels between the myth of Prometheus and Pandora and the myths of Enki which have not yet been treated. These correspondences are found especially in ideas of the creation of Pandora and of the origin and early history of mankind. The Flood story is one of the more recognizable motifs, one which has been discussed to a certain extent, and there are many more parallel ideas and motifs which all point convincingly to Mesopotamia.

Hesiod's works in which most of these parallels are found, the *Theogony* and *Works and Days*, were composed in the early archaic

2 Kirk, *The Nature of Greek Myths*, p.258; Walter Burkert, *Greek Religion*, Harvard University Press, Cambridge (Mass.), and London, 1985, pp.152ff., and *The Orientalizing Revolution: Near Eastern Influence on Greek Culture in the Early Archaic Age*, Harvard University Press, Cambridge (Mass.) and London, 1992, pp.97–9 (this book is the translation and up-date of *Die orientalisierende Epoche in der griechischen Religion und Literatur*, Carl Winter Universitätsverlag, Heidelberg, 1984); Lewis Farnell, *The Cults of the Greek States*, II, Clarendon Press, Oxford, 1896, pp.618ff.; Hans Herter, 'Die Ursprünge des Aphroditecultes', pp.61–76 in *Éléments orientaux dans la religion grecque ancienne*, Travaux du Centre d'Études Supérieures spécialisé d'histoire des religions de Strasbourg, Colloque de Strasbourg, 22–24 mai 1958, Presses Universitaires de France, Paris, 1960; Deborah D. Boedeker, *Aphrodite's Entry into Greek Epic*, Mnemosyne Supplement 32, E.J. Brill, Leiden, 1974, pp.5–6; Paul Friedrich, *The Meaning of Aphrodite*, University of Chicago Press, Chicago, 1978, pp.9–10, 22–3.

3 Jacqueline Duchemin, *Prométhée*; 'Le mythe du Déluge retrouvé dans des sources grecques?', RHR 189 (1976) 142–4; 'Le Zeus d'Eschyle et ses sources proche-orientales', RHR 197 (1980) 27–44; also her, 'Le mythe de Prométhée et ses sources orientales', REG 88 (1975) viii–ix.

period or slightly before, and there are other works of this period in which parallels with Near Eastern, especially Mesopotamian, material have been discussed. Prominent among these works is the *Iliad* of Homer, who is generally believed to have sung his epic shortly before Hesiod composed the *Theogony*. Homer is placed between 750 and 700 BC. The most notable possibilities have been stressed by Walter Burkert. One parallel is that between Okeanos and his wife Tethys and the corresponding Babylonian pair Apsu and Tiamat, respectively the fresh- and salt-water oceans.[4] Okeanos and Tethys are spoken of as the origin of the gods, or even of all (*Iliad* 14.201, 246, 302), and Apsu and Tiamat in the Babylonian cosmological epic *Enuma Elish* are certainly the origin of all, including the gods (Tablet I.1–5).[5] Another parallel is the scene in which Aphrodite is wounded by Diomedes and withdraws and complains to her parents Zeus and Dione in Olympos (*Iliad* 5.311–430) with the scene in the *Epic of Gilgamesh* in which Ishtar is insulted by Gilgamesh and goes off to her parents Anu and Antu in heaven to complain (Tablet VI.1–106). There are several correspondences in these scenes.[6]

In addition to these parallels between Greek and Mesopotamian myths, there are many other correspondences and indications of influence which have been pointed out. Some are complex and even detailed parallels, while others are mere suggestions.[7]

4 Contrast A. Kragerud, who considers them to be the upper and lower waters in *Enuma Elish*: 'The Concept of Creation in Enuma Elish', in C.J. Bleeker, S.G.F. Brandon, and M. Simon, eds, *Ex Orbe Religionum: Studia Geo Widengren*, vol. 1, E.J. Brill, Leiden, 1971, p.41.

5 Walter Burkert, 'Oriental Myth and Literature in the Iliad', in Robin Hägg, ed., *The Greek Renaissance of the Eighth Century BC: Tradition and Innovation*, Proceedings of the Second International Symposium at the Swedish Institute in Athens, 1–5 June, 1981, P. Aström, Stockholm, 1983, p.54; 'Homerstudien und Orient', in Joachim Latacz, ed., *Zweihundert Jahre Homer-Forschung: Rückblick und Ausblick*, B.G. Teubner, Stuttgart and Leipzig, 1991, p.171; Auffarth, *Der drohende Untergang*, pp.131–40.

6 Walter Burkert, *The Orientalizing Revolution*, pp.96–9.

7 See the footnotes above. Additional recent works on the subject: G.S. Kirk, 'Greek Mythology: Some New Perspectives', JHS 92 (1972) 74–85, and *The Nature of Greek Myths*, pp.254, 274; Gerald K. Gresseth, 'The Gilgamesh Epic and Homer', CJ 70/4 (1975) 1–18; Walter Burkert, 'Itinerant Diviners and Magicians: A Neglected Element in Cultural Contacts', in Hägg, ed., *The Greek Renaissance*, pp.115–19; Walter Burkert, 'Oriental and Greek Mythology: The Meeting of Parallels', in Jan Bremmer, ed., *Interpretations of Greek Mythology*, Croom Helm, London and Sydney, 1987, pp.10–40; Christopher A. Faraone, 'Hephaistos the Magician and Near Eastern Parallels for Alcinous' Watchdogs', GRBS 28 (1987) 257–80.

Difficult and hazardous are words which describe the study of Mesopotamian influence in Greek myths, and an appropriate method is essential. To establish influence, or at least the likelihood of influence, there are two main steps. First it is necessary to establish the historical possibility of influence, and then the parallels between the myths of the two areas must fulfil a sufficiently rigorous set of relevant criteria.

There are two main parts to the first step of establishing the historical possibility of influence. First, there must be connections between the two regions involved – for instance, trade and cultural connections. Cultural contact generally follows trade-routes. The second requirement is that the literary material needs to have existed in some form at the time of trade and other contacts between the two regions.

The second step of the method is to demonstrate the existence of parallels of the correct nature between the Mesopotamian and Greek literary material. Parallels must have qualities which conform to a suitable set of criteria in order to indicate influence or its likelihood.

The first concern is therefore to demonstrate the existence of contact between Mesopotamia and Greece and the periods of such contact. There were two periods when Greece was especially open to influence from the Near East, including Mesopotamia, and this existed in trade and cultural contacts. The first period was in the late Mycenaean times of the thirteenth and fourteenth centuries BC, when Greeks established settlements in cities like Tarsus and in the northwest of Syria. The second period of extensive contact is in the first millennium: according to one view, from about 800 BC onwards or, according to another, from about 850 BC onwards, when Greece was especially open to Near Eastern, including Mesopotamian, cultures. These two periods were eras of intensive contact which involved the establishment of entrepôts. Without these signs of extensive commercial activity, less intensive contact existed in the so-called Dark Ages between these periods, although it was comparatively limited. The recent finds at Lefkandi on Euboea, where Near Eastern artifacts dating from the tenth and ninth centuries BC were found, are some of the strong indications of this.[8] Before these

8 Peter Blome, 'Die dunklen Jahrhunderte – aufgehellt', in Latacz, ed., *Zweihundert Jahre Homer-Forschung*, pp.45–7, 58–60; Günter Kopcke, *Handel*, Archaeologia Homerica, Kapitel M, Vandenhoeck & Ruprecht, Göttingen, 1990, pp.90–100; Auffarth, *Der drohende Untergang*, p.142.

recent finds, scholars had already concluded, on the basis of pottery remains and other objects revealing Near Eastern origin or influence, that a certain degree of continuing contact existed between the two periods of more intensive interaction.[9] However, the most visible effects in surviving material in Greece are seen in what is called the Orientalizing period of Greek art, which lasted for about a century from approximately 750 to 650 BC. In the first millennium the Greeks returned generally to the same areas, and to others such as Tell Sukas.[10] Generally speaking, both periods of heightened level of contact with this area of the Near East were times of Assyrian power. Babylonian influence is, of course, not excluded, but the contacts with Mesopotamia in the first millennium especially may have been a result of Assyrian activity, especially the expansion to the West from the ninth century on, but in particular after the mid-eighth century with the activities of Tiglath-Pileser III. Extensive contacts therefore existed between Mesopotamia and Greece at these times, with limited contact possible in the couple of centuries preceding the re-establishment of the notable level of contact in the second half of the ninth century BC.

The second part of the method involved in establishing the historical possibility of influence concerns the literary material which needs to have been in existence at that time. The Mesopotamian works relevant to this study seem to have been extant down to at least

9 Jeffrey H. Hurwit, *The Art and Culture of Early Greece, 1100–480 BC*, Cornell University Press, Ithaca and London, 1985, pp.125ff.; Burkert, *Greek Religion*, p.52; Martin Robertson, *A History of Greek Art*, Cambridge University Press, Cambridge, 1975, p.21.

10 West, *Hesiod: Theogony*, p.28; P.J. Riis, *Sukas I*, Copenhagen, 1970, pp.127, 161–2; Dolores Hegyi, 'Die Griechen und der Alte Orient in 9. bis 6. Jahrhundert v. Chr.', in Hans-Jörg Nissen and Johannes Ringer, eds, *Mesopotamien und seine Nachbarn. Politische und kulturelle Wechselbeziehungen im alten Vorderasien vom 4. bis 1. Jahrtausend v. Chr.*, 25e Rencontre Assyriologique Internationale (1978 Berlin), Berliner Beiträge zum Vorderen Orient 1, Dietrich Reimer Verlag, Berlin, 1982, pp.531–8; Peter Walcot, *Hesiod and the Near East*, University of Wales Press, Cardiff, 1966, pp.53–4; William Culican, *The First Merchant Venturers*, Thames & Hudson, London, 1966, pp.90–4; John Boardman, *The Greeks Overseas*, Penguin Books, Harmondsworth, 1964, pp.61–9; E. Gjerstad, 'The Stratification at Al-Mina (Syria) and its Chronological Evidence', *Acta Archaeologica* 45 (1974) 107–23; J.M. Cook, *The Greeks in Ionia and the East*, Thames & Hudson, London, 1965, pp.64–5; Walter Burkert, 'Oriental and Greek Mythology: The Meeting of Parallels', in Bremmer, ed., *Interpretations of Greek Mythology*, p.13.

NA times, the latest period when they, or rather the ideas which are seen in them, could have influenced the Greek works analysed here. Regarding the Mesopotamian literature, the time of composition and the dates of the extant tablets are included, and discussed where necessary, in the chapters in which the works are analysed. Their dates and existence in the first-millennium libraries will also be discussed in the chapters in which they are relevant to the Greek myths. Tablets of most of the texts of relevance existed in Neo-Assyrian libraries at a time when contact with Greece was intensive.

The literary texts in the libraries were clearly not confined to the use of a few scribes. For instance, a version of the Gilgamesh epic was found in the remains of Hattusha, the Hittite capital. In fact, extended usage of the texts and acquaintance with the stories is indicated: scribes took copies of tablets, and taught private schools of students, who learnt the texts. In addition, no doubt worshippers in the various cults concerned would have known of the stories and myths. Indeed, one would expect extended knowledge of these stories in a form similar to those in the texts, and a thorough acquaintance with the ideas involved in them, since they are part of the basis of the belief system of Mesopotamia. The forms in which the stories and ideas were transmitted from one culture to another and the methods can be manifold. As the subject relates to Mesopotamia and Greece in the present state of knowledge, it is also speculative and is not the concern of this study since it is not essential to the discussion at hand.

The second step of the method involves the discussion of parallels in the myths, and this comprises the major part of this book. In the discussion, very careful adherence to a set of appropriate criteria for parallels and for the indication of influence, if any, is essential. It is all too easy to run eagerly after superficial parallels which cannot really be sustained under a closer scrutiny. Accordingly, the parallels must have similar ideas underlying them and, second, any suggestion of influence requires that the parallels be numerous, complex and detailed, with a similar conceptual usage and, ideally, that they should point to a specific myth or group of related myths in Mesopotamia. Finally, the parallels and their similar underlying ideas must involve central features in the material to be compared.[11] Only then, it would seem, may any claim stronger than one of mere coincidence be worthy of serious consideration. These criteria also require that literary

11 Robin Osborne, 'Orientalism in Eighth- and Seventh-Century Greece', unpublished article, Corpus Christi College, Oxford, 1990.

material be used, as literature is the only source that provides the necessary context to allow the underlying ideas behind the motifs and other features to be identified and adequately defined. In this book, a vast number of parallels emerges from the comparison of the Meso-potamian and Greek myths, and although the criteria of the method are very strict, it is only by adhering to these that any assessment of influence that is the consequence of the study can be considered reliable.

All of the myths analysed here involve journeys carried out by the gods, and the comparisons between the myths are based almost entirely on the structural composition of the journeys and the ideas which are expressed in them. One of the central ideas is the god's acquisition and demonstration of power in the journey. This 'journey for power' is one of the major purposes of the god's performance of the journey sequences, and it is pursued throughout the Meso-potamian and Greek myths. In these myths, it often forms the context in which many other ideas can be understood and defined clearly.

The idea of the journey for power must be thoroughly demon-strated in the Mesopotamian myths before the parallels between the ideas in Mesopotamian and Greek myths can be appreciated. The idea has a special place in the comparison in the Greek myths, and together with the journey sequences it forms the context for the definition of many other features. Since no study of the Meso-potamian myths has yet discussed this idea comprehensively, the analysis of the Mesopotamian myths in the two following chapters concentrates on the exposition of the journey and this accompanying idea. The other features of the myths, which also become important in the discussion of the Greek myths later, are seen in the course of the discussion of the journey and the power involved.

This comparison between the journey myths concentrates on the comparison of ideas or motifs in the journeys, not on their con-cretizations or crystallizations, which vary considerably from myth to myth. For instance, it is not the chariot and trophies of Ninurta on his return journey to Nippur that matter, but the fact that they represent the god's power in the situation and are clearly seen to be functioning with such a significance in the light of surrounding elements. Similarly, the elements of apparel which Ishtar wears in her ascent from the netherworld are not important, but the fact that they, like the chariot and trophies of Ninurta, represent power in the journey is crucial. Again, the importance of the object which Gilgamesh plucks from the bottom of the sea in the *Epic of Gilgamesh* lies in the fact that it is a food of life and another symbol of power. The fact that it is a plant and perhaps may be explained as a piece of coral is not of significance. Once again, the function of the plant as a food of life is clearly demonstrated by the context of the story. In short, it is the ideas which underlie the actions of the gods and the accompanying elements in the stories that are of concern here, for it is they that express the belief system of the peoples concerned. This is one of the keys to understanding the myths in this study.

To help to make the ideas in the exposition as clear as possible, some definitions are necessary. Myth has been defined generally as a 'traditional tale'.[12] A slight qualification is required for this study, in which myths are considered to be tales about the gods and the divine world, or tales involving this world. However, the nature of the Greek myths in this study as 'traditional' is open to question. It depends on the extent to which they were altered by the poets who composed the works in which they are found, and how old they really are. At any rate, the inclusion of the religious aspect in the definition has the purpose of emphasizing the fact that the religious element forms the core of the literary works, in which form the myths are presented, since the material analysed in this study is religious mythological literature. While the literary works may incorporate political, religious, social, historical, cultic, scientific, environmental, folktale and other elements, it is the religious element that forms their core.

The study concentrates on concepts underlying the myths and the material involved in them, and other terms reflect this preoccupation. The term 'motif' is used generally to refer to the idea underlying certain elements in the narrative: for example, the 'noise' motif. This motif lies behind such situations as that where Apollo plays his lyre as he approaches Olympos, and where Ninurta thunders like a storm as he approaches the city Nippur. The term is sometimes used to refer to the concretization of this idea in the myth, but the distinction in usage is always made clear.

The term 'idea' is generally used to refer to a complex concept, like that of the ascent sequence, which usually involves many motifs. However, it is sometimes employed to refer to an element that is otherwise described as a motif, but this occurs when it stresses that the

---

12 Kirk, *The Nature of Greek Myths*, pp.19ff., 30; Burkert, *Greek Religion*, pp.120–1, and *Structure and History in Greek Mythology and Ritual*, Sather Classical Lectures 47, University of California Press, Berkeley, 1979, pp.1ff., 23.

motif is a concept in the myth under discussion. The context makes the relevant meaning of the term clear in the exposition of the myths.

An important key to assist in unlocking the ideas in the myths is the approach which forms the basis of the analysis and is a crucial feature in this study. The ideas are isolated by simple analysis of the primary sources, the myths themselves. Use of various philosophical approaches such as anthropological, sociological, psychoanalytic, Lévi-Straussian structuralist, and so on, is avoided.[13] The intention is to stay as close as possible to the myths and, as far as possible, within them, to define the structures and their elements. It seems to be a general rule in the interpretation of a myth that after the elements have been isolated they are interpreted according to schemes imposed from outside the myth, and from other parts of the culture, or even from beyond the chronological and cultural context of the myth: that is, the elements of the myths are generally understood in terms of possible origins of the material, or of social environment, and by theoretical approaches such as those mentioned above. These have their place in the study of myths, of course, but it appears to be necessary, before leaving the myth, to go one step farther and to look at the underlying ideas of the material, to see from inside the myth what may be causing the effects – the characteristic and repeated patterns.

In other words, the purpose is to let the myths speak for themselves, as far as this is possible: to reveal the structures which reflect the abstract, or belief, system of the people concerned, rather than to impose one upon them from outside. This is at least the aim. While it may be theoretically possible, it is actually difficult, perhaps impossible, to achieve. Nevertheless, one should at least attempt to reach the goal, and in pursuit of this it seems vital to avoid the premises of philosophical theories like those above, since these theories involve modern belief systems. When a philosophical approach of this age is applied to the ancient material, the inherent belief system of a different people and a different age is automatically superimposed on the source. The effect is to rewrite the past and present it in terms which satisfy dogmas of the present day. If such a method helped to reveal the beliefs of these past societies at the same time, it would

---

13 Cf. Kirk on various philosophical approaches: *The Nature of Greek Myths*, pp.38–91, and 'Aetiology, Ritual, Charter: Three Equivocal Terms in the Study of Myths', YCS 22 (1972) 83–102, especially 101–2. Also Malcolm Heath, 'The Structural Analysis of Myth', CR 33 (1983) 68–9, on Lévi-Straussian structuralism and criteria.

possibly be acceptable. However, all it seems to do is to obscure the beliefs of the ancient peoples regarding their religions and societies, beliefs which are subtly presented in the texts and which underlie the narrative of the literary works. There is thus the ever-present danger of misrepresenting concepts which are quite explicit in the myths, and so giving a largely false impression of these ancient societies. It is crucial, therefore, to avoid interpreting the sources according to theoretical premises, and to attempt, instead, to ascertain the abstract system of the peoples concerned by means of straightforward analysis of their texts.

What is possible to achieve, and necessary, is complete objectivity, in the sense of being free of subjectivity to philosophical schema: to be able to stand outside the modern belief systems with all of their assumptions. The suitable method seems to be to analyse the material with a mind clear of preconceptions and then check the results thoroughly for residual contamination by recognizable theoretical premises and emotive responses. Of course, a person of the present era thinks differently from these ancient peoples because of his different mental and physical environment, so that he will never be able to think himself completely out of the present era into another. Total objectivity of this sort appears impossible. However, an objective approach in the terms outlined should bring one as close as it is possible to come to the desired goal. This sort of objectivity is difficult to achieve, but it does not seem to be an unreasonable requirement for this sort of study.

Another point of logic also argues for the avoidance of philosophical premises. Using a theoretical viewpoint which involves assumptions concerning the origin and nature of religion and society as the basis for an interpretation of the deities and their myths, and assuming that the results validate the initial theory, appears to me to constitute a circular argument, a circumstance eminently undesirable. Similarly, the interpretation of the sources using theoretical prior forms is also avoided. To form a theoretical premise of an original state of a literary work, or an original form of a myth, and then interpret it according to this premise, is obviously unsupported assertion. Unfortunately, reasoning of this sort is common.

In both Mesopotamia and Greece, the myths exist as literature. However, while they are of a literary nature, in the sense that they are written and exist in the form of literary works, this study does not approach the myths as literature, in the manner which occurs frequently, as principally *belles-lettres*, without regard to the essential core of a religious belief system. It is important to remember that these are works of religious mythology which express belief systems of great importance to the composers and the audiences. The ideas about the divine world and man's place in it are not literary motifs and conceits which have no other purpose than literary effect. The profound and timeless significance of the ideas discussed in this study is attested by their recurrence again and again over a period of more than two thousand years.

The analysis of the literary works begins with some of the earliest extant mythological material, Sumerian works of the Neo-Sumerian (NS) and Old Babylonian (OB) periods. The material discussed was part of the religious mythological heritage of Mesopotamia which persisted into the latter half of the first millennium BC. The Greek myths are taken from Greek sources, primarily from the Homeric hymns and Hesiod, which belong generally to the early archaic period. Pindar, Aeschylus and other authors also provide valuable material, although sources dating after the early archaic period are used only for confirmation of aspects of the earlier material. Excursions are also made where relevant into the résumés of Apollodorus' *Bibliotheca* for comparison with the material of the early archaic period. The study confines itself for the most part to the discussion of literary works because their context is required for precise analysis and definition of the ideas involved.

This study is intended for a wide range of readers, so before beginning the analysis of the myths, a brief word needs to be said about the Mesopotamian languages and the ways of writing these in transliteration, since some passages from the sources are cited below. There are two Mesopotamian languages, Sumerian and Akkadian, and they both use the cuneiform script. This is usually changed into the roman script, and the results have many idiosyncracies. The Sumerian and Akkadian languages were written with cuneiform signs, mostly on clay tablets. Cuneiform refers to the shape of the signs made by the wedge-shaped end of the reed stylus which was used to inscribe the tablets – Latin *cuneus*, 'wedge'. The signs stood for syllables and words rather than for alphabetical signs. There are often many ways of writing syllables. For instance, there are fourteen ways of writing gu.[14] The Sumerian word gu means 'ox', but the

---

14 For a thorough exposition of cuneiform script used to write Sumerian and Akkadian, see C.B.F. Walker, *Cuneiform*, British Museum Press, London, 1987.

homophone gu is 'thread', and it has a different sign. Numbers are given to the signs to differentiate them, generally according to the relative frequency of occurrence. The word gu, 'thread', is the first sign for gu and it is written without a number. The second sign is marked with an acute accent, so the second gu is written gú. The third is marked with a grave, i.e. gù; the fourth and so on have numbers, e.g. gu$_4$, which is the word meaning 'ox'. Signs can also have several values. Signs representing syllables are linked together into words by hyphens: for instance in the sentence me šu ga-mu-ra-ab-du$_7$, 'I will make the *me* perfect for you', the set of signs linked together is a finite verbal complex. Two diacritical signs which affect the pronunciation are used: the hachek above the *s* as in šu. The word is pronounced as in the English word 'shoe'. The other sign is g̃, which is pronounced like the *ng* in 'sing'. The letter *ḫ* sounds like the *ch* in 'loch'.

Sumerian is an agglutinative language, with each unit of sense, such as a noun or a verb, expressed in an unchanging syllable or poly-syllable. This may be modified by a series of prefixes or postfixes, for instance é, 'house', can become é-a-ni, 'his house'. The verb ku$_4$, meaning 'enter', can become ì-ku$_4$, 'he entered'. The verbal complex ga-mu-ra-ab-du$_7$ is the verb du$_7$, 'to be perfect' or 'to make perfect', with a series of prefixes.

The Akkadian language took over the cuneiform script used for the Sumerian language. There are historical and geographical forms or variants of the main Mesopotamian cuneiform script in different periods: for instance, the Neo-Assyrian script of the first millennium BC. Signs can signify consonant + vowel (e.g. ba), vowel + consonant (e.g. ab), consonant + vowel + consonant (e.g. tam), or logograms, such as KÙ.BABBAR, a Sumerian word which is used to write the Akkadian word *kaspum* meaning 'silver', 'money'. Logograms are always written in capitals and the other signs in lower case. The cuneiform signs are transliterated and joined by hyphens to form words, for instance, a-wi-lum, in the Old Babylonian form. This is then normalized to the Akkadian word complete with vowel lengthening where necessary: *awīlum*, 'man'. There are two dia-critical signs – the macron and the circumflex: the macron lengthen-ing the vowel as in *awīlum*; the vowel contraction, which is marked with a circumflex as in *ukân*. The contracted vowel is pronounced as a lengthened vowel. There are other marks such as the hachek above the *s*, as in *šarrum*, 'king', which signifies that the letter is pro-nounced like the *sh* in ship; the emphatic dot beneath the *t* and *s*: ṭ is conventionally pronounced like the normal *t*, and ṣ is often pronounced *ts* to distinguish it from *s*. The letter *h* is pronounced like *ch* in 'loch'.

According to convention, Akkadian is written in italics, e.g. *ana šībūt sarrātim*, and Sumerian in plain text, e.g. é-a-ni. Akkadian is a Semitic language based on the triliteral root, for instance, the root 'rkb' as in *rakābu*, 'to ride'. The writing system was designed for Sumerian, so it does not suit Akkadian well.

These are, then, the ways of writing the languages in transliteration and it is to be hoped that this brief outline suffices to give the unaccustomed some understanding of the script in the passages which are cited in the following analysis of the Sumerian and Akkadian myths.

2

INANNA

Inanna is the most expansionist-minded of all the Mesopotamian goddesses, so it is perhaps inevitable that her activities should be the first to receive attention in this study, which involves the discussion of power in Mesopotamian journey myths. Inanna is, of course, the most important goddess in the Mesopotamian pantheon and she has the greatest number of myths surviving about her of any of the goddesses. She is most famous as the love goddess, goddess of sexual procreation of humans and animals, but she also features as the great warrior goddess. In Akkadian literature, she is known as Ishtar. In Semitic times, Ishtar, the 'Great Goddess', takes over the roles and attributes of a number of other major goddesses, such as the mother–creatrix Nintu/Mami, and her name comes to be used generally to mean 'goddess'. The process of the exaltation of the goddess seems to be evident already in Sumerian literature.[1]

Better-known myths of the goddess are the Sumerian *Inanna's Descent to the Netherworld*; the Akkadian version of this; *Inanna and Enki*; *Inanna and Ebih*; and *Inanna and Shukalletuda*. There are also various myths in which she participates as a secondary character, myths such as the Sumerian *Gilgamesh, Enkidu and the Netherworld*, and later the great Akkadian work *The Epic of Gilgamesh*. A number of Sumerian hymns to the goddess survive, hymns such as nin-me-šár-ra and in-nin šà-gur₄-ra, both of which are attributed to Sargon's daughter, Enheduanna, en-priestess in the temple of the moon god

---

1 John Gardner and John Maier, *Gilgamesh: Translated from the Sîn-leqi-unninnī Version*, Alfred A. Knopf, New York, 1984, pp.20–2; J. van Dijk, *Lugal ud me-lám-bi nir-ĝál: Le récit épique et didactique des Travaux de Ninurta, du Déluge et de la Nouvelle Création*, vol. 1, E.J. Brill, Leiden, 1983, p.41.

Nanna in the Sumerian city of Ur; and there is also a number of Akkadian hymns to Ishtar. Another group of her myths which should receive a mention are those which tell of her relationship with her lover/consort, the shepherd/herdsman Dumuzi.[2]

Some of these myths involve journeys, and in these myths the goddess travels to various destinations for the purpose of obtaining power of various kinds, after which she returns with the power that she has gained. At the same time, these myths present major motifs and ideas associated with the goddess, and these will be seen in the course of the discussion of the journey and the power involved.

The most important of Inanna/Ishtar's myths for the discussion of these points are *Inanna's Descent to the Netherworld*, its Akkadian version *Ishtar's Descent to the Netherworld*, *Inanna and Enki* and a section of the hymn in-nin šà-gur₄-ra. While the myths of Inanna form the main subject of this chapter, certain liturgies of Damu are also a concern here, specifically edin-na ú-saĝ-ĝá and TRS 8. Damu is closely connected with the goddess, because he is an aspect of, or identified with, the great goddess's consort Dumuzi.[3] These liturgies present journeys which also demonstrate the idea of the 'journey for power', and which, together with other motifs and ideas found in them, will be relevant in the discussion of various Greek myths later. The stories presented in these works of Inanna and of Damu are all different, but the journeys of the gods all result in the acquisition and expression of the power which has been achieved in the journey and by the activities involved in its sequences. In the first myth to be examined, the most important myth of Inanna, the OB *Inanna's Descent to the Netherworld* (hereafter ID), the stated purpose for her

---

2 For a list of sources of Sumerian and Akkadian texts, in the original language and in translation, see Appendix II.

3 Although the cult of Damu, the 'ú-sag-cult', appears to have originally been distinct from that of Dumuzi, the two cults and their attached myths were amalgamated, perhaps in late Sumerian times, with Damu and Dumuzi, and other figures such as the goddesses Geshtinanna (Dumuzi's sister) and Ninazimu'a being identified: see, for instance, Claus Wilcke, 'Politische Opposition nach sumerischen Quellen', in *La Voix de l'opposition en Mesopotamie: Colloque organisé par l'Institut des Hautes Études de Belgique, 19 et 20 mars 1973*, Institut des Hautes Études de Belgique, Brussels, 1975, p.61. On the identification, see also Thorkild Jacobsen, *The Treasures of Darkness*, Yale University Press, New Haven and London, 1976, p.63; and S.N. Kramer, *The Sacred Marriage Rite*, Indiana University Press, Bloomington, 1969, p.159, who also points out that he is directly identified with Dumuzi in a number of his liturgies.

journey is the acquisition of power over the netherworld, and power in the upperworld as well.

INANNA'S DESCENT AND RETURN

Inanna decided to travel to the netherworld. From the 'great heaven' she set her mind to the 'great below'.[4] She abandoned heaven and earth and descended to the netherworld. Dressed in her seven me, her clothes, representing her powers, she set off, giving instructions to her minister Ninshubur on what to do if she had not returned after three days.[5]

Inanna pushed aggressively on the door of the 'palace Ganzir', the entrance to the netherworld, shouting for the doorman, Neti, to open it. She told him that she was travelling east, and then proceeded to lie about her intention of visiting the netherworld. Neti left her waiting and went down to Ereshkigal. Alarmed by Inanna's clothes and her manner of arrival, the netherworld queen issued her instructions to Neti. Descending with Inanna, he opened each of the seven doors one by one, each time taking a piece of her apparel, which he said was according to the customs of the netherworld. Inanna therefore arrived in the netherworld naked and 'subjugated', her garments having been removed and carried away.[6] In anger Ereshkigal rose from her throne, and Inanna immediately sat down on it. The Anunna gods condemned her, so she was killed and hung on a hook.

After three days and nights had passed and Inanna had not

---

4 Useful textual sources: William R. Sladek, 'Inanna's Descent to the Netherworld', Ph.D diss., University Microfilms, Ann Arbor, 1974; A.R. George, 'Observations on a Passage of "Inanna's Descent"', JCS 37/1 (1985) 109–33; see also S.N. Kramer, '"Inanna's Descent to the Netherworld" Continued and Revised', JCS 4 (1950) 199ff., and 'Revised Edition of "Inanna's Descent to the Netherworld"', JCS 5 (1951) 1ff. For another recent translation, see Thorkild Jacobsen, *The Harps that Once . . . : Sumerian Poetry in Translation*, Yale University Press, New Haven and London, 1987, pp.205–32.

5 On her clothes as powers, Sladek, 'Inanna's Descent', p.20, and Chapter 5. Ninshubur is feminine when she is the minister of Inanna, and masculine when An's minister: Gertrud Farber-Flügge, *Der Mythos 'Inanna und Enki' unter besonderer Berücksichtigung der Liste der me*, Studia Pohl Series Minor 10, Biblical Institute Press, Rome, 1973, pp.9–10.

6 There is a discrepancy in the number of garments that she actually put on (nine) and the number taken off (seven or eight), depending on the text; however, the poet views her as naked on arrival.

returned, Ninshubur proceeded to carry out her mistress's instructions. She went first to Enlil in his temple in Nippur, but the enraged god would not help; he condemned Inanna's desire for power in the upperworld and netherworld. Whoever covets the me of the netherworld, he said, 'must remain in the netherworld'. Nanna, in Ur, responded likewise. As Inanna had foretold, it was Enki, the god of wisdom, who answered her appeal. He created two special figures, the kur-gar-ra and the gala-tur-ra,[7] gave them the life-giving plant and water and instructed them on the procedure for ensuring Inanna's revival.

Descending to the netherworld, Enki's creatures sympathized with Ereshkigal, who lay naked in labour, crying out in pain. The pleased goddess offered them gifts, but they refused the offerings and asked instead for Inanna's body.

They sprinkled the water on Inanna and gave her the plant of life to eat: 'and thus Inanna rose' (line 281). As Inanna was rising from the netherworld, however, the Anunna gods seized her, declaring that no-one had ever risen from the netherworld alive, and that she must supply a substitute if she wished to leave.

A crowd of hostile and inhuman demons accompanied the rising goddess. Emerging, Inanna first met Ninshubur, who was clothed in rags and grovelling in the dust. Inanna refused to give the clamouring demons her faithful servant as her substitute. The scene was repeated with Shara at Umma and with Lulal at Badtibira. However, at the great apple tree in the plain of Kulab, Inanna found her husband Dumuzi sitting on a throne and 'clothed in a magnificent garment'. The enraged goddess gave Dumuzi to the demons. Dumuzi pleaded with his brother-in-law Utu, the sun god, to change him into a snake so that he might escape. The text, which is fragmentary here, reveals that the demons pursued and caught him. Inanna, or Ereshkigal,[8] ordained that Dumuzi must spend half of the year in the netherworld, alternating with his sister Geshtinanna. 'And thus Inanna the pure handed over Dumuzi as her substitute' (line 410). The text ends with two lines of praise to Ereshkigal.

---

7 On the nature and role of these creatures in the myth, see Sladek, 'Inanna's Descent', pp.86ff.

8 S.N. Kramer, 'Dumuzi's Annual Resurrection: An Important Correction to "Inanna's Descent"', BASOR 183 (1966) 31, considers 'with reasonable certainty' that these words are uttered by Inanna, by contrast to A. Falkenstein, who had postulated Ereshkigal as the speaker, in Or 34 (1965) 450–1.

Power is the central issue of the journey of Inanna. It is by her performance of the complete journey, the descent and return, that she acquires the power that she seeks. In the various journeys which will be analysed in the course of this study, the type of power that is gained by means of the performance of the journey and the use of it depends on the deity involved and on the purpose of the individual literary work. Here in ID, Inanna descends to extend her power to the netherworld. She already has in the upperworld certain positions of en-ship and lagar-ship, and her me, the divine powers themselves.[9] She intends to increase them, and her intention of gaining power is clearly revealed in the speech of Enlil (lines 190–4), a speech which Nanna repeats (lines 204–8). Enlil is angry at the news of Inanna's descent and her plight in the netherworld:

In his rage [Father] Enlil answered Ninshubur:
"[My daughter] craved the great heaven and she craved
  the great below as well
[Inanna] craved the great heaven and she craved the great below
  as well
The me of the netherworld are me which are not to be coveted,
  for whoever gets [them] must remain [in the netherworld].
Who having gotten to that place, [could then (realistically) want
  to come up again]?"[10]

[a-a-^{d}]en-líl-libiš-bal-a-ni ^{d}nin-šubur-ra-ke
  mu-na-ni-ib-gi$_4$-gi$_4$
[dumu-mu] an-gal al bí-in-du$_{11}$ ki-gal al bí-in-du$_{11}$
[^{d}inanna] an-gal al bí-in-du$_{11}$ ki-gal al bí-in-du$_{11}$
me-kur-ra me al nu-di-da sá bí-in-du$_{11}$-[ga-bi kur-r]e hé-eb-ús
a-ba-àm ki bi sá in-na-an-du$_{11}$ [e$_{11}$-dè] al
  mi-ni-ib-du$_{11}$

The enraged Enlil either does not intend to release her, or does not know the secret for releasing her. Enki is, however, prepared to release her and, being exceedingly clever and knowledgeable, certainly knows the method.

Inanna fails initially in her quest for power. She is killed and hung

9   Sladek, 'Inanna's Descent', pp.17–20, and Chapter 5.
10 The Sumerian and Akkadian texts used in this discussion of ID and AV are those prepared by Sladek, 'Inanna's Descent'.
11 Lines 32ff.; see lines 31a and 31b also. Sladek, 'Inanna's Descent', p.155, n.1.

on a hook. However, she had thought that this would happen and had prepared for it with her instructions to Ninshubur.[11] By means of Ninshubur's efforts and those of the two special creatures sent to her aid by Enki from the upperworld, Inanna returns to life and ascends to the upperworld, thus succeeding in her plan. This pattern of initial defeat, help asked and received from the upperworld or the place of origin, and then victory, is a common and apparently important structure in the journey to acquire power. It seems to be an essential pattern in the activities of the deity, who is confronted on arrival at the destination by a hostile figure. It is also seen, for example, in the myths of Ninurta, such as the Anzu myth and *Lugale*, and with Gilgamesh in the *Epic of Gilgamesh*.[12] It may, of course, be a narrative device to heighten the interest by increasing the difficulties of the hero of the story, and thus his achievements in overcoming them. However, in ID it appears to have more importance than serving as just a narrative device, since it forms an essential part of Inanna's descent and determines the nature of the power that she acquires.

Inanna does achieve the aim of her journey: the acquisition of netherworld powers – though at first glance she appears to fail in her quest for power in the netherworld. Failure is the impression gained when the weakened goddess dies after sitting on Ereshkigal's throne. It is, of course, the 'initial defeat' motif. Her first attempt to gain power over the netherworld via Ereshkigal's throne fails, because she has lost her upperworld powers as a result of her descent through the gates (lines 126–64); this was Ereshkigal's successful stratagem. However, Inanna has a second string to her bow. She has prepared for this situation by her instructions to Ninshubur; and from these it is clear that she never intended to stay in the netherworld, but wanted its powers: the plan was that, if she had not reappeared after a specified time, Ninshubur was to set in motion the process to free her from the netherworld (lines 31ff. and 173ff.).

Inanna's victory lies in her ascent from the Land of No Return, and it is by means of the ascent that she gains netherworld powers. As she planned, she gains the power to rise again; she overcomes the netherworld and its central power, which is to hold all who descend

12 Anzu myth: Tablet II.1–149 and Tablet III obv. i, lines 2–12; *Lugale* lines 151–297; Gilgamesh epic: Tablet V. See fragment of the Hittite recension, in James B. Pritchard, ed., *Ancient Near Eastern Texts Relating to the Old Testament*, 3rd edition, Princeton University Press, Princeton, 1969, p.83.

to it; this was the power of death which belonged to the netherworld gods. It is the ascent that is the important thing; anyone can descend. Indeed, in ascending Inanna achieved what, it appears, nobody had ever before been able to do – to rise again, alive.[13]

The claim of initiator of this descent-and-return journey, this return to life, appears to be made for her in the myth. The words of the Anunna gods indicate this role; as she began to rise (lines 286–7),

> The Anunnaki seized her (saying)
> "Who has ever risen from the Netherworld? Who has
> ever risen from the netherworld alive?"

> ^{d}a-nun-na-ke$_4$-e-ne ba-ab-ha-za-aš
> a-ba-àm lú kur-ta e$_{11}$-dè kur-ta silim-ma-ni e$_{11}$-dè

They are not prepared to give up their prerogatives easily. They manage to retain their power over Inanna to a certain extent, because they stipulate that if she wants to rise she must supply a substitute (lines 288–9).

Another work of the Inanna and Dumuzi corpus, *Dumuzi and Geshtinanna*,[14] also appears to claim for Inanna this precedent: the demons say to Inanna (lines 4ff.):

> "Come on Inanna, go on that journey which is yours alone –
> descend to the netherworld"[15]

> gá-nu ^{d}inanna kaskal-su-šè ní-ba gen-na kur-šè e$_{11}$-dè

The lines which follow refer to her descent, her loss of clothes, and Dumuzi's substitution. The ascent is understood. The text does not actually present the story of Inanna's descent, but concentrates on

---

13 Cf. Sladek, 'Inanna's Descent', p.23. Note also that Kramer suggests, in consideration of Enlil's words (190ff.), that Inanna may have intended to make herself queen of the netherworld: JCS 5 (1951) 16; cf. Sladek, 'Inanna's Descent', p.21. If this is the case, then her first attempt to gain power, consisting of her attempt to take Ereshkigal's position as queen of the netherworld, fails, while she manages to gain power through her second plan. Nevertheless, the view that Inanna seeks to acquire Ereshkigal's throne, her position of rulership of the netherworld, seems to conflict with certain other elements in the work. See Appendix I for a full discussion of this point.
14 This work may instead be part of a different version of ID: Claus Wilcke, private correspondence, 25/10/1990.
15 Translation and Sumerian text: Sladek, 'Inanna's Descent', pp.225–6, 231.

Dumuzi's capture, Geshtinanna's protecting role and her offer to substitute for Dumuzi.[16]

The descent and return, first performed by Inanna, were enshrined in perpetuity in the annual descent and return of Dumuzi and Geshtinanna. Dumuzi's return, like that of Inanna, also has its application in fertility, both in sexual reproduction and in the renewal of vegetable life.[17] Though elements of this aspect are involved in ID it is, however, not important in the work – at least it is not made explicit in the story, as it is, for instance, in the Akkadian version. To judge from the contents of the work, it is concerned rather with Inanna's acquisition of the power to descend and rise, the initiation of the process of substitution, and the perpetual process of the dying and rising – descending and returning – deity which substitution allows.

Inanna's acquisition of power over death, the power to descend and rise again with impunity, which is achieved by means of her own descent to the netherworld and subsequent rise, is seen also in *Inanna and Enki*.[18] Here she gains many of her powers by her visit to the Abzu in Eridu, but two of them are (Tablet II.v.19–20):

e_{11}-dè   Descent (to the netherworld)
e_{11}-da   Ascent (from the netherworld)

The power of the kur-gar-ra, who descends in ID to carry life to Inanna, dead in the netherworld, as well as powers of other elements seen in ID in the descent sequence, are also found in this text following the two cited above (Tablet II.v.21ff.).[19] Bendt Alster suggests that this journey may also be a symbolic descent and return.[20]

Inanna not only overcomes the netherworld, gaining the power to ascend, but she also seems to gain power in the upperworld by means

16 See Kramer, PAPS 107, 492ff., 515ff., for the text and translation. Also Sladek, 'Inanna's Descent', pp.28ff., 225.

17 Claus Wilcke considers that ID is constructed from three originally independent myths, here linked together to make Inanna's quest for power the reason for Dumuzi's death: see 'Politische Opposition nach sumerischen Quellen', pp.59ff. Whether this is the case or not, the question of origins or of the possible previous form(s) of the myth does not concern this present study, which analyses the complete work as it exists, with all its ideas and interrelations intended by the ancient author.

18 For text and translation: Farber-Flügge, *Der Mythos 'Inanna und Enki'*, pp.1ff. See below for treatment of this work.

19 ibid., pp.105–6; Sladek, 'Inanna's Descent', p.95.

20 Bendt Alster, 'On the Interpretation of the Sumerian Myth "Inanna and Enki"', ZA 64 (1975) 23.

of her journey, as Enlil's words indicate (lines 191–2). This power may be demonstrated to a certain extent in this myth in the return or ascent sequence in which she must choose a substitute to descend to the netherworld, and she has the power of life and death over those whom she encounters. This is evident when she meets Ninshubur, Shara, Lulal and Dumuzi (lines 290–349). The first three divine figures show proper respect towards her, mourning and grovelling in the dust at her feet, and she spares them. Dumuzi, however, does not show proper respect, nor does he recognize her power. Instead of being found in mourning and falling into the dust at her approach, he is dressed in beautiful clothes and seated high on a 'magnificent throne', so she consigns him to the netherworld (lines 349–58).[21]

Against the view that this scene demonstrates her power in the upperworld is the fact that she is obliged to choose a substitute in view of the presence of the accompanying demons. So if the episode is meant to suggest her power in the upperworld, the power indicated by Enlil in his speech earlier, it is not a very convincing display, even though she clearly has the power of choice. However, more may lie behind the display of Inanna's power to consign the living to the netherworld than is presented here. Elsewhere Inanna's great power over mortals on earth in both destruction and fertility, and in her omnipresence and omnipotence in human affairs, is expressed at great length. This is portrayed with especial clarity in the hymns nin-me-šár-ra and in-nin šà-gur₄-ra of Enheduanna, but it is clear in many other works as well: she is the queen of heaven and earth and possesses all the me. By the authority of An and Enlil she rules the earth and decrees the fate of all who live on it.[22]

Various symbols of power are presented in ID. The powers here are the me. Inanna's clothes represent power, for they symbolize the me (lines 14–25, 130–64).[23] *Lahar and Ashnan* (line 98) provides

---

21 In another myth which is referred to in two liturgies, e-ne-èg̃-g̃á-ni i-lu-i-lu and ù-u₈-ga-àm-du₁₁, Enlil (variant: the god's mother) is apparently made responsible for Dumuzi's death (variant: her son Damu), according to Inanna, who demands him back: Claus Wilcke, private correspondence, 25/10/1990.

22 For nin-me-šár-ra, see William W. Hallo and J.J.A. van Dijk, *The Exaltation of Inanna*, Yale University Press, New Haven and London, 1968; for in-nin šà-gur₄-ra, see Ake W. Sjöberg, 'in-nin šà-gur₄-ra: A Hymn to the Goddess Inanna by the en-Priestess Enheduanna', ZA 65 (1976) 161–253.

23 Sladek, 'Inanna's Descent', p.20; and Chapter 5.

another example of the me as clothes: me-ni ugun mu-na-ab-ak-e, 'Thanks to me (Lahar) the god Shakan is able to make multicolour work in his me', where 'me refers to nothing but the royal dress as the context shows'.[24] Inanna loses her clothes and thus her upperworld powers as she descends to the netherworld. This dressing motif involving powers is also seen when she puts on the clothes at the beginning of the work (lines 14–25). Ishtar in the Akkadian version of the work (AV) likewise loses her clothes, or powers, during her descent, and regains them during her ascent (lines 42–62, 119–25). Other symbols of power are those of the 'food' and 'water' of life, given to Inanna. They are part of the deity's return to power, at once giving her life and allowing her return, by which she overcomes the netherworld (lines 280–1).

The mythical journey which the goddess carries out to acquire power takes the form of a descent to the netherworld, to Ereshkigal's realm beneath the surface of the earth, and the subsequent return to the upperworld. In the text, however, she actually travels horizontally, that is, across the earth, on her journey to the netherworld entrance. The text states that she abandoned her various temples in a number of Sumerian cities and descended to the netherworld (lines 7–13). The itinerary of the journey, according to one manuscript (Ni 368 and CBS 9800),[25] is Uruk, Badtibira, Zabalam, Adab, Nippur, Kish and Akkad. The general direction, which is along the course of the Euphrates and connecting canals, is therefore northwestward through the cities, except for the initial movement to the east from Uruk to Badtibira. Two interpretations which have arisen from this are those of Sladek and of Buccellati. Sladek considers that Inanna is travelling via the cities to the Zagros mountains in the northeast where the ganzir, the entrance to the netherworld, was situated. That is, she travels east to the mountains after abandoning the cities, since she tells Neti at the ganzir that she is travelling east.[26] Her journey across the land to the mountains is a horizontal one, until she descends vertically through the ganzir to the netherworld.

Buccellati, on the other hand, proposes that the destination of Inanna may be Kutû, the city of the netherworld god Nergal.[27] If the

24 Alster, ZA 64 (1975) 33, n.33.
25 In other manuscripts there is some variation in the sequence and the list of names, or just in the list of names: Georgio Buccellati, 'The Descent of Inanna as a Ritual Journey to Kutha?', SMS 4/3 (1982) 3.
26 Sladek, 'Inanna's Descent', pp.61–63.
27 Buccellati, SMS 4/3 (1982) 3–7.

direction of Inanna's travel is continued beyond Akkad, which is the last city mentioned but is not the destination, this leads in the general direction of Kutû. The city is not referred to in the Sumerian version, but the Akkadian version of the myth refers explicitly to the netherworld as Kutû. When she is about to enter the netherworld, the gatekeeper says to Ishtar: 'Enter, my Lady, that Kutû may rejoice over thee' (obv. 40). Assuming that Kutû does not actually mean the netherworld here, the city would therefore function in a symbolic way as the netherworld. In this case the journey may refer to a cultic 'traditional divine journey', where the statue is carried in procession to the destination city and brought back. The description of Inanna given by Ninshubur in her plea to Enlil, Nanna and Enki also appears to refer to the breaking-up of a statue into its component parts (lines 43–47, etc.).[28] Ninshubur pleads that the gods might prevent this happening to Inanna in the netherworld. This reference to the statue may be a reference to the journey of the statue. However, as Buccellati points out, there is, of course, much more to the work than a simple enactment of the cultic procession and associated ritual. The story is essentially a narrative myth with a complex plot, and the mythical journey is that of a descent to Ereshkigal's realm.

Against Buccellati's view that Inanna's journey in the work is a traditional divine journey is the fact that there is indeed much more to the action of the myth than would be involved in a ritual procession, although the answer to this may, of course, be that the myth was used as the background to the ritual journey of conveying the statue from Uruk to Kutû and its return. However, a more definite argument against the actual destination being Kutû is that Inanna does say that she appears to be travelling east when she arrives at the ganzir (lines 81–2). As Sladek points out, an eastward journey to the mountains, with Inanna having abandoned the civilized cities, would also parallel the journey of Dumuzi to the mountains when he replaces his sister Geshtinanna in the nether-world.[29] If the mountains are indeed the destination, there may be a play on the word kur, 'netherworld' or 'mountains', in the lines which state that Inanna abandoned heaven and her temples and

28 Also A.R. George, 'Observations on a Passage of "Inanna's Descent"', JCS 37/1 (1985) 109–13.
29 W.G. Lambert, 'The Pair Lahmu-Lahamu in Cosmology', Or 54 (1985) 202.

cities in Sumer and descended to the kur (lines 4–5). These are, then, the two main interpretations of the journey. Regardless of which interpretation is followed, however, the mythical journey is the journey of the goddess to Ereshkigal's realm and her return.

In the journey to the netherworld, the places contrasted are the upperworld and the netherworld, the 'great heaven' (an-gal) and the 'great below' (ki-gal) (line 1).[30] The 'upperworld' is identified here as heaven and earth, that is, the surface of the earth (line 5):

> Inanna has abandoned heaven, abandoned earth, and is
> descending to the netherworld
>
> ^{d}inanna an mu-un-šub ki mu-un-šub kur-ra ba-e-a-e$_{11}$

While the journey across the land is a horizontal one, the journey may change into the vertical with the arrival at the ganzir. On a mythical plane the ganzir appears, for instance, in the *Epic of Gilgamesh* and in *Gilgamesh, Enkidu and the Netherworld*, where Gilgamesh's *pukku* and *mekku* fall through it down to the nether-world.[31] In the mythical journey Inanna may, therefore, descend through the ganzir to Ereshkigal's throne. While the mythical journey is the descent and return, if the actual journey referred to in the text is the 'traditional divine journey' of the statue from Uruk to Kutû, as Buccellati suggests, then it would appear that Uruk and Kutû, although on a horizontal plane, would function in the ritual symbolically as upperworld and netherworld respectively.

A comment which should be added here is that, although Inanna travels to the netherworld in this myth, the netherworld is not an essential destination in the process of making a journey to obtain power. In this myth the netherworld is central because Inanna desires to obtain power over the netherworld, and a journey to and from the place is the method by which she achieves it. In addition, the journey to the netherworld and return and the contrast between upperworld and netherworld may be generally important ideas with Inanna, if Bendt Alster's interpretation of a number of other myths where these ideas may be indicated turns out to be the case.[32]

---

30 Kramer translates an-gal as 'great above': JCS 5 (1951) 1; ki can mean either 'earth' or 'netherworld', the place inside or beneath the surface of the earth. In the expression used here, ki-gal refers to the netherworld.

31 *Epic of Gilgamesh*, Tablet XII.i.1–5. The epic repeats *Gilgamesh, Enkidu and the Netherworld*.

32 Alster, ZA 64 (1975) 30ff.

ISHTAR'S DESCENT AND RETURN

The Akkadian version of ID, *Ishtar's Descent to the Netherworld*,[33] here referred to as AV, is much shorter than ID, only a third of its length. As a result of this brevity, the function of many of the episodes and the connections between them are unclear, but most can be understood in the light of the Sumerian original. There are, however, differences in detail and emphasis. In the following résumé of AV, only the parts that are different from ID are discussed in detail.

Ishtar, the daughter of Sîn the moon god, decided to travel to Kurnugi,[34] the dark Land of No Return, whose winged or feather-clad inhabitants eat dust and mud and drink drain water. Ishtar arrived at the door of the netherworld and threatened violence if denied entrance. The doorman descended to Ereshkigal for instructions. At the news of her sister's arrival, Ereshkigal was alarmed and wondered why Ishtar was concerned with the dead, but she ordered her doorman to admit Ishtar and to treat her in accordance with the ancient sacred customs. He led Ishtar down to the netherworld, taking a piece of apparel or adornment at each of the seven gates. Ereshkigal was enraged to see Ishtar in the netherworld, and when Ishtar rushed at her without thinking, she commanded Namtar, her minister, to release sixty diseases against her.

With Ishtar in Kurnugi and presumably dead, there was no fertility, animal or human, on earth. Ishtar's minister, Papsukkal, unhappy, unwashed and clothed in mourning, 'wearily made his way to Sîn his father and wept/ His tears flowed before Ea (Enki) the king' (lines 83–4). He told of Ishtar's descent and the loss of fertility. The wise Ea then created Asushunamir, the *assinnu*, to save Ishtar, and instructed him on the way to go about it.

The seven gates were opened for Asushunamir, and Ereshkigal rejoiced at his presence. After she had sworn a great oath to the gods, he asked her for the waterskin so that he might quench his thirst. Ereshkigal was angry and cursed the *assinnu*. At her command,

33 Source of text, transliteration and translation: Sladek, 'Inanna's Descent', pp.239–62; another translation: Stephanie Dalley, *Myths from Mesopotamia*, Oxford University Press, Oxford, 1989, pp.154–62.
34 Also called here 'the abode of Irkalla' (line 4): see A. Heidel, *The Gilgamesh Epic and Old Testament Parallels*, University of Chicago Press, Chicago, 1949, pp.170–1, for a discussion of Akkadian and Sumerian names of the netherworld.

however, Namtar summoned the Anunnaku and sprinkled Ishtar with 'life-giving' water. As he ascended with her, he re-dressed her, in reverse order to the undressing of the descent.

Ereshkigal commanded him to bring her back if she did not supply a substitute for herself.[35] The story is especially difficult to follow in the last lines (127–38), where it seems to consist merely of a number of episodes with the connections between them unexplained. It seems that Ereshkigal also ordered that Dumuzi should be washed and anointed, and clothed in a red garment; he should play the flute and prostitutes should arouse his sexual desire.

The story switches to Lady Belili (here Dumuzi's sister), who was adorning herself, filling her lap with beads. When she heard of Dumuzi's death, she struck off these ornaments from her lap and her breast, and cried out that her only brother should not be taken from her. The work finishes with a reference to Dumuzi's return (lines 136–8):

> When Dumuzi rises, and when the lapis lazuli flute and
>   carnelian ring rise with him
> When male and female mourners rise with him
> Then let the dead come up and smell the incense.[36]

ina ūmē ^{d}Dumuzi ellânni malīl ^{na4}uqnê šemīr sāmti ittīšu ellânni ittīšu ellânni bākûtu u bākâtu mītûtu lilûnimma qutrin⟨na⟩ liṣṣinū

It can be seen that the story generally follows that of ID, and the same journey to acquire power is involved here. There is also the same emphasis on the irreversible nature of the journey to the netherworld, a feature which Inanna/Ishtar overcomes. Nevertheless, there is a number of differences between the two versions in the material used, and thus in the presentation of the ideas analysed here.

An obvious textual difference is that of AV's omission of the details of Inanna's preparations – the dressing, and the discussion with her messenger. These activities appear to be understood, however, and the working-out of the ideas is not really affected. One difference which has relevance here lies in the 'initial defeat' sequence: only one helper descends from the upperworld to aid Inanna. As with the

---

35 Namtar functions here in a role which parallels that of the gallu in ID. Namtar is sometimes portrayed as a demon: Sladek, 'Inanna's Descent', p.43 n.1.
36 Translation and Akkadian text: ibid., pp.250, 262.

helpers in ID, the creature Asushunamir appears to be sexually abnormal, a feature which seems to make him attractive to the queen of the netherworld.[37] Instead of asking for the goddess's body, as do the kur-gar-ra and gala-tur-ra in ID, Asushunamir makes a request for the 'waterskin' (*halziqqu*) to drink from (lines 98–9). There are different views on just what he is asking for. The usual one is that the waterskin contains the water of life (*mê balāti*) with which Ishtar is to be revived (line 114).[38] The view that Sladek puts forward here is that the waterskin represents the corpse of Ishtar. This would, of course, follow the story of ID, where the helpers ask for Inanna's body. For a parallel motif, Sladek cites the myth of *Inanna and Bilulu*, in which Inanna turns Bilulu (Akk. Belili) into a waterskin for travellers in the desert.[39] Against this, perhaps, is that the name Bilulu appears to be associated with rivers and watercourses, and Bilulu is not, therefore, seen as just a dead body.[40] Asushunamir also wants to drink from the waterskin, which makes one wonder whether it can refer to Ishtar's body. However, this view, that Asushunamir is referring to Ishtar's body, may explain why Namtar rather than Asushunamir sprinkles Ishtar with the water of life.[41]

In ID, the water of life is brought down to the netherworld by the gala-tur-ra, but in AV no mention is made of Asushunamir carrying it down. He may nevertheless have done so, the action merely being another of the details omitted in AV, since water does not seem to exist in the netherworld. The inhabitants receive it in libations from those living on earth. However, despite the questions surrounding it, the water of life has the same function as in ID: the water revives the

---

37 Asushanamir is an *assinnu* (line 92), either a male prostitute or a homosexual. Sladek discusses the *assinnu*, kur-gar-ra, gala-tur-ra and *kulu'u* in Chapter 6, pp.96ff.

38 Cf. Heidel, *The Gilgamesh Epic*, p.126 n.79.

39 Th. Jacobsen, 'Inanna and Bilulu', JNES 12 (1953) 176, lines 110, 121.

40 Thorkild Jacobsen, 'The Myth of Inanna and Bilulu', in William L. Moran, ed., *Toward the Image of Tammuz and Other Essays in Mesopotamian History and Culture, Thorkild Jacobsen*, Harvard University Press, Cambridge (Mass.), 1970, pp.57ff.; Samuel Noah Kramer, *The Sumerians*, University of Chicago Press, Chicago, 1963, p.173: Enbilulu as the 'canal inspector'; similarly, Hermann Behrens, *Enlil und Ninlil. Ein sumerischer Mythos aus Nippur*, Studia Pohl Series Maior 8, Biblical Institute Press, Rome, 1978, p.199.

41 On this inconsistency with ID, see Sladek, 'Innana's Descent', p.41 n.4; and p.41.

goddess and precipitates her ascent.[42] As in ID, it is by means of the helper's descent, bringing aid from the upperworld, that the goddess overcomes the Land of No Return.

The substitution of Dumuzi for the goddess and his annual descent and return are referred to here, in the last lines (127–38). These rather obscure lines may be understood in the light of the events of ID. This last section may be referring to ritual; AV has 'an unmistakable cultic character', perhaps functioning as the ἱερὸς λόγος of a Dumuzi festival.[43] This may be the reason for the emphasis in AV on the dead, those lost to their loved ones above in the world of life, and on their plight: AV also ends with what appears to be a reference to a rise of some nature by the dead (lines 136–8).

Fertility is an important aspect of Ishtar's descent and return in AV. Her descent to Kurnugi results in a dearth of fertility in the upperworld and this serves as Papsukkal's argument to persuade the upperworld gods to aid his mistress (lines 81–90). Sexual fertility aspects are found throughout the work, which is understandable in view of Ishtar's role as goddess of procreation.[44] Presumably fertility returns to the earth with Ishtar's ascent, in the same way as Dumuzi's return from the netherworld to the earth in spring results in fertility of the flocks. 'Sacred marriage' with the goddess is usually a result of the return in this case.[45] This marriage is not seen in Inanna's

---

42 Other omissions from AV are the plant of life and the second helper.

43 Sladek, 'Inanna's Descent', pp.43–5, 50. This interpretation is hypothetical, however.

44 Sexual aspects in lines 34–5, 77–8, 87–90; the *assinnu*, line 92; the cowrie shells, line 116, which appear to have a sexual connotation: Sladek, 'Inanna's Descent', p.42 n.4. Also with Belili, the beads on her breast and in her lap: p.47 n.3.

45 Indicated in Damu texts: see Thorkild Jacobsen, 'Religious Drama in Ancient Mesopotamia', in Hans Goedicke and J.J.M. Roberts, eds, *Unity and Diversity: Essays in the History, Literature, and Religion of the Ancient Near East*, Johns Hopkins University Press, Baltimore, 1975, pp.90–1. The young god returns perhaps in the spring or new year, to couple with the goddess, and the result is life and fertility for the earth, prosperity for the city: Hartmut Schmökel, *Sumer et la civilisation sumérienne*, Payot, Paris, 1964, pp.130ff. Schmökel also points out the importance of the sacred marriage in Sumerian religion. For the sacred marriage and relevant Sumerian texts, see S.N. Kramer, *The Sacred Marriage Rite*; Jacobsen, in *The Treasures of Darkness*, pp.32ff. Bendt Alster has recently made a study of these texts and discusses the content and purpose in regard to the rite and other applications: 'Sumerian Love Songs', RA 79 (1985) 127–59.

encounter with Dumuzi at the great apple tree on her return in ID
(lines 347–8), probably because of the purpose of the work and
Inanna's angry, destructive aspect there. In other contexts, this
encounter of god and goddess under the apple tree can have the
opposite effect, that of fertility. This situation is presented in another
text where Dumuzi and Inanna couple at the apple tree, and
agricultural fertility results: the goddess gives birth to vegetables
and grain.[46]

The 'dressing' motif involving the deity's power appears to be
important in AV. While the Akkadian version tells the story of ID
briefly, the entire undressing scene is preserved, and a re-dressing
scene added (lines 119–25). When Ishtar re-ascends, she puts on her
clothes again, symbolizing her return to power. The order in which
she dons them is the reverse of the order shown in the descent. This
re-dressing scene is omitted in ID, but the resumption of her
garments must have been understood, as she could scarcely return
naked to terrify the gods of the Sumerian cities. The omission in ID
may result from the fact that the ascent sequence concentrates, rather,
on the terrifying aspects of her return, accompanied by demons.

THE LITURGIES OF DAMU

Another journey whose purpose is the power of the god, this time the
power to fulfil his divine functions, is manifest in the liturgies of the
god Damu, a 'dying and returning' deity. Damu, whose specific
function is the fertility of vegetation, is identified with, or is an aspect
of, Dumuzi.[47] He is also identified with a number of other gods,
among whom are Ningishzida and Ishtaran.[48] The story of the death
and return of Damu entails lament for the dead god, the search for
him over the earth and as far as the netherworld by mother or sister
(or mother and sister together, depending on the source), and finally,
his return to the world above and to the city.

Damu's story is told in a number of liturgies. There are, however,

---

46 S.N. Kramer, *From the Poetry of Sumer*, University of California Press,
    Berkeley, 1979, pp.93–4. In SRT 31, Dumuzi and Inanna likewise copulate
    in the apple garden: Alster, RA 79 (1985) 146; the unhappy fate of
    Dumuzi results: p.145.

47 Jacobsen, *The Treasures of Darkness*, p.63; Kramer points out that he is
    directly identified with Dumuzi in a number of his liturgies: *The Sacred
    Marriage Rite*, p.159.

48 Jacobsen, 'Religious Drama', p.91; see TCL XV 8: 121–4.

two main ones: edin-na ú-saḡ-ḡá, 'In the Desert in the Early Grass', which tells of his death, and TRS 8, which speaks of his death and subsequent rise.[49] Other works present versions of his descent, and in these, too, his mother and his sister or sisters participate.[50]

The main liturgy is edin-na ú-saḡ-ḡá, and this is actually a composition of a number of texts put together from many and various sources from the corpus of mythical material about the dying god Dumuzi/Damu and related gods. The liturgy survives in a fragmentary state in OB and NA tablets and it is clear that it had a long history in which it changed considerably, this making the task of re-establishing the text and narrative quite difficult. An example of this is the apparent re-interpretation of one part of the text which in the OB form seems to have dealt with the mother's descent to recover her son, while in the NA material this text has been used to present the descent of Damu to the netherworld. Adding to the complications is the element of compilation, which is apparent from the very beginning: the introduction presents a lament of Inanna for her husband Dumuzi, but the tale which follows deals with Damu and his mother Duttur, with one section about Gunura, Damu's sister. At the end, the sister who joins Damu in the netherworld is named as Mother Geshtin, which seems to be a reference to Geshtinanna, who is specifically Dumuzi's sister. As Alster points out, it is very difficult to arrange the sections in sequence; in fact it is much easier to treat some of the bilingual versions as separate or independent compositions, rather than as duplicates.[51]

The story is based on the mother's search for her lost son and his

49 See also Claus Wilcke for the rise of the god, 'König Šulgis Himmelfahrt', in *Festschrift László Vajda*, Münchner Beiträge zur Völkerkunde, Band 1, Hirmer Verlag, Munich, 1988, pp.246–8. For edin-na ú-saḡ-ḡá: Jacobsen, *The Harps that Once*, pp.56–84, *The Treasures of Darkness*, pp.63ff., 247 nn.40–9, 'Religious Drama', pp.85ff.; Bendt Alster, 'Edin-na ú-sag-gá: Reconstruction, History, and Interpretation of a Sumerian Cultic Lament', in Karl Hecker and Walter Sommerfeld, eds, *Keilschriftliche Literaturen. Ausgewählte Vorträge der XXXII. Rencontre Assyriologique Internationale*, Münster, 8.–12.7.1985, Dietrich Reimer Verlag, Berlin, 1986, pp.19–31; for TRS 8 and its duplicate versions, CT XV pls 26, 27, 30: Jacobsen, *The Treasures of Darkness*, pp.68ff., 247, and 'Religious Drama', pp.90–3.
50 Kramer, *The Sacred Marriage Rite*, p.159. See Jacobsen, *The Treasures of Darkness*, p.67, for one text; for another, CT XV 20–4: see Jacobsen, 'Religious Drama', p.87; and 'Ningizzida and Ninazimu'a'.
51 Alster, 'Edin-na ú-sag-gá', p.26.

recovery from the netherworld and this is built up of many sections, sometimes confusing in their sequence and juxtaposition. Major sections are Inanna's lament, Duttur's lament and search, the young god's journey to the netherworld, the mother's preparation of food and beer, a list of various local incarnations of the god, the section about Gunura, Damu's sister, the mother's determination to go to the netherworld, and the meeting of Damu/Dumuzi and his sister in the netherworld. The presentation of this liturgy follows that of Jacobsen in *The Harps that Once . . .*, with reference to the recent work of Alster, and it is a compilation of the OB and NA tablets.[52]

The text begins with a lament of Inanna for her husband Dumuzi (Damu, Ningishzida, etc.), who has died (lines 12–15):

> The shepherd, Lord Dumuzi, bridegroom of Inanna,
> lord of Arali, lord of 'the shepherd's hill',
> my tamarisk, that drinks not water in the orchard bed,
> the crown of which forms not leafage in the desert.

At the probable beginning of the OB version, the mother goddess, presumably Duttur, weeps for her lost son, her child. Then begins the mother's search in a series of sections in which she vainly seeks to find her child who has been seized. There are various views put forward in the text as to the way in which the young god died. During the goddess's laments which follow, her dead son continually cuts in, trying to dissuade his mother from following, although it is clear that she cannot hear him or does not recognize his voice. He cries that she cannot eat the food which he eats or drink the water, and that he will not be released. In the OB version, the goddess is prepared to descend to the netherworld and sets off in the dying daylight towards the mountains, symbolic of the realm of death (lines 177–80):

> 'If it be required, you lad, let me walk with you,
>   the road of no return.
> Alas, the lad! The lad, my Damu!'
> She goes, she goes toward the breast of the mountains,
> the day waning, the day waning,
>   toward the mountains, still bright.

Since Dumuzi's spirit is like a wind blowing, how can she follow him? Again Damu cries that she should not follow him.

52 Jacobsen, *The Harps that Once*, pp.56–84; Alster, 'Edin-na ú-sag-gá'. The translations used here are by Jacobsen.

At this point the OB text tells of the dead god's meeting with other spirits on the road. He wishes to send a message home to his mother, but they are ghosts and cannot oblige.

Returning to the theme of the mother's search: the mother goddess prepares a meal and brews beer, calling the young god to come and eat and drink. The beer seems to have been considered to have magic reviving properties for the god. Dumuzi wails at this point that he is dead: he has become a ghost and cannot respond to his mother's calling (lines 252–3):

> I am not the one who can answer my mother
> listening in Guedinna (a locality between
> Girsu and Umma)
> my mother who is calling to me in the desert.

A list follows of the god's different incarnations, as various local dying gods, who have been ritually laid to rest in their tombs.

The goddess seems to come to the place where her son was killed and finds his blood (or it may be some vegetable symbolic of his blood). She is encouraged to dig it up, dice it and use it to brew beer which will cheer and warm her dead son. At this point, Damu complains of the unjustness of his fate since he was no enemy.

Following this, a dialogue occurs between brother and sister concerning his loss to the household and its consequent ruin. The sister seems to have joined in the search for the lost son. A section then follows in which the goddess reiterates that she will join her lost child in the netherworld, but the results of this resolution are unclear since the end of this OB section is fragmentary.

The text starts again with a lament by the mother. Finally, at the end of the OB version (SK 27 v 7–16), Damu/Dumuzi greets his sister, who has joined him in the netherworld. She must be sister and mother to him, and he addresses her as Mother Geshtin (ama-^dgeštin), a name which seems to apply specifically to Dumuzi's sister, Geshtinanna. She says:

> Who is your sister? I, I am your sister!
> Who is your mother? I, I am your mother!

The text ends on an optimistic note with her prophesying:

> The day that dawns for you, will also dawn for me,
> The day you see, I shall also see.

The other major composition, TRS 8, and duplicates, presents the god's return.[53] This begins with a lament for Damu, expressing the fear that he will not return to Uruk, with the dire consequences of no flood water, no agricultural fertility or resulting prosperity. His mother sets out in search of him. She adorns her body, dresses in fine linen, puts on her splendid headdress, and then travels to the nurse, a tree, with whom she has left her child. The goddess asks for her child,[54] saying that he sleeps in her core, or in her bark, but finds that he has descended to the netherworld. (Sleep is a symbol of death in these myths of Damu/Dumuzi.)[55] The mother speaks again of her preparations of adornment for the arrival of Damu, and in these lines she identifies herself variously as a cypress tree, a cedar tree of the Hashur mountains, and the black wood of Dilmun.[56] She has adorned herself, she says:

> (To please) him who sails the high waters, the flood . . .
> to please him who comes out of the river,
> I, to please the child who comes out of the river.[57]

She speaks of Damu's lying sleeping in the 'treacherous sleep'. He also lies asleep in the rushes, the grass, the poplar and the tamarisk. The god returns sailing on the flood; but he is also spoken of as coming 'out of the river'.

The text continues with rejoicing in his return.[58] The 'wild bull' Damu is praised under the names given him above, but also as the son of Urash and Enki.[59] The god is accompanied in procession to his

---

53 Jacobsen, *The Treasures of Darkness*, pp.68–71; and above for sources.
54 The child also receives various names here, those of Ningishzida, Ususu, and Igishuba: cf. Jacobsen, 'Religious Drama', p.91.
55 See Jacobsen, 'Inanna and Bilulu', JNES 12 (1953) pp.102–3, lines 1ff., in Moran, *Toward the Image*, where after death the 'wild bull' or 'shepherd' Dumuzi sleeps; Damu, likewise, in SK iv 1ff.
56 The sacred cedar of Eanna, the temple of Inanna in Uruk, was not only considered to mark the god's birthplace, but was also considered to be his mother: Jacobsen, *The Treasures of Darkness*, p.72.
57 ibid., p.69; also Jacobsen, 'Religious Drama', p.91.
58 TCL XV 8: 146–87
59 Kramer, *The Sacred Marriage Rite*, p.159. The god is given various parentages, such as that of Dumuzi, with Sirtur his mother, and Geshtinanna as his sister; or he is the son of Ninisinna and the brother of Gunura of Isin. Identical with this pattern of Damu/Dumuzi, the pattern of mother, sister and dying god, is that of the dying god Lil: his mother is Ninhursag, his sister Egime. The name líl is a Sumerian word meaning 'wind', which is found as a feature of some of Damu's myths. See ibid., pp.159–60, for the liturgy and comments; see also Henri Frankfort,

father. He also receives the names of a series of kings of the Third Dynasty of Ur and the kings of the Dynasty of Isin. The composition ends with reference to Damu's provision of food, and the gifts of prosperity which his return has brought to the land and to the city.

These texts present many motifs and ideas about the god which will be important later in the discussion of parallels in the Greek myths. For the moment, however, it will suffice to confine the discussion to the theme of power in the journey, which is an idea present in these myths of Damu, and also to examine various features which are integral to this journey. The purpose of Damu's descent and return journey is the power to fulfil his divine functions, to provide fertility and prosperity for the city. The purpose of the journey is not stated in the texts as it is, for instance, in ID, as Damu is carried off to the netherworld either against his will or at least without his having any intention of descending. The effect of the god's descent and return in the texts is, however, the fertility and rejuvenation of the vegetable kingdom and of the forest, watercourses and marshes,[60] in the same fashion as human and animal fertility returns with Ishtar's ascent in AV. By his journey Damu gains the power to carry out his divine functions: with his return come life and prosperity.

As in Inanna/Ishtar's journey, Damu's journey is a descent to the netherworld and return. The destination is Ereshkigal's realm beneath the earth, and the same conditions of that realm as shown, for instance, in ID and AV appear to be understood.[61] The netherworld also appears, however, to be represented as kur, 'the mountains'.[62]

The structure of initial defeat and return, with the help descending from the upperworld to give the deity success over the netherworld, is seen in the texts. Damu dies and is carried off to the netherworld by various means (by the demons, by the wind, by boat down the river, or by walking to the mountains accompanying the other ghosts of the

Kingship and the Gods, University of Chicago Press, Chicago, 1948, pp.321–2.

60 Jacobsen, The Treasures of Darkness, pp.68–9 in the texts cited.
61 See also the myth Gilgamesh, Enkidu, and the Netherworld; and S.N. Kramer, 'The Death of Ur-Nammu and his Descent to the Netherworld', JCS 21 (1967) 104ff.
62 See Jacobsen's comments in 'Religious Drama', p.86. See also Moran, Toward the Image, pp.102–3.

dead).[63] In edin-na ú-saĝ-ĝá his death, with his inability to rise when his mother calls him, constitutes his first defeat. His mother cries out for him, but he is unable to answer or rise. After wailing that he is a ghost, he cries that he cannot respond to his mother calling in the desert (SK 26 iv 15–19):

> She will not be answered
> I am not the grass,
> > will not grow up for her again,
> I am not the waters,
> > will not rise for her again
> I am not the grass
> > sprouting in the desert,
> I am not the new grass
> > growing up in the desert!

Claus Wilcke translates the last two lines differently:

> Bist du kein Gras? Wachse in der Steppe!
> Bist du kein Kraut? Wachse überall in der Steppe!

> ú nu-me-en eden-na [m]ú-e
> ú-šim nu-me-en eden-na mú-mú-e

According to this interesting translation, these lines would then seem to refer to the young god's return.[64] However, the impact of the section is the same regarding the god's entrapment in the netherworld at this stage, since he will not return at his mother's call. Instead the goddess, be it mother, sister or both, must descend to the netherworld in search of him before he is able to rise again, his rise perhaps being revealed to the mortal world in ways alluded to. The suggestion in SK 27 v 7–16, where Geshtinanna joins Dumuzi, seems to be her substitution for her dead brother. The last two lines, in which she prophesies of her own experience of the dawn and day that he will see, appear to be referring to the story of the alternative residence of Geshtinanna and Dumuzi in the netherworld, the annual substitutionary cycle established at the end of ID, each god spending six months of each year in the netherworld (lines 407–9). Thus, in edinna ú-saĝ-ĝá, the goddesses, mother and/or sister act as 'helpers' or

---

63 Cf. the statue of Dumuzi carried to the mountains in the east, a cultic re-enactment of Dumuzi's substitution for Geshtinanna: Sladek, 'Inanna's Descent', p.62 and n.4.

64 See Wilcke, 'König Šulgis Himmelfahrt', pp.248–9 n. 26.

substitutes, and in this role they perform a wandering journey over the earth in search of Damu, with an eventual arrival, of one at least, in the netherworld.

TRS 8 and duplicates present the return of the god. His return takes several forms in this text: he appears to return in the vegetation; and this seems to involve the idea of rebirth:[65]

> That child they (the rushes, grass, poplars and tamarisk)
>   have released into the high desert
> released him into the high desert and the low desert
> the desert kept watch over him at the place
>   . . . like a cowherd.

He also returns sailing on the high flood. In the ninth song of TRS 8, the king Ur-nammu, the first king of the Third Dynasty of Ur, and the later rulers in the list function as Damu, sailing on the river to the city.[66] However, in another form of his emergence Damu 'comes out of the river', here apparently symbolic of the netherworld, in his ascent sequence.[67]

THE 'GODDESS AND CONSORT' STRAND

The myths of Damu, and of Inanna and Dumuzi, appear to typify a group of myths in the Sumerian corpus which for convenience may be termed the goddess-and-consort strand. In his article 'Religious Drama in Ancient Mesopotamia', Jacobsen also points out this group of myths, which he entitles 'fertility drama'.[68] A characteristic feature of the myths is that they appear to be concerned with family or personal matters – love, marriage, family relationships such as sister–brother, husband–wife or mother–child, lovers – rather than with, for instance, the feats of the warrior and court scenes, as in the myths of Ninurta. In addition the orientation appears to be towards the female, who plays a central role in the action of the myth, and in some even appears as the dominant figure, as in ID and in the Damu

---

65 CT XXV 27: 43–6: Jacobsen, *The Treasures of Darkness*, p.70; cf. Jacobsen, 'Religious Drama', p.92.

66 Inanna and the Sumerian kings, playing the role of Dumuzi, in the sacred marriage: Kramer, *The Sumerians*, pp.45, 140–1; and Heimpel, JCS 33 (1981) 104; Frankfort, *Kingship and the Gods*, pp.224, 295–9.

67 Jacobsen, *The Treasures of Darkness*, pp.69ff.; also Helmer Ringgren, *Religions of the Ancient Near East*, SPCK, London, 1973, p.13.

68 Jacobsen, 'Religious Drama', pp.65ff.

myths. In many of the myths the male consort, that is, consort generally in the role of husband, lover, brother or son, tends to suffer death or disaster in some form. In some myths the male suffers directly in the relationship. In Dumuzi's case, he suffers at the hands of the angry Inanna as she emerges from the netherworld in ID. In another myth which is referred to in two liturgies, e-ne-èĝ-ĝá-ni i-lu-i-lu and ù-u$_8$ ga-àm-du$_{11}$, Enlil is apparently made responsible for Dumuzi's death, according to Inanna, who demands her husband back, Enlil acquiescing.[69] In the *Epic of Gilgamesh* the goddess is again responsible for Dumuzi's downfall (Tablet VI.46–50).

Damu dies and descends to the netherworld, and in this case the goddess performs the helper role, descending to release him. In these myths, her descent usually takes the form of, or starts with, a wandering journey over the earth. Parallel to her role in the Damu myths is that of Geshtinanna, who performs as substitute for Dumuzi and descends to set him free.

Other gods function in this strand, gods such as Ningishzida and Ishtaran, who are identified with Damu in the myths above; with his mother Ninhursag and sister Egime, the god Lil is a parallel to Damu/Dumuzi; the sun god Utu with Inanna, another sister and brother pair, perform together in this strand, too, as the myth of their journey to the mountain together for the purpose of fertility demonstrates.[70] Similar structures and roles in the sequences are also apparent in the case of Ninurta and his mother, Ninmenna or Mami, in UET 6/1 2, when she seeks a substitute to recover Ninurta after he dies or is overcome in the abzu (lines 55ff.).[71] In Ur, the moon god Nanna (Akk. Sîn) and his wife Ningal appear to have the same myths as Damu/Dumuzi.[72]

Another example of this strand is the myth of *Enlil and Ninlil*.[73] The male deity appears to perform a symbolic descent to the nether-world,[74] an action which comes about as a result of a sexual encounter

69 My thanks are due to Claus Wilcke, who pointed out these two works and their significance to me. See also Wilcke, 'König Šulgis Himmelfahrt', p.246.
70 The myth is in Kramer, *From the Poetry of Sumer*, pp.94–6.
71 The tablets fail at this point of the story.
72 Jacobsen, 'Religious Drama', p.85.
73 For a recent study of this work, supplying text, transliteration, translation and commentary, see Behrens, *Enlil und Ninlil*, pp.1ff., especially pp.213–54; and an even more recent study by J.S. Cooper, 'A Critical Review [on Behrens's *Enlil und Ninlil*]', JCS 32/3 (1980) 175–88.
74 Jacobsen, *The Treasures of Darkness*, pp.103–4; Kramer, *The Sumerians*, p.133.

with the goddess Ninlil. Enlil violates Ninlil and is expelled from the city by the Assembly, after which he performs his journey, comprising several stages. There are two destinations which appear to have netherworld symbolism. One is the 'man-devouring' river of the kur (i_7-kur-ra and i_7-lu-ku-ku, lines 93, 94). Kur is most probably 'netherworld' in this context, but may also be 'mountains'. This is a place which in the cases of Dumuzi and Utu appears also to have netherworld symbolism, so that mountains here may, in the context, amount to the same thing as kur, 'netherworld'.[75] The second is the place of the ferry-boat man on the same river, which the gods appear to cross (lines 119ff.).[76] As Cooper points out, the work uses local toponyms for the netherworld.[77] In the journey, the goddess appears to be following Enlil 'down' to the netherworld, as happens in the Damu myths. At each of the stages during their journey, Enlil and Ninlil meet. By a series of ruses, Enlil each time succeeds in impregnating the goddess with another child. Nanna is conceived in Nippur, and the other three, the netherworld deities Nergal, Ninazu and Enbilulu, on the journey. After each encounter Enlil continues his journey.

The motif of substitution which is important in Damu/Dumuzi myths is also found here. The netherworld deities, or (perhaps more to the point here) the children of Enlil and Ninlil, go down to the netherworld; they appear to have the role of substitutes for Enlil, and probably also for Sîn, the moon god, who himself seems to have had to perform as a substitute for Enlil.[78]

Cooper points out that the literary work's purpose is, superficially at least, 'to tell of the origin of four gods' and that it 'explains why one (Sîn) is shining in the heavens, while the other three dwell in the Netherworld'.[79] The text is also about Nanna's primogeniture. There is some reference to fertility effects, which are a feature of the Damu/Dumuzi myths. The text ends with a hymn of praise to Enlil, and in these lines he is worshipped as the 'lord of abundance' who makes the flax and barley grow, and as lord of heaven and earth.

---

75 Behrens, *Enlil und Ninlil*, pp.192–4, especially p.194.
76 Cooper, JCS 32/3 (1980) 179; Kramer, *The Sumerians*, p.133; and Jacobsen, *The Treasures of Darkness*, pp.103–4.
77 Cooper, JCS 32/3 (1980) 183–4.
78 ibid., pp.175–88, especially pp.179 and 182–3.
79 ibid., p.180.

INANNA AND ENKI

A myth in which Inanna performs a return journey for a similar purpose of power as in ID and AV is that of the OB *Inanna and Enki*.[80] The locales of this 'traditional divine journey' are Uruk and Eridu. The mythical journey is horizontal, rather than from upper-world to netherworld as in ID and AV. However, the journey also involves many of the same motifs as ID and AV, particularly in the expression of the power theme.

Inanna decided to make a journey to Enki's temple Abzu in Eridu, to acquire his me for herself and for Uruk, her city. She prepared for the journey and then directed her steps to the Abzu.[81] The wise god Enki, who held the me of heaven and earth, divined her intentions before she had even come into view. He began his preparations for her arrival and gave instructions to Isimud, his minister.

When Inanna arrived, Isimud gave her refreshments. After this Enki and Inanna drank sweet wine in copious quantities in the Abzu at the Table of An, and Enki, who had become drunk, handed over his me, 'divine powers' or 'divine functions', to Inanna, enumerating the hundred or so of them one by one.[82]

Enki subsequently woke up with a hangover to discover that his me were not in their usual places. His faithful minister told him that he had given them to Inanna, who had already loaded her Boat of Heaven with them and left the quay. Enki ordered Isimud to take the enkum (perhaps temple treasury officials) and recover them. Inanna might return to Uruk, but not with his me.

Isimud overtook Inanna, and the incensed goddess accused Enki of dishonourably breaking his word. Scarcely were the words out of her mouth when the enkum seized her boat. Queen Inanna immediately summoned her own minister, Ninshubur, to come to her aid from her

80 See Farber-Flügge, *Der Mythos 'Inanna und Enki'* and Abdul-Hadi A. Al-Fouadi, *'Enki's Journey to Nippur*: The Journeys of the Gods', Ph.D. diss., University Microfilms, Ann Arbor, 1969, pp.5–14.

81 See Bendt Alster on his view of this introduction section, which introduces the time of the action of the myth, and emphasizes the importance of her sexual powers: ZA 64 (1975) 23.

82 Farber-Flügge, *Der Mythos 'Inanna und Enki'*, p.1; Al-Fouadi, 'Enki's Journey', p.7. On the me, see Farber-Flügge, p.97ff., and also pp.9–10; cf. also Alster, ZA 64 (1975) 33 n.33. Also W.G. Lambert, 'Comptes rendus', RA 70 (1976) 77–8.

temple in Uruk, and recited a charm to help her in this task:[83]

Wasser hat nicht deine Hand berührt, Wasser hat nicht deinen Fuß berührt

a šu-zu nu-tag a me-ri-zu nu-tag

With Ninshubur's help, Inanna succeeded in regaining control of her Boat of Heaven, and took it to safety. At each stage of the journey Enki sent demons, monsters and other figures to try to regain his me. Each time Inanna called Ninshubur from Uruk. Finally Inanna arrived at the quay in Uruk, to a feast and celebrations, and she prophesied good things for the city.

Enki sent Isimud to observe events in Uruk. The text is damaged at this point but after a recitation of the me, the fourth such recitation, and a lacuna of perhaps eight lines, Enki is seen to have arrived in Uruk. The end of the work is badly broken, but from what remains it appears that Enki and Inanna were reconciled with each other.

The motivation of the action of *Inanna and Enki* most closely resembles that in ID, as Farber-Flügge points out. As in ID, Inanna's purpose is to take possession of powers not her own, to increase her authority, and to make herself more attractive sexually.[84] This is the power theme; and to acquire power, Inanna performs the journey to and from the Abzu.

Many of the elements which portray the power theme in the journey are similar to those in ID and AV. As in AV, the goddess's journey entails seven stages; each stage involves power, and in *Inanna and Enki* it involves a dispute over the powers that she has gained in the Abzu. Similarly, in ID the Anunna gods dispute the goddess's return with power. In both works the goddess returns carrying the powers: in *Inanna and Enki* the powers are carried by the Boat of Heaven, whereas in ID and AV Inanna is adorned with them. Other elements of the power theme involved in the encounter in ID and AV are the food and water of life. These allow her to return to the

83 SLTNi 32 Tabl. II col. 1.33 and *passim*.
84 Farber-Flügge, *Der Mythos 'Inanna und Enki'*, p.16; M.W. Green, 'Der Mythos "Inanna und Enki" unter besonderer Berücksichtigung der Liste der me. By Gertrud Farbe-Flügge ...*, (Rezension)', JAOS 96 (1976) 283–4: Green considers that Inanna's purpose in her journey is to acquire sexual allurement. This appears to be at least part of her purpose.

upperworld. In *Inanna and Enki*, food and drink are a part of the scene of hospitality common to the 'traditional divine journey'.[85] The food and drink may be parallel in the thematic action as they occur as part of the 'encounter' at the destination and, as in ID, have a role in the deity's triumph. The comparable situation of eating and drinking with Enki and receiving the me, including the 'me for life' (me u_4-ti-la-ke$_4$) before the return journey is seen in *Ninurta's Journey to Eridu* (col. ii.11).[86]

The motif of help required in the journey before success can be achieved, which appears here in *Inanna and Enki* as well as in ID and AV, is a structural element of the journey and is concerned with the goddess's power. Inanna is attacked by the emissaries of Enki, and her Boat of Heaven is taken from her; but for the help coming from Uruk, which parallels the help coming from the upperworld in ID and in Damu's myths, her setback would have been irreversible. Inanna loses the boat and the me to Enki's servants six times, but each time Ninshubur's help gives Inanna victory. The charm that Inanna recites has the purpose of aiding Ninshubur against the water of the Abzu, in some way facilitating the minister's descent and, apparently, her return.[87]

The journey in this work may possibly parallel the journey of Inanna in ID and AV in another way. Alster points out that the journey to the Abzu appears to be a symbolic descent to a nether realm and a return.[88] The destination, Abzu-Eridu, seems to have a nether-realm significance in the journey. The Abzu, Enki's temple in Eridu, appears to represent, on a mythological level, the Abzu, the nether realm over which Enki rules. Words used in the text also point

85 Jerrold S. Cooper, *The Return of Ninurta to Nippur: an-gim dím-ma*, Analecta Orientalia 52, Biblical Institute Press, Rome, 1978, p.13 and n.1.
86 Daniel Reisman, 'Ninurta's Journey to Eridu', JCS 24 (1971) 3ff., 4, 6. Reisman points out the similarity of the pattern of that myth to *Inanna and Enki*; see Cooper, *The Return of Ninurta*, p.13, and also Al-Fouadi, 'Enki's Journey', pp.4, 5–10, on 'traditional divine journeys'; and Ferrara, op. cit., 1ff.
87 Farber-Flügge, *Der Mythos 'Inanna und Enki'*, pp.15, 85, on this charm; also Alster, ZA 64 (1975) 24.
88 Alster, ZA 64 (1975) 30ff. Alster also presents a structural interpretation of the work. His structure depends somewhat on his reconstruction of the activities of Inanna and Enki in fragmentary sections of the text: for example, the frog episode, and especially the fragmentary conclusion of Farber-Flügge's text. The reconstructions also seem to be influenced by Proppian structuralist theory on folktales: cf. p.27 and *passim*.

to this symbolism. The poet's invariable use of the term Abzu-Eridu, instead of merely Eridu, suggests 'a mythical location associated with the deep ocean, Abzu'.[89] In addition, Inanna *descends* to the Abzu, in lines 26–7 of Tablet I.i:[90]

[ga-ša-an]-an-(na)-mèn me-e ga-(gin) abzu-a(ba)-an-e$_{11}$

I, the queen, let me go, let me descend to the Abzu

The parallels of motif, in particular, the seven stages in the journey, may also suggest that the same sort of journey is represented here symbolically for a cultic purpose in this journey of Inanna to acquire power, with the Abzu-Eridu as a nether locale and Uruk, the city of the 'Queen of Heaven' with its temple of An, as the 'upperworld' locale. The symbolic use of the locales in this 'traditional divine journey' would also parallel the use of Uruk and Kutû in the journey of Inanna in ID as interpreted by Buccellati. However, as in ID and AV, Inanna acquires her powers by meeting the ruler of a nether region, Ereshkigal in ID and AV, and Enki here. (The actual geography of Inanna's journey in *Inanna and Enki* takes the goddess along the Eridu canal for the first five stages and then along the Euphrates to Uruk. The localities mentioned as the stages are not known.)[91]

According to Alster in his commentary on *Inanna and Enki*, the descent-and-return journey appears to be the basis of Inanna's activities in several other of her myths. Besides *Inanna's Descent*, he cites *Inanna and Shukalletuda*, *Inanna and Ebih*, and the hymn *Inanna Nin-egala*.[92] In particular, he refers to *Inanna and Shukalletuda*, which begins in the same way as *Inanna's Descent*. In the introduction, Inanna leaves 'heaven' and 'earth' and travels to the kur, here 'mountains'.[93] There is still a difficulty here, of course, as the beginning of the poem is fragmentary and hinders the exact definition of the usage of the word kur.

---

89 Alster, ZA 64 (1975) 20, 32. Uruk and Eridu represent 'the two extremes of the cosmic journey of the goddess': p.32. See p.33 for the other netherworld associations of Eridu.

90 ibid., p.20, as Alster reconstructs the lines.

91 Farber-Flügge, *Der Mythos 'Inanna und Enki'*, pp.13–14; and see Th. Jacobsen, 'The Waters of Ur', *Iraq* 22 (1960) 181ff.

92 Alster, ZA 64 (1975) 30ff.

93 cf. Wilcke, AfO 24 (1973) 86.

INANNA'S JOURNEY IN THE HYMN
in-nin šà-gur₄-ra

This hymn to Inanna, which may have been composed by the en-priestess Enheduanna, daughter of Sargon of Akkad, makes a brief reference to a situation which involves a gain in power by Inanna after a journey of some nature. In her arrival in heaven Inanna has a threatening effect on the gods in heaven (lines 104–9):[94]

> The Anunna gods bow down their nose, they hurl
>   themselves to the ground,
> You ride *on* seven great dogs, you come out in heaven,
> The great An feared your . . . he was frightened of your
>   dwelling-place,
> He let you take your seat in the dwelling-place
>   of the great An
> (and then) he did not fear you any more. (He said:)
> 'I will hand over to you the lofty royal garza (and)
>   the divine, great garza!'
> The great gods kissed the earth, they served (you)

> ᵈa-nun-na kiri₄-bi gam-e-eš kiri₄ ba-e-dúr-ru-ne-eš
> ur-gal-gal-imin-bi ba-e-u₅ an-na ba-e-è-dè
> an-gal-e MÙŠ-za ní bí-te ki-tuš-zu im-mi-hu-luh
> ki-tuš-an-gal-la-ke₄ dúr ba-e-gar su nu-mu-e-da-zi-zi
> PA.LUGAL-mah PA.AN-gal-g[al] šu-zu ga-mu-un-si
> dingir-gal-gal-e-ne kiri₄ ki-a bí-in-su-ub-bu-uš šu-kin
>   mu-un-dab₅-bé-eš

The translation given to an-na ba-e-è-dè in line 105 is 'you come out/forth in heaven'.[95] In J.V. Kinnier-Wilson's translation, the phrase is translated: 'come out to heaven' or 'rise to heaven'.[96] It replaces Sjöberg's tentative translation of 'you come out *from* heaven',

---

94 For the transliteration and translation of the hymn, see Ake W. Sjöberg, 'in-nin šà-gur₄-ra: A Hymn to the Goddess Inanna by the en-Priestess Enheduanna', ZA 65 (1976) 161–253 (lines 104–9 cited here: pp.188–9). All but one of the texts are of OB date: p.161.
95 Claus Wilcke, private correspondence, 25/10/90.
96 J.V. Kinnier-Wilson, *The Rebel Lands*, Cambridge University Press, Cambridge, 1979, p.19. Similarly 'you come forth in Heaven', or 'arrive in Heaven': Dr J.A. Black, Oriental Institute, Oxford, private correspondence, 5/7/88.

which does not seem to apply in the context of the goddess then taking her seat in An's dwelling-place.

Inanna is a fearful goddess here. She terrifies the Anunna gods and An himself. In her threatening arrival she rides on seven great dogs or, perhaps more correctly, seven lions, which are the animals usually connected with her. The situation may be referring to the idea of Inanna rising as a star (Venus) in the heavens, perhaps from beneath the horizon. What is clear, however, is that she arrives from somewhere else to terrify An and enjoys a gain in power when An hands over the royal and divine garza, apparently to pacify her.[97]

In this journey myth, as in the others in this chapter, the acquisition of power is a perceived result of the journey and seems to be its major purpose. In ID, Inanna seeks power in the netherworld and in the upperworld, as Enlil's words reveal. The same story appears to be followed in AV. In *Inanna and Enki*, the goddess gains the me of Enki in her journey to Eridu, and in in-nin šà-gur$_4$-ra, she receives the garza from An when she arrives in heaven. In his liturgies, Damu acquires by means of his journey the power to perform his divine functions of bringing fertility and prosperity to his city.

Together with this idea of power in the journeys, each of the myths in this chapter presents important ideas and motifs found with the goddess. Of course, Inanna/Ishtar is a great and complex goddess and, especially in later times, a goddess with numerous functions, so one short chapter, which is necessarily limited by the topic to the discussion of the journey myths of the goddess and to specific ideas associated with her in these journeys, cannot hope to do justice to her character, role, and functions, or to the wide scope of her mythology. Nevertheless, each of the myths in this chapter presents important features about the goddess and ideas and motifs of which many are central to her mythology. Similarly, only a number of aspects of her consort Dumuzi have been touched on, but they too are central in his myths.

There are several more myths which need to be considered to complete this treatment of Inanna and her consort satisfactorily for the task at hand. In one other myth Inanna performs a journey with the result of a demonstration of power: in the myth *Inanna and Ebih*,

---

97 On these 'powers', see Farber-Flügge, *Der Mythos 'Inanna und Enki'*, pp.97ff.

she destroys the mountain Ebih. This myth, which seems to refer to the destruction of a foreign land, does not, however, present the acquisition of power, nor does it reveal anything new about the journey for power, and apart from stressing the warrior-goddess aspect of Inanna, it supplies no features which are outstandingly important to the goddess.

The main aspect of the relationship of Inanna and Dumuzi is their love and marriage, although the unhappy fate of Dumuzi which results from it is also important. The complex relationship of the goddess and her consort is also pertinent to the discussion of certain Greek myths, so a general summary of the relevant material is necessary. There is much poetry describing the relationship of the two deities, celebrating their courtship, marriage and coupling, often in graphic detail, and sometimes with the description of results in fertility. There is also a number of texts which concern the sacred marriage of Inanna with kings of various cities, who play the role of Dumuzi as consort and lover of the goddess for the benefit of fertility and their cities' prosperity. As part of Inanna's marriage with Dumuzi, and as part of the ritual sacred marriage, the goddess prepares herself elaborately by bathing, anointing herself with oil, and dressing in 'clothes of power' to meet her lover. There is also a number of love poems focusing on the romantic sexual side of the relationship between the deities. In one poem, SRT 31, which is based on the Inanna and Dumuzi model, a feature indicated by the reference to Dumuziabzu in lines 26 and 30 (referring here to Dumuzi), but which may actually be secular and portray a human *affaire*, the death of Dumuzi as a result of his love for the goddess receives an allusion (lines 18–26).[98]

> My beloved, my man [of my heart],
> I will bring about an evil fate for you,
>   my brother of fairest face,
> Your right hand you have placed on my vulva,
> Your left hand you have stretched toward my head.
> Having approached your mouth to mine,
> Having held my lips toward your head,
> You, for this reason, have been decreed an evil fate,
> Thus it is, 'dragon' of women, my brother of
>   fairest face.

98 SRT 31: Kramer, *The Sacred Marriage Rite*, pp.104–6; and Alster, RA 79 (1985) 142–6.

ki-ig-ga-ág-mu mu-lu-[šà-ab-mà-me-en]
[x n]a-ám erim₂-ma [du₅-mu-ra-an]-mar-mar
   šeš i-b[í šag₅-šag₅-m]u
šeš-mu na-ám-erim₂-ma du₅-mu-ra-an-mar-mar
   šeš i-bí šag₅-šag₅-mu
šu-zi-da-zu gal₄-la-mà bí-im-mar
gùb-bu-zu sag-mu-uš im-ši-ri
ka-zu ka-mà um-me-te
šu-um-du-um-mu sag-za ù-ba-e-né-díb
za-e ur₅-ta na-ám erim₂-ma ku₅-dè-en
ur₅-ra-àm ušum munus-e-ne-kam šeš i-bí šag₅-šag₅

Probably the most famous reference to Dumuzi's unhappy fate is, however, found in the passage of the *Epic of Gilgamesh* (Tablet 6.ii.46–79) which speaks of the disasters which can happen to lovers of the goddess Inanna/Ishtar in myth. After a break, lines 46–50 refer elliptically to the young god's fate:[99]

> For Tammuz, the lover of your youth.
> Year after year you set up a wailing for him.
> You loved the mauve-coloured shepherd bird:
> You seized him and broke his wing.
> In the forest he stands crying, 'Kappi! My wing!'

---

99 Translation: Gardner and Maier, *Gilgamesh*, pp.152–5.

3

NINURTA

Ninurta is the great warrior god of the Sumerian pantheon. His principal cult centre was the temple Eshumesha in the city Nippur. The son of the supreme god of the Sumerian pantheon, Enlil of Nippur, Ninurta functions in several of his myths as the heroic champion of the Assembly of the gods in their confrontations with the terrifying monsters Anzu and Asag in the mountains. The account of Ninurta's defeat of Anzu and his consequent rise to power in the Assembly is the subject of one major myth, while in another important myth he overpowers Asag in an epic battle. There are also other myths in which he defeats threatening opponents, and references to yet others which have not survived. While he is most famous for his martial exploits, he is, however, also portrayed as a god responsible for the irrigation of Sumer by the Tigris and Euphrates rivers, and for agriculture and its fertility.

His myths were assumed to a certain extent by other gods who became important later, gods such as Marduk, the god of Babylon, who is presented in *Enuma Elish* as the supreme god of the Mesopotamian pantheon, Nabû, the son of Marduk, and Nergal, the lord of the netherworld. Marduk's dependence on Ninurta's mythological tradition, especially the Anzu and Asag myths, is clearly seen in *Enuma Elish*, a work which is generally held to have been composed in the last quarter of the second millennium BC, with one commentator dating it at about 1100 BC.[1] In this work he is depicted as the

---

1 W.G. Lambert, 'Studies in Marduk', BSOAS 47 (1984) 1–9; Réné Labat *et al.*, *Les Religions du Proche Orient asiatique*, Fayard/Denoël, Paris, 1970, p.36; Alasdair Livingstone, *Mystical and Explanatory Works of Assyrian and Babylonian Scholars*, monograph of Ph.D. diss., Clarendon Press, Oxford, 1986, p.155. For some aspects of the dependence on Ninurta's

champion of the Assembly of the gods in his battle against the goddess–monster Tiamat. In certain first-millennium texts, Marduk and especially Nabû also directly substitute for Ninurta as the destroyer of Anzu. Nergal is closely associated with Ninurta and also takes over some mythological exploits and martial aspects of the god.

Ninurta was an important god in Mesopotamia and this is especially reflected in his mythological tradition, which is probably second in extent to that of Inanna. The god was also worshipped by the Assyrian kings in the first millennium BC, as a warrior god to help them against their enemies. One example illustrating the importance of the god in first-millennium Assyria is provided by King Assurnasirpal II (883–859 BC), who built in his new capital Kalhu (Nimrud) a temple to Ninurta adjacent to the ziggurat which may also have been dedicated to Ninurta.

Many central ideas expressed in these journey myths of Ninurta which follow, and especially the idea of the acquisition and demonstration of power in the journey, are crucial to the discussion of a number of the Greek myths in the following chapters. Important ideas are found in the nature of the journey sequences themselves, and in events and motifs which occur in the sequences, such as Ninurta's combats, the locales, the temple scenes and his encounters with other gods. All of these ideas will be seen in the course of the investigation of the journey for power and the way in which it is expressed in Ninurta's myths. As with the chapter on Inanna, it is this investigation that is the focus of the present chapter, since these ideas have not been treated in detail before and need to be examined thoroughly in order to prepare for the discussion of parallels in the Greek journey myths, in which it is also found as an important idea. The other ideas which are significant in Ninurta's myths and will be central in the discussion of the parallels in the Greek myths will not be pointed out in this treatment of Ninurta's myths in order not to bias the inquiry into Ninurta's myths and the subsequent examination of parallels which takes place in the following chapters. The

myths, J.J. van Dijk, *Lugal ud me-lám-bi nir-ǧál: Le récit épique et didactique des Travaux de Ninurta, du Déluge et de la Nouvelle Création*, vol. 1, E.J. Brill, Leiden, 1983, pp.3, 26, 27. Cf. also Wilfred G. Lambert, 'Ninurta Mythology in the Babylonian Epic of Creation', in Karl Hecker and Walter Sommerfeld, eds, *Keilschriftliche Literaturen. Ausgewählte Vorträge der XXXII. Rencontre Assyriologique Internationale, Münster, 8.–12.7.1985*, Dietrich Reimer Verlag, Berlin, 1986, pp. 55–60.

discussion must concentrate for the moment simply on the journey for power and its expression in the myths.

The theme of the god performing a journey for the purpose of power is a constant feature in Ninurta's journey myths, in which the power and authority of the young god are a central issue. In the major combat myths, the Anzu myth, *Angim* and *Lugale*, the god makes a journey and carries out heroic activities in the mountains to gain or protect his power in the Assembly amongst the gods. The question of Ninurta's power in the Assembly is treated differently in each of these myths: in the Anzu myth Ninurta rises from obscurity to achieve authority over the established order; in *Angim* the specific issues seem to be the status of Ninurta's power in Ekur and his relationship to his father, the supreme god, as a result of his activities; the protection of Ninurta's and the Assembly's authority over the cosmos appears to be the main concern of *Lugale*. The theme of performing a journey for power can also be seen in the traditional divine journey myths, such as STVC 34, *Ninurta's Journey to Eridu*. Although the end of UET 6/1 2, *Ninurta and the Turtle*, is missing, Ninurta's quest for power also appears to be the subject of this work, in which he travels to Eridu to try to dispossess Enki of the divine powers which had been recovered from Anzu. The first myth of Ninurta in which the theme will be discussed is the myth of Ninurta's confrontation with the terrible bird–lion monster Anzu. A depiction of Ninurta's attack on this opponent, although it may be Asag, was found on a stone relief in the temple of Ninurta at Kalhu. The monster is portrayed as having the head, body and forepaws of a lion and the feathers, wings, tail feathers and hind talons of an eagle.[2]

THE MYTH OF ANZU

There are two versions of this myth, the SB and the OB. Ninurta is the god of the SB version, while Ningirsu who here, as in various places, is seen to be virtually identical with Ninurta, is the god of the OB. The sources for the SB version consist of MA tablets from Assur and Nineveh, and NA tablets from Nineveh and Sultantepe, as well as

---

2 As Anzu: see Stephanie Dalley, *Myths from Mesopotamia*, Oxford University Press, Oxford, 1989, frontispiece with caption; as Anzu or Asag, see Jeremy Black and Anthony Green, *Gods, Demons and Symbols of Ancient Mesopotamia: An Illustrated Dictionary*, British Museum Press, London, 1992, pp.35–6 ('Asag'), ('Ninurta'), 142–3 with depiction.

NB fragments from Nineveh. The first and second tablets of the SB version are quite well preserved, although there are some fragmentary columns at the beginning of the first tablet, while a considerable portion of the third and last tablet remains in fragmentary columns. The sources for the OB version, in which the god is Ninǧirsu, consist of two OB tablets from Susa, presumably the remains of a four-tablet text.[3] While the two versions tell essentially the same story, the more extensive SB version is followed here.

Power is the central issue of the myth of Anzu, specifically the rise to power and authority of the young god Ninurta as a result of his recovery of the Tablet of Destinies after its theft from Enlil by the monster Anzu. Ninurta gains his power by means of the journey to the mountains, by the destruction of the enemy monster there and the regaining of Enlil's lost Tablet.

The work opens with a statement of the poet's intention to praise Ninurta, the son of Enlil and Mami,[4] who became the 'Mighty One' and chief of the Anunnaku as a result of his defeat of Anzu. The story takes place in the mythical time before the sovereignty of Enlil over the Igigi, before the Tigris and the Euphrates irrigated Sumer. The Igigi brought news to their father Enlil of the birth of Anzu in the mountains. In the fragments of columns i and ii, Enlil with Ea beside him encounters Anzu, who, according to Ea, was conceived by the pure waters of the Apsu-gods and the wide Earth and brought forth in the mountain rocks. Ea suggested that Enlil give him a place as guard of the throne in his sanctuary.

From his position at the entrance of the cella, Anzu often saw Enlil bathing in the pure waters, and performing his kingly deeds. He often gazed at his sovereign crown, his divine robes and the Tablet of Destinies in his hands; and he began to covet Enlil's sovereignty.

3 Recent important sources: W.W. Hallo and W.L. Moran, 'The First Tablet of the SB Recension of the Anzu-Myth', JCS 31 (1979) 65–115; M.E. Vogelzang, *Bin šar dadmē: Edition and Analysis of the Akkadian Anzu Poem*, Styx Publications, Groningen, 1988. For additions to Tablet III, H.W.F. Saggs, 'Additions to Anzu', AfO 33 (1986) 1–29; this article presents the text GM 1, which preserves on its reverse side, in sometimes fragmentary state, the text of the three tablets of the Anzu myth. Also, William L. Moran, 'Notes on Anzu', AfO 35 (1988) 24–9.

4 That is: of Nintu, Aruru, Ninhursaǧ, Dingir-mah and Bēlet-ilī. Cf. J.S. Cooper, *The Return of Ninurta to Nippur: an-gim dím-ma*, Analecta Orientalia 52, Biblical Institute Press, Rome, 1978, p.104.

At dawn, when Enlil was bathing in the pure waters stripped of his crown and the Tablet of Destinies, Anzu put out his hand, seized the Tablet and flew off to the mountain whence he had originated. Silence and stillness fell on Ekur and the shrine lost its brilliance. Enlil 'was (also) deadly still'.[5]

The gods assembled in Ekur, and Anu called for a champion to step forth from among the gods, a champion to go forth and slay Anzu and recover the Tablet. He summoned Adad to take up the challenge – to blast Anzu with the lightning-bolt – and offered him unrivalled power in the Assembly. Adad refused, declaring that none could conquer Anzu now that he held the Tablet of Enlil. Girra and Shara were summoned in turn, but they also refused to make the journey on the same grounds.

Then wise Ea thought of a plan and told the troubled gods that he would find a champion. He ordered that Mami be summoned and offered the supreme honour of the title 'Mistress of the Gods'. Ea asked her to give them her son Ninurta as a champion, promising the rewards offered to the previous three (lines 128–32). Mami agreed and persuaded her son to recover the Tablet. She gave him instructions on a plan of action, commanded him to return the Tablet to Enlil once it had been regained and finished by referring to the rewards for doing this. Ninurta obeyed and drove to the mountain of Anzu, where he met his opponent.

In the first encounter Ninurta failed because Anzu, holding the Tablet, shattered with his word the hero–god's arrows into their component parts. Through Sharur, who acted as Ninurta's messenger, Ea advised him to use his wind weapon. He also repeated Mami's instructions, including the command that he should return the Tablet to Enlil. He promised the reward of power – recognition in the Assembly, in the form of receiving a seat or dais, and cultic and political power.

In Tablet III Ninurta defeated Anzu by applying Ea's advice, killing him with an arrow and a javelin. He then destroyed and drenched the mountains. After slaying Anzu he recovered the Tablet of Destinies, and the wind bore Anzu's feathers to the gods as a sign of victory. Dagan announced the news to the gods, recounted Ninurta's achievements and called for Ninurta to be rewarded with the promised position of authority over the established order.

Enlil sent a messenger, Birdu, to summon Ninurta back to the

5 Hallo and Moran, op. cit.

Assembly, and in the fragments of Ninurta's response to Birdu Ninurta may possibly have refused to give the Tablet back to Enlil.[6] However, at the end it is seen that Ninurta has restored the Tablet to Enlil and that he has come into lordship over the established order as a reward for his destruction of Anzu and the mountains, and the re-establishment of Enlil's power. A recitation of the names which he receives in various localities and further praise completes the story.

Power is quite clearly the central issue of the Anzu myth. Ninurta's rise in power is achieved by the performance of a journey to Mount Hibi (which is either in the Syrian mountains to the west or in the Elam mountains to the east), by his destruction of the Anzu bird to recapture the Tablet, and also by his activities after the battle, which presumably ends with his return to Nippur. The possible initial refusal of Ninurta to return the Tablet of Destinies in the fragments of Tablet III suggests steps taken to ensure the fulfilment of the Assembly's promises of reward. The return journey is not clear in the damaged text, but the introduction and the end of Tablet III show that Ninurta achieves both authority in the Assembly and cultic power. From a position of insignificance he becomes the Mighty One, the leader of the Anunnaku, with authority over the established order, and not only is a great warrior god, but also has the important function of god of irrigation and agricultural fertility. The return of Ninurta after the battle is seen on the Neo-Assyrian tablets from Sultantepe (51/19A + 37 and 52/187), which appear to present an independent account of the story.

The major symbol of power in this story is the Tablet of Destinies, the source or symbol of supreme divine power. Both Ea and Mami make it plain that Ninurta should return this to Enlil after its recapture (Tablet II.22–3, 117–18).[7] It is possible that in Tablet III Ninurta disputes this point once he has recovered the Tablet from Anzu, but it is clear at the end of the myth that he does return it to Enlil. Another symbol, or perhaps evidence, of power is the motif of

6 See Vogelzang, op. cit., p.72, G obv ii 22, and her comments; however, Saggs does not see this in the text: AfO 33 (1986) 24. Cf. UET 6/1 2 for a parallel situation where Ninurta is not satisfied with Enki's praises but wants the Tablet of Destinies itself.

7 For what was thought to be seen on this tablet, at least in Sargonid times, see Vogelzang, op. cit., pp.140–1, and see A.R. George, 'Sennacherib and the Tablet of Destinies', *Iraq* 48 (1986) 133–46.

awe-inspiring light. After Anzu steals the Tablet from Enlil, the Ekur loses its 'awesome sheen' (I.86), as evidence of the loss of divine authority. When in possession of the Tablet Anzu also had *melammū*, 'divine radiance' (SB II.37, OB II rev. 82, obv. 2), probably once again evidence of the power conferred by the Tablet. In *Lugale* Ninurta took the fearsome me-lám radiance from the Asag monster after defeating him (lines 289–93).

The complex motif of initial defeat which is found in other journeys to acquire power is also found in this work. Ninurta fails initially, and receives help or advice from the Assembly via a messenger, with resultant success (Tablet II.61 to III obv. i.12). This motif no doubt works as a narrative device to increase the tension, but more importantly it appears to emphasize the difficulty of the task and increase the prestige of the victorious hero, thereby reinforcing his claims to the promised rewards.[8]

ANGIM

The oldest texts of *Angim* are OB and are considered to have been composed in the Ur III period or early in OB times.[9] The OB text is written in Sumerian, and is complete. It consists of 208 lines, some of which are, however, in a fragmentary state; some of the lines can be restored from fragments of later recensions. This text is from Nippur, though it must have been part of the scribal curriculum at other centres as well, for it has also been found in the curriculum at Ur.[10] Other recensions are: MB, of the Kassite period, from Nippur; NA from Nineveh; and NB fragments consisting of six lines. Cooper notes that some of the late texts are closer to the OB originals than the MB. An Akkadian translation was also added to the Sumerian texts in the MB period.

Once again the power and might of a god appears to be the central

---

8 Though not of particular importance to this analysis of the god's quest for power in this myth, a political interpretation has been postulated by Claus Wilcke that the myth may be about Lagash bringing rulership back to Sumer after it had been carried off to the mountains (Gutians).

9 Cooper, op. cit., p.10, notes that the mythological material is undoubtedly old but, because of the absence of textual evidence to the contrary, it is possible that *Angim* may represent a new work created by the author at this date, drawing on Ninurta's myths and traditions. It might simply represent a reworking of older texts to suit a new purpose.

10 ibid., pp.32, 54.

issue in a work involving a journey. In *Angim* the issue appears to be specifically the status of Ninurta in Ekur, and especially his relationship with his father the supreme god after the return from his successful expedition to the kur.

Angim cannot be categorized exactly as a myth. The work may be classified as lying 'between the relatively active narrative of the myths and epics, and the relatively static accumulation of epithets and praise hymns'. The action is slight, occurring after a long section introducing Ninurta's attributes and qualities, praising his powers and great deeds. There is a plot, though at times it is largely obscured by the sheer weight of praise for the deity. It is very simple: Ninurta returns from the kur, the mountains, to confront Enlil in his temple Ekur with his victories and his claims to power, after which he proceeds to his temple Eshumesha to manifest his authority and kingship.[11]

The narrative begins with praise of Ninurta, 'born in the kur', the child of Enlil and Nintu.[12] He receives the title of lugal kur-kur-ra, 'king of the lands' (Akk. [EN m]a-ta-a-ti) (line 7), a title of Enlil; and his divine equality with An and Enlil is stated in the phrases 'created like An, created like Enlil': an-[gim] dím-ma, ᵈen-líl-gim dím-ma (lines 1–2, 7). He is described in lines 25–8 as 'the horned wild bull', and also 'wild ram' and 'stag', but pre-eminently as 'the great bull of the kur' (or 'mountains').

The action of the story begins in line 30, introducing his journey from the kur to Ekur. The monsters he is credited with having vanquished are listed and the way they are all hung on his chariot is described at length. As the story goes, King Ninurta boarded his 'shining chariot', [ᵍⁱˢgigir z]a-gìn-na, and drove toward Ekur, accompanied by several figures including 'Udanne, the all-seeing god', and with the 'Slain Heroes' on his chariot. He travelled with thunderous clamour and destruction towards Nippur; with his retinue, he swept over the land like a deluge, 'howled like a storm at heaven's base'. The Anunna gods fled, 'unable to confront him'.

Nusku, the chancellor of Enlil here, greeted the arriving Ninurta, requesting him not to frighten the Anunna gods and Enlil in his Ekur,

---

11 For text and transliteration: Cooper, op. cit., pp.53–103.
12 For Ninurta's birth in the hur-saĝ (mountain) or the kur, see Cooper, op. cit., p.105, and compare with Hallo, CRRAI 17.30. See also Van Dijk, op. cit., p.35, on Ninurta's birth in the hur-saĝ, and his mother's giving birth to him in the kur.

and suggesting that because of the hero's victory and his great valour, Enlil will offer him gifts – otherwise bribes. Ninurta's response is obscure. He put down his weapons, but then drove his cattle into Ekur and laid out his booty. The Anunna gods were amazed and Enlil humbled. Admiring, Ninlil praised him (line 110):[13]

> O wild bull, with fierce horns raised, son of Enlil, you have
> struck blows in the 'mountains'.

am á huš íl-[íl] dumu [^{d}mu]-ul-líl kur-ba mu-e-tu$_{11}$-tu$_{11}$

Ninurta boasted at length to her, proceeded to list his weapons and rounded this off with an audacious demand that Enlil carry his trophies and weapons into the temple and bathe his (Ninurta's) 'valorous arms' (á nam-ur-sag-gá-mu) with holy water (a-gúb-ba) (line 154). He followed this with a hymn of self-praise, listing his functions and glorious attributes, and claiming power for himself, his city and his temple. Then came his public procession to his temple (which he entered alone) and to his wife, here called Ninnibru, 'lady of Nippur', after which he pronounced favourable words for the city's king. Further praise of his power and kingship is mentioned in connection with his victory over the kur (lines 203–4). *Angim* ends with a restatement of Ninurta's relationship to Enlil (line 207):

> Ninurta, the magnificent scion of Ekur

^{d}ninurta dumu mah é-kur-ra

Ninurta gains power by his activities in the journey, specifically by the defeat of the monsters of the kur. This is demonstrated by his awesome return, in which he terrifies the Anunna gods and destroys the land (lines 71–6). He even appears to alarm Enlil in his temple (line 88). The slain opponents which bedeck his chariot on his return journey are emblems of his might and prowess (lines 51–62). On his return to Ekur he claims power, presumably from Enlil, making his claims for rulership and kingship over heaven (lines 165, 168).[14] His activities in the kur and his frightful return form the basis for his claims to recognition and reward. His somewhat threatening effect

13 Cooper, op. cit., p.27; 'Ninlil' is synonymous with 'Nintu' in line 2. See also ibid., p.104.
14 In the Sumerian version of line 165 the phrase is 'rulership in heaven'; in the Akkadian translation the line simply ends with 'fit for kingship'. Although not all of this line is extant in the OB MS, the half which is parallels that of the MB MS. Cf. ibid., p.89 n.1.

on the gods demonstrates his power and enhances his claim. He also lays out his booty as evidence of his feats and this appears to impress Enlil and the other gods (lines 99–115).

The status of Ninurta's power in Ekur appears to be part of the issue. The work is concerned with the exaltation of Ninurta in Ekur and the lavish praise applied to Ninurta is one of the methods used to achieve this, presenting the young god as the equal of Enlil and An in divinity. The work takes every opportunity to heap praise on Ninurta, beginning with the opening twenty-nine lines of solid praise. Despite the praise heaped upon the god and the exalted nature of some of the epithets, such as 'lord of the lands', lugal kur-kur-ra (line 7), and equality with An and Enlil (lines 1–2), Ninurta is clearly the subordinate of Enlil the supreme god. While Ninurta appears to humble Enlil, and threatens the gods in his return, the work reiterates Ninurta's relationship to Enlil, as his son and as son of Ekur. A good example of this is when Ninurta storms Enlil's temple and boastfully expounds on his victorious deeds and makes his claims for rulership, ending with the brash demand that Enlil carry his weapons and trophies into the temple, as well as putting his 'chariot of supremacy' in a high place (lines 153–9).[15] All of this could have been considered the service of an inferior. However, the work does not refer to Enlil's performance of these deeds, which as Cooper declares is 'one of the enigmas of *Angim*',[16] but instead immediately lays stress on Ninurta's relationship to his father. The work ends in a similar way, with the reiteration of the young god's achievements and his acquisition of power (lines 203–7), but surrounds the passage with a restatement of his relationship to Enlil and Ekur, indicating the continuation of Enlil's authority and Ninurta's position under this authority (lines 202, 208).

The expression of the god's power in the return journey is displayed by elements which closely parallel those of the return of Inanna, particularly in ID and AV, such as the motif of 'dressing in powers', the accompanying retinue, and the terrified gods. The parallels indicate that the same ideas are involved in the journeys as regards the power of the gods.

At the beginning of his return journey (lines 30–113), he adorns his

---

15 See UET 6/1 2 for the motif of Ninurta commanding Enlil on his return to Nippur.
16 Cooper, op. cit., p.13.

'shining chariot'[17] with the trophies of his victories over the kur, which are part of the basis of his claims to power.[18] This 'dressing motif' is found with Ishtar on her ascent as at each of the stages she dresses in clothes and ornaments representing her power (AV lines 119–25). The power connotation of these elements of dress is especially visible in Inanna's descent sequence, where she loses pieces of apparel one by one, to arrive finally in the netherworld powerless and helpless before Ereshkigal (ID lines 14–25, 130–64).

Ninurta is accompanied by a retinue, which precedes and follows him: two figures follow and two precede, and his retinue also includes the company of the 'Slain Heroes' (lines 65–8). Inanna likewise is preceded and followed by a demon and accompanied by a horde of demons (ID lines 291–6).

Ninurta returns from the kur with terrible aspect, thunderous clamour and destruction, and causes the Anunna gods to flee in terror (lines 70–89); and, likewise, the goddess emerges with her retinue to terrify the gods of the cities and Dumuzi, who flees (lines 306ff.). In Enheduanna's hymn, in-nin šà-gur₄-ra, she rises to heaven and terrifies the Anunna, who throw themselves to the ground. An also trembles: she takes her seat in his dwelling-place and he hands over the powers (lines 104–9).[19] This situation is directly parallel to Ninurta's return and arrival in Nippur. In Enheduanna's hymn nin-me-šár-ra, Inanna also terrifies the Anunna, who flee like bats (lines 34–5). In *Angim* also the Anunna are described as fleeing birds, and represented as bulls, and as mice scurrying into refuse heaps at Ninurta's approach (lines 122–3, 174–5).[20] Both Inanna and Ninurta display their power with all these gods whom they encounter.

The destination of Ninurta's journey is the kur, the mountains, not

---

17 Ninurta is also referred to as 'the shining one': the accompanying Akkadian translation of pirig, 'the lion', in line 56 is nam-ru, 'the shining one'. Compare Ninurta's form in his return with that of Inanna in the incipit of the Inanna hymn: (after a blank space) su pirig sa pirig-gá ní im-ma-zi-zi-dè-en, which is translated as 'With a lion's body and a lion's muscles you rise up' (CBS 8530 ii, A. Sjöberg). The lion epithet is also used of kings: Cooper, op. cit., p.119.

18 For the trophies, lines 51–62; for the victorious encounter as the basis of his power, line 90; and because of the victory and the weapons that he bears, lines 128–52.

19 See Ake W. Sjöberg, 'in-nin šà-gur₄-ra: A Hymn to the Goddess Inanna by the en-Priestess Enheduanna', ZA 65 (1976) 188–9, lines 104–9.

20 Lines 71–7 (and note also Cooper, op. cit., p.26) for his aspect; lines 86, 89, 121–2; lines 122, 123, 174–5 for description of the fleeing Anunna.

Ereshkigal's realm as is the destination in Inanna's myths. The mountains seem to have a special significance for Ninurta, as the place where he combats his enemies and grows in glory and power, since these, whether the Zagros or the Syrian mountains, are the destination of the journeys in each of the heroic myths of Ninurta, in the Anzu myth, *Angim* and *Lugale*. The mountainous locale is a distant place, and therefore may be endowed with mysterious or otherworldly overtones, appropriate to a place at which mythical events can occur. A perhaps complementary feature of the kur is the fact that the word appears sometimes to have had a hostile connotation for the Sumerians, with the sense of 'foreign' or 'enemy land'.[21]

The political aspect is an important issue in this work. The myth clearly has a cultic role in the city.[22] Commentators such as Langdon and recently Alster have referred to the double strand in the work, the mythological story and its application in the city's affairs.[23] Beside the purely mythological side, Alster says that it represents a 'paradigm' for the victorious king's return to the city and the temple. The ambivalent character, mythological and political, is expressed in the terms used in the myth: the use of kur and ki-bal, 'rebellious land', terms which are juxtaposed (for instance, in lines 18–19, 119–20, 139, 143) and at times are virtually synonymous. In the same way as ki-bal is juxtaposed with kur, the political aspect appears alongside the mythological in Ninurta's victorious role, where he brings back the trophies of the mythological monsters from the kur and, at the same time, returns like a victorious king with the booty 'of plundered cities'. A similar juxtaposition of kur and ki-bal is provided in the Shulgi hymn.[24] This is the application of the mythology in the city cult, and while it affects the terms used by the mythographers, it does not alter the theme of the young deity's rise in power which is at the centre of the mythological story itself.

---

21 On this aspect of kur, see, for instance, Henri Limet, 'Étude sémantique de ma.da, kur, kalam', RA 72 (1978) 12.
22 Cooper, op. cit., pp.8, 9, 12. *Lugale*, similarly, has a number of levels: mythological, ritual and historical/political. The mythological material is used for a ritual and historical end. See J.J. van Dijk, *Lugal ud me-lám-bi nir-ğál*, op. cit., pp.8 and 28.
23 Stephen H. Langdon, *Semitic Mythology*, volume 5 of *The Mythologies of All Races*, (J.A. MacCulloch, ed.), Cooper Square Publishers, New York, 1964, pp.124ff.; Alster, RA 68 (1974) 54.
24 Jacob Klein, *Three Šulgi Hymns*, Bar-Ilan University, Ramat Gan, 1981, Shulgi D 151–3, 197–9.

UET 6/1 2

The text UET 6/1 2 presents an excerpt from a literary composition which appears to be related to the Anzu myth, though there are great differences between the two.[25] In UET 6/1 2 Ninurta suffers a defeat at the hands of Enki, the hero of the surviving portion of the myth; however, the eventual outcome is unknown as the end of the composition has not been found. In this myth Ninurta performs a journey, and the central issue of his activities is the quest for power, here described as the me (divine powers), giš-hur (plans) or dub nam-tar-ra-bi (tablet of fate) (lines 2–4).

The text opens with a discussion between Ninurta and Anzu, who says that when Ninurta struck him the divine powers returned to the Abzu. Ninurta laments the loss of the me and the power that they represent. He wails that he will not exercise authority in the Abzu as Enki does.

Anzu leads him to the Abzu and to Enki, who praises Ninurta for his feat of regaining the me from the great Anzu and speaks of Ninurta's resultant power in Ekur. However, Ninurta is dissatisfied with Enki's praise and prophecies of the power that he is to assume in Ekur, and secretly plots against him. He attacks the god and his temple with a dark floodwave, but is defeated in ambush and falls into a pit dug by a turtle. The Lord Enki proceeds to gloat over the hero Ninurta's defeat. The fragment ends with the lamentation of Nin-menna, Ninurta's mother, who appears to be considering a substitute for her defeated son.

This composition treats Ninurta in an ironical fashion, and Enki is clearly the hero in the surviving text. This role of Enki is demonstrated in instances where the myth portrays the power and omniscience of wise 'Father Enki', who perceives the envious plot of Ninurta before the culprit has even travelled to Abzu and, after Ninurta's defeat, indulges in self-eulogy and gloats over the abject humiliation of the defeated young hero.

However, Ninurta does perform a journey in the myth, and the purpose of his journey is to acquire power. His envious desire for power, in fact, parallels that of Anzu in the Anzu myth, where that

25 For text and discussion, Bendt Alster, '"Ninurta and the Turtle", UET 6/1 2', JCS 24 (1972) 120–5.

monster covets Enlil's Tablet of Destinies. In the extant text Ninurta fails completely in his quest, although Enki speaks of the authority that Ninurta will gain in Ekur as a result of his defeat of Anzu. Ninmenna appears to be considering a recovery operation after Ninurta's defeat (lines 55ff.) and the end of this may after all be the young god's success in Ekur in accordance with Enki's prophecies.

NINURTA'S JOURNEY TO ERIDU, STVC 34

This myth presents the complete return journey, and in this journey the hero acquires power.[26] Ninurta is the hero of this work featuring Ninurta and Enki, and the hero's journey has the character described by Cooper as the 'traditional divine journey pattern' where power and favours are 'respectfully sought and graciously given', in contrast to the opposite situation where the encounter at the destination has the full antagonistic flavour as seen in the *Myth of Anzu* and UET 6/1 2.[27]

In *Ninurta's Journey to Eridu*, he travels from Ekur to Eridu, that is, to the Abzu, the temple of Enki in Eridu. He is led joyfully to the Abzu by a guide who is not named in the extant text. The guide takes the function of 'carrier' (line 8), presumably carrying the statue of the god: 'In joy he bears Ninurta to the Abzu.'[28] After his arrival and the

26 STVC 34; Daniel Reisman, 'Ninurta's Journey to Eridu', JCS 24 (1971) 3ff.

27 Cooper, op. cit., p.13; note also ibid., n.1, for the 'traditional divine journey' of the gods; and A.J. Ferrara, *Nanna-Suen's Journey to Nippur*, Studia Pohl Series Maior 2, Biblical Institute Press, Rome, 1973, pp.1ff.; more of these are named in Ferrara's bibliography. For the idea of presentation of the me, as opposed to theft, see *Iddin-Dagan's Hymn to Inanna*, where Enki presented the me to her as a gift, and the contrast of her theft of them from Enki in *Inanna and Enki*: Iddin-Dagan hymn, SRT 1. 22–4, and duplicates. Note that Reisman connects all of these myths, basing his connection on two items: the journey, and the motif of the quest of the god for the me; thus he supports the connection of the myths by motif and theme. He also points out that the fact that the action may be presented from different angles in the different myths is 'no reason to reject their essential relationship': op. cit., p.4.

28 Reference to the ritual application of this myth, where the statue of the god is borne in procession from temple to temple, see A. Leo Oppenheim, *Ancient Mesopotamia*, University of Chicago Press, Chicago, 1964, pp.184–5. Cf. also Livingstone, op. cit., p.223: Nabû's statue travelled periodically from his city, Borsippa, to his father's (Marduk's) city to participate in religious festivals. This is much later, of course.

encounter with Enki, Ninurta gains power and displays it: 'The youth who establishes the magnificence of the Ekur' is praised, and sits in assembly with An and Enki (ii.21). Columns iii and iv consist of a hymn to Ninurta, praising his deeds, his attributes as king and hero, and his functions (iii.11–38).[29] The return of Ninurta is indicated in column iii.29, and in column iv he appears to come forth from the Abzu to return to Ekur.[30] The monstrous and terrible aspect he demonstrates in *Angim* on his return from the kur (lines 51–89) is echoed in this section where he comes 'forth from the Abzu, with great noise' (line 18) and in lines 21–2: 'Yo[ur shadow] is lofty, it covers the land/ . . . like a cloth.'

The text also ends in a fashion which recalls *Angim*, for once again his power is limited in relation to Enlil. His deeds and attributes of power are mentioned, but at the same time the author points out that all of these, including his 'determination of destiny' are 'according to the wish of Enlil' (iv.23–8).

Ninurta's clearly stated purpose in travelling to Eridu is to obtain the me, which he gains when he arrives in Abzu and 'encounters' Enki. An interesting point is the description, at this spot in the myth, of the me given to Ninurta: Enki, king of this netherworld realm, gives Ninurta the 'me for life', me u_4-ti-la-ke$_4$ (ii.11).[31]

As they are described in the myth, the powers that Ninurta gains demonstrate his kingship, the power of ruling the land and also foreign lands; and of dispensing destinies, law and order; but, at the same time, he also demonstrates his powers for fertility and abundance of vegetation and animal life (i.7–28).[32] This fertility and creation aspect is another result of victorious encounter in battle;[33] this is displayed with particular clarity in his conflict against Asag and the kur in *Lugale* (lines 349–67).

Another example of the 'traditional divine journey' is provided by the Gudea Cylinder. The journey of the god, here named Ninĝirsu,

29 Reisman, op. cit., pp.3ff.
30 Cf. iv. 20ff.
31 ibid., ii.11; Reisman, op. cit., pp.4, 6.
32 Ninurta is the fierce, invincible king and warrior god, but also the animal and agricultural fertility god. *Angim* concentrates on the warrior aspect. The two aspects are seen together in *Lugale*. Cf. Cooper, op. cit., pp.10–11.
33 See Van Dijk, op. cit., p.23, who points out the connection between the death of Asag and the new creation that follows. A similar sequence is also shown in *Enuma Elish*, involving the battle of Marduk and Tiamat.

who is seen in some works as identical to Ninurta, parallels that of STVC 34. Ninĝirsu's purpose of gaining authority by performing this journey is clear in Gudea's text:[34]

> To the warrior, when he goes to Eridu,
> They will say *bon voyage*
> Ninĝirsu, when he comes back from Eridu,
> The throne in the (well) established city will be firm.

In the various other 'divine journeys' to Nippur the gods who carry out the journey appear to have the purpose of obtaining the power to perform their divine functions for their cities. In each of the journeys the purpose is to receive a favourable destiny from Enlil, and to ensure prosperity and abundance for the visiting deity's city. A good example is the journey of the moon god Nanna-Suen to Nippur.[35]

LUGALE

Lugale is another work which exhibits the complete journey, the hero's journey to the kur and his return.[36] The journey (which is, by contrast to those just discussed, not a traditional divine journey) and the activities of the hero during it have the purpose of securing and protecting the power of the gods, in particular that of Ninurta and Enlil, from the threat of the monster Asag. Ninurta also achieves a gain in power as a reward for his success.

This long poem, consisting of 729 lines, is a complex work. Like *Angim*, it has a number of levels: mythological, ritual and historical/ political. The mythological material is used for a ritual and historical end; this is the purpose of the work.[37] It also appears to combine four myths: '(1) the defeat by Ninurta of the monster Asag, (2) the

---

34 Gudea Cyl. B VIII 13–16.
35 For the divine journeys, see Abdul-Hadi A. Al-Fouadi, '*Enki's Journey to Nippur*: The Journeys of the Gods', Ph.D. diss., University Microfilms, Ann Arbor, 1969, *passim*, and Ferrara, op. cit., pp.1ff. and notes.
36 Van Dijk, op. cit., pp.8, 9, 35; in this epic, the journey begins at line 75, and the return is seen in lines 231, 381, 648ff.
37 Van Dijk, op. cit., p.8: 'Il en résulte que la distribution de la matière mythique, son organisation et sa présentation sont conditionnées par le but rituel et par l'actualisation de la matière mythique dans un contexte historique bien précis'; see also p.28. Cf. the similar purpose with *Angim*: Cooper, op. cit., p.12.

building of the hur-saĝ by Ninurta to benefit mankind, (3) the renaming of Ninurta's mother Ninmah as Ninhursaĝ, "Lady of the Hur-saĝ", and (4) the punning judgement of the stones'.[38] The poem also refers to a number of other mythical labours which are a part of the mythology of Ninurta/Ninĝirsu.[39]

Despite this combination of material, the basic structure behind Ninurta's activities is the journey to and from the kur, the mountains, most probably those of Elam to the northeast. The action begins in Ekur, Enlil's temple in Nippur, where the gods are in assembly. Ninurta receives news via Sharur, his messenger and weapon, of the threat from the kur: the birth of Asag from the union of Heaven and Earth (An and Ki). Sharur reports that Asag has coupled with the kur and has given birth to the stone things; he grows in power continually and threatens to deprive Ninurta of his prerogatives and his privileges received from the Abzu. Ninurta goes forth in anger to meet the monster; at first he has success against the forces of the kur and kills the heroes, but he is then defeated by Asag. After receiving advice and encouragement from Enlil in Nippur, via Sharur, Ninurta returns to the fight and overcomes Asag in a mighty battle. He then changes Asag into the hur-saĝ, mountain, which he heaps up over the kur, and subdues the floodwaters which emanate from the kur. Next, he arranges for the waters to flow into the rivers and canals of Sumer, for the fertility of the earth and for the benefit of the gods (who need no longer work)[40] and of mankind. His mother comes to him in the mountains and he renames her Ninhursaĝ in recognition of her support for him (lines 390–4). As he returns to Sumer from the kur, after crushing Asag, he seems to appear like the sun – after all, in this sequence he is coming from the same mountains from which Utu rises:

38 Dr Jeremy Black, private correspondence, 23/7/87. See also his article, 'The Slain Heroes – Some Monsters of Ancient Mesopotamia', SMS Bulletin 15 (1988) 23. Perhaps even five myths if the return from the kur is to be taken as a separate myth: Claus Wilcke, private correspondence, 25/10/1990.

39 Lines 129–33; Van Dijk, op. cit., p.8. The motif of the 'dead heroes' or 'captive heroes' is also found with Pabilsaĝ, Ninĝirsu, Enzag, Nabû, Marduk, Assur and Nergal; in Van Dijk's view, Ninurta appropriated these labours from Pabilsaĝ and Ninĝirsu, and Marduk and Assur borrowed them from Ninurta: p.17. See pp.17–18 for sources of the motif of 'dead' and 'captive' heroes.

40 Cf. *The Epic of Atrahasis* Tablet I.189–97; also *Enuma Elish* VI.29–49: René Labat *et al.*, *Les Religions du Proche-Orient asiatique*, Fayard/ Denoël, Paris, 1970, p.60 nn.1, 2.

Le Héros avait écrasé la Montagne; lorsqu'il se mit en
mouvement dans la steppe, [il apparut comme le S]oleil(?),
comme (dans) la foule, sous leurs acclamations, il fit son
apparition, majestueusement il s'a[vança].

ur-saĝ-e kur mu-un-sì edin-na di-di-na u[tu-gim   ]
un-gim PA.A.PA-b[a] mi-ni-è á-mah mu-un-[   ]-x

He leaves Eshumesha for another place (lines 648ff.). The text is
silent on the exact final destination, but it is possibly Enlil's Ekur.
This is suggested by line 231, which speaks of his returning to Sumer
on the explicit order of Enlil 'que mon fils rentre avec lui (= l'Asakku)
dans l'Ekur' [dumu-m]u é-kur-ra hu-mu-da-ku$_4$-ku$_4$. Another possible journey and destination is from Nippur to Lagash.[41]

The power theme in Lugale

The power of the god appears to be the purpose of the journey. In
the case of *Lugale* it appears to be primarily retention of power that
is indicated, and mainly for Ninurta, but also for Enlil whom
Ninurta upholds (lines 36, 42, 53–4, 56, 64, 186ff.).[42] This is in
contrast to the Anzu myth, where the purpose of his journey is to
recover Enlil's power, but also for Ninurta to acquire power for
himself at the same time, to be elevated to the position of power seen
at the beginning of *Lugale*. In the latter, Asag and the kur are a
threat to his power and authority, and he preserves both by means of
his journey and its pivotal encounter. Nevertheless, even in this
instance, Ninurta does receive additional power on his return to
Sumer, as a reward for his exploits in the kur against Asag (lines
698–700); besides the blessing of a long life (ti-u$_4$-sù-rá) and a
prosperous reign, he receives 'la force céleste' (line 700):

Roi, que la force céleste soient ta récompense!

lugal usu-an-na nì-ba-zu hé-a

After the encounter with Asag, Ninurta displays his power in
judging the stones and in cosmic organization – the 'second creation',

---

41 Van Dijk suggests these two destinations, op. cit., p.48; cf. also Cooper,
op. cit., p.112, on Enlil's words.
42 Despite the various titles which Ninurta receives in *Lugale*, he is
subordinate to both An and Enlil (lines 12, 16, 19): M.J. Geller, 'Notes on
Lugale', BSOAS 48 (1985) 216.

the creation at the time of the Flood, involving reorganization of the cosmos – and the inauguration of irrigation and agricultural techniques designed for the fertility of the earth (lines 249ff.).

The temple Assembly before the journey

In *Lugale*, as in the Anzu myth, a temple scene involving the Assembly of the gods precedes the hero's journey to the mountains to encounter the monster (lines 17–23). The respective scenes appear, however, to have a different function in relation to Ninurta's power. When the action of *Lugale* begins, Ninurta's power is already established, for he is seen sitting on his throne in the Assembly with An, Enlil and the gods.[43] This forms a contrast to the situation in the Anzu myth, where Anu and Enki promise Ninurta the reward of power in the Assembly and in cult if he successfully challenges Anzu on the mountain and recovers the powers stolen from Enlil. Another difference in Ninurta's role in *Lugale* and Anzu, which may be a result of the difference in Ninurta's initial status, is that in *Lugale* Ninurta issues forth against his opponent of his own volition, not under the orders of another deity. This also forms a contrast to all the other initial situations seen in Ninurta/Niŋirsu myths.

The state of Ninurta's power in the temple scene of *Lugale* is also different from that of *Angim*, a work which may be described as 'the exaltation of Ninurta' in Nippur.[44] The purpose of the *Angim* scene appears to be the assertion of Ninurta's right to power in the Assembly in Nippur and in cult – in view of his activities in the kur and on his triumphant return. In respect of the god's status, *Angim* appears to be a sequel to the situation presented in the Anzu myth, where Ninurta is promised power in return for his success against Anzu.[45] There is also a similarity in Ninurta's actions in the scenes of *Angim* and *Lugale*, where Ninurta's display of power has a slightly menacing edge, so that he frightens the gods. In *Lugale* Ninurta is angry at the news that Sharur brings of the presumptions and threatening actions of Asag, and he terrifies the gods, sending them fleeing (lines 70–4):

43 See lines 12, 17–21, for example.
44 Van Dijk, op. cit., p.4.
45 These scenes are compared merely to analyse the usage of these major elements by the different literary works, to demonstrate the part played in the power theme by the god's role and other elements which occur in these scenes. This is not to suggest any sequential order for the literary works in which the activities of Ninurta are presented.

Le Seigneur cria «u'a»: le Ciel trembla, s'en alla à sa station;
il se tourna vers ce côté (?): Enlil devint confus, s[or]tit de
   l'Ekur,
la Montagne tomba dans le néant; ce jour-là, il fit noir,
   les Anunna tremblèrent.
Le Héros frappa les cuisses avec les poings: les dieux se
   dispersèrent;
les Anunna comme des moutons disparurent à l'horizon.

en-e ù-u'a$_8$ bi-in-du$_{11}$ an b[a]-sìg ki-g̃ìri-ni-šè ba-gub
á-ba i-ni-in-g[i$_4$] ^{d}en-lìl ba-sùh é-kur-ra ba-t[a]-è
kur ba-gul ki-u$_4$-ba ku$_{10}$-ku$_{10}$ ^{d}a-nun-na ba-tar-ra-aš
ur-sag̃-e háš tibir-ra bí-in-ra dingir ba-bir-bir-re-eš
^{d}a-nun-na udu-gim ki-šár-ra ba-e-e$_{11}$-NE-re$_7$^{re}-eš

In both *Angim* and *Lugale* this functions as a demonstration of his
fearful power, but in *Angim* the purpose of the demonstration is to
enhance his claims to power.

Initial defeat

The familiar pattern of the deity's initial defeat by the monster at the
outward destination is seen in *Lugale* (lines 182–297). After the first
battle, where Ninurta defeats the 'dead heroes', or 'captive heroes',
Asag attacks and overcomes the god. Once again a messenger is sent
off to the Assembly: Ninurta sends Sharur, his weapon, to carry the
news of his defeat to Enlil in the Assembly of the gods at Nippur.
There is a break in the text at this point, but when the story is resumed
Sharur has returned conveying Enlil's advice and words of encouragement to Ninurta. The hero returns to the fray and eventually defeats
Asag. This structure of initial defeat, followed by help and advice
from the Assembly and renewed attack resulting in the deity's
success, follows the model seen in ID (lines 166–284) and the Anzu
myth (Tablets I.29 to III obv. i,12); in the *Epic of Gilgamesh* the same
structure is seen, with Gilgamesh receiving encouragement from
Shamash and Enkidu before returning to the fight and reversing his
initial defeat at the hands of Huwawa.[46] The initial defeat motif may

---

46 Fragmentary sections and lines in the Hittite recension of Tablet IV: see
   James B. Pritchard, ed., *Ancient Near Eastern Texts Relating to the Old
   Testament*, 3rd edition, Princeton University Press, Princeton, 1969,
   p.83.

also be reflected in the Marduk epic, in the deity's hesitation and confusion as he first confronts the monstrous Tiamat (IV.67–8).[47]

THE 'HEROIC' STRAND

Ninurta is the type of the heroic warrior deity, representing what may be termed the heroic strand in this study of the power theme in Mesopotamian mythology. Quite a number of deities share the same myths and mythical material with Ninurta: Pabilsağ, Ningirsu, Nabû, Enzag, Nergal, Marduk – the chief Babylonian god who assumes the myths and roles of the major Sumerian deities[48] – and Assur, his Assyrian counterpart. In various places Ningirsu is seen to be virtually identical with Ninurta: 'Ninurta's relationship with Ningirsu ... is not one of sharing or borrowing, but of virtual identity, and these two gods are considered identical throughout [Angim].'[49] The case is the same in the section of the catalogue of names in the Anzu myth.[50] In later theological lists, Ninurta is identified with Ningirsu, Zababa and Nabû.[51] Marduk and Nabû

---

47 Van Dijk, op. cit, p.9; Van Dijk points out that, in addition, the conflict of *Enuma Elish* and its elements reflect both the Anzu myth and *Lugale* encounters of Ninurta. He makes a comparison of *Enuma Elish* and *Lugale*, on the basis of literary composition and elements: pp.9, 18, 21–8, 34.

48 Isaac Mendelsohn, *Religions of the Ancient Near East*, New York, 1955, p.17.

49 Cooper, op. cit., p.11. Others also make this identification. See Thorkild Jacobsen, *The Treasures of Darkness*, Yale University Press, New Haven and London, 1976, pp.128–9; and Wilfred G. Lambert, 'The Gula Hymn of Bullutsa-rabi', Or 36 (1967) 110–11; see also Van Dijk, op. cit., p.4 n. 2, and the sources cited there. On the other hand, Van Dijk is not certain of the identification. Nevertheless, regardless of whether the two names actually refer to the same god or not, on a cultic level they share the same myths, one name simply substituted for the other. Whether this is intentional identification of two deities who were originally different, or whether it is merely witness to the fact that they are identical, is immaterial here. The point relevant here is that they are identified in these works.

50 GM 1 rev. col. v lines 125–62: see H.W.F. Saggs, 'Additions to Anzu', AfO 33 (1986) 2, 25–8.

51 Van Dijk, op. cit., p.7. See also the identification of all these gods in the hymn to the goddess Gula, who sings praises to herself and her spouse, giving him various names in alternative sections: Wilfred G. Lambert, 'The Historical Development of the Mesopotamian Pantheon: A Study of Sophisticated Polytheism', in Hans Goedicke and J.J.M. Roberts, eds,

receive their warrior inheritance from Ninurta, and at times are equated with him; Marduk, Nergal and Nabû substitute for Ninurta as the destroyers of Anzu and Asag.[52] Regarding Marduk, Van Dijk considers that the Asag myth of *Lugale* and mythical motifs in it are important to *Enuma Elish*. Nergal shares many of his martial attributes with his brother Ninurta, as Cooper points out.[53] Errakal in the *Epic of Erra*, a deity in nature like Nergal, is also assimilated to Ninurta.[54] The tradition of the labours of Ninurta/Ninĝirsu is also found with Pabilsaĝ, Enzag, Nabû, Marduk, Assur and others.[55] Some of the slain monsters are also transferred to these other deities.[56] In *Enuma Elish* these heroes become 'captive' or 'dead' gods.[57] In Van Dijk's view, Ninurta appropriated these elements from Pabilsaĝ/ Ninĝirsu, and Marduk and Nabû inherited them from Ninurta.[58] In summary, all these gods share these myths, and together they represent a 'heroic' strand in the Mesopotamian mythology.

In his article 'Religious Drama in Ancient Mesopotamia', Jacobsen

Unity and Diversity: Essays in the History, Literature, and Religion of the Ancient Near East, Johns Hopkins University Press, Baltimore, 1975, p.197; the hymn is found in Lambert, Or 36 (1967) 105–32; another example of identification of Ninurta, Pabilsaĝ and Ninĝirsu can be seen in the Sumerian hymn SLTN 61.

52 Livingstone, op. cit., pp.152–4; Cooper, op. cit., pp.10–11, 153–4; Van Dijk, op. cit., pp.3, 25, 27; J.J. van Dijk, 'Les contacts ethniques dans la Mésopotamie et les syncrétismes de la religion sumérienne', in Sven S. Hartman, ed., *Syncretism*, Almqvist & Wiksell, Stockholm, 1967, p.176.

53 Cooper, op. cit., p.11.

54 ibid., p.11. For Errakal, see Van Dijk, *Lugal ud me-lám-bi nir-ĝál*, op. cit., p.24.

55 Van Dijk, op. cit., p.19. Note also, as Van Dijk points out, there are striking similarities between the labours of Ninurta and those of Heracles: e.g., ibid., pp.17–18, where he compares monsters of Ninurta's labours with those of Heracles. He also points out, however, that the cosmogonic character and connotations are lost in the Greek mythology ('les noms des constellations astrals et la hiérarchie céleste dépendent de ces mythes', Ninurta's labours). There is another difference in the Greek system, in the fact that the myths of the labours belong to divinities in Mesopotamia, whereas in Greece they are associated with the names of heroes who are only semi-divine. On the similarities, see also Black, SMS Bulletin 15 (1988) 25.

56 Van Dijk, op. cit., p.17, and see ibid. for sources.

57 ibid, p.16. See also Labat *et al.*, op. cit., p.54 n.1: The 'dead gods' 'ne sont pas morts au sens strict du terme, comme on le voit au vers 127: ce sont des dieux, vaincus, rélégués dans l'au-delà, où ils vivrent parmi les morts.'

58 Van Dijk, op. cit., p.17.

pointed to these myths as a group, citing the warrior myths of Ninurta and Marduk.[59] Especially characteristic of these myths is the focus on warrior exploits, battle scenes, and court scenes of the Assembly of the gods and the hierarchy of power involved. Jacobsen distinguished between this group of warrior myths in the Mesopotamian mythology and another group of myths which he termed 'fertility drama'. This group of myths corresponds to the group termed, in this study, the 'goddess-and-consort' strand, and exemplified by the myths of Inanna and Dumuzi, and of Damu. Myths of both of these strands have now been discussed, and in all of these myths it can be seen that the gods gain power in the journeys that they carry out.

The purpose of Ninurta's journeys discussed here, and of the major activities involved in them, is specifically the acquisition of power, but also its retention and demonstration. While each myth presents a different story and the question of power receives a different treatment in almost every one, this purpose is remarkably consistent. It appears, therefore, that the idea of carrying out a journey was considered to be an important ingredient in a god's acquisition of power: that is, that in these myths the god achieved his power through the performance of a journey. This conclusion can also be extended to the myths of Inanna and Damu in the foregoing chapter.

The concentration in this chapter has of necessity been on the discussion of the journey for power and the way in which it is expressed in these myths of Ninurta, since these ideas need to be thoroughly established. Nevertheless, many other ideas central to Ninurta's journeys and to the god have been seen in this examination of his myths, and these ideas, like the idea of the journey for power in the context of which these other ideas have been found, are also important in the discussion of certain of the Greek myths which will be treated in the remainder of the book. All of these central ideas, of which the journey for power is just one, take an equal importance in the discussion of parallels in the Greek myths, and it is the combination in the Greek myths of considerable numbers of these ideas, in the

---

59 Thorkild Jacobsen, 'Religious Drama in Ancient Mesopotamia', in Goedicke and Roberts, eds, op. cit., pp.65ff., and especially p.72.

context of the journey for power, that gives real value to the discussion of parallels and raises the question of Mesopotamian influence in these Greek myths.

4

FROM EKUR TO OLYMPOS

The location now moves from Mesopotamia to Greece, and the relationship between Ekur and Olympos epitomizes the connection between the two areas in this study. Ekur is the temple of the supreme god Enlil in Nippur, the temple to which Ninurta returns after performing his great exploits. The name means 'mountain house' and it is the Assembly of the gods. Olympos corresponds to Ekur. Like Enlil, the Greek supreme god Zeus dwells on a mountain, Mt Olympos, and, as with the Mesopotamian god, his abode there, the halls of Olympos, is the Assembly of the gods.

This is a complex parallel with intriguing implications. In the Greek myths analysed here, there are great numbers of such complex parallels, and many parallels of far greater complexity, but unlike this parallel of Ekur and Olympos they are not isolated. Rather, they are usually found in clusters and very frequently in the context of journeys which parallel those in the Mesopotamian myths in nature and purpose. In fact, the same religious mythological ideas expressed in similar motifs are displayed in these Greek myths of the early archaic period. The same structures of the journeys of the gods with the same central idea of the god's acquisition and demonstration of power are presented together; and in the context provided by the journey sequences are found many ideas and motifs similar to those in the Mesopotamian myths. Together, all of the parallels have profound implications for the nature of Greek mythology and its relationship to that of Mesopotamia.

Some works are outstanding for the number of ideas and motifs which they have in common with Mesopotamian myths, and the ways in which they are presented often correspond directly to their presentation in the Mesopotamian material. The Homeric hymns to Apollo and to Demeter especially come to mind in this context, as does the myth of Prometheus and Pandora in Hesiod's *Theogony* and *Works and Days*. However, the other myths discussed here also show similar journeys, together with the idea of the journey for power, and there are many other specific parallels as well.

The long *Homeric Hymn to Aphrodite* is one of these, and it displays many parallels with the myths of Inanna and Dumuzi. This circumstance is not surprising in the case of myths of Aphrodite, since she has long been considered to derive from the same Mesopotamian goddess. If the influence of Mesopotamian mythological ideas is to be found in Greece, one would expect to find it in the myths of Aphrodite. When parallels with the Mesopotamian myths are seen in the journeys and accompanying ideas in the hymns to Apollo and Demeter, it may at first seem more surprising, especially if one looks to originally foreign gods to show evidence of influence. The main gods in these hymns, Leto, Apollo, Artemis, Demeter, Persephone and Hades, are not considered to have any demonstrable connections with Mesopotamia. However, if there are connections with Mesopotamia in these myths, they are connections only of religious mythological ideas and concepts, and have no implications regarding the origins of the deities concerned.

Other myths also show many parallels of idea and motif. In the myth of Athena's birth they are especially strong, but they are also of a very complex nature, and it requires a thorough understanding of the way that the ideas are applied in other Greek myths before their significance can be properly appreciated. Myths of Zeus also show many correspondences to Mesopotamian ideas, especially ideas of the journey for power. These features stand out in the birth myth of Aphrodite too, a myth which, like the story of the *affaire* of Anchises and Aphrodite in the long Homeric hymn to this goddess, shows motifs similar to those in the myths of Inanna.

One of the most striking features of this study of parallels in Greek and Mesopotamian myths is the clear distinction which is apparent in the Greek myths between the two major strands observed in the Mesopotamian mythology. The ideas and motifs of the goddess-and-consort strand and those of the heroic strand are kept almost entirely separate in the Greek myths, mirroring the situation in the Mesopotamian mythology. This is displayed with particular clarity in the brilliant *Homeric Hymn to Apollo*. The clear distinction is one of the especially striking features of this study, but it is just one of the notable parallels. It is when all the parallels are viewed together, and their application in the Greek myths is fully appreciated, that the suggestion of Mesopotamian influence in these Greek myths of the early archaic period becomes insistent. In the hymn to Apollo which follows, the parallels are especially numerous and have many intriguing implications concerning the nature of mythological ideas in Greece.

5

THE HOMERIC HYMN TO APOLLO

'I will remember and not forget Apollo who shoots afar.' In this first line and the next lines of the beginning of the *Homeric Hymn to Apollo*, the poet makes his intention plain: that he will praise Apollo as befitting a mighty Olympian god, the son of Leto and Zeus. He proceeds to carry out his plan in a superlatively imaginative fashion in the two sections which make up the hymn, each section revealing a different set of concepts about his young divine hero. First he hymns the mother Leto's wandering journey to Delos in search of a place to give birth to her son, and the birth and rise of the powerful god on the island; then in the second section, in a completely different manner, he sings of the heroic glory of the mighty son of the supreme god Zeus as he enters his father's Assembly for the first time and then goes forth to establish his illustrious oracle at Delphi.

The genius of the poet is an outstanding feature of the hymn. The poet displays his conceptual and artistic talents throughout the hymn in many different ways and on all levels. As one of the Homeridai who carried on the tradition of Homeric epic poetry, he is not unworthy of his great predecessor, who brought the epic tradition to such glory in the *Iliad* and *Odyssey*. Our poet seems to have composed this hymn during or slightly after the seventh century BC, the century after Homer, whose legacy shows clearly in this poem.[1]

---

1 Some views on dating: Richard Janko, *Homer, Hesiod and the Homeric Hymns: Diachronic Development in Epic Diction*, Cambridge University Press, Cambridge, 1982, pp.132, 195–8; M.L. West, 'Cynaethus' Hymn to Apollo', CQ 25 (1975) 161ff.; Walter Burkert, 'Kynaithos, Polycrates, and the Homeric Hymn to Apollo', in G.W. Bowersock, W. Burkert and M.C.J. Putnam, eds, *Arktouros: Hellenic Studies presented to Bernard M.W. Knox on the Occasion of his 65th Birthday*, Walter de Gruyter, Berlin, 1979, pp.53–62; Karl Förstel, *Untersuchungen zum homerischen Apollonhymnos*, Studienverlag Dr N. Brockmeyer, Bochum, 1979, pp.200–11.

The first real indication of the poet's artistry comes to light in the scene of Apollo's birth on Delos, when he presents many concepts pertaining to the young god in many symbolic ways and by a number of subtle allusions. The poet's methods thus unveiled, many more instances reveal themselves as the story unfolds throughout the poem. His genius is displayed most of all by his handling of the concepts of Apollo and his mythology and the ideas which are expressed about the god in his rise to power in the divine world and over mankind.

The way in which the poem is presented indicates that the story that is revealed in this hymn, and all of its ideas, must have been immediately clear to the ancient Greek audience for whom the hymn was intended; but at first it lies beyond the reach of the outsider, as all we moderns are, because much background knowledge of the mythology and the Greek religion is clearly required, and it is not revealed in any other Greek religious or mythological text.

Amazingly, however, the story becomes immediately clear to a large extent when it is viewed in the light of knowledge of the mythology acquired from the Mesopotamian texts studied above. The poet's clever presentation of the main ideas about the god in both parts of the hymn is also revealed in the light of the motifs and ideas in the Mesopotamian material. It is only when these are known, and their usage in the hymn understood, that the real artistry of the poet and the nature of the story which he is telling begin to be fully appreciated. His presentation of Apollo has two main aspects in the light of the structure of the hymn and the Mesopotamian mythological material, and both aspects are kept virtually distinct in the two main sections of the hymn, the Delian section which comes first (lines 1–178) and the Pythian which follows it (lines 179–546). The separation of the two aspects is a necessity in view of their nature, and this will become apparent in the following examination of the two sections of this hymn.

THE DELIAN SECTION

The Delian section is like a Gordian knot, a puzzle cunningly twisted and tied so that the key to its solution remains concealed in its folds. The ideas seen in a group of Mesopotamian myths seem, however, to provide the key which begins to unravel the knot, at least enough to get a glimpse of the picture which must have been intended for the ancient audience.

The myths which provide the clues are certain of the myths of the goddess-and-consort strand, particularly those of Damu. In the Delian section there are many parallels with central features of these myths, but the main ones consist of the journey and the idea of the 'journey for power' which lies at the heart of it. Both Apollo and his mother, Leto, perform journey sequences, and these constitute most of the narrative line of the section, providing the backbone of the plot. In the light that is provided by the Mesopotamian material, and its central ideas which have been discussed in the previous chapters, the activities of both major deities who are important to this section, but especially of Apollo, are completely transformed and reveal many concepts regarding the young god and his rise to power that otherwise remain completely hidden. The ideas about Apollo seen in this section are only part of the conceptual picture of the god, and it requires the Pythian section to complete this. However, the Delian section provides a fascinating introduction to the poet's complex and subtle picture of Apollo in this hymn.

The hymn begins with the scene of Apollo's arrival in Zeus's temple on Olympos. Apollo walks through the halls of Zeus bending his bow, to the alarm of the gods. His mother, Leto, defuses the situation and presents him to Zeus, who gives him nectar and ambrosia.

The poet then tells the story of Apollo's birth on Delos, where his rise began. Leto wanders over Greece in search of a place to give birth to Apollo, and finally chooses the rocky island of Delos. When she asks the personified island to be the place of her son's birth, Delos is somewhat reluctant. She fears that he will reject her rocky soil and push her down with his feet to the bottom of the ocean. Leto swears by Styx, the great oath of the gods, that her son will build his temple on the island after his birth, before establishing his cult temples and groves over the rest of the earth. Leto thereupon settles down to give birth, surrounded by other immortal goddesses, with the notable exception of Hera.

At this point Leto suffers a setback. For nine days she is unable to give birth to Apollo, because the birth goddess Eileithyia has – through the malice of Hera, inevitably – remained on Olympos in ignorance of Leto's condition. Iris is sent to fetch her, bearing as a gift a special golden necklace nine cubits in length.

Iris escorts Eileithyia back from Olympos and as soon as the birth goddess sets foot on Delos Leto begins to give birth. Beside the streams of Inopos at the foot of Mt Kynthos (lines 117–19):

she threw her arms around a palm tree, kneeled
on the soft meadow, and Earth beneath smiled:
(Apollo) sprang forth to the light, and all the goddesses
raised a loud cry.

ἀμφὶ δὲ φοίνικι βάλε πήχεε, γοῦνα δ' ἔρεισε
λειμῶνι μαλακῷ· μείδησε δὲ γαῖ' ὑπένερθεν·
ἐκ δ' ἔθορε πρὸ φόωσδε· θεαὶ δ' ὀλόλυξαν ἅπασαι.

After his birth Apollo is bathed and dressed in a white garment.
Nectar and ambrosia are given to him, and his might is instantly
apparent, for the golden cords and bands cannot hold him. Apollo
thereupon claims his main attributes of lyre and bow and at the same
time affirms his father's supreme power.

The long-haired Phoebus Apollo begins to walk over the earth, and
the goddesses are amazed. It is then that the whole of Delos blossoms
with gold 'as does a mountain peak with woodland flowers'.[2] He
strides over Mt Kynthos on Delos and then travels through the
islands, establishing his cult, his temples and groves, and his festivals
of boxing, dancing and song.[3]

The journey performed by the two gods is the main structural feature
of the Delian section, and its central purpose is to elevate the god and
demonstrate his power. The power of Apollo is portrayed in many
features in the journey, but the application of the 'journey for power'
theme is not immediately apparent because of the symbolic representation of much of the action in relation to Apollo. The main
subtleties by which the idea is conveyed lie in the symbolic portrayal
of Apollo's journey sequence provided by the birth scene and the
lines which follow (lines 67–75, 119–35, 139–46). The journey for
power will be fully evident only after a thorough and detailed
discussion of the journey sequences of both Leto and Apollo, and of
the ideas that are expressed in them. The significance of all the
relevant features of the complex journeys of Leto and Apollo are
apparent only in the light of Mesopotamian material, specifically
certain myths of the goddess-and-consort strand which are the source
for virtually all of the parallels revealed in this discussion of the Delian

2 Lines 135–9. Lines 136–8 are alternative for line 139 and are consequently
   omitted.
3 Specifically, the festival of the Ionians on Delos: cf. J.D. Niles, 'On the
   Design of the *Hymn to Delian Apollo*', CJ 75 (1979) 37.

section. The parallels are seen for the most part in Damu/Dumuzi's myths, but many are also found in the myths of his wife, Inanna.

To begin, the theme of the god's power is expressed in several motifs in this section: the precocious might of the god in the birth scene after he is bathed by the goddesses and receives divine food from Themis (lines 124–5); his claim of the lyre and bow (lines 131–2) which are employed in other parts of the hymn to portray his power (lines 1–13, 182–206); the activites which the god carries out to establish his cult by founding temples, festivals and rites on Delos and the other islands after his birth (lines 140–52). The journey-for-power context in which these expressions of his power appear, and various other important illustrations of his power, become clear only after consideration of the goddess-and-consort style of journey sequences involved in this section of the hymn.

There are two journey sequences in this Delian section (lines 1–178): first, the wandering journey of Leto in search of a place to give birth to Apollo, a search which ends on Delos; and, second, the birth of Apollo, which appears to involve a symbolic ascent from within the earth. The journey of Leto is straightforward and achieves its aim in the birth of Apollo. Before the successful birth, there is, however, an initial setback, the form of which closely parallels that of the complex initial-setback systems in Mesopotamian myths. The failure typically occurs when the deity reaches the destination of the journey. Only after help is received from the upperworld gods, usually via an intermediary or assistant, is success achieved.

Leto's setback takes place when she arrives at Delos, the destination intended for her by the poet, and fails in the purpose of her journey – to give birth to Apollo (lines 89–92). Help comes from Olympos in the form of Eileithyia, the birth goddess, whose arrival brings Leto the power to give birth. This help comes through the intermediary, Iris, who fetches and escorts the birth goddess from the Assembly.

The same sequence of ideas has been seen in ID, where the goddess Inanna lies dead in the netherworld after encountering the netherworld goddess Ereshkigal, and receives help from the upperworld gods through the efforts of Ninshubur, her minister and messenger, who travels around Sumer and eventually to the god Enki in his temple; help is also received through the substitutes who descend to her, giving her the food and water of life to revive her and allow her 'rebirth' from the netherworld: a 'rebirth' which appears to be represented by a similar motif here in the Greek myth. The help that Eileithyia brings to Leto is the power to give birth, reversing her setback; the purpose of Eileithyia in her journey is actually the same as that of the goddess Leto herself, who travels to Delos for Apollo's birth. In travelling to allow Apollo's birth, Leto also performs the 'helper' role as it is seen in the Damu myths, where the mother goddess sets out to release the child from the netherworld. Other examples of the initial-setback motif in Mesopotamian literature can be seen in the Anzu myth and *Lugale* of Ninurta, and in the *Epic of Gilgamesh*.[4]

Each of these Mesopotamian figures, Inanna, Ninurta and Gilgamesh, receives a setback through the opposition of an enemy, and in Leto's case the enemy is the antagonistic Hera, who tries to prevent the birth of Apollo by keeping Eileithyia in ignorance of Leto's plight.[5] Another element found with Eileithyia is her special golden necklace, which she receives from Iris. This adornment of the Greek birth goddess has remarkable coincidence with the special necklace of the Mesopotamian creatrix and birth goddess, the 'midwife' Mami/ Nintu in the *Epic of Atrahasis* (Tablet III.vi.2–4).[6]

The second journey sequence which may be seen here is an important feature for the elucidation of a number of Apollo's activities in this section. The sequence of actions which constitutes the 'journey' begins with his birth scene. When Apollo is born from the womb of the earth goddess, his mother, he springs forth into the light, and all the assembled goddesses raise a loud shout (lines 115–19). The journey sequence ends with his striding over Delos and spreading his cult and temples around the other islands (lines 119–42). The journey involved is actually an ascent sequence, but it is represented largely symbolically. Delos' function in the 'journey' and her relationship with Apollo as part of it are presented in a highly elliptical way but very cleverly, by a number of symbols of which the significance straightaway becomes visible in the light of Mesopotamian ideas involved in the type of journey which is seen performed in this section by Apollo and Leto.

Though it may seem absurd at first, to anyone without a close acquaintance with the relevant Mesopotamian ideas, to suggest such

---

4 Anzu myth: Tablet II.1–149 and Tablet III obv. i, lines 2–12; *Lugale* 151–297; Gilgamesh epic: Tablet V. See fragment of the Hittite recension, in James B. Pritchard, ed., *Ancient Near Eastern Texts Relating to the Old Testament*, 3rd edition, Princeton University Press, Princeton, 1969, p.83.
5 Cf. also Callimachus' *Hymn to Delos*, 60.
6 On this epic, see Chapter 9 below, on Pandora.

a parallel, the composite journey which forms the basis of the action of the Delian section (from line 30 to line 142), the journey composed of Leto's wandering from Olympos around Greece to Delos and Apollo's symbolic ascent journey, directly parallels the essential journey pattern of the myths of Damu and his mother in edin-na ú-saĝ-ĝá and TRS 8. In these, the mother goddess conducts a wandering search for her son and eventually achieves his release and rebirth from beneath the earth. In the Greek hymn, Leto performs a wandering search over Greece, and her son Apollo performs an ascent sequence for his birth. Leto's search is for a place to give birth instead of a search for the child, but the result is the same, with the birth of the child. In the Greek myth, the young son is born rather than reborn, as Damu is, because it is the myth of Apollo's birth, but the structure is the same: a wandering journey of the goddess and the birth of her son in an ascent sequence. The appositeness of this parallel becomes apparent only after analysis of Apollo's ascent sequence and of all the ideas involved. The parallel is, in fact, a very complex and profound one.

The ascent of Apollo is presented in a clever and highly metaphorical manner in various motifs of his birth. The birth episode follows the pattern seen in the birth of Zeus who similarly emerges from earth as part of his birth sequence. The god's emergence from earth as part of his birth episode, as well as the other motifs seen in the birth and preparation of the god, involve ideas that are perfectly comprehensible in the light of the Mesopotamian ideas which are found in ascent sequences in the myths of the goddess and consort strand and which help to reveal the complexity and profundity of the ascent sequence in the poet's story about Apollo in this scene.

The idea involved in Apollo's birth from his mother is his emergence from beneath the earth on to the sunlit surface of the earth. With this ascent idea, his birth is very like that of Zeus Kretagenes, both in Hesiod's account of Zeus on Mt Aigaios on Crete and in the Palaikastro hymn. In the latter hymn, the young god, who has 'gone to earth' (γᾶν ὃς βέβακες), springs forth (θόρε) from the earth on Cretan Mt Dikte. The birth of Zeus Kretagenes in Hesiod's *Theogony* (lines 468–84) presents the same principles, since, as part of his birth process, he is taken from Rhea and hidden by Earth in a deep cave in the earth on woody Mt Aigaios (lines 482–4); this is another way of saying in the womb of Earth, and from here he must naturally emerge. This is, in effect, a second and symbolic birth of the god. As it is shown at the end of the passage about the birth of Zeus in Apollodorus, Rhea brings him forth in a cave on Mt Dikte which is another representation of the same idea, but here the birth of the god from his mother coincides with the symbolic birth from Earth.[7]

Here in this birth episode of Zeus are many motifs which are repeated in Apollo's birth scene and these similarities are the first indication that the same ideas are involved in both birth situations. In the *Theogony*, the mother goddess, Rhea, journeys to the island to give birth (lines 477–8). The mountain is the place of birth when Zeus is born symbolically from Earth – the cave within the mountain (lines 482–4). In Apollodorus' résumé, Zeus is surrounded by attendants who make a great noise at the god's birth which is deliberately shown as a combination of birth from his mother and symbolic birth from the Earth.

All of these motifs are present in Apollo's birth scene (lines 16–17, 117–22). Leto journeys to the island Delos where she gives birth, at Mt Kynthos (lines 16–17), surrounded by a crowd of attendants (lines 92–5, 119). The motifs of noise, of light, and the springing forth of the god are found directly at the birth of the god (lines 117–19).

In these lines, Apollo's birth from his mother is portrayed as a symbolic ascent from the interior of Earth, directly parallelling the birth of Zeus. The rise from the Earth is suggested immediately by the fact that the earth goddess is mentioned in the scene which reveals many ideas similar to those in the birth of Zeus where the emergence from the earth is explicit. However, most striking is the metaphor presented with Earth in this scene and it is this metaphor which clearly reveals Apollo's ascent from within the earth. Earth's role in the scene is presented by the words 'And Earth beneath smiled' (line 118). Closer inspection reveals the crucial significance of this sentence, which is central in the birth scene. Leto kneels down on the grassy meadow, then beneath her as she gives birth Earth smiles and Apollo springs forth to the light and all the goddesses give a great shout. The motif of the Earth's mouth agape as she smiles is a highly poetic representation of the open interior of the earth goddess, directly beneath the open womb of Leto, and it is at this point that Apollo leaps forth, like the young Cretan Zeus leaping forth from

---

7 Apollodorus I.i.7; for the Palaikastro hymn see Martin L. West, 'The Dictaeon Hymn to the Kouros', JHS 85 (1965) 149–59.

the earth on the mountain – in fact, the same word is used (ἔθορε, line 119) – and like Zeus' birth from the cave within Earth on Mt Aigaios. So in his birth, Apollo is represented as rising from the interior of the Earth at the same time as he is born from his mother, the double idea as found with Zeus at his birth in the *Theogony* (lines 479–84) and Apollodorus (I.i.7). The birth from the earth is clearly symbolic with Apollo just as it is with Zeus.

Before going on, one issue concerning the birth of the young Zeus in the Palaikastro hymn and his birth in Hesiod's *Theogony* needs to be mentioned. Some scholars like to separate the young dying, that is, descending and returning, god of the Palaikastro hymn from Hesiod's Zeus, perhaps chiefly because of the poet Callimachos' famous and fierce rejection in his *Hymn to Zeus* of the idea that Zeus may 'die' each year, accusing the Cretans of being liars because he knows full well that Zeus cannot die.[8] The scholars who do not accept the connection may be right in view of the usual belief of the Greeks that gods are immortal, although the concept of the dying Zeus does not seem to be a purely Cretan belief, so it seems unfair to choose this nation for censure as harsh as that handed out to them by Callimachos.[9] There were, in fact, tombs of Zeus in various parts of Greece, bearing testimony to widespread similar beliefs held by mainland Greeks. However, the consideration that the god of Mt Dikte may not be the Hesiodic Zeus does not affect the interpretation of the motifs which are presented in the birth myths of both the

---

8 *Hymn to Zeus*, 8–9; the quoted words in the hymn are from Epimenides of Crete: see G.R. Maclennan, *Callimachus, Hymn to Zeus*, Edizioni dell'Ateneo e Bizzarri, Rome, 1977, pp.14, 35ff. Cf. also N. Hopkinson, 'Callimachus' *Hymn to Zeus*', CQ 34 (1984) 140. Cf. also West, JHS 85 (1965) 156.

9 On the chthonic Zeus and Hesiod's Zeus, see Walter Burkert, *Greek Religion*, Harvard University Press, Cambridge (Mass.), 1985, pp.200–1; Martin Nilsson, *The Mycenaean Religion and its Survivals in Greek Religion*, Lund, 1968, pp.553–4; M.L. West, ed., *Hesiod Theogony*, Clarendon Press, Oxford, 1966, pp.290–3; H. Verbruggen, *Le Zeus crétois*, Collection d'études mythologiques 10, Société d'Édition «Les belles lettres», Paris, 1981, pp.69–70. On the worship of this Cretan Zeus in early archaic, geometric and earlier periods, see Peter Blome, 'Die dunklen Jahrhunderte – aufgehellt', in Joachim Latacz, ed., *Zweihundert Jahre Homer-Forschung. Rückblick und Ausblick*, B.G. Teubner, Stuttgart and Leipzig, 1991, pp.56–7.

Palaikastro hymn and the *Theogony*, or dim the illuminating light which each sheds individually on those in Apollo's birth scene.

The ascent of Apollo from beneath the earth is illustrated by another feature in the myth, the motif of coming into the light in the birth (line 119) and seeing the light (line 71). This idea parallels the motif of emerging from the gloom beneath the earth into the light of the upperworld sun, seen, for instance, when Persephone releases a figure from the netherworld: the returning figure sees the light. This idea of seeing the light is found also in Pindar, frag. 133, in the case of the return of souls from the netherworld to the light of the sun.[10] A number of ideas may underlie this apparently important motif of Apollo's birth, as it is expressed here, and have much significance for the cult, but one of the ideas therefore appears to be a symbolic ascent from the womb of earth to the surface of the earth, here on Delos at Mt Kynthos.

The careful metaphor in the birth scene and the parallels with Greek mythological material therefore indicate that this is an ascent sequence for the young god who rises from beneath the earth. This ascent sequence is then the second part of the journey begun by the wandering, searching goddess, and the whole journey parallels the journey idea which forms the basis of the Damu liturgies mentioned above. The presence of the ascent sequence is clearly indicated also by the parallels in this hymn with features in the ascent sequence in Mesopotamian myths.

The ascent sequence is illustrated by further motifs in the scene of Apollo's birth on Delos, motifs which must be understood in the light of closely parallel ideas found in the goddess-and-consort myths of the young Mesopotamian descending and returning god Damu/Dumuzi. These motifs are especially important for the expression of the ideas in Apollo's journey for power. The first of these ideas is the alternating ascent and descent of the god and goddess, and the second is the fertility effects of the ascent of the young god. These two features are central to the myths of Damu/Dumuzi in Mesopotamia.

---

10 Christiane Sourvinou-Inwood, 'The Boston Relief of Locri Epizephyrii', JHS 94 (1974) 136. Release of souls to the sun of the upperworld, ἐς τὸν ὑπερθεν ἄλιον, frag. of Pindar from Plato's *Meno*: Ivan M. Linforth, *The Arts of Orpheus*, University of California Press, Berkeley, 1941; cf. frag. 133: B. Snell and H. Maehler, eds, *Pindar Carmina cum Fragmentis*, Part 1, B.C. Teubner, Leipzig, p.111.

Both features are expressed in very subtle and artistic ways in the lines following Apollo's birth. Both also concern Apollo's interaction with Delos, who functions in the ascent sequence as the goddess opposite Apollo, since these particular sequences require a goddess. She seems to replace Leto, who drops out of the narrative immediately on the birth of Apollo, and is nowhere mentioned in the activities which manifest his power in the rest of the Delian section. The two features are referred to in the last part of the Delian section, where the effects of the ascent sequence with the demonstration of the young god's power are the main concern. Now that he is born, the 'far-shooting' Phoebus Apollo begins to stride 'on the wide-pathed earth' (line 133), that is, on Delos (Mt Kynthos, lines 133–42, and 141 especially), who flowers with gold, and then over the islands where he establishes his cult temples, groves and festivals. The manifestation of the god's power – specifically his divine nature and cultic power – can be seen in the reference to his establishment of his temples, groves and festivals, but the demonstration of power is also found here in motifs which involve Delos.

The first feature which expresses an idea seen in the Damu/Dumuzi myths and in other goddess-and-consort myths is Apollo's encounter with Delos. This encounter involves the alternating descent of the god and goddess as it is seen in ID, in both Dumuzi's substitution for Inanna who emerges from the netherworld (lines 281, 285–9, 347–58), and Geshtinanna's replacement of the young god in the netherworld (lines 401–10), but the idea also seems to be referred to at the end of the Damu myth edin-na ú-sağ-ğá.[11] This idea cannot be seen simply by an examination of the lines referred to above (lines 133–42), but it requires other lines from elsewhere in the Delian episode to reveal the whole scenario in the form in which it is presented in the Greek hymn. The form that the encounter takes in the Greek hymn is slightly antagonistic, with the strong male god, who has just risen, 'winning' in the encounter – a characteristic which is entirely in accordance with the nature of Apollo's encounters elsewhere in the hymn (lines 356–62, 375–87) – and then the goddess performing a descent. This encounter is referred to where Delos reveals to Leto her strange fear that the powerful and

---

11 OB version, lines 373–4, in Thorkild Jacobsen, *The Harps that Once . . .: Sumerian Poetry in Translation*, Yale University Press, New Haven and London, 1987, p.84.

scornful Apollo will reject her after his birth and push her down with his feet to the bottom of the sea (lines 71–5), which is a lower region and may be functioning here as a parallel for the netherworld, since Delos is an island. The symbolism of the bottom of the sea as the netherworld is also found in Mesopotamian myth in the context of the descent and ascent journey.[12]

For some reason best known to the poet, the actual performance of the antagonistic encounter is deliberately avoided in the hymn – at this point, at least – as Delos extracts the promise from Leto, in exchange for being Apollo's birthplace, that her son will instead build his temple and establish his cult on the island before setting off to do the same over the rest of the earth (lines 61–88). By means of this, the poet rather cleverly manages to avoid the event but to keep the power-theme results.

Nevertheless, the symbolic performance of the encounter between Delos and Apollo does receive a mention later in the hymn, in the lines referred to above, where he begins to stride over the earth (ἐβίβασκεν ἐπὶ χθονὸς) that is, over Delos (lines 133–5, 139). The image of Apollo striding over Delos (on his feet, of course) reveals the significance in the hymn of the odd motif of Apollo thrusting the goddess down to the nether regions with his feet. Embodied in the simple motif, within the context of Apollo's ascent, are the ideas of the god's encounter with and 'defeat' of the goddess who then descends.

The actual significance of this apparent alternation on the level of cultic belief is not clear, but it should not be automatically interpreted in terms of the Mesopotamian myths, especially since no idea of a cycle of perpetual descent and return is alluded to in these lines, even though other features of the Greek hymn parallel those in the Mesopotamian myths. In fact, the explanation given in the hymn for Apollo's action is, at least in Delos' words, that he will be so great a god that he will scorn her barrenness and rockiness and will, very recklessly, not hesitate to push her under. The explanation is rather trite in view of the complexity and apparent importance of the motif and the author's handling of it, and the motif may have had a deeper

12 In the Dilmun episode of the *Epic of Gilgamesh* (Assyrian version Tablet X.v.1–XI.vi.282) in which the ideas of the goddess-and-consort strand are central features. See below in this commentary on the Delian section for a complete discussion of the relevant ideas in this epic, and the parallels with Apollo's ascent sequence.

significance which was understood. However, as it is incorporated in the action of the hymn, it is used specifically to emphasize the greatness and might of Apollo, and to provide a reason for the establishment of his cult and temple on the island.

The second additional motif which illustrates the ascent sequence and whose depth and complexity is revealed in the light of the Mesopotamian material is the fertility motif of the god in this situation. This involves a motif found in Apollo's interaction with Delos and is one aspect of the god's demonstration of his power. The motif is seen in the context of Apollo striding over Delos: in doing so he causes Delos to flower with gold as does a mountain peak with woodland flowers (χρυσῷ δ'ἄρα Δῆλος ἅπασα/ἤνθησ' ὡς ὅτε τε ῥίον οὔρεος ἄνθεσιν ὕλης).[13] This appears to refer to the fertility effect of the young god's ascent, a feature which is central in the myths of Damu/Dumuzi. This demonstration of fertility in the context of the other motifs which parallel the ideas of the goddess-and-consort strand is in itself a strong indication that the ascent is involved in the birth scene, but the motif also recalls several other ideas of the Damu ascent and display of power. This motif is another example of the poet's cleverness and command of poetic principles, but it also gives witness to his thorough knowledge of the mytho-logical material and his understanding of the underlying concepts; the motif is also highly remarkable for the strength of its evocative qualities, since it conjures up the whole scenario of the young god's rise from the netherworld and its results. The clever motif has a double function, as it also seems to allude to the golden rays of the newly risen sun touching the mountain peak in the early morning and is apparently a reference to Apollo's connection with the sun, an important aspect of the god in later times.[14] The motif of the sun touching the mountain may also concern fertility.

In this motif, involving the mountain and the sunrise in an ascent sequence, another complex parallel with the Damu myths comes to light. In the context of the myths of the goddess-and-consort strand, the mountain has a special significance, and this may be the reason for

13 Lines 135, 139.
14 The same motif of Apollo as the dawn sun seems to be present with his epiphany to the Argonauts, Ap. Rhod. 2, 669–719. Apollo strides past in the darkness, his bow in his hand, and the quiver hanging down his back, and the epiphany is interpreted as a poetic allusion to the arrival of the sun at this part in the epic: see Richard Hunter, 'Apollo and the Argonauts: Two Notes on Ap. Rhod. 2, 669–719', MH 43 (1986) 50–2.

the mountain has a special significance, and this may be the reason for its inclusion in the scene of the birth/ascent of the young god Apollo. In the myths of Damu, the mountain symbolizes the netherworld, the region beneath the earth from which the god rises; the particular mountains from which Damu returns as he comes forth from the netherworld are the mountains of the sunrise to the east of Sumer, the mountains from which Utu, the sun god, rises in the morning.[15] Apollo seems to be doing a similar thing here with Delos, and the motif suggests his similar rise from within the earth. Whatever other symbolism may be found with the mountain in Greece, or the age of worship involving the mountain in various cults, the mountain appears to be combined here with the sunrise to express this ascent idea.

Taken altogether, the complex of motifs involved in the birth scene (lines 119–32) and the following lines (133–42) portrays a complete ascent sequence as part of his birth from his mother. By the employment of these various motifs in Apollo's birth and subsequent striding over Delos, the poet manages to present two ideas in the one scene: the physical birth from his mother, and the idea of the young god's ascent sequence from the gloom within the earth. In doing this, he achieves a poetical *tour de force* by turning a simple motif of birth from the mother into a situation of far greater mythical and perhaps also religious significance. While this ascent sequence is portrayed symbolically, indeed in such a fashion that it is hidden from anyone who does not understand the significance of the motifs, it was probably immediately obvious to the ancient audience for whom the hymn was composed. It may quite conceivably have been well known symbolism, or at least well known to those for whom it was intended, so that just these few brief allusions were capable of conjuring up a whole complex mythological scenario of which the full glory still remains concealed from the modern reader. There is

15 Damu/Dumuzi and the eastern mountains as signifying the netherworld: edin-na ú-sağ-ğá, OB version, lines 177–80, in Jacobsen, op. cit., p.74; 'The Wild Bull Who Has Lain Down', in William L. Moran, ed., *Toward the Image of Tammuz and Other Essays on Mesopotamian History and Culture: Thorkild Jacobsen*, Harvard University Press, Cambridge (Mass.), 1970, pp.102–3 and discussion; and lines 25–6 in Jacobsen, op. cit., p.49, and the discussion on p.47. On the eastern mountains and Dumuzi's journey to and from them, William R. Sladek, 'Inanna's Descent to the Netherworld', Ph.D. diss., University Microfilms, Ann Arbor, 1974, p.62 and n.4; and Wilfred G. Lambert, 'The Pair Lahmu–Lahamu in Cosmology', Or 54 (1985) 202.

also the possibility that the picture may have contained deep religious significance and was presented in such a fashion because it was not meant for all hearers in all circumstances, especially in profane ones. On the other hand, however, it is quite likely that it was well known to anyone interested and, especially in view of the poet's praiseful mention of himself (lines 169–78) – if these two passages were composed by the same poet, and in formulaic tradition one can never be sure – the subtle portrayal of the ascent idea and various associated ideas merely represents the poet's demonstration of his own artistic skill and cleverness, which is, on the evidence of his handling of these motifs and ideas, admittedly not insignificant.

There are several other motifs in the ascent sequence of this section which play an important role in the idea of the journey for power, and they seem at the same time to relate to features found in the Mesopotamian myths of the goddess-and-consort strand. The god's acquisition of power is illustrated in the motifs immediately follow- ing his birth from Leto. The motif of divine food is one of these: Themis pours out nectar and ambrosia for Apollo (lines 124–5) and Phoebus Apollo's consequent might is immediately apparent as the golden cords and bands are unable to confine him (lines 127–9). This motif and the idea underlying its use may be parallel to the motif in ID where food and water from the god Enki is part of the ascent sequence (lines 224–5, 252–3), and it initiates the goddess's rise in power – in her case she gains the power to rise again. However, the motif occurs as part of a scene where the god similarly comes to life and symbolically ascends from beneath the earth, so the context is in these essentials the same.

Further motifs of the power of the strong young rising god follow when Apollo claims his main attributes of lyre and bow, and at the same time affirms the authority of his father, the supreme god. These attributes are used elsewhere in the hymn as part of Apollo's display of power as the son of the supreme god. They do not in fact belong in the context as they are not powers typical of the descending and rising god. This is similarly the case with the idea of fixing the young god's power in relation to that of the supreme god. Instead, these features belong rather to the other aspect of Apollo, which is presented for the most part by the Pythian section, and are here linking devices between the two major aspects of the complete conception of the god and his mythology in the hymn.

Another motif which seems to have a role in the power theme in the ascent, once again in the god's rise in power, is that of the bathing and dressing of the god immediately after his birth. It may also correspond to motifs in the myths of the goddess-and-consort strand, where the motif of bathing and dressing is found with a connotation of power as part of an ascent sequence. The bathing and dressing of the child in the hymn has, of course, its practical purpose, but in the light of its context and of the usage of the motif in a similar context in Mesopotamian myths, it may also have an application as part of the young god's symbolic acquisition of power, particularly as it occurs nowhere else. In the hymn it is part of the preparation of the child by the assembled goddesses, ending in the child's demonstration of power which he has received, so it may have been intended as part of the symbolism seen in the other motifs of the birth scene which increase the god's might. In this function the motif parallels the bathing and dressing of the figure on the ascent journey, as in the case of Ishtar in AV, to take a Mesopotamian example, when she is sprinkled with the water of life and receives clothes as part of her return journey and her return to power in the upperworld (lines 114, 118–25). The motif is, in fact, ubiquitous in this goddess's myths, and in AV it has the same context of an ascent sequence and acquisition of power as seen in the hymn. The motif also plays a role in other myths of Inanna/Ishtar, where it has, again, a connotation of power: in the preparation for the sacred marriage the goddess is bathed and then dressed in 'clothes of power'.[16] One of the results appears to be fertility. In this case the motif has a role in the power of the goddess, but the context is different.

The motif of bathing and dressing is seen in another Mesopotamian myth in the context of a return journey, and the motif of the acquisition of power as a result of the hero's efforts in the journey is also in evidence. In the *Epic of Gilgamesh*, the hero Gilgamesh is bathed and dressed in clean clothes as he begins his return from the island Dilmun to go to the Sumerian city Uruk where he is king, and

---

16 On the bathing and dressing in the sacred marriage rite, S.N. Kramer, *The Sacred Marriage Rite*, Indiana University Press, Bloomington and London, 1969, pp.63–5, 73–7. Some texts on the dressing and bathing: *Iddin-Dagan's Sacred Marriage Hymn*, 180–4, in Daniel Reisman, 'Iddin-Dagan's Sacred Marriage Hymn', JCS 25 (1973) 191; SRT 5 lines 3–7, especially line 7 on the significance of the garments; this poem is in Bendt Alster, 'Sumerian Love Songs', RA 79 (1985) 146–52. On the nature of the clothes, see also the translation in Jacobson, op. cit., p.16: line 7, 'and dressed in the queenly robe, the robe of the queenship of heaven'.

he gains the power for which he has been searching immediately afterwards.[17] The epic is, of course, the story of a semi-divine hero, but the goddess Ishtar plays an important role in it at various places and on various levels, and the underlying ideas and motifs of the goddess-and-consort strand are a central feature in the work, as a recent study has demonstrated.[18] The use of these motifs, which those in Apollo's hymn closely parallel, and their significance in the epic, is complex, so an extended examination is required. Their significance and application in the epic is profound and they are also considerably important for comparison with the hymn, since they help to explain the nature of the motifs which seem to have been inherited by the Greek hymn from Mesopotamian mythology, and to suggest the depth of meaning which may underlie their use by the Greek poet.

In the epic, the hero Gilgamesh undertakes a long wandering journey in search of immortal life. He arrives at the island Dilmun (Tablet X.v.1ff.) across the 'waters of death' (Tablet X.iii.50, X.iv.3ff.) to see his ancestor, the Flood hero Utnapishtim, who lives there, enjoying the immortality which the gods have granted to him alone of all mankind. The discussion between Gilgamesh and Utnapishtim, and Gilgamesh's activities on Dilmun, concern the themes in the epic of immortality and of human mortality. After bathing and dressing, he begins his return journey and at this point is told the secret of the plant of immortal youth, a plant which grows at the bottom of the sea. The hero therefore sinks his boat and dives down through the 'waters of death' to the bottom of the sea and returns with the plant, a food of life, after which he sets off homewards (Tablet XI.258–84). The story has a tragic ending when he loses the plant to a serpent (Tablet XI.285ff.), but this episode concerns the theme of mortality in the epic and not the ideas of the bathing and dressing and acquisition of power in the return.

Gilgamesh therefore performs a journey which appears to corres-

---

17 Tablet XI.238–82. For translations of the epic, see Stephanie Dalley, *Myths from Mesopotamia*, Oxford University Press, Oxford, 1989, pp.39–153; John Gardner and John Maier, *Gilgamesh: Translated from the Sîn-leqi-unninnī Version*, Alfred A. Knopf, New York, 1984, pp.57–271.

18 ibid., pp.17, 20–2, 26, 35; goddess-and-consort motifs in the epic, although examined primarily from a literary point of view: D. Gary Miller and P. Wheeler, 'Mother Goddess and Consort as Literary Motif Sequence in the Gilgamesh Epic', AcAn 29 (1981) 81–108.

pond in certain aspects to the ascent sequence which Apollo performs, and has similar underlying ideas. These are expressed in different ways in the two works, according to their different purposes and themes and the nature of the figures performing the journey. The similarity has, however, certain more profound aspects, which become clear in further investigation of the nature of the journey sequences in this epic.

Here Gilgamesh appears to perform two journeys, and both seem to be symbolic of the descent to the netherworld and return, a theme typical of the goddess-and-consort strand. He travels to the island Dilmun, which lies across the 'waters of death', to try to discover the secret of immortality from Utnapishtim. He bathes and dresses and leaves the island, gaining at the same time the power of immortal life, specifically eternal youth (Tablet XI.270, 280–1). The act of obtaining this power is in itself a descent and ascent journey: he must dive into the 'waters of death' and recover the plant from the bottom of the ocean (Tablet XI.271–6), a performance which is in effect a parallel to what he does in the journey from his city in Sumer to the island of Dilmun and the return. One is merely a vertical journey into the 'waters of death', while the other is a horizontal journey across the same waters. The idea which is being expressed here is, of course, that one must die, that is, go through death, to reach immortality.

The whole underlying conceptual structure of these journeys in the epic seems to have come from the goddess-and-consort strand, since they are merely a version of the ideas seen in ID and AV where Inanna/Ishtar descends, regains life in the netherworld, using the food and bathing motifs in ID (lines 280ff.) and the bathing in AV (118ff.), and returns. She overcomes the power of the netherworld to hold her and achieves the power to return to life in the upperworld. The epic uses different elements, or 'concretizations', to express the same underlying ideas, since the epic has a different subject and is concerned with the human problem regarding mortality and the desire for immortality. ID and AV and the Gilgamesh epic demonstrate the deep significance expressed by the use of these ideas and motifs, and illustrate the different applications to which they can be put.

In view of the parallels with these works, it looks as though certain of these goddess-and-consort motifs and structural concepts have emerged again in the hymn to Apollo, where they appear in a different way in a different narrative and probably with an altered interpretation, but still in the same relation to each other. Apollo seems to perform the same complex series of actions as Gilgamesh carries out in his epic. These ideas are seen, of course, first with Inanna/Ishtar in ID and AV. Gilgamesh performs a return journey symbolic of a return from the netherworld; he bathes and dresses as part of it, with the subsequent gain in power of the sort that he seeks, and the power motif takes the form of food. In the same way, Apollo performs an ascent journey from within the earth – which in other mythological contexts may have received stress as the realm of the dead, the netherworld – he is bathed and dressed, and afterwards clearly gains power, also by the use of the food motif. He then goes on to demonstrate this power in several other ways involving motifs typical of the goddess-and-consort strand.

Here in this hymn, the motifs which seem to express the set of concepts belonging to this strand are few. The poet merely touches on the ascent and its ideas and, indeed, in such a way that they must be unravelled with difficulty like a puzzle. Consequently, scarcely more than the outline is clear to any outsider such as a modern commentator. As a result, little of the depth that is visible in the use of these parallel motifs in the Mesopotamian myths is evident in the presentation here in the hymn. However, one can guess that a complete and profound picture, as it was rendered by the interpretation of these ideas in Apollo's cult and myth, would have been instantly evoked in the minds of the ancient audience for whom the hymn was intended.

The motif of bathing and dressing in a journey which is the centre of the discussion here is also found in Greece in a different context. It may be seen in the ritual in which the statue of Athena is conveyed in procession to the sea at Phaleron, where it is dipped in the water, apparently in a naked state. The goddess then returns in procession to the Parthenon and is re-dressed in new clothes. This may in some way involve the idea of the restoration of the goddess's power. The motif in this illustration is, however, out of the context of the hymn and the Mesopotamian sources, and therefore cannot have much impact on this comparative appraisal.

One other important motif central in the goddess-and-consort myths is found here in this section of the hymn. This is the motif of the trio of mother, sister and young rising god represented in the Damu myths by Duttur, Geshtinanna/Gunura and Damu/Dumuzi. The Greek trio is mentioned at the end of the Delian section, where the poet speaks of the Delians praising their gods in this cult – Leto, Apollo and his sister Artemis (lines 158–9).

There are, therefore, many parallels in the Delian section with Mesopotamian myths, and the major ones are central in the section where they provide the basis of the narrative. The other parallels which can be seen play an important role in the expression of the ideas underlying the activities of the deities. With the exception of one motif (the claim of the lyre and bow) which functions as a thematic linking device connecting Apollo's acquisition of power in the birth scene to the presentation of the 'journey for power' in other parts of the hymn, all the motifs and ideas of the journey in the Delian section which parallel the Mesopotamian material are seen in the same context of the myths of the goddess-and-consort strand, predominantly in the myths of Damu/Dumuzi, but also in the myths of his spouse Inanna. The main parallels are:

1 the complex journey idea of the wandering, searching mother goddess and the subsequent birth of the child in an ascent sequence from within the earth;
2 the idea of the 'journey for power' as the purpose of the journey;
3 the complex initial defeat structure in the journey of the goddess;
4 the alternating ascent and descent of the god and goddess as a result of the complete journey;
5 the demonstration of fertility effects on the earth by the ascending god;
6 the trio of mother, sister and young rising god.

There are also less important parallels, such as the mountain and the parallel motifs expressing the power theme, such as the divine food and the bathing and dressing motifs. In summary, the parallels in the Delian section are therefore numerous, complex and detailed.

One feature which has so far been left out of the discussion of this section is the temple scene at the beginning of the hymn (lines 1–13). Although an important theme in the scene is demonstration of the power and divinity of Apollo, the scene has no concern with the journey of the Delian section. It does not belong to this journey in another way, since it has no parallel in the goddess-and-consort myths of the young returning god Damu/Dumuzi. Rather, it is characteristic of the ideas concerning Apollo which are expressed in the Pythian section, and one of the reasons for its presence in the Delian section will become clear in the discussion of parallels with Mesopotamian myths to be seen in the Pythian section. The Pythian section presents a similar quantity of parallels with Mesopotamian material as has been seen in the Delian section, but, excepting the motif of the 'journey for power', these parallels are seen in an entirely different group of Mesopotamian myths and reveal a very different set of concepts about Apollo as the young son of the supreme god Zeus.

THE PYTHIAN SECTION

The Pythian section of the hymn to Apollo tells the story of the heroic son of the supreme god as it is seen in Mesopotamia. The tale is presented in one of the two major streams of the Mesopotamian mythology, the 'heroic' strand, and the activities of Apollo display ideas and motifs which lie at the centre of this strand.

The picture seen in the hymn of the young divine hero is first depicted in detail in the Mesopotamian tradition with Ninurta, the monster-slaying son of the Sumerian supreme god, Enlil, but its main features were adopted by other Mesopotamian gods, and especially later by the Babylonian god Marduk and then by his son Nabû. The concept of Apollo as the son of the supreme god Zeus parallels the role of Ninurta, and many other parallels are found with important features of this Mesopotamian god's myths. However, the form of many of the motifs follows that seen in later versions of the tradition, chiefly that of Marduk, as it is revealed in his epic *Enuma Elish*, which was composed, according to the general view, in the last quarter of the second millennium BC,[19] and depended to a large extent on the mythology of Ninurta.[20]

One of the striking aspects of the Pythian section is that all of the parallels come from the Mesopotamian heroic-strand myths, and

---

19 Wilfred G. Lambert, 'Studies in Marduk', BSOAS 47 (1984) 1–9; R. Labat *et al.*, *Les Religions du Proche-Orient asiatique*, Fayard/Denoël, Paris, 1970, p.36; Thorkild Jacobsen, *The Treasures of Darkness*, Yale University Press, New Haven and London, 1976, p.167. For a translation of *Enuma Elish*, see Dalley, *Myths from Mesopotamia*, op. cit., pp.228–77; earlier translation: Pritchard, op. cit., pp.60–72, 501–3; for the Akkadian text of the poem, see Wilfred G. Lambert and Simon B. Parker, *Enuma Eliš: The Babylonian Epic of Creation: The Cuneiform Text*, Blackwell, Oxford, 1974.

20 For some aspects of the dependence on Ninurta's myths, J.J. van Dijk, *Lugal ud me-lám-bi nir-ğál: Le récit épique et didactique des Travaux de Ninurta, du Déluge et de la Nouvelle Création*, vol. 1, E.J. Brill, Leiden, 1983, pp.3, 26, 27. Cf. also Wilfred G. Lambert, 'Ninurta Mythology in the Babylonian Epic of Creation', in Karl Hecker and Walter Sommerfeld, eds, *Keilschriftliche Literaturen. Ausgewählte Vorträge der XXXII. Rencontre Assyriologique Internationale, Münster, 8.–12.7.1985*, Dietrich Reimer Verlag, Berlin, 1986.

articulate many central concepts which are expressed there, while there are no features which correspond to those seen in the Mesopotamian myths of the goddess-and-consort strand. The heroic-strand myths characteristically portray the glory of the heroic god and his rise in power to receive a position of authority in the Assembly of the gods and in cult. The idea is expressed typically in exploits of a martial nature and in temple and court scenes. His power is demonstrated especially in these scenes and in the establishment of temples and rites, in which prophecy has an important role.

The ideas and motifs of this strand form a contrast to those of the goddess-and-consort strand, which is concerned chiefly with the role of the goddess and her interaction with the young god, the idea of fertility, and the dying and returning deity. These ideas are expressed in motifs which are usually quite different from those of the heroic strand. The journey of Leto and Apollo in the Delian section demonstrates these characteristics and forms a complete contrast to the journeys in the Pythian section.

In the Pythian section, the major parallels with Mesopotamian myths exist, first, in the style of the journey sequences which constitute the basis of the whole action of the section, and in the activities of the gods in these sequences; and, second, in the expression of the god's growth in power and the demonstration of his power, which are central ideas of the sequences. The journey sequences complete the god's rise to power, a rise started in the journey of the Delian section. Although it is important in the Delian section too, the journey-for-power idea receives especial stress in the Pythian section, and this reflects the concerns of the Mesopotamian heroic-strand gods whose activities parallel those of Apollo here. In the light of the parallels, this section completes the poet's apparent purpose in the hymn, which in its entirety succeeds in presenting a complete concept of divinity as it is seen from the perspective of the Mesopotamian religious mythological tradition. Ideas central to both strands seem to be united in the hymn to explain the god and to establish him in authority and power.

Apollo travels from Delos to Delphi with his lyre, wearing perfumed immortal garments (ἄμβροτα εἵματ' ἔχων τεθυωμένα, line 184). From Delphi he travels to the Assembly of the gods, passing from earth to Olympos. He arrives playing his lyre, and the gods sing and dance, captivated by his music. He shines, and his feet and chiton also gleam.

Apollo descends from Olympos and wanders over the earth in search of a place to build his temple and establish his cult. Rejecting a number of places, he passes through Onchestos, Poseidon's splendid grove, where there is a rite involving a horse pulling a driverless chariot, which runs through a woody grove risking the destruction of the vehicle.

Apollo decides to build his temple and grove at the stream Telphousa. However, she is jealous of her spot, so she cunningly persuades him that Mt Parnassos in Crisa would be ideal. Apollo arrives at Delphi and decides to build his temple here below the peak.

Nearby, at the spring, Apollo performs his celebrated feat of destroying the monstrous female serpent of Pytho.[21] Here appears the story of the birth of Typhaon, the monster which, in the *Theogony*, Zeus overcame to complete his power. Hera bore Typhaon after she became angry with Zeus for dishonouring her, his wife, as she saw it, by giving birth to Athena without her help. So she descended from Olympos to Earth for a year to give birth to Typhaon, whom she gave to the great serpent at Pytho to rear. Like the Pythian serpent, Typhaon made a habit of devastating the region around Delphi. As regards the monstrous serpent of Pytho, Apollo shoots her with an arrow and she lies drawing great gasps of breath and writhing over the land; blood flows from her and Apollo gloats over his deed.

Suddenly, Apollo realizes that Telphousa has tricked him. Storming angrily to the stream, he throws down a mountain on her, hiding her beneath a shower of rocks. Then he builds his altar and grove beside the stream which issues forth from the steep mountain.

After these conflicts, Apollo completes the establishment of his Pythian oracle. Casting around for suitable priests and officials, he espies a ship of Cretans sailing from Knossos in Crete to Pylos. These he meets in the ocean, assuming the form of a monstrous dolphin. He springs on to the ship and guides it towards Delphi. At the shore of Crisa, now taking his own form, he leaps forth flashing fire, and speeds to Delphi. As he enters his shrine a flame flares up in the famous tripods, and his splendid shafts of light stream forth from the

21 In the hymn the serpent Python is unnamed. Elsewhere it is called Πύθων, Δελφύνη (feminine), Δελφύνης (masculine): see T.W. Allen, W.R. Halliday and E.E. Sikes, *The Homeric Hymns*, 2nd edition, Oxford University Press, Amsterdam, 1963, p.247, for sources. In Euripides' I.T. 1245 and Pausanias X.6.5 the serpent is unnamed also, and its sex changed to male.

temple. His radiance fills all Crisa, causing the women and maidens of the Crisaians to cry out at this outburst of Phoebus. He then leads the still-bemused Cretan sailors in procession from the ship to Delphi, instructing them in his rites.

The Pythian section therefore concentrates on Apollo's arrival at Olympos and the establishment of his cultic seat at Delphi. There are three journey sequences involved. They all closely parallel the type of journey sequences in the heroic-strand myths, and have many parallels in concepts and content with features in the heroic-strand myths. These journey sequences and the activities in them express many ideas about the god but, as in the Mesopotamian myths, where they are also central features, they are employed to establish and express the god's power.

The first journey sequence is composed of a journey from Delos to Delphi and Apollo's arrival at the temple of Zeus on Olympos (lines 179–206). In the concepts involved, the sequence closely parallels the return journeys of Ninurta when he returns with power to the supreme god's temple and Assembly of the gods. Apollo has acquired might and divinity in his birth scene, and he displays his power in the journey, and in the Assembly scenes as one of the Olympians and as the son of Zeus when he arrives at the Assembly of the gods.

In this hymn, there are two Assembly scenes in which he encounters the gods and expresses his power. One scene is found at the beginning of the Delian section (lines 1–13), and the second here at the beginning of the Pythian section (lines 186–206), at the end of Apollo's journey from Delos. These two temple scenes have caused endless trouble for interpreters, but their function in the hymn becomes clear in the light of the Assembly scenes of the myths of Ninurta, the son of the supreme god, and in the light of indications in the hymn itself. The two scenes are actually two versions of the one scene, that is, of the first arrival of Apollo in the temple of the supreme deity, his father, which also constitutes the Assembly of the gods as in Mesopotamia. The journey which begins in the Delian section with his birth and his striding over Delos and other islands ends in the Assembly scene in the Pythian section. This is clearly the first arrival of the god. The action of the first scene of the hymn occurs chronologically after the events of the Delian section, since this tells of his birth, and the poet's words reveal that the scene is actually a duplication. He shows that the Delian temple scene is in effect the same as the first arrival of Apollo on Olympos at the beginning of the Pythian section when he says, in line 11, that Zeus is 'shown his dear son', δεικνύμενος φίλον υἱόν.[22]

There is a number of reasons for the presence of the two scenes, and they are striking indications of the poet's skill in working out his themes in the hymn to present the concept of Apollo as the young heroic god. One of the reasons for this duplication becomes evident in view of the temple scenes of Ninurta, with whom they are a feature central in demonstrating his power and authority among the gods. The two scenes of Apollo are actually similar to the two types of temple scene found with the young Ninurta on his journeys. The first is the threatening encounter in the temple, as seen in *Angim*, where the powerful returning god alarms the Assembly of the gods (lines 63ff.). This is one expression of his authority and a demonstration of his might. In *Angim*, Ninurta arrives terrifyingly at the Assembly, causing the gods to fear him; the minister, Nusku, and Ninurta's mother, Ninlil, defuse the situation, Nusku by offering gifts of recognition and authority from Enlil, Ninlil by her praise since she is impressed by her mighty son; and the supreme god gives Ninurta power in the Assembly, as revealed in Nusku's promises (lines 63–176).[23] The events in the Delian scene closely follow the ideas in this sequence of events: Apollo strides through the halls of Zeus bending his bow, and the gods spring up from their seats in alarm. His mother, Leto, releases the tension, taking his bow and quiver from his shoulder and hanging them on a golden peg. She bids him sit, and Zeus gives his son nectar and ambrosia. Like Ninurta, Apollo's might has been recognized by the gods and he has been received into the Assembly. Like Ninlil, Leto rejoices in her mighty son, who has similarly displayed his power in his arrival. With this array of motifs, the scene is without analogy in Greek mythology, while it is quite similar to the arrival scene of the young Ninurta in *Angim*.[24] The second type of encounter is the friendly type like that in *Ninurta's Journey to Eridu* (STVC 34), which is a traditional divine-journey myth in which the gods celebrate and the

---

22 See also Josef Kroll, 'Apollon zu Beginn des homerischen Hymnus', *Stud-ItalFilolClass* 27–8 (1956) 181, 183–4, who also points out that this is the first arrival of the new god.

23 The meeting of Ninurta's demands for recognition is implied: Jerrold S. Cooper, *The Return of Ninurta to Nippur: an-gim dím-ma*, Analecta Orientalia 52, Biblical Institute Press, Rome, 1978, p.28.

24 See also Kroll, op. cit., pp.183–4.

travelling god receives powers as a gift (col. ii.10ff.).[25] Apollo's arrival in the Pythian section is, in a similar way, a friendly encounter where the gods sing and dance together and Zeus and Leto look in delight at their son. By making these two scenes two versions of the first arrival in the Assembly, and separating them by the whole Delian journey, the poet manages to portray these two contrasting Assembly-scene ideas concisely in the same hymn.

The second major reason for the two scenes involves the powers given to Apollo at his birth in the Delian section. The significance of these powers of the god in the divine world and as part of his divinity is explained as a result. In the two scenes, the two powers claimed by Apollo at his birth (lines 131–2) are displayed, and both affect the gods: the warrior power symbolized by the bow in the first scene, with its alarming effect, and the power of Apollo's lyre music in the second. Both express Apollo's power over the gods and are seen here as part of his relationship with the other gods.

This motif of the lyre music, together with another power motif, is found in the journey to Olympos, and there are parallel motifs in the return of Ninurta to the Assembly in *Angim*. Apollo's journey to Olympos is, in effect, a sequence of the same nature as Ninurta's return journey. Like Ninurta, his destination is the Assembly of the gods, where he demonstrates the powers that he has gained. This is the return sequence of the journey for power as seen in Mesopotamia with the heroic young god. The noise of the lyre which he plays on this journey to the Assembly parallels the noise motif found with Ninurta as he returns to the Assembly. In his case, he roars awesomely across the earth like a thunderstorm. The noise of both gods has an effect on the respective Assemblies, demonstrating the power of the young god. So while the concretization is different, the underlying idea and purpose are the same.

The second motif which parallels a feature in Ninurta's return in *Angim* is the clothes of Apollo. Clothes are seen as a representation of the god's power in the birth scene (lines 121–2), and they clearly have the same function in Apollo's journey to Olympos: wearing divine perfumed garments, he comes to Olympos (ἄμβροτα εἵματ' ἔχων τεθυωμένα, line 184). The ambrosial quality of the garments stresses the power aspect in this scene, which is concerned especially with the divinity of the god. The dressing idea is used for a similar purpose in Ninurta's return, though expressed in a different way. Ninurta

25 Daniel Reisman, 'Ninurta's Journey to Eridu', JCS 24 (1971) 4–6.

adorns his chariot with the trophies of his success in the mountains, trophies which represent his claim to power, as he begins his return to the Assembly (*Angim* 51–68). One other feature which demonstrates the returning god's power is the same in *Angim* as in Apollo's scene. As the gods dance to his irresistible music, Apollo and his symbols of power in the hymn, his lyre, chiton and feet, shine with radiance (lines 201–3). This closely parallels Ninurta on his return, as his radiance (me-lám) covers Enlil's temple and his chariot, a symbol of his power in *Angim*, shines (lines 51, 82, 124). In almost all of these parallels, the concretizations are different, but the ideas and their purpose are the same. For example, in the case of Ninurta, the noise takes the form of a thunderstorm approaching the Assembly, while it is lyre music with Apollo. However, in both cases, it is a motif of noise, and its purpose is to express the god's power as he travels towards the Assembly. This is the case with the other parallels.

The motif of obtaining power in the temple scene, as presented with Ninurta in *Angim* and *Lugale* when he returns, is also seen here.[26] Apollo receives a form of power from the supreme god in the Delian section when Zeus gives him nectar and ambrosia. These have been seen already as symbols of the acquisition of power and divinity in the Delian birth scene (lines 124–5). In the Pythian scene, he just demonstrates his power over the gods, who are captivated by his music.

After his arrival in Olympos and the display of his power over the gods, he carries out a journey to establish his temple and cult in Delphi, and in doing so he performs two heroic exploits through which he achieves cultic and oracular power. Leaving the Assembly of the gods, Apollo enacts a wandering journey in search of a place for his oracle, at the end of which he encounters and defeats both the Pythian serpent and Telphousa.

All the main ideas of this journey sequence are seen in the heroic-strand myths. The sequence directly parallels the situations in the myths of Ninurta and later Marduk where these gods set out from the Assembly and overcome a monstrous enemy and thereby achieve power. In addition, the two feats which Apollo performs, the first the shooting of the Pythian monster, and the second the burying of Telphousa beneath a mountain, parallel two versions of the heroic-strand combats seen in these same Mesopotamian myths. Both types are found with Ninurta and repeated with Marduk, and as they are

26 *Angim*, 90, 156ff.; *Lugale*, 684–700.

central to the acquisition of power of these gods they are similarly central features of Apollo's journey for power.

The idea of the journey for power is the same in Apollo's myth as in the Mesopotamian myths. Ninurta and Marduk demonstrate their warrior capabilities and acquire power by means of victory in combat with the opponent, as in the Anzu myth and in *Enuma Elish*. Likewise, Apollo achieves cultic and oracular power, and in his encounter with the monstrous serpent at Pytho he specifically proves his might in combat. By contrast to Ninurta and Marduk, who are each the champion of their respective Assemblies, Apollo is not the champion of the Olympians. In Greek religion, this role belongs specifically to Zeus, who overcomes a parallel opponent in Typhaon, a monster which is closely associated with the Pythian monster in this hymn. However, like Ninurta and Marduk, Apollo achieves cultic power and sets up his cultic apparatus as a result of his conflicts.[27]

Apollo's state of power at the beginning of this journey sequence parallels that especially of Ninurta in the Asag myth, where Ninurta is seen accepted and in his position in the Assembly before setting out on a journey which results in the defeat of the monster. Marduk's case in *Enuma Elish* is similar, since he has received power in the Assembly before setting out against the monstrous Tiamat, although, of course, his is supreme power over the universe, since he is supreme god, unlike Apollo in the hymn (Tablets III.116–IV.34). In this sense, Apollo is closer to Ninurta as the son of the supreme god, and it is this aspect that Apollo shows most strongly in the Assembly scenes in the hymn.

The journey of Apollo differs slightly from those of Ninurta and Marduk in the sense that these two gods set out intentionally to defeat a monster. However, the difference in motive of the gods is immaterial, since the main purpose and features of Apollo's journey sequence are the encounter, or encounters, and the consequent setting-up of Apollo's cult in Delphi, and it is clearly the poet's intention to bring these events about.

The two types of encounter which are found with Apollo in this journey sequence are also found with both Ninurta and Marduk, and Apollo's encounters show various important parallels to features in the Mesopotamian combats. With Ninurta, the two types of battle are, first, his combat with Anzu and, second, the combat against Asag and the kur in *Lugale*.[28] Both are repeated in Marduk's epic, *Enuma*

---

27 *Angim*, 156, 193ff.; *Enuma Elish*, Tablet VI.49–80.
28 *Myth of Anzu*, Tablets II.35–149, III. obv. i.2–12. *Lugale*, 70–297.

Elish. The Anzu kind, where Marduk shoots Tiamat, supplies the majority of the motifs of the encounter between Tiamat and Marduk in the main combat of *Enuma Elish* (Tablet IV.93–104), although the Asag combat is represented in the role and activities of Tiamat in the lead-up to the encounter, as well as its aftermath; the motif of the encounter of Asag and Ninurta is also referred to in the myth mentioned in the catalogue section where Marduk, in the passage on the SIR.SIR epithet, buries the river Tiamat under a mountain (Tablet VII.70–5).[29] The form and the elements of the encounter myths in the hymn resemble the Marduk form of the tradition rather than the earlier Ninurta myths.

The motifs of the Pytho combat recall in a general way the main Marduk–Tiamat conflict of *Enuma Elish*, which is principally a variation of the earlier Ninurta–Anzu combat. Beside the stream, Apollo shoots the fat, or bloated, Pythian serpent with an arrow, so that she dies with blood pouring from her; and this is, of all the Mesopotamian combat stories, closest to that of the Marduk–Tiamat conflict where the female monster Tiamat, who is swollen by the winds of Marduk, is shot with an arrow (Tablet IV.96–102). Tiamat's blood also pours forth, but the blood is in her case streams of water borne away by the wind (Tablet IV.32, 131–2). The elements that are parallel in the actual fight are limited to those of the combat against a female monster and the monster's death by the arrow. A further similarity is the serpentine nature of the Pythian monster. Although this is not the form of Tiamat, it does parallel the monstrous serpents of the encounter between Marduk and Tiamat (Tablet III.23–36), and this particular form does not occur in Ninurta's Anzu and Asag combats. In addition, Tiamat does, however, seem to have a river aspect, as she is called Mother Hubur (Tablet I.132), Hubur being a river.[30] This aspect is found with the Pythian serpent in the hymn: she appears to be connected with the river beside which the battle occurs, while she is certainly closely connected with the river in Callimachus' *Hymn to Delos* (line 92), specifically the river Pleistos at Delphi.[31]

The pairing of male and female monsters, the Pythian monster and

---

29 Also in Tablet V.57.
30 Tiamat as Mother Hubur: Samuel Noah Kramer and John Maier, *Myths of Enki: The Crafty God*, Oxford University Press, New York and Oxford, 1989, p.140.
31 The river Pleistos at Delphi: see A.W. Mair and G.R. Mair, *Callimachus, Lycophron, Aratus*, Heinemann, London, 1955, p.92 n.b.

Typhaon, in the long digression consisting of the story of Hera and Typhaon, also recalls a feature in *Enuma Elish*. There the goddess Tiamat and her monstrous son, Qingu, form a pair of enemies of the hero, Marduk (Tablet III.37–49). The male and female monsters are split between the two parallel Greek versions.[32] In the hymn, Apollo is opposed by the female monster; and Zeus fights against the male form of the monster, Typhaon. In the *Theogony* (line 821) and Apollodorus I.39, the latter is called the son of Gaia, who, like Hera in the hymn, is angry with Zeus. This male-monster side of the tradition is also found with Apollo in Euripides' *Iphigeneia in Tauris* 1245 and Pausanias X.6.5, and in Callimachus' *Hymn to Apollo* 100, where the unnamed Delphic serpent is presented as male. However, as the presentation of the story is in the hymn, it is closely parallel to Marduk's combat regarding the sexes of the opponents. It is also parallel in that the male monster is subordinate to the female.

In this version the Pythian serpent and Typhaon are the two major forms of the heroic deity's opponent, which in Mesopotamia are the Anzu or Asag type as seen with Ninurta, the other type being the female monster–goddess, the enemy of Marduk. Typhaon parallels Anzu and Asag, while the Pythian monster parallels Tiamat. In view of the Mesopotamian epic, a role like that of the enemy–goddess in the Mesopotamian epic is evident here in the Greek myth in the combination of Hera and the Pythian serpent. The goddess Hera and the female monster of Pytho present the two aspects that are found in *Enuma Elish* in the one mythical figure, the goddess and monster Tiamat. In addition, the two roles – the role of mother of the male monster played by Hera, and that of nurse of the male monster played by the Pythian serpent – are found with Tiamat herself. In the Babylonian epic she is the mother of Qingu, while in the texts of the Assyrian period she also functions as the nurse. In this role of nurse, Tiamat was equated with Ishtar, the battle goddess, with whom nursing is also a strong feature.[33] Ishtar also plays the hostile role of enemy of her consort, as Hera does here. The ideas with Tiamat are, therefore, manifold, and the complex situation in the hymn presents parallels with them of a rather indefinable, but very suggestive, nature.

---

32 J. Fontenrose, *Python: A Study of Delphic Myth and its Origins*, University of California Press, Berkeley, 1959, p.252, considers that these Greek myths are derived from the Near East (p.176).

33 Alasdair Livingstone, *Mythical and Mythological Explanatory Works of Assyrian and Babylonian Scholars*, Clarendon Press, Oxford, 1986, p.234.

Apollo's second combat is against Telphousa, who is clearly a personified stream. Apollo buries Telphousa beneath a mountain and a shower of rocks, and her streams issue from beneath the mountain. The motifs of burying the opponent under the mountain, and the stream flowing forth, parallel specifically the Asag combat, where Ninurta changes his opponent into a pile of rocks – the mountain, hursag̃, which he builds over the kur, also the enemy of Ninurta in the myth; the waters of the kur flow out as a river (*Lugale* 326, 334–59). The situation is more complex in this conflict than in the Telphousa encounter, but the parallels of idea are striking. The ideas of this combat of Ninurta are also repeated briefly in the *Enuma Elish* catalogue section (Tablet VII.70–5). Here Marduk throws down a mountain over Tiamat; the text also speaks of Marduk crossing her, like a river, by a bridge.[34] The arrangement of the ideas in this work is quite close to the situation found with Telphousa. Closely parallel to Tiamat, who seems to be represented here as a river buried under a mountain, Telphousa is a spring and stream buried under the mountain crag and shower of rocks, her stream flowing forth as Tiamat's seems to do. By contrast, Telphousa is not like Asag or the kur, which seem to be inanimate opponents, so the Greek version appears to be closer in this respect too to the later ideas found with Tiamat and Marduk.

The Telphousa story is odd in that Apollo meets Telphousa before fighting the Pythian serpent, but the defeat of Telphousa is delayed until after the destruction of the serpent. The presentation suggests that there is a special reason for the arrangement, since the poet's use of Telphousa to send Apollo to Pytho is unnecessary. However, whatever may be the motive for this arrangement, the scenario in which Telphousa is buried under the mountain after the destruction of the monster parallels another major idea found with the Asag combat in *Lugale* and Marduk's combat in *Enuma Elish* against Tiamat, and in the aftermath of each combat. In these Mesopotamian myths, the controlling of the waters by a mountain follows the combat against the monsters. This is a major cosmological motif and represents the gods' formation of the Tigris and Euphrates rivers to irrigate Mesopotamia. A cosmological motif is not visible in Apollo's encounter, which is used merely as a basis for demonstrating Apollo's establishment of his cult at Telphousa. Despite this, the relationships

---

34 For another Greek example of the mountain thrown down on the river, this time by the warrior Ares: Callimachus, *Hymn to Delos*, 133ff.

between the motifs here in the hymn still faithfully parallel those seen in the Mesopotamian myths, despite the apparent difference in usage. If there is any deeper significance to these motifs with Apollo, perhaps indicating a cosmological aspect of the god's activities, as there is with Ninurta and Marduk in the parallel usage of the motifs in Mesopotamia, it is not revealed explicitly in the hymn.

Beside the stories of the Pythian monster and Telphousa, there is the story of another locale in this journey of Apollo: that is, the tale of the rite at Onchestos, Poseidon's famous grove. This is another feature of the hymn which has caused commentators problems. Here the horse, yoked to a riderless chariot, races through the trees of the grove, sometimes smashing the chariot. This episode presents very little information and is really just an allusion. One would expect that the Greek audience would know the story behind it, but, because of the brevity of the reference, the exact significance of the episode to the hymn is out of the reach of anyone without the background knowledge required. The story seems at first a strangely irrelevant inclusion in a hymn to Apollo where everything else pertains to the god and his rise to power; however, the poet's accuracy in the choice and use of material in other places suggests that there must be a particular reason for the inclusion. The episode might be an allusion to a myth behind the rite, one which has a clear connection with this journey of Apollo and its consequences of power, but there is not sufficient material in the hymn to reveal its exact significance to a modern commentator.[35] However, so far in this section the major episodes have paralleled the heroic strand of Ninurta and Marduk, and the inclusion of Poseidon also recalls a feature of this strand, since Enki, the Mesopotamian god of the ocean, plays an important and, in fact, a central role in the mythology of both Ninurta's and Marduk's rise to power. If this myth of Apollo owes anything to the influence of Mesopotamian ideas, this in itself would be sufficient reason to include Poseidon in some way in the myth of Apollo's birth and rise to power.

---

35 For various interpretations of the rite, see A. Schachter, 'Homeric Hymn to Apollo, lines 231–8 (The Onchestos Episode): Another Interpretation', BICS 23 (1976) 102–13. See also Georges Roux, 'Sur deux passages de l'hymne homérique à Apollon', REG 77 (1964) 6–22.

In the light of Mesopotamian ideas, the journey of Apollo from the Assembly to the encounters with his opponents is an 'outward' journey. At the end of this journey sequence, the story is still incomplete, since a return sequence with a temple or Assembly scene is required after it. After his outward journeys away from the Assembly to defeat the monster, Ninurta performs a return journey to the Assembly and/or to the temple where he displays his power. In the Anzu myth, in the Asag myth and in *Angim*, Ninurta does this each time, returning to the Assembly and to his temple.[36]

The 'return' sequence with Apollo, following his encounters, is provided by the final journey of the hymn. In this journey sequence, he travels from the sea to his temple in Delphi, displays his power and completes the establishment of his cult. This journey is simply added on to the end of the previous journey sequence, but connected with it by the theme of the establishment of the cult in Delphi. The addition of the 'return' sequence is indicated by the poet's presentation of it in the hymn. At Delphi, Apollo becomes aware of Cretan sailors in their ship, and suddenly appears before them, in the shape of a great dolphin springing on to the ship. There in no mention of any 'outward' journey from Delphi to the sea, but the return journey to Delphi is narrated at length and displays many elements typical of the return sequence as this is seen with Ninurta.

The idea of the journey from the sea to his temple does parallel situations in the myths of Ninurta and Marduk. The idea is seen in a symbolic way with Ninurta. In the work *Ninurta's Journey to Eridu*, which presents a divine journey, the god returns from the Abzu temple of the god Enki in Eridu to his temple in the city Nippur. The temple in Eridu, the 'Abzu house', e-abzu, appears at times to be symbolic of the freshwater nether-sea, the Abzu, of which Enki is the master. It appears to be seen with this connotation also in *Inanna and Enki*, in which Inanna journeys, specifically descending, to the Abzu temple in Eridu to visit Enki, takes his powers, and returns to her temple in Uruk.[37] Similarly, the Abzu temple seems to symbolize the nether-sea in UET 6/1 2, in which Ninurta 'descends' to the Abzu temple in Eridu following the Tablet of Destinies which the Anzu

---

36 *Angim*, 75, 177, 185; *Lugale*, 648ff.
37 Descending to the Abzu: *Inanna and Enki*, Tablet I.i.26–7. On these lines, see Bendt Alster, 'On the Interpretation of the Sumerian Myth "Inanna and Enki"', ZA 64 (1975) 20.

bird dropped in the fight and which seems to have dropped down to Enki.[38] In this work, Enki prophesies that Ninurta will return to Nippur with power, so a return is indicated here as well. The situation appears in a different way in *Enuma Elish*. After he defeats Tiamat, the sea, Marduk performs various cosmological acts and then founds his temple and cult in Babylon (Tablet VI.47–80). There is no journey mentioned because of a different cosmological arrangement in the epic by comparison to the myths of Ninurta, but the sequence of events is similar.

The sea therefore has a role at the same point in these myths, as the place of the outward destination. The sequence of ideas underlying the action is similar in Apollo's last journey sequence too. After the encounter with the monster or with the god from whom the powers are obtained, the hero of the journey goes on to demonstrate his power in his temple and cult. Apollo meets the stunned Cretan sailors in the sea and returns to Delphi, where he establishes his cult at his temple and displays his power. Of course, the actual motifs of the concretization of the ideas, the encounter with the shipful of Cretans in the sea, and Apollo appearing as a dolphin, are not found in any myth of the heroic strand in Mesopotamia. In the hymn, they are probably expressing ideas which are concerned with other aspects of Apollo in his cult at Delphi, besides those already seen in the hymn. This is particularly the case with the motif of the dolphin, which also appears with Dionysos, who is found together with Apollo at his cult in Delphi; dolphin, δελφίς, is a play on Delphi.

In this last journey of Apollo, he travels to his temple at Delphi, rather than to the Assembly of the gods at Olympos. By comparison, in the myths of Ninurta the temple to which the god returns is the Assembly of the gods, where he holds his power and cult daises, although in *Angim* he does travel on to his temple, which is also in Nippur. The last two journeys of the hymn are, however, concerned with the founding of Apollo's temple and cult at Delphi, so it is to this temple that he returns, rather than to the Assembly at Olympos. Nevertheless, like Apollo in this return to Delphi, Ninurta is also concerned in his journeys with establishing his own power and cult.

In Apollo's return, light is an important feature demonstrating his power. It is typical of the return sequence in the hymn, in which it

---

38 *Ninurta and the Turtle*, or UET 6/1 2, lines 1–8.

appears several times. It is also a feature which parallels those found with the returning, radiant Ninurta. In the Assembly scenes in the hymn, the god returning with power shines with radiance, and his symbols of power also shine – his bow, lyre, feet and the shining immortal chiton of divinity all emit radiance (lines 4, 201–4). The parallels of the radiant Apollo and his shining symbols of power with Ninurta and his radiant symbols have already been demonstrated in the discussion of the Assembly scenes on Olympos. The situation is parallel in the last journey, the return from the sea, where, bright as a star, Apollo radiates light as he springs from the boat and as he enters his temple, and his shafts of radiance fill it and all of Crisa (lines 440–5). This burst of light demonstrates his power and here gives authority to him, to his temple and to his cult in Delphi.

The motif of light in the return has also been seen in the ascent sequence of Apollo in the Delian section, in the imagery of the mountain peak flowering with gold, which appears to be an allusion to the golden rays of the rising sun touching the mountain. This is a different appearance of the motif of light with the god and suits the context of the other motifs, which parallel those in Damu's myths. Here the motif is relevant to the return of Damu/Dumuzi from the mountains of the rising sun. This is essentially the same motif with Damu/Dumuzi and with Ninurta, but is expressed in different ways. The two gods are, in fact, linked in this return, since they both return from the eastern mountains where the sun rises. Ninurta is seen returning like the sun in *Lugale* after his defeat of Asag in the mountains (line 648). However, Ninurta's radiance seems to be the result of other features as well, features which are not seen with Damu/Dumuzi, since it probably refers to the god's me-lám, the symbol and evidence of the returning god's power. This is seen in *Angim* with Ninurta, where he and his symbols of power shine on his return, and in the case of the Asag myth he seems to be returning with it after he takes the fearful me-lám radiance from the defeated Asag (*Lugale* 289–93).

The noise motif occurs together with the light motif in this last journey sequence of Apollo, as it does in both the journey from Delos to the Assembly and the ascent sequence in the Delian birth scene. Once again it is evidence of the god's power in this returning situation. Here at the end of the hymn, it again takes the form of the din of startled or amazed women, forming a thematic link with the parallel situation in the Delian scene. Apollo's burst of light startles all of the daughters of the Crisaians, so that they cry out in alarm (lines 145–7). This feature is found in the instances of the birth of Apollo and his striding on the earth, similar situations of return and power, when all the goddesses raise a cry (line 119) and are amazed by the rising god.

One other feature in this last journey sequence in the hymn has a Mesopotamian parallel. It is, however, not a parallel with a mythological feature in Mesopotamian myth, but rather a parallel with a cultic fixture concerned with temples. In entering his temple in Delphi, Apollo passes between the two tripods, which flame up as he goes by (lines 443–4). The tripods are the subject here. In the hymn they are considered to stand on either side of the entrance to the temple. These fixtures directly recall the tripods that flank the doors of some Assyrian temples. They are seen especially in Neo-Assyrian times, but they are probably found earlier too. In the hymn, the description of Apollo's temple probably accords with an actual temple in existence at the time of the composition of the hymn and is not necessarily a mythological reference, so that it is probably not found in the heroic-strand myths.

These are, then, the ideas in the three journey sequences of the Pythian section which parallel features presented in the Mesopotamian heroic-strand myths. In this section, Apollo performs as the heroic son of the supreme god, closely paralleling Ninurta in his role as the son of the Sumerian supreme god. The poet who composed the hymn uses motifs and ideas to present concepts of the god which are very similar to those in the same circumstances in the Mesopotamian heroic-strand myths. Apollo closely parallels Ninurta especially in the Assembly scenes, and performs three journey sequences which correspond to journey sequences found with Ninurta. The major motifs of these journey sequences, above all the Assembly scenes of the first return sequence of the section, and the two encounters of the outward journey sequence from the Assembly, but also many other parallels, show detailed similarities to those found with Ninurta, and also with Marduk in his epic, *Enuma Elish*, which was strongly influenced by the myths of Ninurta.

In all of these journeys, the idea of the acquisition of power and its demonstration is one of the central purposes. In the first journey sequence, Apollo displays his divinity as a powerful Olympian god, and shows his power in the Assembly and over the gods. In the second, he gives evidence of his warrior might in defeating his opponents and begins the establishment of his cultic seat, displaying his authority as a god. In the third, he completes the establishment of his cult at Delphi with the acquisition of the Cretan sailors as priests, and shows his power in the journey and in his temple. The acquisition and demonstration of power in these journey sequences is also displayed by means of motifs which have been seen in the Mesopotamian myths, where they occur with the same purpose and in the same context.

In summary, the major parallels between the Pythian section and the Mesopotamian heroic-strand myths are:

1 the return-journey sequence, with its destination as the Assembly of the supreme god;
2 the young god's outward journey from the Assembly, with its encounters typical of the heroic strand of myth;
3 the last return sequence from the sea to the temple;
4 the two types of Assembly scene of the heroic son of the supreme god;
5 the combat of the heroic son of the supreme god with the monster;
6 the burying of the stream beneath the mountain in the same sequence;
7 the journey of power as the purpose of the journey sequences;
8 the motifs expressing power in the two 'return'-journey sequences: motifs of food, dressing, noise, radiance and 'weapons';
9 the establishment of the young deity's cult and temple as a result of the journeys.

These are all complex and detailed parallels, and at the same time they are central in the hymn, as they are in the Mesopotamian myths of Ninurta and Marduk. Together they present the concept of the god as the heroic son of the supreme god, as seen with Ninurta in the Mesopotamian heroic-strand myths.

The parallels of this section are even more numerous than those of the Delian section, which also supplies an array of striking parallels. Together, the parallels in both sections present a compelling argument for influence from Mesopotamia in this hymn. The parallels more than adequately fulfil the criteria for the indication of influence. They are numerous, complex and detailed, and play a central role in the myths of the two areas. The same underlying ideas are present, and the motifs of the Delian section are found together in the same context in the one group of Mesopotamian myths, myths belonging to Inanna and Dumuzi/Damu, while those of the Pythian section are also found in one group of myths where they are used in the same way.

Many aspects of the presentation stress the case for influence, but none more than the poet's clever handling of the concepts and the motifs which express them. The virtually complete separation of the material which compares to that of the two different strands into the two sections which focus on different locales emphasizes this, but other clear indications are the birth/ascent sequence of Apollo in the Delian section and the careful arrangement of the three journey sequences of the Pythian section, all presenting, in their correct sequences, ideas of the young heroic god as he is seen in Mesopotamia. Another fine example is the way in which the poet adds the final sequence to complete the god's journey for power, showing that he is conscious of what he is doing and is master of the situation. In fact, the poet seems to demonstrate that he has an intimate knowledge of the concepts and material which are seen in the Mesopotamian myths of both strands. Not only does he appear to know the motifs and ideas which belong to this material, but he seems to recognize what concepts they express, so that he can assemble them in such as way as to present his own story about Apollo without once misrepresenting the material and the concepts which underlie it as these are all seen in the Mesopotamian myths, or confusing the issues.

In the hymn, the presentation of the ideas seen in the Meso-potamian material is often brief and consists of allusions; this feature indicates that the poet composed the hymn for an audience thoroughly conversant with the concepts revealed in this comparative study and with the significance of the motifs which express them. This indicates that these ideas were certainly known by the worship-pers of Apollo and most probably were known generally, since the hymn was meant for public praise of the god. Similarly, the presenta-tion of the material does not look as though it is concealing secrets known to just a few, but rather explaining the god in well-understood terms. Indeed, the poet makes it clear at the end of the Delian section, which is full of symbolism, that this hymn which speaks of Delos is meant for all (lines 174–5):

And we will carry your renown as far as we roam over the earth
among the well-placed cities of men.

ἡμεῖς δ' ὑμέτερον κλέος οἴσομεν, ὅσσον ἐπ' αἶαν
ἀνθρώπων στρεφόμεσθα πόλεις εὖ ναιεταώσας·

Influence is indicated by the parallels in the hymn, and this conclusion is not disallowed by the other two factors on which the possibility of influence depends, the existence of contact between the two areas and the availability of Mesopotamian material at a time of possible influence.

The relevant Mesopotamian goddess-and-consort material for the Delian section seems to have been extant down to at least NA times, about the time of the Orientalizing period. The relevant works are ID, AV, Damu's myths edin-na ú-saĝ-ĝá, and perhaps also TRS 8 (=TCL 15). More accurately, AV and edin-na ú-saĝ-ĝá are extant in NA versions in the first-millennium Assyrian libraries, while ID and TRS 8 exist only in OB versions. However, it can be assumed that the ideas in ID were known in the later period, because knowledge of the Sumerian myth is necessary before one can understand the events of the Akkadian AV. This work is basically a summary of the ideas and events of the Sumerian version, although, as one scholar points out, there are also differences and expansions which make it more than just a summary of the earlier work.[39] The myth of Damu/Dumuzi, edin-na ú-saĝ-ĝá, is important for the Delian section and seems to have the major ideas of the Damu myths which are found in the hymn. Although TRS 8 is known only from the OB version, it may perhaps be assumed, in view of the existence of edin-na ú-saĝ-ĝá, that knowledge of other Damu stories such as TRS 8, as well as the ideas involved in them, existed in these later periods. This may be the case with other material such as the sacred marriage texts and the love songs of Dumuzi, especially since the quantity of the Mesopotamian literature extant is not large and some aspects of the literature are poorly represented while others have abundant texts. These other works are, however, not essential to the parallels in the Homeric hymn. The *Epic of Gilgamesh* first appears on OB tablets and is an important work, especially in the SB version produced in the second half of the second millennium BC. Texts appear down to the latest Akkadian times, the NA and NB eras in the first millennium BC.

The major works relevant to the Pythian section are the Anzu myth, *Lugale, Angim* and *Enuma Elish*. These were all known down to the first millennium, into NA times and later. Other sources which are not so important, but are cited in the comparison, are *Ninurta's Journey to Eridu* and UET 6/1 2. Both are Sumerian myths and the

---

39 Ph. Talon, 'Le mythe de la Descente d'Ištar aux Enfers', *Akkadica* 59 (1988) 15, 23–4.

copies extant are OB. In view of the knowledge of other myths of
Ninurta in the first millennium, and the importance of these in
the general mythology, as well as the fact that Ninurta was worshipped in NA times, it is likely that these were known in the first
millennium too.

As discussed in the introduction to this study, intensive
trade contact and therefore cultural contact is known to have existed
between Greece and the Near East, the Hittite areas, the north of
Syria and the areas beyond this, in the thirteenth and fourteenth
centuries BC. There is evidence of intensive contact again, in the same
places and in Phoenicia, after about the late ninth century BC, while
indications exist of continuing contact with the Near East, though
comparatively limited, during the so-called Dark Age between
the twelfth and early ninth centuries BC.[40] Influence could then
have occurred at these times, and the parallels in the Homeric
hymn provide compelling support for the view that it actually took
place.

If it is a case of influence, which seems likely, the hymn appears to
attest to a general awareness of important Mesopotamian ideas in
Greece in the seventh century BC during the early archaic period.
Although dating by diction does not seem to be extremely reliable,
studies in the diction of the two sections suggest that the poem
reached its present state sometime in the seventh century or slightly
after. Depending on the views regarding unity, the latest date of
composition appears to be just after the end of the Orientalizing
period, around the end of the seventh century, while an earlier date in
the first half of that century is sometimes suggested for part of the
hymn. A later date, at the end of the sixth century, has been
considered, but judging by the diction, combined with other elements
of the poem, this seems too late.[41] The poem appears then to have
been composed during or at the end of the period of strong Near
Eastern influence in Greece as evinced by the Orientalizing style of

40 The periods and extent of contact between Greece and the Near East,
   are discussed in detail in the first chapter. For the sources see p.6 n.10 and
   p.147 n.45.
41 Some views on dating: Janko, op. cit., pp.132, 195–8; West, CQ 25 (1975)
   161ff.; Burkert, 'Kynaithos, Polycrates, and the Homeric Hymn to
   Apollo', pp.53–62; Karl Förstel, op. cit., pp.200–11.

Greek art which was popular between approximately 750 and 650 BC. The apparent general openness in this period to Near Eastern culture, an openness which is indicated by the material evidence, provides the general climate for a wide acceptance in the seventh century of Mesopotamian ideas, which is suggested by the presentation of the material in the hymn, assuming as it does the audience's understanding of the significance of the motifs and material in both sections.

The knowledge of these Mesopotamian ideas may have been present earlier, at least with a few people if not generally. The hymns to Demeter and to Aphrodite, which will be discussed in the next two chapters, show similar parallels, and although they also appear to have been written in the seventh century BC, their stories are older, since they date back to before Homer and Hesiod. Both of these poets refer to the *affaire* of Aphrodite and Anchises, the basis of *Homeric Hymn V*, an *affaire* which presents many parallels with Mesopotamian mythological and religious ideas. The story is referred to in Homer's *Iliad* (2.˅19–21) and in Hesiod's *Theogony* (lines 1008–10), anᴠ thes works seem to have been composed between approximately 750 and 700 BC. Likewise, in *Theogony* (lines 912–14) Hesiod mentions the story of Demeter's hymn, a hymn which matches this hymn to Apollo for the depth of the parallels with Mesopotamian myths. The stories of Aphrodite and Demeter are referred to in these works of Homer and Hesiod in a way which suggests that they are already traditional, so they may be considerably ·lier than these two revered poets. While the story in the hymn to ⅃ᴧollo is not attested earlier than the seventh century, the ideas in it and the general acceptance of them which is indicated by the poet's delivery, may be considerably older. This point will be discussed in more detail after the investigation of the parallels in other archaic Greek literary works belonging to the Homeric tradition and to Hesiod.

The results of the discussion of parallels in the hymn with Mesopotamian ideas add another dimension to the support for the unity of the hymn, which is the major contentious issue concerning the hymn. Since the time of Ruhnken in the late eighteenth century, there has been much debate as to whether the hymn is one work composed of two sections, two separate hymns united at some stage, or one section a subsequent extension of the other.[42] The discussion of parallels adds weight to the conclusions of recent studies on the literary and linguistic composition of the hymn, which have emphasized that one single poet is responsible for the form of both sections of the hymn as we have it. The hymn is, of course, a work of the Homeric tradition and is based on inherited material and on inherited formulae which have their origin in oral tradition. It is, therefore, likely that more than one poet had a hand in the growth of the hymn to its existing state.

Many features support the case for the unity of the hymn, and not least the foregoing discussion of parallels. However, this discussion presents new information on the composition of the hymn which indicates that the unity of construction by one poet seems to be the only reasonable conclusion. In both sections, the poet shows the same complete understanding of the ideas and material that have

---

42 Recent literature on the discussion of unity: studies supporting unity, Niles, op. cit., p.36 n.2; W. Appel, 'Ultrum hymnus Homericus ad Apollinem unus sit in duas partes dividendus', *Meander* 40 (1985) 21–5, and 'Das Problem der Zerteilung des homerischen Apollonhymnus', *WZ Rostock* 34 (1985) 6–8; Andrew M. Miller, 'The Address to the Delian Maidens in the Homeric Hymn to Apollo: Epilogue or Transition?', *TAPhA* 109 (1979) 173–86, and *From Delos to Delphi: A Literary Study of the Homeric Hymn to Apollo*, Mnemosyne Supplementum 93, E.J. Brill, Leiden, 1986, *passim*, especially pp.111–17; Jenny Strauss Clay, *The Politics of Olympos: Form and Meaning in the Major Homeric Hymns*, Princeton University Press, Princeton, 1989, pp.18–19; Cora Angier Sowa, *Traditional Themes and the Homeric Hymns*, Bolchazy–Carducci Publishers, Chicago, 1984, pp.172–93; Matthias Baltes, 'Die Kataloge im homerischen Apollonhymnus', *Philologus* 125 (1981) 25–43; Wolfhart Unte, 'Studien zum homerischen Apollonhymnos', doctoral diss., Philosophische Fakultät der Freien Universität Berlin, A. Wasmund-Bothmann/Höpfner, Berlin, 1968, pp.202–10; a good thematic review, Camillo Cessi, 'L'inno omerico ad Apollo', *Atti del Reale Istituto Veneto di Scienze, Lettere ed Arti* 87/2 (1927–28) 865–83; Allen, Halliday, and Sikes, op. cit., pp.183ff.; studies asserting division, Förstel, op. cit., pp.272–84 (this book supplies a résumé of scholarship on the issue back to Ruhnken (1782), although from the point of view of the author, of course); A. Hoekstra, *The Sub-Epic Stage of the Formulaic Tradition: Studies in the Homeric Hymns to Apollo, to Aphrodite and to Demeter*, Verhandelingen der Koninklijke Nederlandse Akademie van Wetenschappen, AFD. Letterkunde, North Holland Publishing Company, Amsterdam and London, 1969, pp.20, 28; West, *CQ* 25 (1975) 161–70; Joachim Schröder, *Ilias und Apollonhymnos*, Verlag Anton Hain, Meisenheim am Glan, 1975, p.10; Janko, op. cit., pp.99ff.; earlier, Engelbert Drerup, 'Der homerische Apollonhymnos: eine methodologische Studie', *Mnemosyne* 5 (1937) 81–134.

Mesopotamian parallels. He employs the material with the same purpose of demonstrating the rise of the young god to power, which is the major theme of the work. The journey for power is also completely consistent in both sections, and it is presented with many similar motifs and in thematically linked ways. This is seen, for instance, with the powers which Apollo claims at his birth, the lyre and bow, which are used in the two Assembly scenes, which belong thematically to the activities of the Pythian section. Other devices which link the expression of power in the two sections are the motifs of dressing, noise and light. These are essential to the presentation of the journey for power and are consistent throughout.

Both sections have many parallels to features of Mesopotamian myths, and these have the same nature. The same style of presentation of the ideas seen in Mesopotamian myths is followed in both the Pythian and the Delian sections. The ideas are largely suggested symbolically, and the audience's knowledge of the motifs and its understanding of their significance appears to be assumed. In addition, the material is used for an aetiological purpose in both sections, in the Delian portion to explain the setting-up of Apollo's cult and festival on Delos, and in the Pythian to explain the establishment of his cult at Delphi. Even more indicative is the fact that the parallels with Mesopotamian material in each section come from different strands. It needs both sections to present a whole picture of the god. Together, the sections present a complete idea of the deity from the point of view of the two strands in Mesopotamian religious mythology, since these strands tell different stories of the rise of the deity to divinity and his acquisition of his functions and his power in the religion. This picture presented by the whole hymn coincides with the idea in line 29 which speaks of the rise of the god, referring to Delos, 'where his rise began'. It takes the two sections, both sets of material and the concepts involved to complete his rise and establish him as the powerful divinity in the style of the heroic strand, which is foreshadowed in the first Assembly scene but not explained there, and as the son of his wandering, searching mother Leto in the style of the myths of the goddess-and-consort strand.

The presentation of this complex idea of divinity, as it is seen in the two strands of Mesopotamian myths, necessitates the separation into two parts, or rather the use of two different situations to present the two different sorts of journey and the concepts involved. When the myths of Apollo's birth in the Delian section and the two encounters in the Pythian were attached to these locales, whether the connection was invented by the poet or already assigned by tradition, is the question. If they were traditional, then it was the poet's task to mould them to suit his purpose, but if the poet himself brought about the connection, then one of the major reasons, beside the desire to laud these two cult places, must have been the requirement for two different environments to present his two different sets of journeys and their attached ideas.

The virtually complete separation of the material that has parallels with the two distinct strands agrees with the view that a conscious effort was made by one poet to present both sets of concepts about the god in one hymn, whereas a mixture of the two in both sections would suggest that the sections were not composed as part of a complete design, since they would then be theoretically capable of existence in their own right as hymns presenting the whole deity. At the same time, material which does coincide in both sections clearly has the purpose of linking the two independent sections. Examples of these linking devices are the powers which Apollo claims at his birth. These are parallel with the powers of the heroic-strand divinity and stand out from the context of the goddess-and-consort motifs in which they are found. These symbols link the journey-for-power theme in this birth scene with the journey sequence of the Pythian section, where their exact significance becomes apparent. The Assembly scene in the Delian section is another linking device. It clearly has no connection with the journey that comprises the rest of the Delian section, and it also links this section with the Pythian section in terms of the parallels with the heroic-strand material in this scene and in the Pythian section.

The placement of this Assembly scene is, in fact, an example of the conceptual cleverness of the poet in creating the structure of the whole hymn. The positioning of the scene at the beginning of the Delian section allows him to present concisely in the same hymn the two types of Assembly scene of the young heroic god, and both in the form of the new god's first arrival in the Assembly, but it also permits him to introduce strongly the theme of the entire hymn: the demonstration of his mighty divine hero as a major divinity of the Olympian Assembly. In this scene, his authority is at the same time defined in terms of the supremacy of Zeus, who calmly receives the powerful new god in the Assembly. While the demonstration of his hero's might is the main theme of this religious work, when discussing authority in the divine world the supremacy of Zeus over all the gods is also of major importance.

In her detailed study of literary themes in the Homeric hymns and other works, Cora Angier Sowa points out that both sections of the hymn are linked on a literary and linguistic level. They are closely intertwined by a framework of parallel events and repetition of verses, and the forms of some of these are unique to this hymn.[43] Key words and other elements also link the sections. Words for fire, light, the sun and shining things are common to the Delian and Pythian parts. The usage of these particular words is, of course, in accordance with the theme of the god's power that the poet is concerned with demonstrating throughout the hymn. Other key words with this purpose, such as words for lordship and honour, are generally distributed throughout the hymn.[44]

Several points concerning the themes and content of the hymn have been advanced to support the argument for the separation of its two sections. These are, however, not tenable in the light of all of the evidence, including the indications of this comparative study.

Lines 177–8 have often been cited as the termination of the Delian section, an indication that this was the end of a hymn to Delian Apollo. However, these lines are not irrefutable evidence for a complete termination. For one thing, they are not a standard type of hymnic close. Indeed, they can be understood in the sense that the poet does not intend to cease his singing about Apollo at this point, but rather that he is preparing to go on to the Pythian story of Apollo's great exploit:[45]

> But I will not cease singing of far-shooting Apollo
> of the silver bow, whom lovely-haired Leto bore.

> αὐτὰρ ἐγὼν οὐ λήξω ἑκηβόλον Ἀπόλλωνα
> ὑμνέων ἀργυρότοξον, ὅν ἠΰκομος τέκε Λητώ.

After these lines the Pythian story begins. The lines, therefore, function as a transition – a comma rather than a full-stop.

43 Sowa, op. cit., p.183.
44 ibid., pp.185–6.
45 See A.M. Miller, 'The Address to the Delian Maidens in the Homeric Hymn to Apollo: Epilogue or Transition', TAPhA 109 (1979) 173–86; also the similar understanding of the lines by Cessi, op. cit., pp.869, 871; Ann L.T. Bergren, 'Sacred Apostrophe: Re-Presentation and Imitation in the Homeric Hymns', *Arethusa* 15 (1982) 93–4; Cf. also Sowa, op. cit., p.173; Förstel, op. cit., p.162; Alfred Heubeck, 'Gedanken zum homerischen Apollonhymnos', in *Festschrift für Konstantinos J. Merentitis*, Athens, 1972, pp.138–40. Contrast F. Càssola, *Inni omerici*, Mondadori, Milan, 1975, p.97; Janko, op. cit., p.253.

The lines seem, in effect, to be a clever and artistic device to indicate the end of a topic, but at the same time the continuation of the song. Their presence here in the hymn does indicate an end of some sort, and this is entirely consistent with the nature of the parallels in this hymn, since the poet is now going on to sing a completely different song about Apollo, the song of the heroic son of the supreme god as it is seen in the myths of Ninurta. This story forms a complete contrast to the story of the myths of the goddess-and-consort strand that supply the parallels for the Delian section. The following lines (179–81) at the beginning of this Pythian section are an invocation to Apollo, as Camillo Cessi stresses, not a prologue, and it does not indicate the beginning of a new work, but rather a change of topic.[46] This is expected in view of the great change in the type of story involved. Homer similarly puts a fresh invocation to the Muses before the section on the catalogue of ships in the *Iliad*. Likewise, Hesiod also puts three separate invocations to the Muses in the introductory *prooimion* to the *Theogony*.

The different geographical basis and different religious interests in the two sections have also been advanced as reasons for there being two poems instead of one. Both, however, are completely understandable in terms of the poet's purpose and of the two different types of material which he seems to be presenting together in this hymn. Even without the indications which this comparative study provides, these points would not be indicative of two poems, since the poet is merely singing of two areas of importance to Apollo, and that does not require two separate poems.[47] In terms of the parallels, the reason for the two different places can be seen clearly. Another reason offered to support the case for the division of the hymn is that the Pythian section is aetiological in flavour. The Delian section is, however, also aetiological, since it is explaining the reason for Apollo's famous cult and temple on this barren and unprepossessing island.

The linguistic composition of the hymn has been the ground for much contention, and this is the the most difficult aspect of the argument to discuss, since it really needs a large and comprehensive linguistic study to deal thoroughly with all of the issues raised by this study of the parallels in the hymn. However, the linguistic composition of the hymn is consistent with the unity of the hymn in view of the formulaic-tradition nature of the work. All of the apparent

---

46 Cessi, op. cit., pp.781–3.
47 Cf. Förstel, op. cit., p.163; Miller, *From Delos to Delphi*, pp.112–13.

irregularities of the poem can be explained in terms of this feature and the artistic ability of the poet, which is a major consideration.

Some have contended that the diction – that is, the use of formulae, words, verses and other linguistic devices – is different in the two sections. However, as Unte points out, there is no significant stylistic difference in the use of language in each section. Both present a mixture of traditional epic elements and creative innovation. In each section, the parallels with Homeric epics in long and short formulae and in words are consistent. The main differences do not exist between the sections but, rather, between the parts within the sections. For instance, the highest number of linguistic parallels in the hymn with the Homeric epics is in the Cretan segment of the Pythian section (lines 388–544), while, relatively speaking, the fewest are found in the same section, in Apollo's search for a place for his oracular seat and temple (lines 216ff.). At the same time, there are many parallels with Homer in the dialogue scene between Leto and Delos in the Delian section, but they are lacking in the same section in the scene after his birth (lines 120–39) and in the description of the Delian festival (lines 140–76). Again, linking the two sections are the long Homeric formulae, the greatest number of which are found in the birth scene (lines 89–119) and in the Typhaon story (lines 300ff.). Likewise, non-Homeric words are spread throughout the hymn. With identical implications, the same style of adjective-and-noun unit is most strongly found in the dialogue between Delos and Leto in the Delian section and in the description of Apollo's wanderings in the Pythian section.[48] Similarly, as Sowa points out, various linguistic features, such as the repetition of stems, words and verbal patterns, cut across the division of the sections, and in addition to this some words and formulae which are found in both the sections are not attested elsewhere in the extant Homeric corpus.[49]

As part of the discussion of the differences in diction between the two sections, one argument put forward to support the case for two separate hymns is that the Delian section is most like Homeric epic in its ideas, and the Pythian section is concerned with ideas which are seen especially in Hesiod's works, such as aetiological ideas. While both sections have aetiological concerns, the parallels with Hesiod in certain features are a definite aspect peculiar to the Pythian section. For instance, as Sowa points out, the Pythian portion of the hymn

48 Unte, op. cit., pp.207–8.
49 Sowa, op. cit., pp.183, 186.

'is remarkable for its folk etymologies, plays on words and other tricks of sound, such as alliteration and the juxtaposition of cognate words. It shares this interest with the *Theogony* of Hesiod.'[50] However, while this is a feature of the Pythian section, the same section also has passages with the highest number of parallels in formulae and verses with the Homeric epics (lines 388–544). In the Delian section, by contrast, the first scene of Apollo stretching his bow in the Assembly on Olympos (lines 1–11) has few parallels with Homer, like the description of the Delian festival and the farewell to the Delian maidens in the same section (lines 140–76).

As a number of scholars have concluded,[51] the explanation for this difference between passages lies for the most part in the subject of each. In effect, the frequence of parallels of formulae, words and verses is largely determined by the subject in each passage in each section. In addition, the theme, style and tone of each part affect the diction and the devices employed. Also of importance here is the question of the extent to which the ideas and material presented in the poem are traditional and of how great the poet's innovative and creative efforts needed to be in order to present the story and its themes as they are in the hymn. Whatever the answer, everything shows that the whole poem as it stands is a unity and the creation of a single poet whose creative hand is seen in every part. As Wolfhart Unte sums it up: 'Das alles spricht dafür, daß der Apollonhymnos in der Form, wie er uns vorliegt, einmal gedichtet worden ist, und kein Konglomerat aüßerlich adaptierter Einzelgedichte ist.'[52]

A difference in style exists between the two sections. This feature has sometimes been cited as an indication that the poem is two different hymns.[53] The Delian section has a lyric quality, while the Pythian is more epic in style. It is, in fact, one more piece of evidence for the poet's artistic genius, which is clearly displayed in all aspects of the hymn.[54] The different styles have been cleverly used to present the different subjects of the two sections, marking once again the poet's awareness of the significance of his material. Each story is told in a style highly suitable to its content. The lyric and emotional style is used for the story of the wandering, searching mother and the birth of her child, which ends in the cheerful description of the festival of

---

50 ibid., p.189.
51 Förstel, op. cit., p.47; Unte, op. cit., pp.206ff.; Cessi, op. cit., p.874.
52 Unte, op. cit., p.209.
53 Cf. Förstel, op. cit., pp.272–84.
54 Baltes, op. cit., pp.40–1.

the Ionians on Delos. The epic style is extremely suitable for the description of the great heroic exploits of the hero in the Assembly and in his martial conflict with the Pythian monster. It is also apt for the momentous establishment of an oracular cult of such eminence as the Delphic oracle.[55]

Some who separate the composition into two hymns date the Delian and Pythian sections differently. Basing their conclusions on an assessment of diction, most place the Delian portion in the first half of the seventh century and the Pythian at the end of the second half of the century. This would suggest some more points that would need to be considered regarding the composition of the hymn, were it not for the fact that dating the hymns on the basis of diction is clearly not an exact science. Another view held is that the Pythian section was composed before the Delian, a conclusion which indicates that dating by means of diction is imprecise and that the results of the studies are open to a number of interpretations which are to a greater or lesser extent subjective.[56] The differences between the various parts – and it is a question of a difference not simply between the Delian and the Pythian sections, but between the smaller parts within the two larger divisions – really depend on many things, such as content, style, subject, inherited material, region, artistic manipulation by the poet and so forth. All of these are hard to define and appear to make the task of dating by means of the diction and the development of the formulaic tradition an art rather than a science. It seems that a lot more work needs to be done on this aspect of the formulaic tradition before any reliable understanding of the situation can be achieved. Above all, a study of diction should be allied to a careful and sensitive appreciation of the hymns as works of art composed by talented and ingenious poets open to a variety of influences.[57] One requirement seems to be that the methods used in linguistic studies should be sufficiently sensitive and finely tuned to be able to take into account the actual individual usages by the poet of the elements being investigated.

One final aspect of the hymn that the study of parallels affects needs to be mentioned before concluding. The hymn is, of course, a

55 Cessi, op. cit., pp.874–5.
56 Studies presenting these two views on the relative composition and date of the two parts: Janko, op. cit., pp.99ff., 198; Marchinus van der Valk, 'A Few Observations on the Homeric *Hymn to Apollo*', AC 46 (1977) 441–52; Förstel, op. cit., pp.282–4; West, CQ 25 (1975) 161–70; Schröder, op. cit., pp.1, 10.
57 Cf. Miller, *From Delos to Delphi*, pp.114–15.

work of the Homeric tradition, but it is not necessarily a work of oral tradition in the sense that it was composed during performance.[58] In fact, the profundity of the ideas which the poet presents in clever and complex ways and often places carefully at different parts of the hymn, as well as the extremely high artistry seen, for instance, in the presentation of the two styles of the different sections, indicates that much premeditated composition was involved before performance. One example of the complexity that indicates much prior preparation is the subtle presentation of the motif of the submersion of Delos by Apollo after his birth. The motif is first alluded to in lines 70–6, and it is explained only in lines 133–5, 139, in such a way as to preclude spontaneous invention. This whole scene of the birth of Apollo is, in fact, carefully constructed to present all of the correct motifs in their proper order for the portrayal of the journey for power as it is seen in the Mesopotamian myths. The precision of the poet in placing all the ideas and motifs in the context of the correct journeys, and the sequential presentation of the complex and detailed story of the heroic son of the supreme god by means of this material, also suggest that much time was required for premeditated creation of the hymn. The clever positioning of the first Assembly scene to present the theme of the power of the god in a way to be explained only much later on in the poem is another strong indication, as is the creation of this scene as a duplicate for the second scene of the first arrival of the new god in his father's Assembly, and its separation from its explanatory sequence and placement at the beginning of the hymn.

The study of the hymn in the light of the Mesopotamian ideas therefore also illuminates to a certain extent the poet's methods of composition. This manner of composition seems to be necessary for the nature and profundity of the presentation of the ideas which the poet wants to express in his story, and it is really another indication of the level of the conspicuous skills which manifest his genius in many ways throughout this hymn to Apollo, not least his clever and imaginative use and presentation of the ideas and material which appear to derive from Mesopotamia and form the basis of the hymn. Whoever he may have been, this great work of art suggests that he must have been an inspiration to many poets and to others who knew the story of Apollo and all of the ideas which give his hymn so much depth and meaning.

---

58 See Janko's definition of oral formulaic literature (op. cit., p.18), and his discussion of oral composition in relation to the Homeric hymns (ibid., pp.18–41).

6

THE HOMERIC HYMN TO DEMETER

In the Homeric corpus the *Homeric Hymn to Demeter* stands unsurpassed in the emotional depth of its subject. The poem highlights the relationship between the mother Demeter and her daughter Persephone. The love and devotion of the mother goddess for her lost child, snatched away unbeknownst to her by Hades, the lord of the netherworld, to be his wife, eventually results in the discovery of her daughter's whereabouts and her return to the upperworld, at least for part of each year.

This hymn constitutes the earliest evidence for the Mysteries of Eleusis: not of their rituals, of course, which were secret and would not be revealed in a work for public consumption like this one, but of their existence and their highest prize, the gift of blessed immortality to those who undertook the secret initiation rites.[1] The Mysteries must surely have provided great hope to the initiates of archaic times, if they believed themselves to be condemned to the compulsory

---

1 This study is concerned only with influence on the myth, especially as it is represented in the hymn, and not with the discussion of the Eleusinian Mysteries and possible Mesopotamian influence on these and the cult. The relationship of the hymn to the Mysteries and cult is highly problematic, and it is not the concern here. On these questions, see, for instance, N.J. Richardson, *The Homeric Hymn to Demeter*, Clarendon Press, Oxford, 1974, pp.12–30; André Cheyns, 'La structure du récit dans l'*Iliade* et l'*Hymn homérique à Déméter*', *Revue belge de philologie et d'histoire* 66 (1988) 33–5; Larry J. Alderink, 'Mythical and Cosmological Structure in the Homeric Hymn to Demeter', *Numen* 29 (1982) 1ff.; Fritz Wehrli, 'Die Mysterien von Eleusis', *Archiv für Religionswissenschaft* 31 (1934) 77ff.; Kevin Clinton, *The Sacred Officials of the Eleusinian Mysteries*, American Philosophical Society, Philadelphia, 1974, and 'The Author of the Homeric Hymn to Demeter', *Opuscula Atheniensia* 16 (1986) 43–9.

immortality of the sort portrayed in the picture of Hades presented in other Homeric works, and summed up in the *Odyssey* in the passionate words of the great hero Achilles in his response to Odysseus in the netherworld: it is better to be a poor serf on earth among the living than to be the king of the dead in the underworld (11.487–91). In Book 11 of this work the dead are seen in the gloom at the edge of Hades as feeble ghosts, pitifully squeaking and fluttering around Odysseus' sacrifice to drink the blood of the slain sheep. There is no evidence in these early Greek works of the paradise for ordinary mortals offered to the Orphics of later times.[2]

The hymn, which bears a close relation to the oral tradition of the epic works, is, with 495 lines, almost as long as the *Homeric Hymn to Apollo* and not much shorter than the longest surviving Homeric hymn, the hymn to Hermes. Its time of composition is disputed, although it is placed in either the seventh or the sixth century BC.[3] The myth involved is, however, clearly much older, since Hesiod's *Theogony* (lines 912–14) preserves the earliest reference to what seems to be the story of the Greek hymn. The section of the *Theogony* in which these lines occur is usually considered to be authentic.

The hymn is outstanding for the striking number and the nature of the parallels with Mesopotamian myths. Indeed, numerous motifs and underlying ideas are not only closely similar but are complex features central to the Mesopotamian myths as they are to the Greek hymn. Just as significantly, they are also found in a specific group of Mesopotamian myths, that is, among the myths of the goddess-and-consort strand representing the cult of Inanna and her consort

2 On various places of paradise and the Orphic beliefs, see, for instance, Bruno Zannini Quirini, 'L'aldilà nelle religioni del mondo classico', in Paolo Xella, ed., *Archeologia dell'Inferno*, Essedue Edizioni, Verona, 1987, pp.282–90.

3 Richardson, *Demeter*, pp.5ff, 11ff.; also comments by A.W. James, 'The Homeric Hymn to Demeter, Ed. by N.J. Richardson ... [review article]', JHS 96 (1976) 165–8; Richard Janko, *Homer, Hesiod and the Hymns: Diachronic Development in Epic Diction*, Cambridge University Press, Cambridge, 1982, p.183; Walter Burkert, 'The Homeric Hymn to Demeter, Ed. by N.J. Richardson [review article]', *Gnomon* 49 (1977) 442–3; Cheyns, *Revue belge*, 66 (1988) 82.

Dumuzi, and of Damu, who is identified with him.[4] There are many parallels, especially in the central structural ideas of the journeys carried out by the gods and in the accompanying idea of the power involved in the journey, but there are also striking parallels of motif with similar underlying ideas; so many, in fact, that the conclusion of Mesopotamian influence is, even at first sight, hard to avoid, and on closer inspection, compelling.

Other scholars have recognized the parallels between elements in the *Homeric Hymn to Demeter* and features in Near Eastern myths, including Mesopotamian mythical material. G.S. Kirk, in *The Nature of Greek Myths*, points to the motif of Demeter's disappearance or withdrawal from Olympos, with the resultant loss of fertility and drought on the earth, as a performance which follows that of the drought-causing deities Inanna, Dumuzi and Telepinu.[5] Walter Burkert has also pointed out more recently this parallel between Demeter's action and its consequences and features in Near Eastern myth.[6] Kirk remarks that the motif of drought appears to be inconsequential in the Greek context and inappropriate in a Greek myth in view of the Greek environmental background, but it is a typical motif for Mesopotamia, subject as that region is to occasional natural disasters such as flood and drought. He also comments on the parallel between Persephone's annual descent and Adonis' seasonal disappearance to the netherworld. However, as he points out, these are not sufficiently complex or detailed mythical parallels to indicate influence, and he therefore concentrates on other deities such as Apollo, Artemis and Aphrodite.

However, a close analysis of both the Greek hymn to Demeter and the myths of Inanna and Dumuzi/Damu offers many more parallels to consider. Here the parallels are numerous, complex and profound, and appear to indicate much more than simple coincidence. They do

4 The world of the heroic-strand myths stands far away. Karl Deichgräber notices the distance of the ideas in the hymn from the world of warriors and martial exploits of the Homeric epics, although he naturally ascribes a different reason to the phenomenon: 'Eleusinische Frömmigkeit und homerische Vorstellungswelt im Homerischen Demeterhymnus', *Akademie der Wissenschaften und Literatur in Mainz, Geistes- und Sozialwissenschaftlichen Klasse* 6 (1950) 513–14.

5 G.S. Kirk, *The Nature of Greek Myths*, Penguin Books, Harmondsworth, 1974, p.254.

6 Burkert, *Gnomon* 49 (1977) 443–4. See also Ioannis Loucas, 'La déesse de la prospérité dans les mythes mésopotamien et égéen de la Descente aux Enfers', RHR 205 (1988) 239–40.

not exist merely on the level of motif, but are supported by the presence of complex underlying ideas which indicate a similar religious conceptual understanding of the motifs and of the gods and their activities. A résumé of the hymn is necessary at this point before a detailed examination of the parallels is possible.

The story begins with the scene of Persephone, the daughter of Demeter and Zeus, gathering flowers with other goddesses in a meadow on the plain of Nysa, here a mythical place at the edge of the world beside the streams of River Ocean. According to the will of Zeus and to please Hades, Earth produced the marvellous, radiant Narcissus to snare the girl; a hundred sweet-smelling heads grew from the flower's root, and Earth, wide Heaven and the Sea laughed aloud.

When the amazed girl grasped the plant, the 'wide-pathed earth' yawned and Hades thundered out, driving his four-horse chariot. He seized the lamenting maiden, who cried out shrilly. Only Hekate in her cave, Helios and Demeter heard her.

Demeter rushed over the sea and earth in search of her child for nine days. At dawn on the tenth day she went, accompanied by the goddess Hekate, to the sun god Helios, who sees all, and stopped his horses. The sun god revealed what had happened, and added his opinion that Hades, who ruled a third of the universe, was no unfitting husband for Kore (Persephone).

The angry Demeter abandoned Olympos and, disguising herself as an old woman, roamed for a long time over the earth. By the Maiden Well in Eleusis, the daughters of King Keleus met the goddess as she was resting. Demeter told them a tale of how she had been kidnapped by pirates, and the girls offered her the position of nurse to their newly born brother Demophoon. In the palace Demeter nursed Demophoon, who grew like an immortal being. She fed him with ambrosia and, secretly at night, hid him like a brand in the hearth fire. However, his mother Metaneira, growing suspicious, caught her at it and cried out in sorrow. Demeter was terribly angry. She snatched the child from the flames and threw him to the ground, saying that Demophoon would be a king, but not immortal. The goddess now returned to her own form.

Demeter sat in the temple that the Eleusinians had built for her and yearned for her daughter. In that year she caused a cruel famine over the earth, and would have destroyed mankind and deprived the gods of their sacrifices if Zeus had not perceived the situation. First he sent Iris to her, commanding her to return to Olympos, and then all of the other immortal gods were summoned to entreat her. However, Demeter would not reverse her policy unless she saw her daughter again.

Zeus dispatched the messenger Hermes down to dark Erebos with the instruction to Hades to release Persephone into the light. Hades acquiesced, but pointed out to Persephone that he was a fitting husband for her and decreed that, as long as she were with him, she would rule over all the living and have the greatest honours among the immortal gods. He surreptitiously ensured that she would return to him by giving her a pomegranate seed to eat.

Persephone returned from the netherworld, driven by Hermes in Hades' chariot over the seas and earth to the temple in Eleusis. Mother and daughter embraced. Demeter said that if she had eaten any netherworld food she must return to dwell in Hades for a third of the year, coming forth in the verdant spring.

Zeus sent Rhea to bring Demeter to the assembly of the gods, promising her honours of her choice among the immortals, and at the same time confirmed Persephone's destiny of perpetual descent and return. Demeter made the earth bloom again and taught her mysteries to the Eleusinians. The two goddesses then joined the immortal gods on Olympos.

Similarities between the hymn and the relevant myths of Inanna and Dumuzi/Damu are found in various motifs, but the main parallels exist in the journeys which the gods carry out. These journeys are the central structure of both the hymn and the Mesopotamian myths, and are a feature on which the episodes of the stories are built.

A major parallel, which seems so far to have been overlooked, is the complex narrative idea of the journey of the bereft mother goddess wandering over the earth in search of her lost child who has been carried off to the netherworld. The discovery of the child's whereabouts is followed by an attempt by the goddess to obtain the child's release. This is also the basic story-line of the major part of the Sumerian myth of Damu in the series edin-na ú-saǧ-ǧá, which has been discussed in the chapter on Inanna. This fragmentary work, put together from OB and NA tablets, is a compilation of a number of texts taken from the myths about Dumuzi/Damu and related gods, and the separate sections present various ideas about the deities involved. Built on to the story of the lamenting mother searching for her lost child are various features such as Inanna's lament for her lost husband Dumuzi/Damu (lines 1ff.), the identification of Damu with various local incarnations of the descending god, Damu's meeting on the road to the netherworld with other ghosts of the dead (lines 202ff.), the mother's preparation of food and beer, of which the purpose is apparently to revive her son (lines 233ff.). At various points there appears to be dialogue of some nature between the lost child and his mother and his sister, who at one stage also helps in her mother's search. Nevertheless, the basic story-line of edin-na ú-saĝ-ĝá is that of the mother's desperate wandering search for her lost child, who has descended to the netherworld, followed by an attempt at a recovery operation. Damu descends to the netherworld. His bereft mother, Duttur, searches for him from place to place and eventually discovers that he is in the netherworld. She decides to go after him, declaring that she will even go to the netherworld to secure his release.[7] She carries out several acts which appear to have the purpose of achieving the child's return. In the end the sister, Geshtinanna, is seen in the netherworld with her brother Dumuzi/Damu and there appears to be some reference to the annual sub-stitutionary cycle which is otherwise established at the end of ID (lines 407–9). Damu's return is also seen in TRS 8, where it is achieved simply by the mother's search, apparently with no other assistance, and in the text the return's result in the fertility of vegetation is stressed.[8]

A look at the Greek hymn shows that the journey of Demeter closely parallels that of Duttur. She wanders despairingly over the earth in search of her lost child, ignorant of the fact that she has been carried off to Hades. No one can tell her the fate of the child. Like the Mesopotamian goddess, she is unwashed. Finally there is a point in her wandering journey where the goddess discovers her child's fate.[9] The OB version speaks of her determination to descend to the

---

7 SK 26.iv.1–9. For a translation, see Thorkild Jacobsen, *The Harps that Once . . .: Sumerian Poetry in Translation*, Yale University Press, New Haven and London, 1987, p.71: OB version 177–80.
8 Duplicate versions of TRS 8: CT XV pls 26–7, 30. For translation of some of the lament, and discussion of the story, see Thorkild Jacobsen, *The Treasures of Darkness: A History of Mesopotamian Religion*, Yale University Press, New Haven and London, 1976, pp.68–72.
9 *Homeric Hymn to Demeter*, 64–74.

netherworld, and she sets out to do so.[10] Similarly, Demeter removes herself from Olympos and the Assembly of the gods and goes to earth, wandering through the cities and fields of men, determined on her child's release (lines 91–4):[11]

Being angry thereafter with the black-clouded Son of Kronos,
she abandoned the assembly of the gods and high Olympos,
and went away to the cities and rich tilled fields of men,
disguising her form for a long time.

χωσαμένη δὴ ἔπειτα κελαινεφέι Κρονίωνι
νοσφισθεῖσα θεῶν ἀγορὴν καὶ μακρὸν Ὄλυμπον
ᾤχετ᾽ ἐπ᾽ ἀνθρώπων πόλιας καὶ πίονα ἔργα
εἶδος ἀμαλδύνουσα πολὺν χρόνον·

Olympos is an ambiguous term, and can be used with the sense of heaven. An example of this idea is seen, for instance, in the *Homeric Hymn to Apollo*, where the god Apollo goes from earth to Olympos and then later back down again, clearly leaving earth and returning again (line 186, ἔνθεν δὲ πρὸς Ὄλυμπον ἀπὸ χθονός, and line 216, Πιερίην μὲν πρῶτον ἀπ᾽ Οὐλύμποιο κατῆλθες·). The idea is seen especially in the *Iliad*: Zeus is styled as the god of Olympos or heaven. Martin Nilsson pointed out that in the *Iliad* 'Olympos and the Heavens appear as identical'; in accordance with this, the Greek gods are called 'the Olympians' ('Ολύμπιοι), and 'the Heavenly Ones' (Οὐρανίωνες), or the 'Heavenly Gods' (δεοὶ Οὐρανίωνες).[12] Olympos can be found referring to οὐρανός, meaning the sky, in the *Odyssey* (20.103). If Olympos is separated from earth here with the sense of heaven, as it surely is, the idea of a descent is involved, and this constitutes a parallel to the idea in the OB version of the descent of Damu's mother, who at this point in the myth declares her intention of going to the netherworld to regain her child. There is a difference, of course, in that Demeter's descent is from heaven to earth, whereas with Damu's mother it is from earth to the nether

---

10 SK 26.iv.1–9. Jacobsen, *The Harps that Once . . .*, p.71: OB version 177–80.

11 Demeter's nine-day search seems to have been limited to the world of the gods. However, if this is not the case and she has already been wandering over the earth, the idea of the abandonment is mentioned at this point.

12 Martin P. Nilsson, *The Mycenaean Origin of Greek Mythology*, Sather Classical Lectures 8, University of California Press, Berkeley, 1932, pp.228–30.

world.[13] Nevertheless, the similar idea at the same point in the journey is a remarkable parallel. Indeed, as Richardson points out, in other references to the Greek story 'there are traces of a version in which Demeter herself went down to Hades in order to recover her'.[14] In this version Demeter is given a guide in the shape of the Eleusinian Eubouleus. This then parallels the idea of the mother goddess's descent that is seen in the OB version of edin-na ú-saĝ-ĝá.[15] However, in the hymn Demeter does not descend to the netherworld, just as, in fact, the Mesopotamian mother goddess never reaches the netherworld in the surviving text. It is another figure who descends to the netherworld with the result of the child's ascent.[16] In the same way, in the Greek hymn it is another deity who descends to Hades to achieve the child's release.[17] The mother's wandering search is the first part of the complex parallel. The other elements of the parallel are the goddess's discovery of her child's descent and the recovery operation. The first event is seen in the hymn when, after her nine-day search, Demeter discovers from Helios that her child is in the netherworld (lines 74–87). The discovery is followed at the end of the Eleusinian section by attempts by the mother goddess to recover her child (lines 301ff.).

An objection to the parallel of the searching goddess and lost child may at first seem to exist in the sex of the child, since Damu is male and Persephone is female. However, part of the Mesopotamian myth involves the descent of the sister, Geshtinanna, who, like Damu/Dumuzi, descends and returns every year. It is this idea of the female's descent and return that is picked up in Persephone's myth. Moreover, the idea of the descent and return of the goddess is also found in ID and AV, in which there are parallels for a number of other features of Persephone's descent and return journey. In

---

13 The upperworld is seen as heaven and earth in ID 1–5: the goddess leaves the 'great heaven' to go to the 'great below'; she leaves heaven and the land of Sumer and goes to the netherworld.

14 Richardson, *Demeter*, p.84.

15 Bendt Alster, 'Edin-na ú-saĝ-ĝá: Reconstruction, History, and Interpretation of a Sumerian Cultic Lament', in Karl Hecker and Walter Sommerfeld, eds, *Keilschriftliche Literaturen. Ausgewählte Vorträge der XXXII. Rencontre Assyriologique Internationale*, Münster, 8.–12.7.1985, Dietrich Reimer Verlag, Berlin, 1986, p.26.

16 The sister Geshtinanna: SK 27.v.7–16. For translation, see Jacobsen, *The Harps that Once . . .*, pp.83–4: OB version 366–74.

17 Hermes: lines 334–46, 377–85.

addition, a feature of the Eleusinian cult seems also to be the importance of the goddesses and a concentration on them, while the male gods seem by comparison to take a secondary role. Nevertheless, the inclusion of the young male is seen in other evidence of the cult, for instance in the form of the κοῦρος, usually Ploutos. An anonymous male child, perhaps Ploutos too, seems also to be born to the goddess (πότνια) as part of the rites of the Mysteries.[18] In addition, the triad of mother, sister and male child – parallel to the group Duttur, Geshtinanna and Damu – is shown in Greece on pottery, where a standard tableau is the group of Demeter, Persephone and a male child, perhaps Ploutos, as the returning child of plenty.[19] This triad is indicated at the end of the hymn, where Ploutos is mentioned in connection with the two goddesses: they send Ploutos into the house of the man whom they favour, taking wealth with him (lines 488–9).[20]

The encounter of Demeter and Hekate with Helios, in which the discovery of Persephone's whereabouts occurs, follows the pattern of the Mesopotamian intercessory encounter with the sun god. The interceding god should approach the sun god as he comes forth from the netherworld.[21] This occurs here, for the goddesses approach Helios at dawn on the tenth day as he comes forth from the netherworld (lines 51–61). Hekate's presence in the scene may reflect her important mediating role, which she displays in Hesiod's *Theogony*,[22] but it also parallels to some extent the role of the sister in the OB version, who helps the mother goddess search for the lost child.[23]

18 R. Seaford, ed., *Euripides Cyclops*, Clarendon Press, Oxford, 1984, pp.42–3; Richardson, *Demeter*, pp.26–7; Michael H. Jameson, 'The Homeric Hymn to Demeter', *Athenaeum* 54 (1976) 444; Martin P. Nilsson, 'Die eleusinischen Gottheiten', *Archiv für Religionswissenschaft* 32 (1935) 97–101.

19 Richardson, *Demeter*, p.317; on the κοῦρος Ploutos and Dionysos, see ibid., pp.26–8, 231, 316ff. Cf. also William D. Furley, *Studies in the Use of Fire in Ancient Greek Religion*, Ayer, New Hampshire, 1981, pp.82ff.; Ugo Bianchi, *The Greek Mysteries*, E.J. Brill, Leiden, 1976, pp.22–3 and plate 27; Nilsson, 'Die eleusinischen Gottheiten', p.81.

20 Another triad may exist in the hymn as well, Rhea, Hekate and Helios (lines 56–62, 74–5): see Cora Angier Sowa, *Traditional Themes and the Homeric Hymns*, Bolchazy–Carducci Publishers, Chicago, 1984, p.314.

21 R. Caplice, 'É.NUN in Mesopotamian Literature', Or 42 (1973) 303 n.20.

22 Jenny Strauss Clay, 'The Hecate of the Theogony', GRBS 25 (1984) 35ff.

23 Jenny Strauss Clay, *The Politics of Olympus*, Princeton University Press, Princeton, 1989, p.218.

An important aspect which should be taken into account is that both the Greek cult and the Mesopotamian have fertility as one of their basic concerns. Demeter is the goddess of corn, the staple food of life, and an important element in the prosperity of the people, a feature which is expressed with Ploutos at the end of the hymn.[24] Persephone's return also results in fertility of the earth (lines 302ff., 331–3, 450–6, 470–3). Agriculture, particularly with the gift of corn, is important in versions of the story: for instance, in the version popular in Athens in the classical period, in which Triptolemos received the gift of corn and the knowledge of agriculture from Demeter. The later epic poet Panyassis also made allusion to this, replacing King Keleus by Triptolemos as the son of Eleusis.[25] Parallel with the dispensation in the Homeric hymn that Persephone should return every year in the verdant spring (lines 401–3), Damu's return from the netherworld results specifically in vegetable fertility, as seen in TRS 8, and his return is essential to bring prosperity to the city.[26] In the fifth song this liturgy begins with a lament for Damu, expressing the fear that he will not return, with the dire consequences of no flood water, no agricultural fertility or resulting prosperity. Eventually, after the mother's search, Damu returns, bringing gifts of food and prosperity to the land and to the city. He also returns on the high flood, which ensures the agricultural prosperity of the cities; in the ninth song of TRS 8, the king Ur-nammu, the first king of the Third Dynasty of Ur, and later rulers in the list, function in the ritual as Damu, sailing on the river to the city.[27] In another form of his emergence Damu 'comes out of the river'.[28] Of course, in the wider cult of Dumuzi and Inanna/Ishtar, the concern is also for human and animal fertility, as seen particularly in AV 87–90, but Damu's

---

24 Nilsson, 'Die eleusinischen Gottheiten', pp.101–8.
25 Richardson, *Demeter*, pp.75–6.
26 Last fragmentary lines of TCL XV 8. See Jacobsen, *Treasures of Darkness*, p.72. The young god returns perhaps in the spring or in the new year, and the result is life and fertility for the earth, and prosperity for the city: Hartmut Schmökel, *Sumer et la civilisation sumérienne*, Payot, Paris, 1964, pp.130ff.
27 Inanna and the Sumerian kings, playing the role of Dumuzi in the sacred marriage: S.N. Kramer, *The Sumerians*, University of Chicago Press, Chicago, 1963, pp.45, 140–1; W. Heimpel, 'The Nanshe Hymn', JCS 33 (1981) 104; Henri Frankfort, *Kingship and the Gods*, University of Chicago Press, Chicago, 1948, pp.224, 295–9.
28 Jacobsen, *The Treasures of Darkness*, pp.69ff.; also Helmer Ringgren, *Religions of the Ancient Near East*, SPCK, London, 1973, p.13.

function seems to be limited specifically to the fertility of vegetation, at least in these myths. In the Greek pantheon it is Aphrodite who occupies the area of human and animal fertility, as seen, for instance, in *Homeric Hymn V* (lines 1–6). It has long been the generally held view that this goddess had her origins in the same great Mesopotamian goddess discussed here with Demeter and Persephone.[29] However, the point is that both the Eleusinian cult and that of Damu are concerned with fertility.

The story of Persephone's journey to Hades and her return combines major features of both ID and AV as well as of the liturgies of Damu. While her role in combination with that of Demeter, and elements such as her unwilling descent at the hands of Hades, parallel those of the lost child Damu, many features of her descent parallel those of Inanna/Ishtar's descent in ID and AV but are not found with Damu. Such features are, for example: the concern of the journey with the goddesses' achievement of power in the netherworld and upperworld, including the motif of the rulership of the netherworld (ID 165–6); receiving help to return to the upperworld from a figure who descends from the Assembly to the netherworld (ID 245ff., AV 92ff.); the motif of food taken immediately before her return (ID 280); and the journey's result in the instigation of the perpetual descent-and-return cycle (ID 407–10; AV 126–38).

The concern of the journey with the goddesses' achievement of power is important in the hymn, and this idea of power acquired in, or as a result of, the journey forms a major parallel with the ideas in the Mesopotamian myths, especially as they are portrayed in ID and AV. One of the aims of the hymn is, of course, to praise the goddesses, and the mention in the hymn of the goddesses' power may perhaps be expected, but it is significant for this investigation of parallels and influence that power is achieved directly as a result of the journeys, and by means of the activities involved. In addition, it is especially significant that in the case of Persephone the powers are exactly parallel in nature and scope to those of Inanna in ID, and are acquired in a similar way as well as at precisely the same point in the journey. In fact, both Demeter and Persephone gain power in their journeys. As a result of her activities in the journeys, Demeter is

---

29 For instance, Walter Burkert, *Greek Religion*, Harvard University Press, Cambridge (Mass.), 1985, pp.152–3; Kirk, *The Nature of Greek Myths*, pp.113, 258. For a thorough discussion, see Chapter 7 below on Aphrodite.

promised τιμαί, powers and privileges, of her choice among the gods on Olympos (lines 460–2) and she returns to Olympos.[30] On her part Persephone receives power over the netherworld, as its queen, and powers over the living in the upperworld (lines 360–9). Similarly, Inanna's purpose in descending to the netherworld is to acquire power there and also, it seems, in the upperworld, as revealed in the supreme god Enlil's words to Inanna's minister (lines 190–2):

> In his rage [Father] Enlil answered Ninshubur:
> "[My daughter] craved the great heaven and she craved the great below as well."

> [a-a-ᵈ]en-líl-libiš-bal-a-ni ᵈnin-šubur-ra-ke₄ mu-na-ni-ib-gi₄-gi₄
> [dumu-mu] an-gal al bí-in-du₁₁ ki-gal al bí-in-du₁₁

While it is not Persephone's purpose to achieve power, as her descent is involuntary, it is definitely the purpose of the author of the hymn. The establishment of the ruling pair is also an effect of the journey. While rulership of the netherworld is an issue of the Mesopotamian myth *Nergal and Ereshkigal*, it is also a feature of Inanna's journey in ID, in which the goddess sits on Ereshkigal's throne, an action which appears to be an attempt to usurp Ereshkigal's position (lines 165–6).[31] Although she fails to obtain the rulership, as her attempt is part of the 'initial defeat' structure, an important feature of many Mesopotamian journey myths (and, in any case, the throne is already the possession of Ereshkigal, the netherworld queen in the pantheon),

---

30 Jean Rudhardt also points out their gain in τιμαί in his article, 'A propos de l'hymne homérique à Déméter', MH 35 (1978) 7ff. The goddesses increase their power: see also Alderink, *Numen* 29 (1982) 6–9. Persephone's power: Cheyns, *Revue belge* 66 (1988) 65.

31 See O.R. Gurney, 'The Sultantepe Tablets: The Myth of Nergal and Ereshkigal', AnSt 10 (1960) 105–31; and, more recently: Manfred Hutter, *Altorientalische Vorstellungen von der Unterwelt. Literar- und religionsgeschichtliche Überlegungen zu «Nergal und Ereškigal»*, Orbis Biblicus et Orientalis 63, Universitätsverlag, Freiburg, 1985, pp.1ff. Regarding queenship, S.N. Kramer suggests, in consideration of Enlil's words (190ff.), that Inanna may have intended to make herself queen of the Netherworld: 'Revised Edition of "Inanna's Descent to the Netherworld"', JCS 5 (1951) 16; cf. also William R. Sladek, 'Inanna's Descent to the Netherworld', Ph.D. diss, University Microfilms, Ann Arbor, 1974, p.21.

she does obtain power over the netherworld, which she achieves by means of her descent and return, as Persephone achieves power here. Inanna gains a certain power over the netherworld, and perhaps even the upperworld, by means of gaining the power to rise again. She thus overcomes the netherworld's major power, which is to hold all who descend to it. She does this after her helpers descend to her, bringing aid from the upperworld gods, thus reversing her defeat (ID 254ff.). A similar feature appears to be repeated in the Greek hymn, as Hades gives Persephone her powers over the netherworld and upperworld only after she gains the power to rise again – and this occurs after the helper, Hermes, descends from the upperworld Assembly to her aid, reversing her initial defeat at the hands of Hades, and her entrapment in the netherworld (lines 360–9). It is at this point that Hades offers her the powers. The goddess therefore receives her powers, as does Inanna, as a result of having obtained the right to ascend again.

Persephone has power over life and death. This can be seen when, for instance, she sends Alkestis back to life in the upperworld, and when in Pindar, frag. 133, she sends the dead back to life: ἐς τὸν ὕπερθεν ἅλιον κείνων ἐνάτῳ ἔτεϊ ἀνδιδοῖ ψυχὰς πάλιν.[32] This return of the dead from the netherworld is seen with Ishtar and Dumuzi at the end of AV, where the dead perform an ascent of some nature with Dumuzi (lines 136–8):[33]

> When Dumuzi rises, and when the lapis lazuli flute
> and carnelian ring rise with him
> When male and female mourners rise with him
> Then let the dead come up and smell the incense

32 B. Snell and H. Maehler, eds, *Pindari Carmina cum Fragmentis*, Part 1, B.G. Teubner, Leipzig, 1975, p.111. For Alkestis, see Euripides' *Alkestis*, and Apollodorus I.105–6. II.129. See also C. Sourvinou-Inwood, 'The Boston Relief of Locri Epizephyrii', JHS 98 (1978) 136, who also refers to Persephone's release of the souls to the upperworld sun.

33 The belief in blessed life after death for the initiate that is indicated in lines 480–2 is also suggested in Pindar Ol. 2. 53ff., in connection with Eleusis, where he speaks of Ploutos and eternal life. Cf. T.W. Allen, W.R. Halliday and E.E. Sikes, *The Homeric Hymns*, 2nd edition, Oxford University Press, Amsterdam, 1963, p.180. Richardson, *Demeter*, p.318. For one interpretation of the rise of the dead in AV, see also Ph. Talon, 'Le mythe de la Descente d'Ištar aux Enfers', *Akkadica* 59 (1988) 23–4, who suggests that this may be a reference to the *kispum* ceremony.

ina ūmē ^dDumuzi ellânni malīl ^{na4}uqnê šemīr sāmti
ittīšu ellânni
ittīšu ellânni bākûtu u bākâtu
mītūtu lilûnimma qutrin<na> lissinū

Another parallel with ID is that Persephone's journey results in the instigation of the perpetual annual descent-and-return fertility cycle (lines 398–400, 463–5), as seen in ID (lines 407–9) with Geshtinanna and Dumuzi. Although the substitutionary idea seems also to be suggested at the end of edin-na ú-saǧ-ǧá, the instigation of the cycle is not mentioned in this text.[34] The hymn also presents the same motif as that clearly expressed in ID, the partition of the year – although here it is a tripartite division, rather than bi-annual as in the case of Dumuzi and Geshtinanna. However, the earlier Greek divisions appear to have been bi-annual, so Persephone's stay in the netherworld for a third of the year may represent a change from the two-part to the three-part year. The division into three may also be a reflection of the cosmological idea of the tripartite universe, a motif mentioned in Hades' one-third share of the cosmos.[35] Instead of the substitutionary system performed by Dumuzi and Geshtinanna, each spending half of the year in the netherworld, Persephone descends and returns by herself. Her annual journey with its results of fertility is like the annual journey of Damu. Her residence in the netherworld has the effect of dearth of fertility and prosperity on earth: similarly, at the beginning of TRS 8 Damu's mother fears that her son will not return, with the consequence of loss of fertility and prosperity. This is, of course, the application of the journey for power with Damu in his myths: by his annual descent and return he has the power to fulfil his functions of bringing fertility and resulting prosperity to the inhabitants of the land. Although Persephone's annual return coincides with the return of fertility of the earth in spring, the aspect of her power in bringing fertility and prosperity every year as a result of her performance of the perpetual cycle is not stressed in the hymn. The concern is rather with the establishment of Persephone's power in the netherworld and upperworld, as seen likewise in ID and AV. The function of bringing prosperity, seen with Damu in his myths, seems to lie specifically with the young male Ploutos in the hymn,

34 SK 27.v.7–16. For translation, see Jacobsen, *The Harps that Once . . .*, pp.83–4: OB version 366–74.
35 Richardson, *Demeter*, p.284. Cf. also Allen, Halliday and Sikes, *Homeric Hymns*, p.375. See also Sowa, *Traditional Themes*, pp.312–13.

rather than with Persephone, as can be seen at the end of the hymn, when the statement is made that the goddesses send Ploutos who gives abundance (ἄφενος) to mortal men (lines 488–9).

In these myths of the goddesses, the great netherworld oath of the gods seems to have a certain role concerning the acquisition of life. In the Demophoon episode, Demeter swears the netherworld oath, the oath of Styx, which is the highest oath of the gods, and she swears it when she angrily states that she would have made Demophoon immortal (lines 259–61):

> For know that, oath of the gods and pitiless water of Styx,
> I would surely have made your dear son unageing all his days
> and granted him imperishable honour.

> ἴστω γὰρ θεῶν ὅρκος ἀμείλικτον Στυγὸς ὕδωρ
> ἀθάνατόν κέν τοι καὶ ἀγήραον ἤματα πάντα
> παῖδα φίλον ποίησα καὶ ἄφθιτον ὤπασα τιμήν·

In the *Homeric Hymn to Apollo*, Leto also swears, at the island-goddess Delos' bidding, the great oath in a similar situation – before the birth of the child Apollo (lines 83–6):

> And Leto swore the great oath of the gods:
> 'Now know this, Earth and broad Heaven above,
> and flowing water of Styx, which is the greatest
> and most terrible oath of the blessed gods,
> surely there will always be here a fragrant altar of Phoebus
> and a precinct, and he will repay you above all others.'

> ... Λητὼ δὲ θεῶν μέγαν ὅρκον ὄμοσσε·
> ἴστω νῦν τάδε Γαῖα καὶ Οὐρανὸς εὐρὺς ὕπερθεν
> καὶ τὸ κατειβόμενον Στυγὸς ὕδωρ ὅστε μέγιστος
> ὅρκος δεινότατός τε πέλει μακάρεσσι θεοῖσιν·
> ἦ μὴν Φοίβου τῆδε θυώδης ἔσσεται αἰεὶ
> βωμὸς καὶ τέμενος, τίσει δέ σέ γ' ἔξοχα πάντων.

The netherworld oath is seen in the Mesopotamian mythology in a comparable situation: the netherworld queen Ereshkigal swears it before the revival – the return to life and to the upperworld – of Inanna (ID 271):

> They made her swear this [by heaven and earth]

> [zi-an-na zi-ki-a] mu-ni-in-pà-dè-eš

Another motif which occurs in this Eleusinian episode is that of the goddess's deliberate lie. Demeter declares that it is fitting for the girls to know the truth about herself and about her journey, and promptly proceeds to tell them the lie of her Cretan origins (lines 120ff.).[36] Deception also occurs in ID, as Inanna too gives a false account of her presence at the gate of the netherworld (lines 78–89). Another Greek example of the goddess's lie is Aphrodite's lie to Anchises in the *Homeric Hymn to Aphrodite* (lines 107–42).

The resounding scream of Persephone when she is seized by Hades parallels Geshtinanna's great scream. The scream takes place in the same context of the carrying-away of the young person by a denizen or denizens of the netherworld. Persephone's great supernatural scream is a special feature in the hymn: as long as she is still above the earth, the mountains and the sea-depths ring with her immortal cry (lines 38–9). This parallels Geshtinanna's great supernatural scream echoing over the earth in the composition *Dumuzi's Dream*, which tells of Dumuzi's descent as the substitute of Inanna when this goddess has returned after her descent to the netherworld, having completed the journey which is the subject of ID. In *Dumuzi's Dream*, the cry is concerned with the descent of the young male: Geshtinanna utters her great scream when Dumuzi takes refuge at her 'holy fold', where he is captured by the pursuing netherworld *gallu*-demons, dies and is presumably carried off to the netherworld:

> Geshtinanna let screams draw near unto heaven,
> > draw near unto the netherworld;
> the sum of screams covered like a cloth the base of heaven,
> > veiled it like a linen sheet.[37]

There is therefore the same cosmic scream associated with the death or disappearance of the child to the netherworld, and it seems to be a special feature in this context. It should be noted that Persephone parallels Geshtinanna also as the female child who descends, so it is in one way the corresponding figure who utters the scream. In the case of the Homeric hymn, Persephone utters the scream and it is applied to her own descent as the child of the mother goddess. The same ideas

---

36 Another Cretan tale is seen in the *Odyssey* 13.253ff., where Odysseus tries to deceive Athene. Crete is probably a customary place to use for a false tale: Richardson, *Demeter*, p.188.

37 *Dumuzi's Dream*, 240–1; Jacobsen, *The Harps that Once . . .*, p.44. This is followed by actions which are generally part of lamentations for those who have died (lines 242–5). Cf. ibid, p.44 n.20.

therefore underlie the motifs in this complex parallel, and they are carefully used in the same context.

An important element of the journey in Mesopotamian myths is the initial-setback structure. In this the deity at first fails in his purpose or suffers a setback before succeeding. There are two general types of initial defeat in the Mesopotamian myths studied here. In ID and AV, the goddess fails and is killed. Helpers descend from the Assembly of the gods, bringing food and water of life to the goddess to return her to life and to the upperworld (ID 254ff.; AV 91ff.). This form is seen also in myths of Ninurta, where the warrior god fails in his first attempt to destroy the monster Anzu in the mountains and must receive help – in the form of advice and encouragement brought to him from the Assembly – before he overcomes the opponent at the second attempt.[38] The same pattern is followed in *Lugale*, in which he fights the monster Asag (lines 151–297).[39] The other type is that seen with Damu – he receives a setback at the beginning by being carried off to the netherworld and cannot rise again.[40] He receives help from the goddess, who achieves his release from the netherworld.

The Homeric hymn presents the initial setback of the Damu style, but both forms of the helper role are combined in achieving the goddess's release. In a parallel way to that of Damu in edin-na ú-saǧ-ǧá, Persephone suffers initial defeat when she is overcome by Hades and taken to the netherworld, where she is trapped and is not able to return. Her mother performs the helper role of the Damu myths, in which the goddess searches over the earth and eventually discovers her child, and sets out to achieve his release. The method of achieving his release is not spelled out in the Mesopotamian myth, but it may

---

38 Anzu myth: Tablet II.1–149 and Tablet III obv. i, lines 2–12. For the Anzu myth: W.W. Hallo and W.L. Moran, 'The First Tablet of the SB Recension of the Anzu-Myth', JCS 31 (1979) 65–105; E.A. Speiser and A.K. Grayson, in James B. Pritchard, ed., *Ancient Near Eastern Texts Relating to the Old Testament*, 3rd edition, Princeton University Press, Princeton, 1969, pp. 111ff., 514ff. For additions to Tablet III, see H.W.F. Saggs, 'Additions to Anzu', AfO 33 (1986) 1–29; also M.E. Vogelzang, *Bin šar dadmē: Edition and Analysis of the Akkadian Anzu Poem*, Styx Publications, Groningen, 1988, for all the texts except the additions to Tablet III by Saggs.

39 For *Lugale*, see J.J. van Dijk, *Lugal ud me-lám-bi nir-ǧál*, E.J. Brill, Leiden, 1983.

40 OB version. See Jacobsen, *The Harps that Once . . .*, p.76: OB version, 252–9.

involve the method of substitution in the netherworld.[41] In any case, the Greek hymn combines the helper role of the mother goddess with the helper role seen in ID and AV: the helper descends from the upperworld Assembly to confront the netherworld figure, and the goddess is immediately released (ID 254–81; AV 93ff.). Hermes does this here as he descends from Zeus and the Assembly on Olympos to the netherworld and conveys Zeus' command to Hades to release Persephone, with the consequence for the goddess of the power to rise to the upperworld (lines 334–69). She rises from Erebos to meet her mother at Eleusis and together they travel to Olympos (lines 375ff.). The Homeric hymn is closer to the Mesopotamian material in this aspect than another, later version which is found in Orph. Hy. 43.7. There Persephone is brought back to earth by the Moirai and Charites, as well as the Horai, her dancing-companions, rather than by Hermes. However, these also perform the helper role.

The food which Kore (Persephone) eats has the same place in the myth as does the food of life in Inanna's myth. In ID the goddess returns after receiving the food of life (lines 280–1), as Kore does immediately after eating the pomegranate seed (lines 371–80). An interesting feature in the Damu myth is the beer which seems to have the purpose of reviving the child in the netherworld. This brings to mind the κυκεών in the hymn, a drink which has a function in the Mysteries. Perhaps the notion of revival or of some connection with life of the initiates was associated with this drink too. If so, the use of this feature may derive from this Mesopotamian cultic background.

In Kore's myth the food also serves as the cause of the goddess's compulsory return to Hades, and of the institution of the perpetual cycle of the descending and returning fertility deity. In ID the instigation of the perpetual cycle is caused by the Anunnaku gods in the netherworld, who resist the idea of the goddess reascending and require a substitute in place of her (lines 285–9). This episode is not found in the Greek myth, of course, as in any case the Greek underworld has no comparable group in Hades, but the same resistance to the ascent of the goddess is present,[42] and the motif of the pomegranate seed is used to achieve the same resulting cycle of the

---

41 SK 27.v.15–16. For translation, see Jacobsen, *The Harps that Once . . .*, pp.83–4: OB version, 373–4.
42 Rudhardt, MH 35 (1978) 8.

perpetually descending and returning deity.[43] The motif of the substitute descending to replace the ascending deity, the motif found in ID and AV in this context, is not used; rather, here is seen the helper role of the wandering mother goddess of the Damu myths, as well as the descending helpers in ID and AV.

While the hymn to Demeter shows these parallels to the ideas in this group of myths of Inanna and Dumuzi/Damu, there are major features which are quite different, features such as: the conspiracy between Zeus, Earth and Hades to bring about the marriage of Hades and Persephone, the initial cause of the entire action of the hymn; Earth's creation of the narcissus, followed by Hades' terrible emergence as he drives his four-horse chariot out of the gaping earth to snatch the girl up; the deliberate famine-producing strike by Demeter to force the return of her child; the nine-day duration of Demeter's search. The Eleusinian episode, with Keleus' royal family, the construction of the temple, and Demeter's magical activities with Demophoon, also finds no echo in the Mesopotamian material.

Similarly, the Mesopotamian works of literature and their story-lines appear superficially quite different from the Greek hymn and have many features which are not found in this Greek hymn: in edinna ú-saĝ-ĝá there are features such as Damu's meeting with the ghosts on their way to the netherworld, the episode where the mother prepares the reviving beer, and the descent of the sister, which is necessary for the substitutionary system employed in the Mesopotamian cult, but not in the Greek. Other less important features are also not paralleled in the Greek hymn. In addition, there are quite a number of features in ID and AV which are not found in the hymn; for instance, the goddess Inanna/Ishtar deliberately descends to the netherworld to obtain power, employing stratagems to achieve this aim; the Anunnaki, a group of gods, here shown in the netherworld, for which there is no comparable group in Greek religion; the dressing-and-undressing routines of the goddess; the Mesopotamian divine system; and other features.

Nevertheless, the basic and central ideas of the journeys involved in these myths and important structural ideas coincide closely. In summary, these ideas are:

43 The pomegranate seed has been variously interpreted as symbolic of blood and death or of marriage and fertility: Richardson, *Demeter*, p.276; cf. Allen, Halliday and Sikes, *Homeric Hymns*, p.170.

1 the idea in ID and AV of the descent to the netherworld and return of the goddess, with the acquisition of power in the netherworld and above;

2 the recovery operation for the release of the goddess and her return in ID and AV;

3 the instigation of the perpetual seasonal journey as a result of the descent in ID and AV, an idea which also seems to be present at the end of edin-na ú-sağ-ğá;

4 the complex idea of the bereft mother searching for her lost child who has descended to the netherworld, followed by attempts at recovery and the eventual return of the child;

5 the structural features found especially in the release of Inanna/ Ishtar with the descent of the 'helper' from the Assembly of the gods after the 'initial defeat' of the goddess, and similarly the wandering 'helping' role of the mother goddess.

These are all central structural features of the journey stories of these myths, and it is these that are repeated in the Greek hymn, where they form the basis of the story. There are also other features which are parallel: the concern of the cults with seasonal fertility; the concern with the fate of the dead, as well as prosperity in mortal life; and less far-reaching but still important motifs such as the goddess's great oath, the goddess's deliberate lie in the journey, the food which is eaten in the netherworld immediately before the goddess's return, the scream and other ideas.

On balance it does seem as though there must have been influence from Mesopotamia. The parallels between the Greek and Mesopotamian material fulfil the careful and precise above mentioned criteria for the indication of influence in the discussion of parallels: the parallels are numerous, and often complex and specific as well as detailed; and many are central features and have a similar conceptual usage. They are also found in Mesopotamia in a group of related myths, certain myths which belong to the cult of Inanna and Dumuzi, which like the Greek cult has as one of its basic concerns the fertility of agriculture.

While the conclusion that influence is involved in this case would appear to be unavoidable, it also seems reasonable to conclude that it is not a case of textual influence, because the literary works are quite different from the Greek hymn and its versions. It seems most likely that the stories or ideas travelled in an oral form, rather than by direct transmission of literary material. In addition, it is not the complex literary stories that are reproduced in the Greek myth, but instead crucial journey ideas involved in the stories which present basic ideas of the cult. Together with these journey ideas in the Greek hymn are other features which parallel ideas and motifs expressed in the literary works, and these seem to have been transmitted at the same time.

It is also clear that, if influence has occurred, the Greek hymn is not a case of the slavish copying of material and ideas, but rather a creative process of combining presumably native Greek material with the Mesopotamian journey ideas which seem to be used as the basis of the narrative, together with transformation of the Mesopotamian material to agree with the Greek cult and to suit the Greek environment.[44] There is no doubt also that rejection of much associated material must have been involved.

The date of influence is a difficult matter and really can be little more than speculation. It also depends on the periods during which influence from Mesopotamia was possible, when there were demonstrable contacts between the two areas, and when the Mesopotamian material existed and could have been the source of influence, if members of the cult were not the source.

The relevant Mesopotamian material seems to have been extant down to at least NA times, about the time of the Orientalizing period. The relevant works are ID, AV, Damu's myths, edin-na ú-saĝ-ĝá and perhaps also TRS 8 (=TCL 15). The same works are relevant to the Delian section of the *Homeric Hymn to Apollo*, and their existence down to the first millennium BC has been discussed at the end of the preceding chapter. One other work which appears in the discussion of the hymn to Demeter is *Dumuzi's Dream*. In view of the existence of edin-na ú-saĝ-ĝá and other stories of Dumuzi/Damu, it may be assumed that the knowledge of stories such as *Dumuzi's Dream*, as well as the ideas involved in them, existed in the later periods.

Since Greece was in contact with the Hittite and North Syrian areas, and through them with Mesopotamia to varying extents from the late Mycenaean period down, with limited, but still observable, influence in the so-called Dark Age, the stories and the religious ideas contained in them could therefore have influenced Greece from the

---

44 Cf. Christoph Auffarth, *Der drohende Untergang: 'Schöpfung' in Mythos und Ritual im Alten Orient und in Griechenland am Beispiel der Odyssee und des Ezechielbuches*, Walter de Gruyter, Berlin and New York, 1991, pp.127, 131.

late Mycenaean period onwards.[45] The major conclusion indicated by the study of parallels in the literary material regarding the possible time of influence is that the sharpness or clarity of the journey structures and ideas which seem to be repeated in the hymn, combined with the complex motifs, underlying which the same profound ideas are also strongly represented, argues against an earlier, second-millennium date, since it is likely that the oral tradition in Greece would change and blur the material over a long period of time. Consequently a first-millennium date seems more probable. If a first-millennium date is correct, it must have been quite early. Hesiod's *Theogony* preserves the earliest reference to what seems to be the story of the Greek hymn (lines 912–14). The date of the Homeric Hymn is disputed, although it is placed in either the seventh or the sixth century BC,[46] but the *Theogony* appears to have

45 The periods and extent of contact between Greece and the Near East, as well as the main places involved, are discussed in detail in the introductory chapter of this book; Günter Kopcke, *Handel*, Archaeologia Homerica, Kapitel M, Vandenhoeck & Ruprecht, Göttingen, 1990, pp. 90–100; M.L. West, ed., *Hesiod Theogony*, Clarendon Press, Oxford, 1966, p.28; P.J. Riis, *Sukas I*, Copenhagen, 1970, pp.127, 161–2; Dolores Hegyi, 'Die Griechen und der Alte Orient in 9. bis 6. Jahrhundert v. Chr.', in Hans-Jörg Nissen und Johannes Renger, eds, *Mesopotamien und seine Nachbarn. Politische und Kulturelle Wechselbeziehungen im Alten Vorderasien vom 4. bis 1. Jahrtausend v. Chr.*, 25e Rencontre Assyriologique Internationale (1978 Berlin), Berliner Beiträge zum Vorderen Orient 1, Dietrich Reimer Verlag, Berlin, 1982, pp.531–8; Peter Walcot, *Hesiod and the Near East*, University of Wales Press, Cardiff, 1966, pp.53–4; William Culican, *The First Merchant Venturers*, Thames & Hudson, London, 1966, pp.90–4; John Boardman, *The Greeks Overseas*, Penguin Books, Harmondsworth, 1964, pp.61–9; E. Gjerstad, 'The Stratification at Al-Mina (Syria) and its Chronological Evidence', *Acta Archaeologica* 45 (1974) 107–23; J.M. Cook, *The Greeks in Ionia and the East*, Thames & Hudson, London, 1965, pp.64–5; Walter Burkert, 'Oriental and Greek Mythology: The Meeting of Parallels', in Jan Bremmer, ed., *Interpretations of Greek Mythology*, Croom Helm, London, 1987, p.13; Jeffrey H. Hurwit, *The Art and Culture of Early Greece, 1100–480 BC*, Cornell University Press, Ithaca and London, 1985, pp.125ff.; also Burkert, *Greek Religion*, pp.125ff.; Peter Blome, 'Die dunklen Jahrhunderte – aufgehellt', in Joachim Latacz, ed., *Zweihundert Jahre Homer-Forschung. Rückblick und Ausblick*, B.G. Teubner, Stuttgart and Leipzig, 1991, pp.45–7, 58–60.

46 Richardson, *Demeter*, pp.5ff., 11ff.; also comments by James, JHS 96 (1976) 165–8; Richard Janko, *Homer, Hesiod and the Hymns*, Cambridge University Press, 1982, p.183; Burkert, *Gnomon* 49 (1977) 442–3.

been written as early as the late eighth century BC.[47] Therefore, if this hymn is a case of influence from Mesopotamia, it must have been a result of transmission quite early in this period of renewed intensive contact with the Near East, or late in the period of lesser activity just preceding it.

Various features in the hymn lack logical links and have no clear motivation for the events which occur. In view of the strong probability of influence, a comparison with this Mesopotamian material of the Inanna and Dumuzi cult can profitably be used to suggest solutions to some of the problems in the hymn. Similarly, a comparison with the Mesopotamian material also helps to clarify many points concerning the interpretation of the hymn in the light of the same ideas and their similar expression and usage in what appears to be the original context.

The conspiracy between Zeus, Earth and Hades to bring about the abduction of Persephone (lines 4ff.) is one feature which presents difficulties for comprehension because of the poet's reluctance to provide the background to the activities of the gods involved. The reason for the omissions can be better understood in the light of Mesopotamian influence. The major problem for the reader of the hymn is that the motivation of all involved to pursue their secret plan is lacking in the hymn. Why Zeus takes this course of action is unexplained. It may be said, if one admits only the introduction as evidence, that Zeus merely gives Hades permission to wed Persephone, but the words of Helios later (lines 77–80) suggest that Zeus acquiesced in the actual abduction. The variant version in which Zeus intervenes with his thunderbolts to drive back Athena and other goddesses who try to prevent Hades from carrying the girl off agrees with this.[48] The understanding seems to be that Zeus is culpable. Of course, Zeus surely has the prerogative as the father and as supreme god to give away the hand of his daughter. However, if the reason for the subterfuge is that Demeter is against the marriage, the plan would only exacerbate the problem. But what is indicated is that Demeter was not asked for her advice or permission. No reason is given for the omission; nor is there any apparent reason for her hostility in the

---

47 West, op. cit., pp.45–6.
48 Richardson, *Demeter*, pp.79–80. See also Fritz Graf, *Eleusis und die orphische Dichtung Athens in vorhellenistischer Zeit*, Walter de Gruyter, Berlin, 1974, pp.151–8.

event of a marriage.[49] Earth's motivation for her part in the plan is also lacking. Similarly, the reason for the creation of the narcissus, as well as its exact role in the situation and its connection with Hades' emergence, is not made clear. Other versions of the story add nothing to explain this situation.

This conspiracy is, of course, the initiating factor of all the following events in the hymn, and as such it fulfils its purpose admirably. Nevertheless, as it is presented in the hymn it leaves unexplained more questions than it answers. It may be, however, that this presentation in the hymn is only a summary of a complex myth, which was simply used here for the purpose of starting the narrative. Indeed, this part of the Greek hymn has no parallel with the Mesopotamian material, which may indicate that it was a pre-existing Greek myth used to introduce the following story which is based on the Mesopotamian journey ideas. If this precipitating conspiracy is a summary of a myth about how Persephone became the goddess of the netherworld, it does in fact indicate that the actual journey myths of Demeter and Persephone were considered to be the really important feature of the hymn, with the conspiracy serving only to initiate the ensuing action of the hymn. Such a conclusion about the conspiracy story and Hades' spectacular abduction of the girl and its role in the hymn does not necessarily mean that Persephone was not already a descending and returning goddess. In fact, if she already had this function, this would have encouraged the adoption of the Mesopotamian myth.

A feature which the Mesopotamian material helps to explain is the apparent delay in the plot between Demeter's discovery of her daughter's whereabouts and her action to recover her (lines 74ff., 305ff.).[50] The scene in which Helios reveals the facts of the case to Demeter is followed by the Eleusinian section. In the hymn the delay between the discovery of the abduction and Demeter's implementation of the drought to force the return of the child is not explained. One interpretation is that this Eleusinian section may be an implant in the basic story of the loss of the child and the mother's search for

---

49 Bruce Lincoln, 'The Rape of Persephone: A Greek Scenario of Women's Initiation', HThR 72 (1979) 226–7, for the male role in granting permission to marry.

50 Richardson, *Demeter*, p.260. Contrast Clay's opinion: *The Politics of Olympus*, pp.225ff.

and recovery of her.[51] This explanation is supported by the Mesopotamian material, in which there is nothing comparable to the Eleusinian section and in which the mother begins her activities to recover the child immediately on learning the truth of the matter.[52] The actual means used to bring about the return of the child are different in edinna ú-saǧ-ǧá, but the return to ensure the survival of the inhabitants of the land is the same in this Mesopotamian myth and in AV. Although there is no 'strike' in the Damu myths, the threat of famine if the child does not return is also a strong theme.

The Eleusinian section has no parallels in motifs or ideas with the Mesopotamian material, beyond the possibility that the figure of the male child of the cult may be the reason for the inclusion of Demophoon. The idea connected with the male child in the cult – the triad of the mother, sister and male child, seen later on in the hymn (lines 488–9), which parallels the concept of the triad in the Damu myth and elsewhere in the Mesopotamian cult of the returning child – may have some relation to Demophoon, but if it has, it is certainly not presented in the Eleusinian section. This episode of the hymn is obviously the incorporation of the story of the crone or old witch as it appears with Demeter but the question raised is where the material in this section could have come from, since the events do not parallel those found in the myths either of Inanna and Dumuzi/Damu or of any other deity. There is the story of the Egyptian goddess Isis' search for the dead Osiris in Byblos, which is presented in Plutarch's work *On Isis and Osiris* (Περὶ Ἴσιδος καὶ Ὀσίριδος), and some scholars have looked to this as a source for the Eleusinian events in view of the many strong parallels with the hymn. However, it is clear rather that the opposite is the case: the parallels in the story of Isis and Osiris, which is presented in much later Greek sources, are a result of the influence of the *Homeric Hymn to Demeter* on this Egyptian/Phoenician story. The earliest attestation to the material which

---

51 Lincoln, HThR 72 (1979), 231; Clay, *The Politics of Olympus*, p.223, although Clay disagrees on p.226; cf. Nancy Felson Rubin and Harriet M. Deal, 'Some Functions of the Demophoon Episode in the Homeric Hymn to Demeter', QUCC 34 (1980) 7–8. On Demophoon's thematic role in the hymn, and connection with Persephone, Robert Parker, 'The *Hymn to Demeter* and the *Homeric Hymns*', G & R 38 (1991) 11.

52 Clay, *The Politics of Olympus*, pp.225–6, holds the view that the events in the Demophoon section are directed to the recovery of the child. If this is so, it may be seen as an attempt to aid the unity of the poem. The section still, however, appears to be an implant in the basic story-line.

parallels the hymn is not earlier than Plutarch in the second century AD. Although Plutarch is particularly concerned in his work to equate Isis and Demeter, his story of Isis' search for Osiris in Byblos is probably not his own invention, since he is not the most original of writers, but goes back to one of his Greek Hellenistic sources, from which he received much of his material on the cult and myth of Isis.[53]

In the Byblian episode of the Egyptian myth, the inspiration from the Homeric hymn of the search of Demeter and her activities in Eleusis is clear to see. The Egyptian myth is told in Plutarch 356A–357B. After the death of Osiris as a result of a trick by Typhon (Seth) and his fellow conspirators, the goddess Isis sets out in search of her dead husband. She hears that the coffin of Osiris has been cast up by the sea at Byblos, where there seems to have been a cult of Isis as early as the seventh or sixth century BC, although the evidence for the cult of Osiris is earlier. The coffin comes to rest near a tree, which quickly grows around it and hides it in its trunk. Admiring the tree, the king of Byblos cuts it down and uses it for a pillar in his palace. Isis hears of this, and arriving in Byblos she sits down near a fountain, dejected and tearful, just as Demeter on her arrival at Eleusis sits at the Maiden's Well, sorrowing for her child (lines 98–9). The maids of the queen of Byblos talk to her, with the result that the queen sends for her to be the nurse of her young son. This, of course, parallels Demeter's meeting with the young maidens of the house of King Keleus, who take Demeter to their mother, the queen, to be the nurse of her young son, Demophoon (lines 105–10, 141–2, 164–5). The motif of the goddess's fragrance is also present: Demeter breathes her fragrant breath on Demophoon (line 238), while Isis breathes fragrantly on the young maids of the queen. Like Demeter (line 236), Isis does not give her breast to the child, and both use fire on the child (line 239). The fire is found in a similar situation in another Greek myth with Thetis, who tries to make Achilles immortal (Apoll. Rhod. 4.865–79). When the queen sees Isis burning the child, she shrieks and thereby deprives him of immortality, a sequence of events for which the hymn is clearly the prototype (lines 242–62). As with Demeter's subsequent self-revelation (lines 275–6), Isis reveals herself. She then

53 J. Gwyn Griffiths, *Plutarch's De Iside et Osiride*, University of Wales Press, Cardiff, 1970, pp.54, 320–1 and *passim*; Jean Hani, *La religion égyptienne dans la pensée de Plutarque*, Société d'édition «Les belles lettres», Paris, 1976, pp.74–5.

demands the coffin, and when she falls on it in her grief her loud wail results in the death of the queen's young son, just as the child Demophoon dies in the account preserved in Apollodorus (I.31) as the result of his mother's cry of grief. The elder son also dies later as a result of Isis' anger. The Egyptian myth continues after this episode, and there are no further parallels with the hymn.

The influence of the hymn in this episode is clear, although some slight alterations have been made. The story of the hymn may have been brought into association with the Osirian myth because of the general parallel of Osiris' death and revival with the descent and return of Persephone, although the parallels are not close. The use of the hymn in the myth of Isis and Osiris may also be a result of the fact that Demeter was identified by the Greeks at some time with Isis, perhaps on the general basis that each had the functions of earth and mother goddess. The earliest identification with Isis seems to be that by Herodotus (2.144, 156) in his book on Egyptian religion, in which he identifies many Greek gods with Egyptian deities, although for reasons which he does not make very clear.[54] Similarly, the cult of Demeter later had a strong presence in Egypt after Alexander's conquest, and the cult of Osiris and Isis received much influence from that of Demeter, especially in the shaping of the Egyptian cult's rites, which became full mysteries in the Greek sense.[55] This is, however, all much later than the Homeric hymn and is therefore not of great concern to this discussion of the implications of the possible influence of the Mesopotamian myths on the Greek hymn.

The Mesopotamian material also helps to clarify the question of motivation for the instigation of the perpetual cycle in the hymn. The reason for the instigation of Persephone's perpetual annual descent and return and for the seasonal nature of the length of stay in the netherworld is not really explained and appears to be arbitrary, at least on the information supplied in the hymn. However, in ID the reason for the annual descent and return of Dumuzi and Geshtinanna is made clear: Inanna must supply a substitute, and the cycle, including the length of stay in the netherworld, comes about as a result of Geshtinanna's offer to share with her brother the period of what is considered to be incarceration. In the hymn the events appear

---

54 For instance, Herodotus 2.43, 46, 48, 50, 60, 62–3. He also states that most of the Greek gods came from Egypt (2.5): J.G. Griffiths, *Plutarch's De Iside*, p.309.

55 ibid., pp.67–8, 322; Hani, *La religion égyptienne*, pp.74–5.

merely to be following the arrangements established in the Mesopotamian cultic stories: the instigation of the child's descent-and-
return cycle with its seasonal implications, although the seasonal stay
has been altered to suit the three-part year.

The barrier between the upperworld and the netherworld, the
presence of which is indicated by the fact that Demeter wanders
about on earth and must force Zeus to order Hades to release the girl
rather than herself descending to confront Hades, seems to be a
Mesopotamian idea taken over here rather than a native Greek
concept, as unimpeded descents by various other Greek divine or
semi-divine figures indicate.[56] In the Mesopotamian stories the
journey is irreversible without a substitute (ID 286–9):

> The Anunnaki seized her (saying),
> 'Who has ever risen from the Netherworld? Who has
> ever risen from the Netherworld alive?
> If Inanna wants to rise from the netherworld
> Let her furnish a substitute for herself.'

> ^{d}a-nun-na-ke$_4$-e-ne ba-ab-ha-za-aš
> a-ba-àm lú kur-ta e$_{11}$-dè kur-ta silim-ma-ni e$_{11}$-dè
> u$_4$-da ^{d}inanna kur-ta ba-e$_{11}$-dè
> sag-dili sag-gá-na ha-ba-ab-sum-mu

In other Greek myths Hades may be penetrated with no penalty. For
instance, Dionysos descends to Hades to fetch his mother; Orpheus
descends to collect his wife; and Heracles descends to Hades to seize
Kerberos and other booty. All return.[57] Similarly, in Hesiod's
Theogony the gods who break the great oath descend to Tartarus and
return after nine years (lines 793–804). In Mesopotamia, Inanna's
return from the netherworld is a great feat because of the nature of
Ereshkigal's realm as the Land of No Return. With the exception of
messengers and the possible exception of the sun god, there is no
descent and return. With regard to messengers, it is interesting that in

---

56 On this barrier, see Rudhardt, MH 35 (1978) 8–9; Clay, *The Politics of
Olympus*, p.212.
57 Nothing in the hymn suggests that the netherworld was inaccessible
before the time of these events of the hymn. The concept of the barrier
and the irreversible nature of the journey for the gods is limited to this
hymn. Of course, mortals do not in general return, except in particular
cases and in reincarnation: see above.

the hymn the gods' messenger, Hermes, is able to descend and return with impunity, just like the Mesopotamian messengers.[58]

One feature which is not explained in the hymn is Demeter's rejection of Helios' advice. The sun god argues that Hades, as lord over one-third of the cosmos, is a worthy husband (lines 83–7). Demeter clearly does not accept this, but no reason for her reaction is given in the text. It is clear, however, in view of the Mesopotamian tales, that the story must nevertheless continue until the eventual recovery of the child.

Another feature, and one which is much discussed, is the nature of Persephone in the hymn as a young girl rather than as the awful netherworld queen portrayed by Homer in the *Iliad* and *Odyssey*.[59] This portrayal of her youthful, innocent nature is continued after her return to her mother (lines 405ff.), even when she is clearly now the wife of Hades (lines 342–3). This treatment is easily explicable in terms of Mesopotamian origins of the basis of the story. Persephone's nature in the hymn accords naturally with her role as the child of the searching mother goddess as portrayed in the Mesopotamian myth edin-na ú-saĝ-ĝá. The lack of any description of her as the awful netherworld queen is probably due to the fact that the netherworld queen Ereshkigal is quite a different figure from Geshtinanna or Gunura in Mesopotamia and is presented as the dread netherworld queen in a different work. She is seen, for instance, in *Nergal and Ereshkigal*,[60] and even though she appears in ID and AV, she appears there as the opponent of the descending and rising goddess, and her role and nature are incompatible with those of the descending goddess Inanna/Ishtar and the child of the mother goddess, Geshtinanna or Gunura.

Another question which may be discussed in the light of the underlying Mesopotamian ideas has been raised recently in a thesis which places the hymn and the other major Homeric hymns in the framework of a scheme that includes the Homeric epics and Hesiod's *Theogony*. The thesis may be summarized as saying that the idea at the core of the Homeric hymns is, like that of the Homeric epics and

58 Hutter, *Altorientalische Vorstellungen*, pp.79–81; Cf. Clay, who also notices the messenger's privilege in the hymn: *The Politics of Olympus*, p.212.
59 See Richardson for the aspects of Persephone's dread power which lie behind Hades' statement of her power on earth and in the lower spheres of the cosmos in lines 360–8: *Demeter*, pp.270ff.
60 Source: Hutter, *Altorientalische Vorstellungen*.

the *Theogony*, the presentation of a 'panhellenic' religion with the divine world ordered by and under the domination of Olympian Zeus, the supreme god, and that the purpose is to replace an earlier, fragmented and perhaps locally based religious system.[61]

While this thesis may be arguable in other material, the *Homeric Hymn to Demeter* does not support it. There is no evidence of any previous religious system's concepts or structure identifiable to indicate a change from an earlier religion. The panhellenic religion, as it is called, is already in existence in the hymn; that is, it is assumed, and Zeus' dominance and power in dispensation are not a crucial feature of the hymn.[62] In fact, it may be said that the opposite scenario occurs, with the discomfiture of Zeus. The purpose of the myth is rather to demonstrate the power and authority of Demeter and the establishment of Persephone's position. Instead of being dominant and dispensing his order in unquestioned authority, Zeus is culpable and is powerless against Demeter, to whose wishes he is eventually forced to bow (lines 334ff.). The actual situation at the end of the hymn, with the return of Persephone and the institution of the perpetual cycle, is a result of Demeter's actions,[63] rather than any plan of Zeus that is apparent in the text.[64]

One interpretation of the hymn with which the indication of

---

61 Clay, *The Politics of Olympus*, pp.8–15, 256–65, 268.

62 Cf. ibid., p.207. However, there is no definite textual evidence, either in the hymn or in works composed before it, to indicate any change of the nature required. Of course, Herodotus (2.53) states, perhaps rather naively, that Homer and Hesiod were responsible for forming the divine world as seen in their works, in which they established the characters and functions of the gods, religious mythological conceptions believed generally by Greeks following them in time, but he does not say that they created a new 'panhellenic' religion. The MB cosmological work *Enuma Elish* indicates what is necessary regarding the methodology to verify a thesis such as the one proposed: it is possible to see that the Meso-potamian work is presenting or advancing a major religious change, because (1) previous literary works exist showing the previous system (NS and OB); (2) the change is therefore clear in the work; and (3) the supremacy of the major god in the new system and the establishment of his order are the central theme. However, even in this work it is not possible to determine whether it instituted the change or was merely giving authority to a long-established religion, because there is a 600-year gap at least since the earlier works.

63 Cf. Demeter's dispensation of Persephone's fate (lines 393ff.), which is agreed to by Zeus in lines 463–6: νεῦσε δέ σοι . . . , (line 463).

64 Contrast Clay, *The Politics of Olympus*, pp.8–15, 256–65, 268.

influence and the nature of the originating stories do not agree is the concept of the hymn as the initiation of a girl into female adulthood, specifically initiation by rape, in the sense of the violent sexual act. This interpretation is not supported in the hymn or by the Mesopotamian stories, and it misses the point of what is essentially a Greek religious work which has the purpose of celebrating the deities of Eleusis and the Eleusinian Mystery cult in Attica.[65] It is a work which discusses questions of the divine world and the place of the goddesses in this world, not questions of the human social world, or what are imagined to be the conditions of the human social world at the time of the composition of the myth. In addition, in the reunion scene Persephone is presented as the same figure as before the abduction. She is clearly the daughter of the mother goddess Demeter, and still a young girl, little more than a child. She shows no sign of now having become an 'experienced', 'initiated' woman.[66] In fact, quite the reverse is seen in her tripping sentences as she innocently tells her mother the tale of her abduction (lines 405–33). Indeed, the author has taken pains to portray her as still a young girl, overjoyed at being with her mother once again and at pains to tell her that it was not her fault and that she was doing nothing wrong when she was abducted. At the same time it is clear that no violent sexual act is involved. For one thing, in these lines Persephone makes no allusion to such, nor is her attitude to Hades hostile; second, the author makes no allusion to any such thing. In fact, quite the contrary is the case in the scene that takes place in Hades when the messenger Hermes enters the presence of Hades and his wife sitting together in bed (lines 342–4). The scene may be best described as relaxed:

> And he found that lord within his house,
> sitting in bed with his revered wife,
> much reluctant because of longing for her mother.

---

65 For an example, see Lincoln, HThR 72 (1979), 223–35, especially 228–9, 233. For the mistaken view of rape in the sense of the violent sexual act, instead of the sense of 'abduction' which is the meaning of the word 'rape' (from Latin *rapere*) in the title often given to the hymn, 'The Rape of Persephone', see ibid., pp.228–9, 233; Marylin Arthur, 'Politics and Pomegranates: An Interpretation of the Homeric Hymn to Demeter', *Arethusa* 10.1 (1977) 7–47; and, rather ambiguously, C. Kerényi, *Eleusis*, Routledge & Kegan Paul, London, 1967 (originally published in 1960), pp.34–5.

66 Contrast Lincoln, HThR 72 (1979) 233.

τέτμε δὲ τόν γε ἄνακτα δόμων ἔντοσθεν ἐόντα,
ἥμενον ἐν λεχέεσσι σὺν αἰδοίῃ παρακοίτι,
πόλλ' ἀεκαζομένῃ μητρὸς πόθῳ·

The two sitting in bed seems at first to indicate that they are now god and wife, but this may not necessarily be the case, since one possible interpretation of the scene, in view of the last line of the quotation, is that the marriage has not been consummated: to Hades' chagrin, the 'very unwilling' (πόλλ' ἀεκαζομένῃ) young girl is still obstinately digging her heels in through yearning for her mother, and even possibly freely applying her own pressure in order to be released so that she may see her mother again. This implies Hades' forbearance. However, if the other interpretation is correct, that the tableau of the two sitting in bed is meant to indicate that they are now completely married, there is in this scene still no indication of the sadistic tyrant and rapist that one would expect in the light of some studies. Indeed, the evidence indicates quite the opposite of violence. While Hades is indeed masterful, the relaxed and even compassionate nature of his demeanour is emphasized especially by lines 357–69. In addition, Persephone is certainly no maltreated or hostile victim here. The picture presented is rather that of a homesick girl, reluctant certainly but, as stated in the text, for the simple reason that she longs to see her mother, from whom she has been separated without warning (line 344). This accords with the thematic basis of Persephone's role in the hymn and is also in concert with the Mesopotamian origins of this cultic story of the lost child of the mother goddess in the netherworld, which appears to be the primary foundation stone of the whole work and is borne out in every passage which has to do with Persephone.

The pomegranate seed, a motif which often receives a stressed position in interpretations, is necessary in this religious story for the instigation of the perpetual descending and returning fertility cycle. Persephone must return to the netherworld for part of each year because she has eaten netherworld food, and this is made clear in the text (lines 393–403). However, there seems to be an additional significance to this motif, beyond that of the compulsory return, and it is a feature which is subtly expressed by the type of food chosen for Persephone. The food which Hades gives to Persephone is not just any netherworld food, but the pomegranate seed, and it seems to have a connotation complementary to the story of which it is a part – the journey to the netherworld and return of the young girl Persephone whom Hades wished to make his wife. Since she is the revered goddess of the Mysteries, it seems logical that this aspect of the story was intended as a love-story. As Faraone's study indicates, the pomegranate seed is a love-charm:[67] its purpose is to induce the loved one to reciprocate. As the text says, Persephone is 'very reluctant', and is clearly not reciprocating. Hades gives her the seed as a charm to induce her to love him, to reciprocate his love and desire for her. This charm, which is a symbol of love, much more than just an erotic symbol, is in keeping with the scene in Hades and the girl-like innocence that Persephone exhibits throughout the hymn, especially in the following scene of her reunion with her mother (lines 385–433). With this significance, the motif is highly suitable to the context of the story of the young child of the mother goddess, the theme which motivates the hymn. The motif is suitable in another way too, as love-charms of this type closely parallel similar charms seen in the NA texts.[68]

This little red pomegranate seed has in the past been endowed with a great range of symbolic meaning by interpreters,[69] and especially recently with purely sexual connotations, often of great complexity and inordinate subtlety. However, these connotations are not really borne out by the rest of the literary work or by the nature of the Mesopotamian religious material. It is important, rather, to remember its major and obvious significance for the instigation of the cycle, and to keep the interpretation of the motif within the bounds of Persephone's demonstrable role in this profoundly religious work.

67 C.A. Faraone, 'Aphrodite's ΚΕΣΤΟΣ and Apples for Atalanta: Aphrodisiacs in Early Greek Myth and Ritual', *Phoenix* 44 (1990) 219ff.
68 ibid., 239ff.
69 Richardson, *Demeter*, p.276; Clay, *The Politics of Olympus*, p.253; Lincoln, HThR 72 (1979) 234; Arthur, *Arethusa* 10.1 (1977) 29.

7

MYTHS OF APHRODITE AND HER ORIGINS

Delightful, charming and imaginative are probably the words which best describe a large proportion of Aphrodite's myths. One of this calibre is the myth of her *affaire* with the warrior god Ares, where she was trapped *in flagrante* under a golden net by her artful husband, Hephaistos, to the merriment of the gods. Another is the story of her wounding at the hands of the hero Diomedes, who scornfully told her to keep out of battle and stay with things that she knew about. The cameo situation of her assistance to Hera, to help the goddess to prepare herself enticingly for her husband Zeus's bed, also comes to mind, while the birth myth of the powerful love goddess who arrives in Olympos to entice the gods presents many disturbing ideas about the goddess and about Greek mythology in general. Especially close to the ethos of this goddess, however, is the story of her *affaire* with the mortal Trojan herdsman Anchises, which came about as the revenge of Zeus in response to her favourite game of causing him and other gods to fall in love with mortals. He had turned the tables on her: never more would she be able to gloat over the gods' discomfiture without fear of their scorn in return.[1]

This myth, in particular, and the myth of her birth are of especial concern to the ideas pursued here. They both involve journeys and at the same time have features which are parallel to those in various of the Mesopotamian myths discussed above. The correspondences in these two myths do not, however, occur with the same numerical intensity as they do in the hymns to Apollo and to Demeter. Of course, in the case of the birth myth this is due primarily to brevity.

---

1 Sources for these stories: Homer's *Odyssey*, 8.266–369, and *Iliad*, 5.311–51, 14.198ff.; Hesiod's *Theogony*, 188–206; *Homeric Hymn VI*; and *Homeric Hymn to Aphrodite*.

However, there are quite a number of parallels, especially in the myth of the goddess's *affaire* with Anchises, and these are of a specific nature. In addition, the journeys of Aphrodite result in the increase and demonstration of power in the myths. Since Aphrodite is the goddess of sexual love, the way in which she demonstrates her power is chiefly in the ability to cause desire in gods and mankind. Nevertheless, despite the peculiarity of this goddess, there still exists the connection between the journey and the idea of increasing and demonstrating the deity's power, while one myth has the added purpose of establishing the deity's authority in the divine and human spheres.

Although Aphrodite is presented entirely as a Greek goddess from the earliest literature down, she is generally considered to be of Near Eastern extraction, and there are many indications to support the idea. However, this view has been disputed by a number of studies, including several in recent years, particularly by those who look for Indo-European origins to Greek mythology. The Near Eastern derivation of the goddess does not necessarily help to support the case for the parallels in the literary works which are being discussed, since it is the myths that are of concern here and the influence of mythological material from the Near East does not necessitate the deity's similar origins; but it does help to make it much more logical that the parallels are present in her mythology. If that is her origin, it would be natural then that they should be found attached to this particular goddess. Consequently, the various ideas about Aphrodite's origins need to be considered, since they have a bearing on the discussion of the ideas at issue in this study.

Aphrodite is held by most people to derive from the Near East. Ancient sources, especially Herodotus and later Pausanias, and much independent modern research agree on the Near Eastern origin of certain aspects of Aphrodite.[2]

---

2 G.S. Kirk, *The Nature of Greek Myths*, Penguin Books, Harmondsworth, England, 1974, p.258; Walter Burkert, *Greek Religion*, Harvard University Press, Cambridge (Mass.), and London, 1985, pp.152ff. and *The Orientalizing Revolution: Near Eastern Influence on Greek Culture in the Early Archaic Age*, Harvard University Press, Cambridge (Mass.), and London, 1992, pp.97–9 (this book is the translation and up-date of *Die orientalisierende Epoche in der griechischen Religion und Literatur*, Carl Winter Universitätsverlag, Heidelberg, 1984); Lewis Farnell, *The Cults of the Greek States*, vol. II, Clarendon Press, Oxford, 1896, pp.618ff.; Hans

The clearest indication of Near Eastern derivation in ancient sources can be seen in Pausanias, when he speaks specifically of Aphrodite Ourania (1.14.7): 'The Assyrians were the first among mankind to worship Ourania, and after the Assyrians the Paphians in Cyprus and the Phoenicians in Askalon.' Similarly, at a much earlier date, Herodotus mentions the most ancient temple of Aphrodite Ourania among the Syrians (i.e. Phoenicians) in Askalon and also the temple in Cyprus which was established by the Phoenicians from the one in Syria (i.e. Askalon). He also points out that the Persians worshipped Ourania, having learnt to do so from the Assyrians and the Arabs. He adds that the Assyrians name Aphrodite Mylitta (1.105, 1.131).

Herodotus' assertion that the temple of Aphrodite in Paphos was established by Phoenicians from Askalon seems to contrast with modern archaeological evidence which indicates that the Paphian temple was established at the end of the Mycenaean times in the Mycenaean settlement. Phoenician presence becomes evident in archaeological remains only at the beginning of the first millennium BC. However, the adoption of a foreign deity does not automatically require the settlement of foreigners in the locality, so this does not hinder the adoption of the goddess by the Mycenaeans in Paphos earlier than the Phoenician's actual *en masse* settlement at the beginning of the first millennium. The case for adoption without settlement is supported by evidence in historical times. The adoption of Cybele in the Dionysiac cult in Athens and Thebes was not accompanied by the wholesale settlement of Phrygians in these cities in historical times. Such an event is not seen in the archaeological record or reported in textual evidence. Regarding Herodotus on the founding of the temple in Paphos from the one in Askalon, this statement is probably due to the situation on the island in historical times after the Phoenician settlement, but it does not mean that the idea of influence from Askalon, held presumably by other Greeks besides Herodotus, is incorrect.

One must, of course, always view with caution the Greeks' attempts at equating Greek and foreign gods, and especially Herodotus' attempts, since he has a habit of equating gods of the different

Herter, 'Die Ursprünge des Aphroditecultes', in *Éléments orientaux dans la religion grecque ancienne*, Travaux du Centre d'Études Supérieures spécialisé d'histoire des religions de Strasbourg, Colloque de Strasbourg, 22–24 mai 1958, Presses Universitaires de la France, Paris, 1960, pp.61–76.

areas with Greek gods for very dubious reasons, or of simply calling them by the same names.[3] However, Pausanias is much more reliable, since he is not equating Aphrodite with a foreign goddess but rather is speaking of the origin of a specific aspect of the goddess. This is quite different and much more plausible.

Though only this one designation of Aphrodite, specifically Aphrodite Ourania, is directly connected with the Near East by these historical sources, the Near Eastern aspect of Aphrodite seems to be central to the goddess in the early Greek sources, since her epithet Kypris is the most commonly given to her in the *Iliad*, and her connection with Cyprus is also especially stressed in *Homeric Hymns V* and *VI*.

The ancient sources agree with the general modern opinion that Aphrodite owes much to her Near Eastern forerunners, specifically Ishtar of the Babylonians and Assyrians, by way of her derivative Astarte/Ashtoroth in the Phoenician region.[4] Important correspondences found in character, cult and iconography which are pointed out by one respected modern scholar are:[5]

1 The most important characteristic of Aphrodite as the goddess of love, especially of sexual desire and its physical expression, is exactly parallel with the character of Ishtar/Astarte as goddess of love.
2 More strikingly, like Ishtar and Astarte, Aphrodite is androgynous.[6]
3 Aphrodite is called Ourania, as Astarte is the Queen of Heaven, and as Ishtar is in Mesopotamia.[7]

---

3 For instance, in Book 2.43, 46, 48, 50, 60, 62, 63; Dionysos is Osiris, Pan is Mendes, etc. In fact, according to his view in this book, most of the Greek gods came from Egypt: Poseidon, the Dioskoroi, Hera, Themis, the Charites, etc.: see 2.50.
4 Cf. Burkert, *Greek Religion*, pp.152ff., and *The Orientalizing Revolution*, p.98; Kirk, *The Nature of Greek Myths*, p.258; Farnell, *The Cults of the Greek States*, II, 618ff.
5 Cf. Burkert, *Greek Religion*, pp.152ff.
6 See, for instance, Hans Herter, *Die Ursprünge*, pp.71–6 for a discussion of the androgynous characteristic and the nature of Aphrodite's androgynous aspect. See also Brigitte Groneberg, 'Die sumerisch–akkadische Inanna/Ištar: Hermaphroditos?', WO 17 (1986) 25–46.
7 Inanna/Ishtar is the queen of heaven and earth, but she is also specifically the 'Queen of Heaven': cf. the poem quoted by S.N. Kramer, *From the Poetry of Sumer*, University of California Press, Berkeley, 1979, p.96: 'Enlil gave me heaven, he gave me earth/ I, the Queen of Heaven am I!' See also the opening lines of the hymn nin-me-šár-ra, especially line 12: ibid., p.87.

4 Sacrifices of doves and incense are made to Aphrodite alone in Greece, and Astarte receives the same.
5 Aphrodite may be armed and bestow victory, while Ishtar is the Mesopotamian warrior goddess.
6 Prostitution seems to be found in connection with Aphrodite, particularly at Corinth (Strabo 378),[8] and this is, of course, a notorious feature of the goddess in Phoenicia and in Mesopotamia.

Taken altogether, the parallel is complex and has many specific features. It seems to confirm the ancient authors' indications of the Near Eastern origins of this goddess. Of course, peripheral aspects and connections may have been added from elsewhere, such as the 'Mistress of Animals' idea and connections with Ida, which may have come from Cybele in Phrygia.[9] Similarly, certain features may have been invented in Greece. This whole process may be considered to be natural in the development of a living religious figure.

However, not all agree on Aphrodite's Near Eastern origins. The other main viewpoint is that of the Indo-European origin of the goddess. Boedeker is the most important of the more recent of those who, against the general trend, have attempted a longer study with the purpose of supporting the idea of Indo-European origins of Aphrodite. After much enthusiastic argument, she feels confident enough to ascribe an Indo-European origin to the goddess, even though she concedes early in the book that in 'certain aspects of cult and iconography, the similarities between Aphrodite and the Great Goddesses, especially Astarte, are not to be disputed'.[10]

In her view, however, these have been overestimated and misinterpreted, although in what aspects and in what ways is not made clear. Nevertheless, evidence of Aphrodite's Indo-European origins is accordingly sought primarily in linguistic material, since there is no archaeological material in Greece to support the view.

There are several main points to the argument, and if these were well supported they would suggest at least a partial Indo-European origin for Aphrodite. They would never be able to demonstrate a completely Indo-European origin, because Aphrodite does have aspects which only Semitic derivation can properly explain. Unfortunately, the

8 Cf. also Pindar frag. 87, and Athenae. 573 C. Temple prostitution on Cyprus, Herodotus 1.199.
9 Cf. *Homeric Hymn V*, 69–74.
10 Deborah Boedeker, *Aphrodite's Entry into Greek Epic*, E.J. Brill, Leiden, p.6.

arguments advanced are too often highly speculative, appear to be based on tenuous connections, and fail to take into account largely contradictory indications. Nevertheless, the main problem in the book is that the postulation of an Indo-European prototype dawn goddess creates a circular argument: the existence of a prototype with which Aphrodite allegedly has similarities, derived largely from attributes and linguistic features, is supposed to prove that Aphrodite is Indo-European; yet proof that Aphrodite and Eos, the Greek goddess of the dawn, are Indo-European dawn goddesses would be necessary, surely, to postulate an Indo-European prototype. One major difficulty in the proposition is that in historical times, that is, in the extant sources, the attributes of Aphrodite are shown to be almost entirely different from those of either Eos or Ushas, the Vedic goddess who is compared to Eos and Aphrodite.[11] An attempt is made to overcome this by 'reconstruction' of supposedly original meanings of words and epithets, and of associations between them. The dependence on hypothetical origins is a major problem in the study.

More recently, Paul Friedrich carried out a synthetic work on Aphrodite, *The Meaning of Aphrodite*, which includes a section on origins of the goddess.[12] His thesis in this book is that Aphrodite is a composite figure who is indebted to a number of different areas of religious culture for her origins. He posits the various areas – prehistoric Old European, Sumerian and Semitic, proto-Indo-European and pre-Greek, Minoan and Mycenaean, as well as Egyptian – as places of origin for his composite Aphrodite. However, the arguments are for the most part speculative and not supported by concrete, defined and reliable evidence, so that the conclusions unfortunately remain hypothetical. Indeed the connections made between Aphrodite and her alleged sources are usually extremely tenuous.

The Near Eastern derivation of the goddess Aphrodite appears to have the much stronger case, in view of the support in the form of extant literary sources and a respectable number of demonstrable parallels in character, cult and iconography, many of which parallels are of a specific and central nature. The Indo-European and other suggested origins rely on the reconstruction of a hypothetical pre-historical character and development of the goddess and theoretically

11 ibid., pp.15–16.
12 Paul Friedrich, *The Meaning of Aphrodite*, University of Chicago Press, Chicago and London, 1978, pp.9–54.

constructed prototypes which do not apply to the historically attested nature of the goddess. In addition, the methods which are used to debate and rally support for the contentions are in the vast majority of cases of very dubious value.

In both the birth myth of Aphrodite and the myth of the goddess's *affaire* with Anchises there are parallels to motifs found with Inanna/Ishtar. This is a circumstance which may be expected in view of the apparent Near Eastern origins of the goddess. However, it is necessary to stress that the motifs do directly parallel those of the Mesopotamian goddess rather than motifs found extant with Astarte. It is accordingly quite possible that these Greek literary myths, both of which belong to the early archaic times, have been influenced directly by the Mesopotamian myths rather than indirectly through the myths of an intermediate deity. In fact the nature of the myth of Anchises in particular makes it probable that, if there has been influence from the Near East, it is directly from Mesopotamia, in view of the absence of any motifs which may be recognized as parallel to Phoenician ones.

The birth myth has some features which parallel those found with Ishtar in her myths, and *Homeric Hymn V*, which presents Aphrodite's *affaire* with Anchises, contains many more. Most striking are the motifs which recall the relationship of Inanna/Ishtar and her young lover the herdsman/shepherd Dumuzi. In both of these myths there is also the theme of power involved in the journeys which form an important part of the goddess's activities in both cases and strengthen the parallel with the Mesopotamian mythological ideas. It may be a significant aspect in the myth in which Anchises plays a major role that the motifs are entirely of the goddess-and-consort strand, presenting another parallel with the situation in the Inanna and Dumuzi myths. There is nothing of the court-and-warrior scenes and allied concepts, as found in the myths of Ninurta and Marduk, which constitute, of course, a completely different context in Mesopotamian mythological and religious terms. It should also be noted at this point that the parallels between the Greek and Mesopotamian myths are parallels of motif and of idea. The myths of Aphrodite are in no way the Greek versions of myths of Inanna/Ishtar or of Dumuzi. In fact, the narrative lines of both Greek stories are quite different from any myth of the great Mesopotamian goddess and of her consort.

In her birth myth Aphrodite travels from the sea to Olympos via Kythera and Cyprus. Hesiod's *Theogony* tells of Aphrodite's birth from the severed genitals of Ouranos after Kronos' violent separation of Heaven and Earth (lines 188–206). Born in the sea, she was blown via Kythera to Cyprus, where she stepped ashore and grass grew beneath her slender feet as she emerged from the sea (lines 188ff.). This motif of grass growing beneath the goddess's feet may express her power of fertility.

The account of the birth myth in *Homeric Hymn VI* (lines 1–21) presents her journey from Cyprus to Olympos. At Cyprus the gold-filletted Horai, the Seasons, received her joyfully and dressed her in divine clothes. On her head they placed a beautifully wrought crown of gold and added ornaments of mountain copper and precious gold to her pierced ears. Around her neck and on her silver-shining breast they arranged golden necklaces. This dressing completed, they led her to the immortals, who were so amazed at her beauty that each god prayed that he might lead her home to be his wedded wife.

While this myth has no parallels of narrative to those myths which survive about the Mesopotamian goddess, it is fitting, in view of the apparent origins of Aphrodite, that there is a number of motifs, central to the narrative as well as to the nature of the goddess, which recall those of Inanna/Ishtar.

The dressing motif, for instance, is a feature of her birth myth, and the clothes and accoutrements are a physical representation of her power – they make her even more attractive. The dressing motif is found elsewhere with Aphrodite and seems to be an important motif of the goddess. It is its function in the myth in the attractiveness of the goddess that is of importance here, as it is elsewhere.[13] This motif of dressing is found in a number of places with Inanna/Ishtar. One example of the motif occurs in a hymn to Inanna, in which the preparation of the goddess takes place on the island Dilmun and is parallel to the dressing on Cyprus here.[14] The motif in the Mesopotamian hymn may also involve the goddess's power. This can be seen in the sacred marriage dressing-scene where she is spoken of as

13 Other examples: *Homeric Hymn V*, 61–5, 161–3; also a scene in the *Iliad* 14.169ff. in which Aphrodite plays a role.
14 Réné Labat, André Caquot, Maurice Sznycer and Maurice Vieyra, *Les Religions du Proche-Orient asiatique*, Fayard/Denoël, Paris, 1970, pp.247ff. for the hymn.

dressed in 'clothes of power'.[15] Other sources in which the motif of dressing is found involving the power of the goddess are ID and AV. In AV Ishtar gradually regains her powers as she is dressed on her return journey to the upperworld (lines 114–25).[16] And like Ishtar (line 125), Aphrodite is adorned with a beautiful crown (lines 7–8). However, while this dressing motif of Aphrodite is obviously also a feature with the Mesopotamian goddess, and is connected in both cases with the power of the goddess, the context of the motif in ID and AV is different to a certain extent since, although both myths involve a journey, the journey in the Greek hymn is not a return from the netherworld.

The motif of beautiful clothes and adornments which express Aphrodite's powers of attraction and love is essential also to Ishtar as seen in an OB hymn in which this goddess's qualities of love, attraction and seductiveness are presented as her clothes, and express the goddess's greatness and power (lines 3–6):

> Chantez Ishtar, la plus imposante des déesses,
> que soit glorifiée la maitresse des femmes, la plus grande des Igigi.
> Elle est revêtue d'allégresse et d'amour,
> Elle est parée d'appas,[17] d'attirance et de charme.[18]

Aphrodite's power is a central feature in this journey myth, in which she travels from the sea via Kythera and especially Cyprus to arrive in Olympos, where she demonstrates her power in befitting terms. The hymn is primarily concerned with the goddess's power, her τιμή, and this is natural in her birth myth, which also has the

---

15 For power connotation of the bathing and dressing of the sacred marriage, e.g. SRT 5, lines 1–7, especially line 7, in which the power significance of the clothes is referred to: 'and dressed in the queenly robe, the robe of the queenship of heaven': Thorkild Jacobsen, *The Harps that Once . . .: Sumerian Poetry in Translation*, Yale University Press, New Haven and London, 1987, p.16. Also Bendt Alster, 'Sumerian Love Songs', RA 79 (1985) 150.

16 See the chapter on Inanna for the discussion on the clothes as symbols of power. This feature in the Mesopotamian myth is seen especially in ID, in which Inanna wears the me, divine powers, as clothes. When she is deprived of the clothes in the netherworld, she is without power and 'subjugated'.

17 In-bi, '(sexual) attractiveness and power'.

18 Source: Marie-Joseph Seux, *Hymnes et prières aux dieux de Babylonie et d'Assyrie*, Les Éditions du Cerf, Paris, 1976, p.39.

added purpose of praise of the goddess. What is significant is that it is expressed once again in a myth based on a journey during which she manifestly increases in power, specifically in the preparation scene on Cyprus. At the end of the myth, her power is expressed in her attractiveness to the gods (lines 16–18). As the goddess of love, this is part of her τιμή. The motif used to present her increase in power is the 'dressing sequence' and her clothes and jewellery are the symbols of power, adding to her attractiveness and consequent power over the gods on her arrival at the Assembly of the gods on Olympos. The idea of the journey, with its intimate connection with the power of the god – an idea first found in Mesopotamian myth – appears, therefore, also to be present here in this myth of Aphrodite, and this seems to constitute another parallel. This time the parallel is of what is, in effect, a structural idea.

Not all of the motifs in Aphrodite's birth myth have Meso-potamian parallels. One example of the differences is the important motif of Aphrodite's birth in the sea from the severed genitals of Ouranos. Interestingly, the event which precedes Aphrodite's birth – the separation of Heaven and Earth, involving Heaven's loss of his genitals (*Theogony*, 178–82) – is, of course, found in Hurrian/Hittite myth. Kumarbi castrated Heaven in the myth and in so doing sent Heaven upwards, that is, away from earth. However, the simple motif of the separation of Heaven and Earth is found in Mesopotamian myth, where it is an event brought about by Enlil (the son of An = Heaven), to whom Kumarbi actually owes his position in the Hurrian/Hittite pantheon. Kumarbi has the same position in the procession of kingship in the Hurrian/Hittite cosmological myth as Enlil has in the generations of the gods in Mesopotamia, and as Kronos has in the Greek theogony and line of kingship. All three separate Heaven and Earth in their respective traditions. Also perhaps of significance in terms of the Mesopotamian input into these myths is that the Hurrian/Hittite god of heaven is Anu, who is actually the Mesopotamian god of heaven and the Akkadian word for heaven (from the Sumerian an). This may indicate a close relationship between the Hurrian/Hittite cosmological myth and Mesopotamian belief.

Another example of the difference between the Greek and Meso-potamian myths is the group of attendants in the dressing-scene. While the preparation of the goddess on the island Cyprus is parallel to that of Ishtar on the island Dilmun, the Mesopotamian myth has no group of attendants who carry out the dressing of the goddess as the Seasons do in the Greek myth (lines 5–15).

Despite these differences, there are several features of this myth which parallel those in the myths of the Mesopotamian goddess. In addition, they seem to have much the same underlying idea of power and are used in a similar context of the goddess's journey resulting in the establishment and demonstration of the goddess's power. In view of these considerations, it would take an over-hasty commentator to dismiss out of hand the possibility of influence of ideas and motifs from Mesopotamia in this myth of Aphrodite, a goddess who herself appears to constitute definite evidence of Mesopotamian influence.

In *Homeric Hymn V*, Aphrodite performs another journey, presenting similar motifs and aims. She gains power in the activities of the journey, using the same dressing motif which gives to her her irresistible attractiveness. The myth which is the core of this hymn, the *affaire* of Aphrodite and Anchises, contains, in addition, many motifs and ideas which correspond directly to motifs and ideas found with Inanna/Ishtar and the young herdsman/shepherd Dumuzi. When all the relevant motifs are taken together, they repeat the relationship between the Mesopotamian goddess and her mortal consort. The number and specific nature of the parallels, and the fact that most are central to the myths of both the Mesopotamian and the Greek pairs, suggest a Mesopotamian origin for the main feature of this myth, the relationship between the love goddess and her lover Anchises. The hymn appears to be one of the earliest, if not *the* earliest, of the Homeric hymns, and the myth which is its core appears to be of great antiquity, since it was referred to by both Homer in the *Iliad* (2.819–21) and Hesiod in the *Theogony* (lines 1008–10).[19]

The story goes that Zeus was angry at Aphrodite's overwhelming him and other immortals with desire for mortals. He revenged himself on her by causing her to fall in love with a handsome Trojan herdsman named Anchises. She saw the young man and, struck with love, withdrew to Cyprus to prepare herself. Here the motif of bathing and dressing in beautiful clothes is used. The Seasons bathed her and poured immortal oil on her. She dressed in beautiful clothes and adorned herself with golden jewels and necklaces (lines 61–5, 161–3), after which she sped back to Troy.

As she met Anchises her clothes shone more brightly than blazing

---

19 Early date of the hymn, E.J. Bickerman, 'Love Story in the Homeric Hymn to Aphrodite', *Athenaeum* 54 (1976) 229; cf. T.W. Allen, W.R. Halliday and E.E. Sikes, eds, *The Homeric Hymns*, 2nd edition, Oxford University Press, Adolf M. Hakert, Amsterdam, 1963, pp.350–1.

fire, her embroidery shimmered like the moon, and her necklaces shone at her throat (lines 86ff.). Anchises was overwhelmed with desire, and it was for this that she carried out her preparations. Anchises recognized her divinity, and Aphrodite had to overcome this impediment to her desire with a lying story. Before the other herdsmen returned with their oxen, she woke the young hero and revealed her divinity to him, at which he was greatly afraid, fearing the consequences of lying with a goddess. She calmed him and told him of the child, Aineias, who would result from their liaison. At the end he was warned that he should not reveal his *affaire* with Aphrodite, or Zeus would smite him with a smoking thunderbolt.[20]

Certain features in this myth recall the relationship of Inanna and Dumuzi. The purpose of Aphrodite's activities is her coupling with Anchises, the mortal herdsman of Ida, and this may reflect the sacred union of the goddess Inanna with her mortal herdsman Dumuzi. The motifs of bathing and dressing are also a feature of the preparations for this sacred union.[21] As Aphrodite does in the Homeric hymn, Inanna bathes herself, anoints herself with oil, dresses and puts on jewellery for her 'sacred marriage' encounter with the 'wild bull',

20 The stories of Ganymedes and of Tithonos included in Aphrodite's speech are the *affaires* of other gods and are not integral to the story of the relationship of Aphrodite and Anchises. They are included by the poet as part of Aphrodite's discussion of her shame at lying with a mortal, and of the question of whether she should apply for immortality for Anchises. These concern the themes of the literary work. For a discussion of these, see Peter Walcot, 'The Homeric *Hymn to Aphrodite*: A Literary Appraisal', *Greece and Rome* 38 (1991) 148ff.; also Peter M. Smith, 'Aeneiadai as Patrons of *Iliad* XX and the Homeric *Hymn to Aphrodite*', *Harvard Studies in Classical Philology* 85 (1981) 51–2. Similarly, the introductory section on Athena, Artemis and Hestia is also not part of the Aphrodite–Anchises action, but is concerned with defining Aphrodite's power. On these introductory lines, see Friedrich Solmsen, 'Zur Theologie im großen Aphrodite-Hymnus', in Friedrich Solmsen, *Kleine Schriften*, vol. 1, Georg Olms Verlagsbuchhandlung, Hildesheim, 1968, pp.55–67. Comparisons of aspects of the story with Homeric epic: Tilman Krischer, 'Der homerische Aphroditehymnus als poetische Konstruktion', *Hermes* 119 (1991) 254–6.

21 S.N. Kramer, *The Sacred Marriage Rite*, Indiana University Press, Bloomington, 1969, pp.59, 63–5, 73–7. Some texts on the dressing and bathing: *Iddin-Dagan's Sacred Marriage Hymn*, 180–4, in Daniel Reisman, 'Iddin-Dagan's Sacred Marriage Hymn', JCS 25 (1973) 191; SRT 5, lines 3–7, especially 7 on the significance of the garments. On this poem, see Jacobsen, *The Harps that Once . . .*, p.16: line 7, 'and dressed in the queenly robe, the robe of the queenship of heaven'.

Dumuzi.[22] These motifs of bathing and dressing are important with Aphrodite and are found elsewhere with the goddess. It is their function in the attractiveness and power of the goddess that is of importance here, as is the case in other examples of their usage.[23] This appears to be the only case of the bathing and the dressing together, and it specifically recalls the Mesopotamian usage.

The motif of the male suffering as a result of the amorous encounter with the goddess is another parallel. After Aphrodite reveals herself to him in her epiphany, Anchises pleads with the goddess not to leave him feeble, as he well knows that disaster comes upon men who have loved the immortal goddesses (lines 185–90) and that he 'runs a serious risk of being killed'.[24] The threat of disaster hangs over the end of the poem, in the shape of Zeus's thunderbolt: Anchises will suffer its effects if he boasts about his *affaire* with the goddess. Other sources reveal that disaster eventually befalls him, when Zeus's thunderbolt leaves him lame, or blind.[25] In the context of the threat of the thunderbolt to Anchises in the hymn, and in its effect related later in other sources, it becomes clear that Anchises' fears of being left 'feeble' involve some concrete disaster, not just a loss of vitality.[26] In Mesopotamia, disasters of various kinds are the result of enjoying Ishtar's favours. In the *Epic of Gilgamesh* (Tablet VI.ii.46–79), Gilgamesh insults and enrages the goddess by reciting a list of her lovers who have suffered as a result of her love, and he

22 These motifs of dressing or bathing are found elsewhere in connection with Aphrodite: *Iliad*, 14.169ff:, *Odyssey*, 8.362ff.

23 *Homeric Hymn VI*, 5–13; see above for the discussion of the dressing motif in this hymn; also *Odyssey*, 8.362ff.

24 N. van der Ben, 'Hymn to Aphrodite 36–291: Notes on the Pars Epica of the Homeric Hymn to Aphrodite', *Mnemosyne* 39 (1986) 20.

25 Allen, Halliday and Sikes, *Homeric Hymns*, p.372; cf. P. Smith, *Nursling of Mortality: A Study of the Homeric Hymn to Aphrodite*, Studien zur klassischen Philologie 3, Verlag Peter D. Lang, Bern, 1981, p.98, on the early source for these later accounts: Soph. frag. 373; Hyginus, *Fabulae*, 94. In the hymn no harm comes to him from Aphrodite, who is shown as free from blame in this case; he will bring disaster on himself if he boasts. Nevertheless, the unhappy fate is a result of the *affaire*.

26 For just a loss of vitality, see Anne Giacomelli, 'Aphrodite and After', *Phoenix* 34 (1980) 1–19. Anchises' feebleness in the passage (lines 188–90) needs to be taken in the context of the whole myth. Regarding the suggestion that Anchises' disaster occurs as a result of the 'incommensurate' nature of the spheres of mortal and immortal activity, a 'basic tenet of the Olympian religion', p.18, the *affaires* of Zeus and other gods, as well as those of Aphrodite in this hymn, seem to disagree with this

refuses to add himself to the number. Dumuzi, in particular, dies as a result of loving Inanna/Ishtar.[27] The same fate for the lover of Aphrodite may underlie the statement of Anchises, who declares that he would choose to lie in love with her even if it meant going afterwards to Hades' realm (lines 153–4). This statement must be seen, also, in the context of the scene later in the hymn, where he fears disaster or death as a result of lying with the goddess (lines 187–90).[28] This love-and-death or disaster motif is quite specific and is especially reminiscent of Dumuzi and Ishtar, with whom it is a famous feature.

Certain other features in this myth resemble those found with the Mesopotamian goddess. The motif of Aphrodite bathing and dressing on Cyprus is paralleled by Inanna in the hymn that has already been referred to in the discussion of Aphrodite's birth myth.[29] In his literary/structural analysis of *Homeric Hymn V*, P. Smith considers that the purpose of the bathing-and-dressing scene is to supply a touch of realism to the narrative.[30] This may be an effect which the poet also desired to convey, but he makes use of religious mythological elements and uses the effects of these elements to further his story. While the hymn is a work of literature, and its literary nature is important for an understanding of the poem and of the author's purpose in presenting the story, it is relating the activities of a goddess who is much more than just a woman preparing for an assignation;

view. On the nature of the disaster, there is no mention of castration or impotence such as is the fate of Attis. The idea is more complex than this. Cf. R. Mondi, who compares Anchises' fate with that of Attis: 'Greek Mythic Thought in the Light of the Near East', in Lowell Edmunds, ed., *Approaches to Greek Myth*, Johns Hopkins University Press, Baltimore and London, 1990, p.147.

27　See also Kramer, *The Sacred Marriage Rite*, pp.104–6; Alster, RA 79 (1985) 142–6: lines 18–26, 30 of the love poem SRT 31.

28　While there are scenes in the *Iliad* and the *Odyssey* in which people want something so badly that they are prepared to die for it, the motif of love-and-death is found only in this hymn. For examples of the scenes in Homer referred to, see Van der Ben, op. cit., p.19. Compare also J.C. Kamerbeek, 'Remarques sur l'*Hymne à Aphrodite*', *Mnemosyne* 20 (1967) 392: love-and-death motif here. For an analysis of this situation in literary terms, see also Walcot, *G&R* 38 (1991) 144ff.

29　Labat, *et al.*, *Les Réligions*, pp.247ff., for the hymn.

30　Smith, *Nursling of Mortality*, p.41. Similarly another study which treats the Aphrodite myth predominantly from the angle of literature and folktale, and to a large extent from a secular point of view: E.J. Bickerman, 'Love Story in the Homeric Hymn to Aphrodite', *Athenaeum* 54 (1976) 234ff.

therefore elements and ideas like these are not just literary conceits arbitrarily created for this work but are part of the religious mythology which belongs to the goddess and are being used to further the ideas being presented about her in the action of the myth.

Another parallel with the Mesopotamian goddess can be seen in the coupling of the animals which fawn around Aphrodite on Mt Ida near Troy (lines 68–74) and in her function as goddess of sexual reproduction of human beings (lines 1–6). She reproduces here the sexual–fertility aspects of Ishtar, as seen in AV for instance (lines 76–90).[31] It is, however, also apparent in this specific example in the myth, the fawning of wild animals around the goddess on Mt Ida, that there has been an admixture of ideas in this myth from another or other sources. Such an idea is the aspect of the 'mistress of animals' which is found with the goddess on her arrival at Mt Ida. The 'mistress of animals', especially of beasts of prey as these in the hymn are, and the idea of 'mother of the mountain',[32] which may be involved here, are traits that are associated with Cybele, the Phrygian goddess, a form of the Anatolian Great Goddess, and Aphrodite may have received these in the myth through some association with Cybele.[33] The latter goddess appears to have also been taken up, with similar traits attached, in the worship of Dionysos in Athens and Thebes, as may be seen in later times in Euripides' tragedy the *Bacchae*.[34] Nevertheless, the specific form that the motif of Aphrodite's association with the animals takes here in this myth, the fertility and sexual

31 See also Thérèse Ory, 'L'animal et le végétal dans l'*Hymne Homérique à Aphrodite*', LEC 52 (1984) 251, on the importance in the hymn of the goddess's power in terms of sexual reproduction.

32 Of course, μῆτερα θηρῶν in line 68 in the hymn refers to Mt Ida rather than to Aphrodite. Cf. Van der Ben, *Mnemosyne* 39 (1986) 8.

33 Burkert, *Greek Religion*, p.154. One unsound view, held especially in the early part of this century, was that the story of Aphrodite and Anchises was derived entirely from that of Cybele and Attis: cf. H.J. Rose, 'Anchises and Aphrodite', CQ 18 (1924) 11–16. See also, for a more recent view on Ishtar and Cybele, Silvio Ferri, 'L'inno omerici a Afrodite e la tribu anatolica degli Otrusi', in *Studi in onore di Luigi Castiglioni*, vol. I, G.C. Sansoni Editore, Florence, 1960, pp.294ff.

34 Especially lines 78–82. Cf. G.S. Kirk, ed., *The Bacchae of Euripides*, Cambridge University Press, Cambridge, 1979, p.35. The hero of the play, Pentheus, hides in a tree to spy on the Bacchic women's rites and is dragged from this tree by the frenzied women and slain (lines 1066–127); cf. a report, though much later, from Firmicus Maternus, Halm, p.120: 'in sacris Phrygiis quae matris deum dicunt, per annos singulos arbor pinea caeditur et in media arbore simulacrum iuvenis subligatur'.

interplay of the animals, is true to the picture of Aphrodite,[35] but also especially to the image of her forerunner Ishtar, who appears to function also as the goddess of sexual reproduction of animals.

Another parallel with Mesopotamian mythology is the idea of the increase and demonstration of power as part of the journey. The motif of power is an important feature in this journey myth, and its increase and display seem to be an integral part of the journey of the goddess. Aphrodite appears to become more potent as a result of her activities in this journey, and her display of power reaches its climax at the end of her journey to Mt Ida. The goddess's power is that of sexual desire which overwhelms and deceives the mind, and it is a central feature of the hymn, which emphasizes the virtually universal nature of her power (lines 1–6). The seductive beauty of the goddess expresses her power, and her preparations in Cyprus have the effect of enhancing this. The adornment and the application of the immortal oil with which Aphrodite anoints herself increases her beauty and potency so that she arrives at Mt Ida with overwhelming beauty. In a parallel way, Apollo grows in power when he is bathed and dressed and takes immortal food and drink.[36] The goddess's power in her beauty and irresistibility is displayed in the encounter with the hero, and it is displayed in a way typical of the return part of the journey: beautiful clothes, ornaments, face all radiant, and a golden peplos brighter than blazing fire (lines 86ff.). The power represented by the clothes and accoutrements is expressed in the light motif in a similar way to that with Apollo as he presents himself at Olympos after his birth, when his clothes, lyre, chiton and feet, which are symbols of power in that myth, shine.[37] The light motif is also seen with Zeus in Crete after his birth, where it symbolizes the young god's growth in power and might.[38] One of the ways in which Aphrodite's radiance is described in the hymn has a close similarity with a reference to Inanna's radiance after she has bathed and adorned herself in a Sumerian hymn: 'Dumuzi pushed (open) the door, and like a moonbeam she came forth to him out of the house' (ii.20). When Aphrodite met Anchises the decorations on her breast shone like the moon (lines 89f.).[39]

Radiance can also be an aspect of the epiphany of a divinity, as can

35 As seen also in *Homeric Hymn V*, 3–5 concerning the mating of animals.
36 *Homeric Hymn to Apollo*, 124–9.
37 ibid., 201–3.
38 Hesiod, *Theogony*, 492–3.
39 Jacobsen, *The Harps that Once. . .*, p.21.

be seen in the case of Demeter's epiphany when she enters the home of Metaneira in *Homeric Hymn II* (lines 488–91). While this creates awe in the viewers, the situation is, however, different in Aphrodite's hymn: here the goddess's radiance is expressed in terms of clothes and ornaments in which she is re-dressed, and in the journeys this is, in the context of her other actions in the hymn, an expression of power. It is noticeable that, by contrast with her appearance here in the situation where she overwhelms Anchises, radiance is not a feature of her subsequent epiphany when, after she has lain with Anchises, she reveals herself as a goddess to him. The only features mentioned – her height, with her head touching the roof-tree, and her beautiful eyes and neck – are those representing her divinity (lines 172–5, 181). Aphrodite is recognized in a similar way by Helen – by the sight of her beautiful eyes, neck and breasts – when the goddess translates Paris back from the battle to Helen's chamber, thereby saving him from death at the hands of Menelaos.[40] The radiance of Aphrodite in the Homeric hymn appears to indicate the goddess's power.

In summary, Aphrodite obtains power in her journeys in both myths discussed here, and this is expressed in her apparel, her adornments and her personal attractiveness. The main form her power takes in these myths is the power to cause sexual desire in gods, men and animals. Because of the careful and specific usage of the motifs to express the power theme, it seems as though the idea of the journey for power was known by the author and was being deliberately employed. Indeed, in the myth of the goddess's *affaire* with Anchises the dressing-and-bathing procedure through which Aphrodite enhances her power seems to be the sole reason for her journey to Cyprus. Its result is also immediately apparent at the end of the return journey on her arrival at Ida, where her might is expressed in symbolic ways typical of other examples of the power theme at work, and her major attribute, that of causing sexual desire in gods, humans and animals, is amply demonstrated.

The various motifs in this myth point to the great Mesopotamian goddess, as they do in the myth of Aphrodite's birth. In particular, her relationship with the herdsman Anchises recalls that of Ishtar and her lovers: especially her consort Dumuzi, the shepherd and herds-

---

40 *Iliad*, 3.396–7. In a similar way the angry Achilles recognizes the divinity of Athena by her terrible shining eyes: *Iliad*, 1.199–200.

man, with whom she performs the 'sacred marriage'. Although the narrative is once again apparently Greek, and the specific purpose of the hymn, according to one view, may be to explain why unions between gods and mortals no longer take place,[41] many of the ideas and motifs used suggest that the author has not hesitated to rely strongly on traditional features of Aphrodite's mythological corpus, many of which may conceivably have their origin, as does the goddess herself, in Mesopotamia. Another feature which also points to some connection with Mesopotamia is, of course, the presence of the idea of a journey for power. In view of the nature of the parallels, which are specific and complex, especially in the myth of her *affaire* with Anchises, with many motifs corresponding directly to the Mesopotamian motifs and being central in the myths of both areas, some influence directly from Mesopotamia must be the answer. The influence would not, of course, have come from Mesopotamia in the form of literary works in the foreign script, but most probably as myths and ideas transferred orally to Greece, where aspects seem to have been assimilated as part of the mythological tradition of Aphrodite, Ishtar's Greek counterpart. This influence from Mesopotamia appears to be the case despite the admixture of features in the myth which seem to have some connection with the Phrygian goddess Cybele. To the Greeks, however, must be attributed the imagination to create new, delightful and rather sophisticated myths, while working old and possibly foreign ideas and material from divergent sources, predominately Mesopotamia in the myth of Aphrodite and Anchises, into the framework of the Greek religious, social and environmental context.

If Mesopotamian influence in these hymns is the case, as seems likely, there remains the question of the probable time of influence. The earliest evidence for Aphrodite in the Greek and Mycenaean area is the temple in Paphos. This appears to have been founded in the twelfth century, apparently at the time when the locality was settled by Mycenaean Achaeans, at the very end of the Mycenaean age.[42] The

---

41. Although William G. Thalmann objects to this explanation, in CPh 86 (1991) 146. Perhaps the union of gods and mortals will still occur, but Aphrodite will no longer be able to boast about it: Ann L.T. Bergren, 'The *Homeric Hymn to Aphrodite*: Tradition and Rhetoric, Praise and Blame', *Classical Antiquity* 8 (1989) 2. See also Robert Parker, 'The Homeric *Hymn to Demeter* and the *Homeric Hymns*', G&R 38 (1991) 4.
42. Vassos Karageorgis, *The Ancient Civilization of Cyprus*, Nagel, Geneva, 1969, pp.62–7, and see also pp.135–50; Burkert, *Greek Religion*, p.153.

goddess may have been already present in Mycenaean Greece owing to Mycenaean contacts with the Near East in the previous two centuries, unless the period after the end of the Mycenaean age – especially the time of the beginning of lesser, but still appreciable, contact – was responsible for the adoption of the goddess. Whatever the period, if the goddess's adoption in Greece was a result of influence from Phoenicia – and in the initial period at the end of the Mycenaean era this remains open to question in view of the Mycenaean contacts with the North Syrian and southern Hittite areas – these myths were not apparently part of it, since the parallels visible in the hymns, especially in the larger hymn to Aphrodite, directly parallel features found with Ishtar, unmixed with any recognizable Phoenician elements. However, this leaves open the date at which influence could have occurred. There are various possibilities, but no conclusive answers. The nature of the parallels in the *affaire* of Anchises and Aphrodite is specific, central and, to some degree, complex, and this may suggest a later date. Of course, the time of influence is clearly some time before the composition of the *Iliad* by Homer, which occurred approximately between 750 and 700 BC, since the story, is referred to there (2.819–21). The way in which it is mentioned indicates that it is already an accepted story, which dates it some time before that. The birth myth occurs in the *Theogony*, which was composed at approximately the same time as Homer's epics, and it also appears to be an accepted story. The dressing motif involved in it appears to be specific, which suggests that it is not much older than these compositions. There is a connection of Aphrodite's birth with motifs having parallels with Hittite ideas, but this connection may have come about at any date.

An early date depends on the extent to which the oral tradition is conservative, so as to allow the preservation of the relationship of the ideas to one another. The various ideas of the journey for power are closely interrelated in their expression with Aphrodite and follow Mesopotamian patterns. Similarly, the ideas of the journey for power are integral to the relationship of Aphrodite and Anchises, and this also repeats the situation in the Mesopotamian myths of Ishtar and her consort. The question of whether whole myths of Ishtar and Dumuzi arrived in Greece at this early time and only some aspects were taken up, or whether just a few ideas were transmitted, is unresolvable. A termination date for the influence of foreign ideas would hinge on the time that is necessary to allow the assimilation of the material to the extent seen in the myths so that they are accepted as part of the mythological tradition of Aphrodite. However, in the case of the myth of her *affaire* with Anchises in particular, the most likely time of influence seems to be the first millennium BC, and not too long before the Homeric epics, owing to the specific and complex nature of the parallels.

A study of Aphrodite would not be complete without a reference to Adonis, the other lover of Aphrodite who suffers disaster. He may be another example of Mesopotamian influence, since he seems to be the West Semitic derivative of Dumuzi and to have come to Greece from the Phoenician religion, an origin which is supported especially by his name and his cult in Greece.[43] Although attestation of his myths is late, the god seems to have been taken up at quite an early time by the Greeks: he and his unhappy fate are attested in the sixth century on Lesbos in a poem of Sappho (frag. 140), and according to Apollodorus he is also mentioned by Hesiod in the *Catalogue of Women* or *Eoiai* (Hes. frag. 139).

The myth of Adonis' birth in Apollodorus (III.183–5) presents various parallels with the Mesopotamian stories of Dumuzi/Damu, the consort of Aphrodite's counterpart in Mesopotamia. According to Hesiod, Adonis was the son of Phoinix and Alphesiboia, but Panyassis says that his parents were Theias, the king of the Assyrians, and his daughter Smyrna. Because Smyrna did not honour her, Aphrodite caused the girl to fall in love with her father, with whom she lay secretly for twelve nights. When her father perceived that it was his daughter, he drew his sword and pursued her. Just as she was about to be caught, she prayed to the gods to make her invisible, but they changed her into a tree instead, the smyrna tree. In the tenth month, the tree split open and Adonis was born. Although still a child, he was so beautiful that Aphrodite fell in love with him, concealed him in a larnax and gave him to Persephone. When this goddess saw him, she would not give him back. After Zeus had been asked to arbitrate on the affair, it was decided that Adonis should spend one-third of the year with Persephone, another third with Aphrodite, while the remaining third he might have to himself. He decided to spend his third with Aphrodite. Adonis was later killed by a pig while hunting, owing to the anger of the huntress Artemis.

43 Walter Burkert, *Structure and History in Greek Mythology and Ritual*, Sather Classical Lectures 47, University of California Press, Berkeley and London, 1979, pp.105–11; Ernest Will, 'Le rituel des Adonies', *Syria* 52 (1975) 93–105; Oswyn Murray, *Early Greece*, The Harvester Press, Brighton, 1980, pp.85–6.

There are certain themes here which have parallels with Mesopotamian ideas of Dumuzi/Damu, from whom Adonis is descended.
The Near Eastern derivation of the story is evident for a start in the
name of the god: Adonis appears to come from the West Semitic
word for 'lord'. Similarly, Hesiod's name for his father, Phoinix, also
suggests a Phoenician origin, and his father according to Panyassis is
an Assyrian and explicitly Mesopotamian.

The most obvious motif in this brief résumé in Apollodorus to
have Mesopotamian parallels is his annual residence in Hades with
Persephone, a motif which he shares with Persephone. Of course, he
is parallel with Dumuzi/Damu who also spends a part of each year in
the netherworld, as seen in ID, AV, edin-na ú-saĝ-ĝá, and TRS 8. Like
Persephone, he remains in the netherworld for one-third of the year,
rather than half a year as is the case with the Mesopotamian god. This
may be due to influence from Persephone, or simply to the customary idea of the three-part seasonal year in Greece.

A less obvious, but significant, parallel with Dumuzi/Damu is his
birth from a tree. In TRS 8, the Mesopotamian vegetation god is left
by the mother goddess in the care of a tree and sleeps within her bark.
When the mother comes to collect her son, she finds that he has
descended to the netherworld. However, he is released from the
netherworld and is born symbolically every year in the vegetation, as
Adonis is born from the tree. The motifs are not in an identical
arrangement, but the same ideas appear to underlie the story. The
mixing of motifs may be a result of transmission through the Syrian
or Phoenician form of the god, which seems more likely than
transmission directly from Mesopotamia.

However, it must be noted that the myth comes from Apollodorus
and is very late.[44] It would then involve questions of Near Eastern
influence which lie outside the scope of this study, an investigation
which confines itself to the discussion of the question of influence in
early Greek myths of Aphrodite. There is nothing here to add to the
case for influence from Mesopotamia on the goddess Aphrodite and
her myths in the archaic or earlier times, with the exception of the
adoption of Adonis himself as an apparent derivative of Dumuzi; and
this seems, at the most, to be only indirect influence by way of
Phoenician religion.

---

44 Versions of the story are found later in Christian authors, beginning with
   Aristides, and these present similar motifs: Burkert, *Structure and
   History*, pp.109–10.

8

JOURNEYS OF HERMES AND ZEUS

The corpus of surviving Greek mythological works of the formulaic poetry tradition preserves myths of Zeus and Hermes which involve journeys. The *Homeric Hymn to Hermes* is the longest of the four long Homeric hymns which have survived, and it presents a series of journeys carried out by Hermes and Apollo. In the myth of Zeus' birth in the *Theogony* (lines 477–500), Zeus and his mother, Rhea, carry out journeys which parallel those found in the long Homeric hymns to Apollo, Demeter and Aphrodite.

In the *Theogony*, Zeus also performs as the champion of the Assembly and defeats the monster Typhoeus (lines 820–70). This monster, which is mentioned in the *Homeric Hymn to Apollo*, parallels Apollo's opponent, the Pythian serpent, which Apollo overcomes with the similar effect of establishing his power.[1] In fact, the general situation of the Typhoeus combat and Zeus' role in it parallels the situation in the monster-combat myths of Ninurta and Marduk in the heroic-strand myths of Mesopotamia, as well as the corresponding events in Apollo's myths.

The Near Eastern derivation of aspects of the *Theogony* has been generally recognized, and in keeping with this the myth of Zeus' birth and the Typhoeus episode show some specific parallels with Mesopotamian myths. The birth myth has parallels in the ideas of the journey and in some motifs, while the correspondences of the

---

1 Typhaon and Typhoeus are considered by the author of the *Homeric Hymn to Apollo* to be the same monster: lines 339, 367–8. See also *Theogony*, 306–7, 821. For a discussion of the different traditions of the parentage of Typhoeus and Typhaon, see Alain Ballabriga, 'Le dernier adversaire de Zeus: le mythe de Typhon dans l'épopée grecque archaïque', RHR 207 (1990) 3–30.

Typhoeus myth in Hesiod to Near Eastern, including Mesopotamian, myths is confined to a small number of motifs. In the later account of the combat in Apollodorus, which is included for the sake of comparison with the Hesiodic version, many Near Eastern ideas and motifs are visible.

The hymn to Hermes presents a number of journeys which are especially important for comparison with those of the Homeric hymns to Apollo, Demeter and Aphrodite. It forms a significant contrast to these three long Homeric hymns, since it shows no signs whatsoever of parallels with the Mesopotamian myths in this study, and if there are parallels with other Mesopotamian material they are not obvious.

THE HOMERIC HYMN TO HERMES

The hymn is of considerably later date than the other hymns, and this may have something to do with the absence of parallels. The text is in places very corrupt and the date of composition is difficult to determine with anything approaching precision, since there is little external or internal evidence to assist. The estimates of date vary, and the poem is placed as late as the fifth century or afterwards. A time of composition at the end of the sixth century BC is probably the most acceptable.[2]

The character of the hymn is also different from the others, in that it has a rambling style of story. In addition, Hermes is treated with less reverence than the gods in the other long hymns; however, this may be a result of the youthful god's character and functions as they are displayed here in the story.

Hermes, the precocious son of Zeus and the nymph Maia, is born at dawn, plays his lyre at midday and steals Apollo's cattle in the evening. Shortly after he springs forth from the womb of Maia, he steps forth from his mother's cave and finds a tortoise. Using its shell, he constructs a harp and sings marvellous songs about his mother and Zeus as he strums its resounding strings.

As the sun sinks beneath the earth towards Okeanos, he hurries to

2 Richard Janko, *Homer, Hesiod and the Hymns: Diachronic Development in Epic Diction*, Cambridge University Press, Cambridge, 1982, pp.133, 134.

Pieria and cuts out fifty cattle from Apollo's herd and, by various tricks, tries to disguise the tracks on his way to the river Alpheios near sandy Pylos. On the way, he attempts to bribe an old man tending his vineyard, who sees him driving the cows backwards.

At Alpheios he kindles a fire, demonstrates his strength in slaying two of the cows, and then sacrifices them, enjoying the rich odour of the roasting flesh. After this, he goes back to his mother's cave at Kyllene and climbs back into his cradle, wrapping the swaddling clothes around himself to appear a feeble baby. His mother knows that he has been out and scolds him for his shameless robbery, but Hermes retorts that he will bring honour to her and to himself, and declares that if Apollo causes any trouble, he will make that god sorry for it.

Meanwhile, Apollo has been searching for his cattle, and after discovering the truth from the old man in the vineyard, he follows the tracks of Hermes and the cattle and duly arrives at Maia's cave. After searching the cave for his cattle, he threatens to throw Hermes, who pretends to be an innocent baby, into Tartaros if he does not own up and return the cattle. Hermes swears that he knows nothing of the beasts, and that he is too young even to know what cattle are.

Apollo carries him off to the Assembly on Olympos for Zeus to judge the case. Apollo explains the situation, but Hermes again swears his innocence and deviously states his own view of the affair. Zeus laughs at the child's impudence and orders him to take Apollo to the cattle and to settle the quarrel.

At Pylos, Hermes drives the cattle out of their hiding-place. He is too strong for the ropes of osier with which Apollo binds him. He bursts them, and they fall off and begin to grow rapidly, covering all of the cattle. Then Hermes starts to play his lyre, and the astonished and delighted Apollo barters his cattle for the instrument and the skill to play it.

Afterwards, the two return to Olympos and Zeus makes them both friends.[3] At the urging of Apollo, Hermes, the prince of thieves, swears that he will steal no more from Apollo, who then gives him the

---

3 These lines, 510 or 512 to the end, have been considered by some to be added to the hymn. Against this, however, is that the lines do continue the theme of the rest of the hymn, and add important details to the explanation of Hermes as a divinity. Various verbal patterns and repetitions also continue into the last lines, strengthening the case for the hymn's unity: Cora Angier Sowa, *Traditional Themes and the Homeric Hymns*, Bolchazy–Carducci Publishers, 1984, pp.194–7; Janko, *Homer, Hesiod*, p.133.

gift of divination through birds. Hermes shall be lord over birds of omen, as well as over various creatures of the wild and over flocks. Finally, he is also appointed as the messenger of Hades.

The hymn to Hermes stands out from the other three long Homeric hymns in this study of journeys of the gods and of the theme of the acquisition and demonstration of power which plays an integral role in the journeys. Although Hermes and Apollo travel to and fro in the hymn, the journeys are quite different in structure and purpose from those of the other hymns and the idea of the journey for power as it is seen in these other hymns, is not present. Hermes does display his power and divinity in the hymn, since this is a theme of the Homeric hymns which are concerned with praising the gods, but it is not presented as an integral part of the journeys.[4] There may be a general idea that the demonstration of the god's power occurs in connection with a journey, but it is not of the sort seen in the other hymns or in the Mesopotamian works, since the structures of the journeys, as well as their content, do not compare in any way.[5]

The journeys have no patterns of the sort seen in the Meso-potamian myths or the other hymns. As can be seen, there is no parallel either with the journeys of the myths of the goddess-and-consort strand or with the journeys of the heroic-strand myths. The journeys are, in fact, quite haphazard, and show no conscious organization to present any underlying ideas. At the same time, there is no connection between the demonstration of power and the journeys, since the exhibition of power and the receipt of gifts do not occur as parts of the sequences as they do in the other myths. For instance, there is no wandering journey of the goddess, no ascent sequence and demonstration of powers closely involved, and there is no journey of the powerful god to the Assembly to demonstrate his power and assert his authority. Instead, Hermes demonstrates his cleverness in creating his lyre after he steps forth from the cave; he shows his strength in killing the two cows later, when he sacrifices

---

4 A good example of this is Hymn 28, to Athena.
5 On the origin and nature of Hermes, see, for instance, Hans Herter, 'Hermes: Ursprung und Wesen eines griechischen Gottes', *Rheinisches Museum für Philologie* 118 (1975) 193–241; A.J. van Windekens, 'Réflex-ions sur la nature et l'origine du dieu Hermès', *Rheinisches Museum für Philologie* 104 (1961) 289–301; Walter Burkert, *Greek Religion*, Harvard University Press, Cambridge (Mass.), 1985, pp.156–9.

them near the Alpheios river. Similarly, he displays his deceitfulness and cunning throughout, but once again not in any connection with the journeys themselves. To confirm the absence of Mesopotamian ideas in this hymn, there are no accompanying motifs that parallel Mesopotamian mythological material.

There appears to be one parallel with the *Homeric Hymn to Apollo*, and it is another feature which demonstrates the difference in the ideas involved, because the material is not used in the same way or with the same purpose. The elements of the birth of Hermes seem to allude to Apollo's birth in his hymn (lines 119–32). At dawn, Hermes springs forth from his mother's womb, and emerges shortly afterwards from his mother's cave (lines 20–4). He then invents the lyre and sings marvellous songs about the relationship of Zeus and his mother Maia (lines 25–61). The springing-forth and the idea of the dawn, as well as the suggestion that he comes forth from the earth, after which he acquires the lyre, may be an allusion to the motifs in Apollo's birth story, an allusion which is consistent with the large part that Apollo plays in the hymn alongside Hermes. The hymn to Apollo was famous and must also have been known to the author of this hymn, which was composed in the same Homeric tradition as the hymn to Apollo, though at a later date. However, while these motifs may be an allusion to Apollo's birth, it seems to be an allusion purely on a literary plane. The motifs are not used for the same purpose, since there are no accompanying motifs showing the power theme or any other motifs defining an ascent sequence. If this is an allusion to Apollo's birth scene, it does seem, however, to confirm the importance of these ideas, which are presented in Apollo's hymn, and which are also found with Zeus Kretagenes in his birth, as discussed in the chapter on Apollo.

The lack of parallels with Mesopotamian myths in both the journeys and the accompanying motifs in the hymn to Hermes is highly significant to this study of parallels in Mesopotamian and Greek journey myths. This difference in the hymn emphasizes the fact that the ideas of the journeys and accompanying motifs in the other hymns are no accident. In the hymn to Hermes, there are several journeys, but they completely lack both the underlying ideas and the motifs which parallel those in Mesopotamian myths. By contrast, the other hymns have journeys which show the same structural ideas as the journeys in the Mesopotamian myths, and have large numbers of motifs which directly parallel those in the same myths. This fact stresses what has already become abundantly clear in other ways, that the other hymns appear to be a result of conscious creation relying on Mesopotamian ideas and material. The journeys involved are specific journeys with clear-cut aims and ideas which are expressed in characteristic motifs. The hymn to Hermes also confirms that these structures and ideas seen in the Mesopotamian material are specific and do not apply generally to any sort of journey. Rather, the journeys in the Mesopotamian myths and in the three other hymns are the result of deliberate construction, of which the purpose is to portray certain definite and profound religious ideas about the divine world and the deities involved.

THE JOURNEYS OF ZEUS

The Near Eastern origin of major aspects of Hesiod's *Theogony* has been recognized from the time of the discovery of the Hittite texts *Kingship in Heaven* and *The Myth of Ullikummi*. The succession myth forms the backbone of the *Theogony*, and this idea is generally considered to have been derived from the Near East. It closely parallels similar ideas found in Hittite, Ugaritic, Phoenician and Mesopotamian myths, but the motifs of the myth are in general most like those in the Hittite epics. The parallels and the issues have been discussed in great detail in recent decades and there is no need for further discussion of these here.[6]

6 Hans Gustav Güterbock, 'The Hittite Version of the Hurrian Kumarbi Myths: Oriental Forerunners of Hesiod', AJA 52 (1948) 123–34; W.G. Lambert and P. Walcot, 'A New Babylonian Theogony and Hesiod', *Kadmos* 4 (1965) 64–72; P. Walcot, *Hesiod and the Near East*, University of Wales Press, Cardiff, 1966, *passim*; M.L. West, ed., *Hesiod Theogony*, Clarendon Press, Oxford, 1966, pp.19ff.; G. Komoróczy, 'The Separation of Sky and Earth', AAntHung 21 (1973) 21ff.; G.S. Kirk, *The Nature of Greek Myths*, Penguin Books, Harmondsworth, 1974, pp.26–7, 116ff.; Jacqueline Duchemin, *Prométhée: Histoire du mythe, de ses origines orientales à ses incarnations modernes*, Société d'édition «Les belles lettres», Paris, 1974, pp.33ff.; Jacqueline Duchemin, 'Les mythes de la Théogonie hésiodique. Origines orientales: Essai d'interpretation', in Jean Hani, ed., *Problèmes du mythe et de son interprétation*, Actes du Colloque de Chantilly (24–25 avril 1976), Société d'édition «Les belles lettres», Paris, 1979, pp.51–67; Albert I. Baumgarten, *The Phoenician History of Philo of Byblos: A Commentary*, E.J. Brill, Leiden, 1981, pp.94–139; Henry Podbielski, 'Le mythe cosmogonique dans la *Théogonie* d'Hésiode et les rites orientaux', LEC 52 (1984) 207–16; Robert Mondi, 'The Ascension of Zeus and the Composition of Hesiod's *Theogony*', GRBS 25 (1984) 342ff.; M.L. West, 'Hesiod's Titans', JHS 105 (1985) 174–5; Gérard Naddaf,

However, there are also parallels in certain parts of the rise of Zeus to power which have not been pointed out. Most of these are found in the birth myth of Zeus. The ideas in this myth correspond to many features seen in Mesopotamian myths and take a form very similar to their appearance in the birth of Apollo in his Homeric hymn. Other parallels with Mesopotamian myths are found in Zeus' combat against the monster, named Typhoeus, Typhaon or Typhon, although the parallels in the case of this combat in Hesiod's *Theogony* are only of a general nature.

As with Apollo, Zeus' myths have parallels with the Mesopotamian myths of both strands. On one side, Zeus performs as the heroic champion of the gods who defeats the monster, like Marduk in *Enuma Elish* and, on the other, he seems to be involved in sequences which parallel those of the goddess-and-consort myths of Damu. As with Apollo, the parallels with the latter occur in the myth of his birth.

The birth episode in the *Theogony* resembles a Homeric hymn, as Mondi points out.[7] It also follows the same principles as are seen in the birth of Apollo, and various features parallel those in the myths of the goddess-and-consort strand and in Apollo's birth on Delos. Hesiod's account is typically brief, and seems to consist mostly of references to the events and ideas of the myth.

Rhea crosses to Crete for the birth of her son. When he is born, the vast Earth receives him from Rhea, for she is to nurse and rear him. Earth carries him through the black night, first to Lyktos, and then to woody Mt Aigaios, where she hides him in a deep cave under the earth. As a substitute for Zeus, Earth hands to Kronos a great stone wrapped in swaddling clothes. He takes it and gulps it down, because he has learnt that he is destined to be overcome by his own son.

Swiftly, Zeus's radiant limbs grow and his might increases (μένος

'Hésiode, précurseur des cosmogonies grecques de type «évolutioniste»', RHR 203 (1986) 339–64; Friedrich Solmsen, 'The Two Near Eastern Sources of Hesiod', *Hermes* 117 (1989) 413–22; Robert Mondi, 'Greek Mythic Thought in the Light of the Near East', in Lowell Edmunds, ed., *Approaches to Greek Myth*, Johns Hopkins University Press, Baltimore and London, 1990, pp.151ff. and *passim*; Christoph Auffarth, *Der drohende Untergang: 'Schöpfung' in Mythos und Ritual im Alten Orient und in Griechenland am Beispiel der Odyssee und des Ezechielbuches*, Walter de Gruyter, Berlin and New York, 1991, pp.129–30.
7 Mondi, GRBS 25 (1984) 336ff.

καὶ φαίδιμα γυῖα, line 492). The year passes and Kronos is beguiled by the great wisdom of Earth. Vanquished by the arts and force of his son, he vomits up his other offspring, whom he had swallowed to prevent the destiny revealed to him, bringing forth first the stone that he had swallowed last. Zeus places it in the wide-pathed earth at Delphi, beneath Parnassos.

The general form of these journey sequences appears to follow the ideas of the goddess-and-consort myths, specifically the Damu myths edin-na ú-saĝ-ĝá and TRS 8: the goddess performs a journey, and it results in the birth of the child from the earth.[8] The form of the sequences here follows that of the Delian section of the hymn to Apollo. The same combination of ideas of birth from the earth, or Earth goddess, is found here. Rhea herself is an earth goddess, and the transferral of the child to Earth is just another way of articulating the idea of birth from the earth, which Zeus does when he emerges from the cave deep in the earth on Mt Aigaios (lines 482–4). As in the hymn to Apollo, the mountain symbolism is involved in the birth. In Apollo's myth, it seems to have the symbolism of the emergence from beneath the earth, an emergence which is quite explicit in this birth of Zeus. In any case, as Apollo is born from the earth goddess Leto's womb, as well as from the island/mountain Delos (at Mt Kynthos), so Zeus is born from his mother Rhea and symbolically from the womb of the Earth herself at Mt Aigaios on Crete. The Hellenistic Palai-kastro hymn about the young returning god presents similar ideas to those in these myths, with the same birth from within the earth.[9] This has been discussed in the chapter on Apollo.

Two other motifs found with Apollo's birth-and-ascent sequence are repeated here: the great noise at the birth, and the radiance of his limbs, symbolizing the power of the god. The Kouretes make a frightful din and clash their shields. Similarly, Apollo's nurses cry out in amazement at his birth in his Homeric hymn (line 119). Zeus'

8 For edin-na ú-saĝ-ĝá, see Thorkild Jacobsen, *The Harps that Once . . .: Sumerian Poetry in Translation*, Yale University Press, New Haven and London, 1987, pp.56–84; TRS 8, duplicate version CT XV pls 26–7, 30. For translation of some of the lament and discussion of the story, see Thorkild Jacobsen, *The Treasures of Darkness: A History of Mesopotamian Religion*, Yale University Press, New Haven and London, 1976, pp.68–72.
9 For the hymn, see M.L. West, 'The Dictaean Hymn to the Kouros', JHS 85 (1965) 149–59.

limbs shine with radiance as he grows in might (*Theogony*, 492–3); this motif is parallel to the radiance of Apollo's feet, weapons, lyre and chiton, all of which express his power in the journey sequence as he travels to Olympos after his birth (lines 4, 202–3). Like the light at Apollo's birth, and the light at his ascent in the Pythian section, there is a great blaze of light at Zeus' birth in the mountain cave.[10]

The birth of Zeus is followed by a journey to Olympos, which also parallels the situation in Apollo's hymn. As the powerful Apollo travels to Olympos after his birth, Zeus makes his way to Olympos, where he displays the might into which he has come in the ascent-sequence birth by defeating his father, Kronos. This sequence is only briefly referred to in the *Theogony* (lines 490–7). However, in this sequence, he grows in power as he overcomes his father and succeeds to kingship.[11] Lines 490ff. refer to Zeus' return to Greece and his overthrow of his father. In line 499, Zeus is seen in Greece at Delphi. Kronos is overcome by the arts and force (τέχνῃσι βίηφί τε) of his son.[12] In Ol. 5.17, Pindar indicates that Zeus dispossessed Kronos of Olympos: Σωτὴρ ὑψινεφὲς Ζεῦ, Κρόνιόν τε ναίων λόφον – 'Saviour Zeus high in the clouds, dwelling on the hill of Kronos'. Various lines in the *Theogony* suggest that Zeus' overthrow of Kronos was a violent encounter between the two of them alone, as the Titans are nowhere mentioned in these passages, and nor are Zeus' brothers and sisters (lines 71–4, 490–1). References to the affair in the *Iliad* (14.202–4, 8.10–16) and in other sources support the single-handed overthrow of Kronos by Zeus.[13] In any case, he displays and increases his power in this journey sequence which ends at Olympos.

In Mondi's view, this final part of the myth, involving his expulsion of Kronos and acquisition of his father's kingship, seems to be suppressed in Hesiod's account, which refers only to Earth's deception of Kronos, who vomited forth his offspring, and alludes to

---

10 See the chapter on Apollo for a discussion of these points with Apollo. The Eleusinian divine child, the κοῦρος, is also born to the accompaniment of a great blaze of fire: Nicholas Richardson, *The Homeric Hymn to Demeter*, Clarendon Press, Oxford, 1974, p.318.

11 Mondi, GRBS 25 (1984) 339; cf. Jean Rudhardt, 'A propos de l'hymne homérique à Déméter', MH 35 (1978) 4ff. on Zeus' power (τιμή).

12 Line 146 is included, as it appears to be an integral part of the story. Cf. Mondi, GRBS 25 (1984) 340.

13 ibid., pp.340ff.; see also M.L. West, *Hesiod Theogony*, p.302, on the combination of stratagem and singlehanded physical force; also Podbielski, LEC 52 (1984) 207.

Zeus' defeat of his father (lines 493–6). According to Mondi, the suppression of this part of the myth is necessary in view of Hesiod's desire to include the episode of the Titanomachy, another tale of Zeus' acquisition of kingship, in the sequence of events ending in Zeus' supremacy over the gods. The encounter with Kronos, and the resultant transfer of kingship would have rendered 'a subsequent narrative of an alternative tale of Zeus' rise to power – the Titanomachy – nonsensical'.[14] This may be the case, but on the other hand, the brevity of the reference to Zeus' defeat of his father so that he vomits forth his children is in keeping with the brevity of the rest of this story.

In his combat against Typhoeus (*Theogony*, 820–68), Zeus performs deeds which parallel the activities of the heroic-strand gods Ninurta and Marduk. Like both of these gods, he is the champion of the Assembly. However, he is especially like Marduk, who achieves supreme power over the cosmos. In a similar way to Marduk, he is in power as the king of the Assembly before he goes forth to defeat the monster. This also parallels Ninurta's position of power before he goes out to defeat the Asag monster in *Lugale* (lines 1ff.), but of course Ninurta is not supreme god in the Assembly.

The combat of Zeus against Typhoeus corresponds directly to the combats of Marduk against Tiamat and of Teshub against Ulli-kummi in their rise to power over the cosmos, since these both take place after they come to power as chief god in the Assembly. However, in Hesiod's account, there are no specific parallels with *Enuma Elish* of Marduk or any other Mesopotamian myth. This may be due to the brevity of Hesiod's presentation of the myth, which appears to be merely a reference.[15] The emphasis is on verbose heroic description of the god and his opponent, rather than on the details of the combat.

---

14 Mondi, GRBS 25 (1984) 344. See also Solmsen on this section of the *Theogony*: op. cit., pp.413–22. Cf. also, on the Mesopotamian parallels with the Titans, Walter Burkert, *The Orientalizing Revolution: Near Eastern Influence on Greek Culture in the Early Archaic Age*, Harvard University Press, Cambridge (Mass.), 1992, pp.94–5.

15 On the authenticity of this episode in the *Theogony* and its purpose: Suzanne Said, 'Les combats de Zeus et le problème des interpolations dans la *Théogonie* d'Hésiode', REG 90 (1977) 183–210; Fabienne Blaise, 'L'épisode de Typhée dans la *Théogonie* d'Hésiode (v. 820–85): La stabilisation du monde', REG 105 (1992) 349–70.

Typhoeus is born from Gaia and Tartaros, as a result of Gaia's anger at the Titans' destruction by Zeus and his generation. Typhoeus is described as a terrible monster. He has a hundred serpent heads growing from his shoulders. The noise that he makes varies: at one time it is that of a roaring lion, at others of a bellowing bull, hissing serpents and yelping dogs.

Zeus springs down from Olympos on to the monster, attacking him with thunder, lightning and his thunderbolt. He defeats his monstrous enemy by burning all of his 'marvellous' heads and lashing him with strokes. He hurls him down to earth, on the mountain (line 860), and then throws him into Tartaros. From Typhoeus in the netherworld destructive winds blow over the sea and earth.

One general parallel with Marduk's combat is the lack of initial defeat of the hero (Tablet IV.35–104). Like Marduk, Zeus is the invincible deity and does not suffer initial defeat in his encounter with the monster. This is in accord with Hesiod's purpose in the *Theogony*, which is the elevation of his hero to supreme power; for the same reason and in the same way, the *Enuma Elish* presents the invincible Marduk's unimpeded rise to supremacy. By contrast to the invincibility of Marduk and Zeus, the Hittite god Teshub appears to undergo initial defeat in his combat. He returns to defeat Ullikummi after the intervention of Ea, the helper in this initial-setback structure.[16]

The weapons of Zeus in this combat are those particularly his own in his function of weather god: thunder, lightning and his ubiquitous thunderbolt (lines 853–4). Lightning is found as the weapon of Adad, the storm god, who is urged in the Anzu myth to use it against the

---

16 James B. Pritchard, ed., *Ancient Near Eastern Texts Relating to the Old Testament*, 3rd edition, Princeton University Press, Princeton, 1969, p.125; see pp.121–5 for the whole myth. Regarding the structural elements, the Hittite myths are often considered to be the source of the Typhoeus combat in the *Theogony*: for instance, Said, REG 90 (1977) 204; Duchemin, *Prométhée*, p.33. However, Walcot points to Marduk and *Enuma Elish* as the source, on the basis of comparable structural elements, and the position and nature of Zeus in the *Theogony*: Walcot, *Hesiod and the Near East*, pp.25ff. Said points out the similarity of the structure of Teshub's and Zeus' struggle against the monster after they have gained supreme power, REG 90 (1977) 207. However, this is also the case in *Enuma Elish*.

monster Anzu and save the Assembly (Tablet I.96–7).[17] This is also the weapon of the Assyrian god Assur, who replaces Marduk in the Assyrian version of *Enuma Elish*. Ninurta is depicted on a stone relief at the temple of Kalhu, erected by King Assurnasirpal II in the ninth century BC, attacking Anzu or Asag with the lightning weapon.[18] It is this weapon that Zeus uses rather than the bow and arrow which Ninurta uses against Anzu in the Anzu myth (Tablet II.59–60), and which Marduk uses against Tiamat (*Enuma Elish* Tablet IV.101–3). The bow is the weapon of Apollo, and with it he shoots the Pythian serpent in his version of the heroic-strand combat.[19]

Zeus's defeat of the monster is found in far greater detail in the résumé of Apollodorus, where the monster is named Typhon. This version is, of course, much later in date, at the earliest the first millennium BC. The sources for Apollodorus' account seem to be Hellenistic, but it may still be of interest to examine the later form of this myth, which first appears in Hesiod.

In Apollodorus' version there are many parallels with Near Eastern myths, both Hittite and Mesopotamian. It may be of value to examine the myth to see how far it compares with the Mesopotamian material, although, of course, no conclusions about the parallels with Mesopotamian myths or influence in early archaic times can be based on this examination of so late a source.

Although the version of Apollodorus is much more extensive than that of Hesiod, it is still a résumé of a longer story and most likely includes only features which struck the compiler as necessary, specifically the action of the myth rather than its purpose and the more abstract themes, whether these are stated or not in the original source.

In this account, Zeus and Typhon carry out a journey, fighting their way from Egypt to Syria, through Thrace to Mt Etna in Sicily.

17 For depictions of Adad (Ishkur) with his lightning weapon, see Jeremy Black and Anthony Green, *Gods, Demons and Symbols of Ancient Mesopotamia: An Illustrated Dictionary*, British Museum Press, London, 1992: Ishkur (pp.110–11).

18 The stone relief is depicted in Stephanie Dalley, *Myths from Mesopotamia*, Oxford University Press, Oxford, 1989, frontispiece with caption. She considers that the monster is Anzu; as Anzu or Asag, see Black and Green, *Gods, Demons and Symbols*: Asag (pp.35–6), and Ninurta (pp.142–3) with depiction.

19 *Homeric Hymn to Apollo*, 356–8.

Despite such a summary, the journey is, however, not a simple one, for it is, rather, constructed of a series of episodes which take place at different locations. The power of Zeus is naturally an aspect of the myth, since it forms part of his rise to power, at least as it appears in the account in the *Theogony*. It appears to be a matter of retention of power in the face of a serious threat rather than of a rise of any sort to power. The idea of a journey for power does not seem to be involved. Instead, it appears to be simply a tale of the god's heroic activities in defeating a great and terrible monster. Interestingly, however, there are several features concerning the power of the god which parallel those in various Near Eastern monster-combat myths.

Apollodorus I.vi.3 relates that the defeat of the Giants angered the earth goddess Gê, so she coupled with Tartaros and gave birth to Typhon,[20] the strongest and most terrible of all her children. The monster's form was a mixture of man and beast, and he was so huge that his head reached higher than the mountains and often touched the stars. From head to thigh, he was human in form; and his hands reached from the east to the west. Attached to each of his hands were a hundred vipers' heads.[21] From the thighs down grew great coils of vipers, which writhed upward to his head and hissed mightily. His body was winged, and his head and cheeks covered in matted hair, which floated in the wind. Fire flashed in his eyes.

Typhon hurled red-hot rocks at the sky itself, and rushed towards it hissing and shouting, and a great storm of fire boiled forth from his mouth. The gods saw him coming and fled towards Egypt to escape. As Typhon pursued them, they changed themselves into animal shapes.[22]

Zeus threw thunderbolts from a distance and, when he had drawn closer, tried to cut him down with an adamantine sickle. Typhon took flight and fled to Mt Casios, above Syria, but Zeus followed on his heels. Seeing that the monster was badly wounded, the god made

---

20 As in Hesiod's *Theogony*, 820–2.

21 In Pindar, P.i.16, the hundred serpents spring from Typhon's shoulders instead of from his human head. Aeschylus also describes Typhon as Pindar does, with a hundred serpents' heads, in *Prometheus Desmotes*, 351–72. The same idea seems to be involved in Apollodorus' description, where the snakes' heads rise around his head.

22 As in Pindar, frag. 91; and Ovid, *Metamorphoses*, 5.321–31. Considered a motif of Egyptian origin: cf. West, *Hesiod Theogony*, p.380. The transformation of the gods into different animal shapes as they cross the sky may have its origin in their crossing the lines of the Zodiac.

the mistake of engaging in hand-to-hand combat. Typhon entwined Zeus in his coils and, holding him fast, seized the sickle and cut out the sinews from Zeus' hands and feet. Setting the god on his shoulders, he carried him across the sea to Cilicia and deposited him in the Corycian cave. He then hid the sinews in a bearskin and placed Delphyne – half-maiden, half-dragoness – as guard.

However, Hermes and Aigipan stole back the sinews and surreptitiously replanted them in Zeus. The god, now strong again, appeared suddenly from the sky, driving a chariot drawn by winged horses. He hurled thunderbolts at Typhon and chased him to Mt Nysa. The Moirai there deceived the monster, giving him some of Mt Nysa's ephemeral fruit to eat, which they persuaded him would give him strength. With Zeus pursuing, Typhon fled from there to Thrace and, while fighting around Mt Haimos, threw whole mountains at Zeus. When the god pushed them back on to him by means of his thunderbolts, a great quantity of the monster's blood flowed out on to the mountain. (This is, allegedly, the reason for its name of Haimos.) Typhon fled again, now through the Sicilian sea, and Zeus finished him off by bringing Mt Aetna down on him. It is said that Aetna still erupts fire from the thunderbolts which Zeus threw.

In Typhon, Zeus overcomes the last threat to his kingship and power. An interesting motif of the power theme in this myth is that of Zeus' sinews (ἶς), of which he is deprived by Typhon who thus renders him powerless. This motif appears to be a result of a pun on the homophone ἶς, which means 'strength', 'force'. This motif is important regarding the theme of power of the god, and it parallels motifs found with the Mesopotamian heroic-strand gods: it reiterates the idea of the powers themselves, the me and the Tablet of Destinies, that are lost and gained by the Mesopotamian deities.

A number of motifs of this myth of Typhon parallel motifs in extant combat myths of the Near East. Parallel features are found in Marduk's epic *Enuma Elish*, in Ninurta's myths, in both the combats against Anzu and Asag and also, to some extent, in the Hittite myths concerning Illuyanka and Ullikummi.

One such motif is the idea of the threat of the monster to the Assembly of the gods before the champion goes forth to defeat the menace. This general structural motif is found in the *Enuma Elish* (Tablets II.1–IV.34). A far stronger parallel is that of the initial defeat of the hero, a complex structural feature which is seen in the Anzu and Asag myths of Ninurta.[23] In these Mesopotamian myths the god is defeated in the mountains, receives help, and then returns to the fight to defeat the monster. In a similar way Zeus receives his initial defeat at Mt Casios when Typhon overwhelms the god and takes away his sinews, his 'powers'; helpers, Hermes and Aigipan, come to the aid of the defeated Zeus, and with his sinews restored Zeus returns to the fray and defeats the monster. The element of this combat that is not found as part of the initial defeat in the Mesopotamian myths is the theft of the 'powers' from the monster by the helpers. The parallel for this is found in the later version of the Hittite Illuyanka myth.

The helper role of Hermes in the sequence parallels that of Sharur, the weapon and messenger of Ninurta in the Asag myth. Aigipan, of course, plays the same helper role as does Hermes. His name recalls the deity Pan, the half-goat inhabitant of mountainous regions.[24] However, it also recalls, in the context of this myth where he helps in returning power to Zeus, the *aegis* of Zeus, variously his goatskin shield, weapon and emblem. As such he is a parallel figure to Sharur, who is both the weapon and the helper of Ninurta.

Following the initial setback and the receipt of help, the deity then returns to defeat the monster. His strength restored, Zeus bursts forth from heaven in a chariot drawn by winged horses and hurls his weapon at the monster. The motif is especially reminiscent of the tableau in *Enuma Elish* of Marduk driving forth from the abode of the gods in the Assembly against Tiamat in his 'storm-chariot' drawn by four mighty horses (Tablet IV.48–60).

Besides the initial defeat, little else in the journey of Zeus and Typhon corresponds to the journey structures in Mesopotamian combat myths. Nevertheless, various features in the episodes of the combat itself parallel other features of Near Eastern myths. The motif of the Graces' tricking Typhon into eating the ephemeral fruit which grew on Mt Nysa may have a Hittite parallel, as the motif of food in the defeat of the monster is seen in the older version of the myth of the dragon Illuyanka.[25] The goddess Inara persuaded Illuyanka and his brood to come to a feast, and when the bloated Illuyanka was unable to return to his lair, the mortal hero of the myth caught and

23 Anzu myth: Tablet II.1–149 and Tablet III obv. i, lines 2–12; *Lugale*, 151–297.
24 Keith Aldrich, *Apollodorus: The Library of Greek Mythology*, Coronado Press, Lawrence, 1975, p.118.
25 Pritchard, *Ancient Near Eastern Texts*, pp.125–6.

trussed him with rope and he was then killed by the storm god. The only similarity between the Hittite myth and that of Typhon is this motif – the tricking of the monster into eating the food, and the part played by the food in the defeat of the monster – so the correspondence is not very strong.

However, there is another motif which may parallel a Hittite example: the theft of the god's bodily parts. This motif occurs in the later version of the Illuyanka myth, in which Illuyanka vanquishes Teshub and takes his eyes and heart. Against the correspondence of the myths, however, is the fact that the parts are quite different and the method by which they are regained to allow the god's return to destroy the monster is also quite different.[26]

The last two episodes of Typhon's defeat, those at Mt Haimos and at Mt Etna, present two examples of the monster's defeat which have similarities to the events portrayed in the Asag myth of Ninurta, and in the catalogue section of *Enuma Elish* under the SIR.SIR epithet (Tablet VII.70–5). The main motifs are those of bringing the mountain down on the monster, and of water or blood issuing forth from beneath the mountain. In his epic, Marduk brings down a mountain on the river Tiamat. Earlier in the epic in the main combat, Tiamat's blood, in the form of water since she is the salt-water ocean, flows from the defeated monster (Tablet IV.32, 131–2). In the Asag myth, Ninurta lays waste the mountainland and then transforms the defeated Asag into a pile of rocks, the mountain hursağ which is built over the kur (*Lugale* 327, 349–52). Waters of the kur flow out from beneath it, over the earth (lines 354–9). The motif in the Greek myth corresponds in a vague way to these Mesopotamian examples: Typhon, now in the Thracian mountain regions, throws mountains at Zeus, but the god pushes them back on top of him, and Typhon's blood (αἷμα) flows forth, although in this myth it is limited to flowing over the mountain Haimos. Similar to Ninurta's placing the mountain over the kur is Zeus' feat in bringing down Mt Etna on top of Typhon as he flees through the sea.

A motif found with the defeated Typhon in Pindar's first Pythian ode (lines 15ff.) seems to give Typhon a water-monster nature and parallels a motif found in a Mesopotamian creation myth. Here Typhon lies under Aetna, but also under Cumae, and it is at Cumae that the sea-dykes are set over him. In particular, this recalls the scene

---

26 See ibid., p.126; and cf. West's comments in *Hesiod Theogony*, pp.380, 391–2.

of Ea and the Apsu in the *Epic of Atrahasis* (Tablet I.15–18), where Ea erects dykes, or bars, over the nether-sea Apsu to keep it in its place.

The myth as it appears in Apollodorus therefore has similarities with features of the main Near Eastern monster-combat and other myths. Indeed, it seems to be a pot-pourri of motifs recalling elements of those myths. The initial-setback structure is the strongest parallel, but the motifs of burying the monster under a mountain and fixing the sea-dykes over Typhon seem also to be quite strong correspondences. Apart from these, however, the other motifs which parallel Mesopotamian and Hittite material are not at all specific, but rather general, in the same way as the description of Typhon is vaguely reminiscent of Mesopotamian monsters but does not recall any one monster. There are, in addition, a host of features which do not parallel any in Mesopotamian and Hittite monster combats. Consequently, if this myth does owe anything to Near Eastern material, it would seem to be a construct of vague recollections of various Mesopotamian combat myths, including some Hittite material, combined with much non-Mesopotamian material, rather than being influenced by any one single myth.

Although it is interesting to note that there are many parallels with Near Eastern myths, it must be stressed that this discussion has no bearing on the parallels between early archaic Greek myth and the Mesopotamian myths, or on the question of influence, since the account of Apollodorus is of a much later date. The length and detail of the story does suggest, however, that there was much more to the older story of Zeus and Typhoeus than Hesiod included in his brief reference in the *Theogony*.

9

PANDORA, PROMETHEUS AND THE MYTHS OF ENKI

We come now to one of the most fascinating of the Greek myths, the myth of Prometheus and Pandora, which involves the creation of Pandora, the first woman. Hesiod presents this myth in both the *Theogony* and *Works and Days*, in two versions which differ in some respects. However, Pandora's creation is only part of the myth of Prometheus' rebellion against Zeus and its results, and the entire myth is of concern here. There is a great deal of depth to the ideas involved in this myth. The story of Pandora is the most outstanding part: it is, in effect, like the melody of a song, the pretty and attractive part of a complete musical composition, with the chord progressions, base and harmonies that provide its basis going largely unperceived. The creation of Pandora is in reality only part of a whole set of beliefs concerning the creation and early history of mankind which in Hesiod's versions has been used to emphasize another aspect of the supremacy of Zeus. The beliefs are seen in the myths of Pandora and other material related to the creation and early history of mankind, some details of which are found outside the story of Prometheus and Pandora in the *Theogony* and *Works and Days*. These details are seen in other places in Hesiod's work and in other sources.

The myth of Prometheus and Pandora presents many ideas on the creation of mankind, but it also contains an ascent sequence with an intriguing application of the idea of the journey for power. In all aspects of the myths many detailed parallels with Mesopotamian myths can be seen, particularly parallels with the myths of the important god Enki. These myths of Enki involve the Mesopotamian tradition of the creation and early history of mankind.

Some years ago Jacqueline Duchemin pointed out a number of similarities, especially those concerning the parallel functions and

197

characteristics of Enki and Prometheus.[1] There are, however, many more points of correspondence than have been noted by Duchemin and other scholars, and they go far beyond similarities between Prometheus and Enki. The additional points of correspondence involve especially the myths of the creation-of-mankind tradition and Pandora. In fact, the comprehensiveness of the parallels between the myth of Prometheus and Pandora and the myths of Enki is phenomenal. In particular, there are numerous and extensive similarities with the *Epic of Atrahasis*, the most comprehensive work of the Mesopotamian tradition of the creation and early history of man, and these have yet to be pointed out.

Creation-of-mankind ideas are found in Hesiod's *Theogony* and *Works and Days*, not in the creation of men, but rather in the creation of Pandora, the first woman, as lines 590–3 in the *Theogony* state quite clearly:[2]

> For from her is the race of very female women,
> [for of her is the destructive race and tribes of women][3]
> a great calamity for mortal men with whom they dwell,
> not companions in accursed poverty, but in wealth.

---

1 Jacqueline Duchemin, *Prométhée: Histoire du mythe, de ses origines orientales à ses incarnations modernes*, Société d'édition «Les belles lettres», Paris, 1974, 'Le mythe du Déluge retrouvé dans des sources grecques?', RHR 189 (1976) 142–4, and 'Le Zeus d'Eschyle et ses sources proche-orientales', RHR 197 (1980) 27–44; also 'Le mythe de Prométhée et ses sources orientales', REG 88 (1975) viii–x.

2 This is the accepted interpretation of the lines: cf. M.L. West, ed., *Hesiod Theogony*, Clarendon Press, Oxford, 1966, p.305. Heinz Neitzel put forward the view that Hesiod does not mean that Pandora was the first woman, comparing the passage to Semonides' work on the different types of women: 'Pandora und das Faß', *Hermes* 104 (1976) 411–13. But this is a much later and quite different work with a different purpose. In addition, the real force of Hesiod's disapprobation of womankind, and he means all of womankind in this passage, as the alternative line indicates (line 591), depends on the literal interpretation of Hesiod's naming of Pandora as the first woman. On the inconsistencies between the various sections of Hesiod's poems, see Robert Mondi, 'The Ascension of Zeus and the Composition of Hesiod's Theogony', GRBS 25 (1984) 325ff.

ἐκ τῆς γὰρ γένος ἐστὶ γυναικῶν θηλυτεράων,
[τῆς γὰρ ὀλοίιόν ἐστι γένος καὶ φῦλα γυναικῶν,]
πῆμα μέγα θνητοῖσι, σὺν ἀνδράσι ναιετάουσαι,
οὐλομένης Πενίης οὐ σύμφοροι, ἀλλὰ Κόροιο.

Lines 570–89 in the *Theogony* and lines 60–89 in *Works and Days* present the story of Pandora's creation.

The version in the *Theogony*

The god Prometheus matched his wits with the mighty son of Kronos, and angered the supreme god by playing a trick on him when the immortal gods and mortal men were separated at the feast of Mekone. The wily god divided an ox into two portions. He covered the flesh and entrails with the ox-stomach and placed this before mankind, while he dressed up the bones in white fat to look good, and placed this before Zeus. When the supreme god commented on the unfair manner of dividing the portions, Prometheus cunningly offered him the choice of the portions. Zeus, 'who knows immortal counsels', nevertheless did not fail, Hesiod says, to discern the trick. Having chosen the superficially more attractive portion, he lifted up the white fat, and reacted angrily when he saw the bones beneath. (Because of Prometheus' distribution, the tribes of men burn bones on their altars to the gods.)

In retaliation for the clever Prometheus' trick, Zeus withheld fire from the 'Melian race of mortal men'. Undeterred, however, Prometheus stole the fire and gave it to mankind.[4] When Zeus saw that man had fire, he was very angry and planned an evil thing for men as its price. According to his will, Hephaistos moulded from earth the likeness of a maiden. Gleaming-eyed Athena adorned her with silver-shining raiment and covered her head with a long embroidered veil, a wonder to see. She placed on the maiden's head a beautiful golden crown, wrought by Hephaistos to please Zeus. On it were sculpted many curious and wonderful things, many wild creatures of land and sea, marvellous things like living creatures with voices.

When he had made the beautiful evil, Hephaistos led her out to where the gods and men were; the maiden exalted in the adornments

---

3 This line, 591, is alternative for line 590. Cf. West, *Hesiod Theogony*, pp.329–30.

4 Aeschylus says that the fire was stolen from Hephaistos: *Desmotes*, 7, 38.

that Athena had given to her. The gods and men marvelled at what was a sheer inescapable trap for mankind.

For from Pandora comes the race of women, a calamity for mortal men, companions only in wealth, not in poverty, who feed like drones on the labour of others. Zeus made women to be an inescapable evil for men, to afflict them with painful toils, and to be a source of unabating grief.

Thus it is not possible to cheat or outwit Zeus. Not even clever Prometheus escaped his heavy anger. Zeus bound him with painful bands, drove a pillar through his middle, and set on him a long-winged eagle, which would eat his liver during the day. Since he was immortal, his liver would grow back at night. However, Heracles later killed the eagle and released the son of Iapetos from his evil distress, according to the will of Olympian Zeus who rules on high (lines 321–2).

The version of *Works and Days*

Hesiod tells generally the same story in *Works and Days*, but it differs in some respects, particularly in the treatment of the creation of Pandora, and of her effects. While Hesiod's main purpose in the *Theogony* account is to illustrate another aspect of the authority of Zeus, the initial purpose of his narration in *Works and Days* is to explain why men have to toil so hard for their living.

After Zeus had hidden fire and Prometheus had stolen it for mankind, Zeus angrily declared revenge (lines 54–8):

> Son of Iapetos, surpassing all in cunning plans,
> you are pleased that you have deceived my mind;
> > but to you and to mankind it will be a great distress.
> To them, for the price of fire, will I give an evil in which all
> who see it may rejoice in their spirit while they lovingly
> > embrace the evil.

So said Zeus, the father of gods and men, and laughed aloud. He commanded Hephaistos, urging him to hasten, to mix water and earth and create a lovely maiden with a face 'like the immortal goddesses'; Athena was commanded to adorn and teach her, and Aphrodite to pour attractiveness and painful desire over her; but he ordered Hermes to put in her a shameless mind and a wily character.

Accordingly, Hephaistos moulded earth into the image of a revered maiden; Athena clothed her; Peitho and the Charites adorned her with golden necklaces; and the Seasons crowned her head with spring flowers. Athena fitted each adornment on her. In her breast, however, Hermes put lies, wheedling words and a crafty character. He also gave her speech, and called her Pandora, because each of the gods on Olympos gave her a gift.

When he had finished the utterly irresistible snare, Zeus sent Hermes to lead the gift to Epimetheus. Although his brother, Prometheus, had warned him never to take a gift from Zeus lest it be harmful to men, Epimetheus ('Afterthought') took it and understood the evil only once he possessed it.

Before this event, men lived free from evils, hard toil and painful diseases, but the woman took the lid off the jar (*pithos*) and scattered all of its contents, except for hope (or expectation). Consequently, countless miseries and diseases roam about among mankind, silent because Zeus took their voices away. So it is not possible to escape Zeus.

The myth of the creation of Pandora in Hesiod strongly recalls the creation-of-mankind myths of Enki. The combination of god and goddess, Hephaistos and Athena, in the creation, and the method of creation presented here, directly parallel the ideas in the myths in which Enki creates mankind, in co-operation with the creatrix and birth goddess Ninmah (also named Mami, Ninhursağ, and so forth). In the mythological work *Enki and Ninmah*, for example, Enki plans the fashioning of figurines of men from clay, and the mother goddess, accompanied by Ninmah and various birth goddesses, gives them birth, and their fate in society is decreed (lines 30–44).[5] In the Atrahasis epic also, another work in which Enki is the hero, Enki co-operates with Mami to create mankind, and the method used is also directly parallel to the method used in the creation of Pandora. Enki kneads clay and models figurines of men and women, and the goddess brings them to birth, with the assistance of other birth goddesses.[6]

5 Carlos Benito, '*Enki and Ninmah* and *Enki and the World Order*', Ph.D. diss., University Microfilms, Ann Arbor, 1969; Samuel Noah Kramer and John Maier, *Myths of Enki, the Crafty God*, Oxford University Press, New York and Oxford, 1989, pp.31–7, 211–15.
6 Tablet I.189–260 and K 3399+3934 obv. iii lines 1–14. Text and translation: W.G. Lambert and A.R. Millard, *Atra-hasis: The Babylonian Story of the Flood*, Clarendon Press, Oxford, 1969; translation: Stephanie Dalley, *Myths from Mesopotamia*, Oxford University Press, Oxford, 1989, pp.1–38.

The same process is followed in Hesiod: Hephaistos mixes earth and water to make clay, and models the figurine of a woman, and Athena completes the task of creation by dressing and adorning her (*Theogony*, 571–84); in *Works and Days* she is assisted by other goddesses (lines 60–6).

A similar idea of the goddess's role in the creation to that found with Mami is seen clearly in the account of Pandora's creation in Hyginus, who states that Athena gave Pandora *anima* (*Fabulae*, 144). Likewise, in *Enki and Ninmah*, the goddess gives life to men and women by bringing them to birth (lines 30–7);[7] and in the Atrahasis epic Mami also completes the task and gives life to the figurines of men and women. In the Atrahasis epic, however, the goddess completes the creation in a more complex way than in *Enki and Ninmah*, as she uses Mesopotamian midwifery techniques and the help of birth goddesses to bring them to birth.[8] Nevertheless, while the method of Mami in the Atrahasis epic differs, the purpose of her actions and their effect are the same as Athena's.

In the Pandora myth, the creation is specifically of the first woman, and this seems to be a feature of *Enki and Ninmah*. The same idea of woman's creation taking place after the creation of man is involved here, as the prior existence of men appears to be assumed in the *Theogony*. In *Enki and Ninmah*, the creation of the child-bearing woman is a result of a competition between Enki and Ninmah, at a feast which is being held to celebrate the creation of men to take over the gods' burden of toiling for food (lines 83–7).[9] In the Atrahasis epic, men and women come into existence at the same time.[10]

An important feature strongly reminiscent of the Babylonian cult of Marduk can also be seen in the form of the creation scene in Hesiod's accounts. Zeus's role in the creation is identical to that of Marduk in the creation scene of the Babylonian epic *Enuma Elish* (Tablet VI.1–48). This work takes over the mythology of Enki's

7 Wilfred G. Lambert, 'The Relationship of Sumerian and Babylonian Myths as seen in Accounts of Creation', in *La Circulation des biens, des personnes et des idées dans le Proche-Orient ancien, XXXVIIIe R.A.I.*, Éditions Recherche sur les Civilisations, Paris, 1992, pp.130–1.

8 K 3399+3934 obv. lines 3–14.

9 For the text of *Enki and Ninmah*, see Benito, '*Enki and Ninmah*', pp.20–44. See also Bendt Alster's comments and interpretation in '"Enki and Ninhursağ", Creation of the First Woman', UF 10 (1978) 26–7.

10 K 3399+3934 obv. iii lines 9–14.

creation of man as it is in the Atrahasis epic,[11] and attempts to attribute it to Marduk. As the tradition is seen in the OB Atrahasis epic, Enki (who is presented as the skilful god of craft, the clever god of wisdom, and the benefactor of mankind) conceives the idea of the creation and the method of bringing it about, and constructs mankind with the help of the goddess (Tablet I.189ff.). In Marduk's epic, Enki, or Ea as he is called there, still does the actual creation – he mixes clay and water, moulds mankind, and so on – but the epic attributes it, rather clumsily, to Marduk, claiming that he thought of it first and planned it (Tablet VI.4–7, 48). This same configuration of roles is found here in Hesiod: Zeus orders the creation and it is presented as his plan (*Works and Days*, 83–4 even claims that Zeus created Pandora), while Hephaistos and Athena, in accordance with the pattern in the Enki myths, actually do the manual labour of creation. The co-operation of the creating god and goddess in Hesiod corresponds to the tradition as it is seen in Enki's myths, rather than Marduk's epic, for the goddess is omitted, for some reason, in the creation scene of *Enuma Elish*. The various elements of the Greek account therefore recall the versions of the tradition represented in these different sources.

The Pandora material also presents the other creation method of the creation of mankind which is attested in Mesopotamian myths, the agricultural method, where man ascends like plants from beneath the earth, as though from the womb of Earth. Hesiod's accounts of Pandora's creation do not show this aspect, but it appears in the pottery depictions of the myth, on which Pandora is seen emerging from the soil.

The Mesopotamian tradition can be seen in, for example, *Enlil and the Pickaxe* :

> (And Enlil) drove his pickaxe into the *uzu-e*
> In the hole (which he thus made) was the vanguard
> (sağ: head) of mankind,
>
> (And) while (the people of) his land were breaking up
> through the ground (like plants) toward Enlil
> He eyed his black-headed ones in steadfast fashion.[12]

11 J. Bottéro, *Mythes et rites de Babylone*, Slatkine–Champion, Paris, 1985, pp.153–4.

uzu-è ᵍⁱˢal-a-[ni mi-n]i-in-dù
sag nam-lú-ulú ù-šub-ba mi-ni-gál
ᵈen-líl-šè kalam-ma-ni ki mu-un-ši-in-dar<-re>
sag-gi₆-ga-ni-še igi-zi nam-mi-in-bar

And in *Enki's Journey to Nippur* (lines 1–4):

In those remote days, when destiny was determined,
In a year (full of abundance), which An (Heaven) had created,
When people sprang up from the earth like herbs (and) plants,[13]
(Then) the Lord Enki, lord of the Abzu . . . (built his temple in
Eridu).[14]

u₄-ri-a nam ba-tar-ra-ba
mu hé-gál an ù-tu-da
un-e ú-šim-ginₓ ki-in-dar-ra-ba
en-abzu lugal ᵈen-ki-ke₄

Pandora's agricultural creation, or birth from within the earth, is in
the scene on a volute crater of about 440 BC, on which the figures are
named. The crater depicts Epimetheus holding an agricultural
implement, a clod-breaking mallet, and Pandora rising fully dressed
out of the earth with her arms raised. Epimetheus is clearly receiving
the woman, looking down at her as she is still waist down in the earth,
and holding out his hand to her as she looks up at him. Zeus is
depicted on the other side of Pandora, seeming to give instructions to
Hermes: Zeus faces Hermes, who is looking back at the supreme god,
poised for departure. A period of time clearly intervenes between the
events portrayed by the two pairs of figures: Zeus speaking to
Hermes, and Epimetheus receiving the rising Pandora.[15] This follows
the account in *Works and Days* (lines 83–5).

12 Translation and Sumerian text: Thorkild Jacobsen, 'Sumerian Mythology:
A Review Article', JNES 5 (1946) 128–52. For the article, see also William
L. Moran, *Toward the Image of Tammuz and Other Essays on Mesopotamian History and Culture, Thorkild Jacobsen*, Harvard University
Press, Cambridge (Mass.), 1970, pp.112ff.
13 Or, more correctly, 'when (people) split open the ground like herbs and
plants': Dr J.A. Black, The Oriental Institute, Oxford University, private
correspondence.
14 For translation and Sumerian text, see Abdul-Hadi A. Al-Fouadi, *'Enki's
Journey to Nippur*: The Journeys of the Gods', Ph.D. diss., University
Microfilms, Ann Arbor, 1969, pp.69–85.
15 Oxford 525 volute crater; M.L. West, ed., *Hesiod Works and Days*,
Clarendon Press, Oxford, 1978, p.165; ARV 1562 no.4; for the scene,

The same rise of Pandora, with similar agricultural overtones, is shown on a London red-figured amphora of the third quarter of the fifth century BC, on one side of which a woman rises from the earth, half out of the soil, with her arms raised to a male figure, presumably Epimetheus, who stands holding a pickaxe. On the other side, Hephaistos stands looking at a woman's head emerging from a *pithos*.[16]

A similar idea is presented in a scene on a black-figured vase on which the huge head of Pandora rises from the ground, while two satyrs, fertility figures, standing on either side, strike the emerging head with mallets.[17] This scene may symbolize a number of ideas in connection with the rising Pandora, but it is especially reminiscent of the idea of the emerging head of mankind in Enlil's myth of the creation of mankind, *Enlil and the Pickaxe*, in which the god strikes the earth with his pickaxe, an agricultural implement, and the 'head of mankind' emerges.

The birth of mankind from the meeting of Heaven and Earth, or from the Earth fertilized by the rain of Heaven, is one version of the agricultural method of creation in Mesopotamia. This can be seen in the passage: [18]

> Après que le déluge eut ravagé (la terre) . . .
> que l'espèce humaine fut créée à jamais,

JHS 21 (1901) 3, pl. 1. The find-spot of the volute crater is not recorded. According to Beazley, the painter is Alkimachos II, ARV 1562.

16 London, British Museum, F 147, officially stated to have come from the Basilicata in South Italy; see William Berg, 'Pandora: Pathology of a Creation Myth', *Fabula* 17 (1976) 20, for a drawing of the scene; likewise A.B. Cook, *Zeus*, vol. III, Cambridge University Press, Cambridge, 1940, p.352 (comments on pp.349–53).

17 Find-spot unknown. C. Kerenyi, *The Gods of the Greeks*, Thames & Hudson, New York, 1951, p.219, for the scene and comments; Charles Lenormant and Jean J.A.M. de Witte, *Elite des monuments céramographiques, matériaux pour l'histoire des religions et des moeurs de l'antiquité, etc.*, tome I, Paris, 1844, pl. 52. Cf. bell crater, Stockholm 6, from Magna Graeca, ARV 1053 no. 40 (by Polygnotos and his group).

18 Source BM 23103: J. van Dijk, *Lugal ud me-lám-bi nirğál: Le récit épique et didactique des Travaux de Ninurta, du Déluge et de la Nouvelle Création*, vol. 1, E.J. Brill, Leiden, 1983, pp.31–2. For Sumerian, see E. Sollberger, 'The Rulers of Lagaš', *JCS* 21 (1967) 280–1 (lines 1–5). See also Marie-Joseph Seux, 'La création du monde et de l'homme dans la littérature suméro–akkadienne', in Fabien Blanquart, ed., *La Création dans l'Orient ancien*, Congrès de l'Association Catholique Française pour l'Étude de la Bible, Lille, 1985, Les Éditions du Cerf, Paris, 1987, pp.60–1.

que la semence de l'humanité fut déposée (par le Ciel
dans la Terre)
que le peuple, les têtes-noires, d'eux-mêmes eurent
surgi (de la Terre)

[e-gir a-m]a-ru ba-ùr-ra-ta
[ù gi]l-le-èm kur-ra-gé ba-an-g̃ar-ra-ta
n[am]-l[ú]-lu$_8$ da-re-eš i-nà-a-ba
numun nam-lú-[l]u$_8$ im-mi-in-tag$_4$-a-ba
ukù sag̃ g̃i$_6$-ga im-bi-a im-mi-in-íl-la-a-ba

This can also be seen in Hesiod's account, especially in the *Theogony*.
The existence of men before the creation of Pandora is assumed in the
Theogony, and in the Pandora episode the existing men appear to be
called 'the Melians' (lines 563–4).[19] In this context Hesiod appears to be
thinking of the Melian nymphs (tree nymphs), the nymphs born from
Heaven and Earth; and the race of men from the Melian nymphs are the
first known to the ordinary Greek tradition.[20] The Melian nymphs are
a source of mankind in *Works and Days* (line 187) also, as the origin of
the bronze race. In the *Theogony* (lines 174–87), the Meliai are born as
a result of the meeting of Heaven and Earth: when Kronos castrated
Heaven, as Heaven descended to lie on Earth, drops of blood showered
over Earth, and among the creatures to whom Earth gave birth as a
result were the Meliai. Both ideas of the creation of mankind by
Heaven and Earth – the meeting of Heaven and Earth, and Earth's
fertilization by Heaven – are therefore represented in the creation of
the Melian nymphs, and this parallels the Mesopotamian tradition.
This reference in Hesiod to the birth of men from the earth via the
Meliai is also consistent with the reference in Pindar (N. 6. 1ff.), who
speaks of the common origin of men and gods from Mother Earth.[21]

An ascent idea, a rise from the netherworld – that is, from the
region beneath the surface of the earth – appears to be involved in the
creation of Pandora and her delivery to Epimetheus. This can be seen

19 Even omitting the corrupt line 564, this must be the sense of lines 562–3.
20 West, ed., *Hesiod Theogony*, p.221. Melian nymphs the mothers of
     mankind: M.L. West, 'The Prometheus Trilogy', JHS 99 (1979) 130–48.
     Contrast N.B. Booth's treatment of μελιῆσι in 'The Chorus of *Pro-
     metheus Pyrphoros* and Hesiod *Th*. 563', JHS 105 (1985) 149–50.
21 Also *Works and Days*, 108 on the common origin of man and gods: see
     Duchemin, RHR 189 (1976) 142–4; cf. Reynal Sorel, 'Finalité et origine
     des hommes chez Hésiode', RMM 87 (1982) 30, on line 108; and G.S.
     Kirk, *The Nature of Greek Myths*, Penguin Books, Harmondsworth,
     1974, p.272.

with particular clarity on the pottery depictions of the myth as it is told in Hesiod's accounts. In all of these scenes mentioned above, Pandora is seen ascending from beneath the earth. A further example of her rise is shown on an Apulian crater of the third quarter of the fourth century BC, on which she rises from the earth holding a torch, her head adorned with 'the diadem and flowers mentioned in Hesiod's account'.[22] Pandora rises in these scenes, emerging from the soil in the same way as Gaia, Pherephatta (Persephone) and Aphrodite are depicted in other pottery scenes.[23]

That this idea also underlies Hesiod's accounts of the creation of Pandora is expected in view of the pottery depictions where the ἄνοδος from beneath the earth is clearly evident, and it is also shown by several features in Hesiod's accounts. However, as the ascent sequence appears in Hesiod it lacks the agricultural aspect, and in fact many ideas found attached to it in Pandora's myth closely follow ideas seen in the ascent of Inanna/Ishtar in ID and AV. One of the major ideas found with the ascent sequence in ID and AV is the connotation of birth and coming-to-life in the upperworld, and this appears to be its main usage with Pandora. In the Mesopotamian myth, the goddess is revived and returns to the upperworld, the land of the living (ID 279–90; AV 118–26). The similar usage of the ascent with the idea of coming to life has already been seen in Greek myth in the birth of Apollo in the Delian section of the *Homeric Hymn to Apollo* (lines 119–42). This has been demonstrated in the discussion of the Delian section in the chapter on Apollo. The idea is also found with Zeus Kretagenes, when the god is born from the earth in an ascent sequence (*Theogony*, 477–500).[24] The idea of coming to life in an ascent sequence by being 'born' from the earth is conspicuously apparent with Pandora, with whom it can clearly be seen in the pottery scenes.

---

22 See *Theogony*, 576–7; quotation from Berg, *Fabula* 17 (1976) 22. For this scene, see A.D. Trendall, 'Three Apulian Kraters in Berlin', *Jahrbuch der Berliner Museen* 12 (1970) 168–70, figs 10 and 12. Cf. ARV 612 no.1, c. 445 BC, Ferrara T. 579 from Spina, in *Hesperia* 24, pl.88, b and *Rheinisches Museum* 47, 124.

23 Patricia A. Marquardt, 'Hesiod's Ambiguous View of Woman', CPh 77 (1982) 285–6, 290–1. N.J. Richardson, *The Homeric Hymn to Demeter*, Clarendon Press, Oxford, 1974, p.285. West, ed., *Hesiod Works and Days*, pp.164ff.; Martin Nilsson, *Opuscula Selecta*, Lund, 1951–2, pp.611ff.

24 Zeus' birth is also discussed together with that of Apollo in the chapter on Apollo. See also the chapter on the journeys of Zeus.

A number of features indicates the presence of the idea of the ascent sequence in Hesiod's accounts, and these features parallel those found in the ascent sequence of Inanna/Ishtar in ID and AV.

The escort in the journey is a feature of the ascent sequence, and the ascent sequence in Hesiod's accounts, where the audience's knowledge of it seems to be otherwise assumed, appears to be referred to by means of this motif. The motif is found connected with the dressing in the ascent in both Pandora's myth and in Ishtar's, and the figure who acts as escort in one account of Hesiod is closely similar to the figure in AV. In her ascent, Ishtar is dressed as she is led to the upperworld, and so too is Pandora led, after she is dressed, on a journey to the gods (lines 118–25) and Epimetheus. Ishtar is escorted by the netherworld figure Namtar, while in *Works and Days* Hermes, the *psychopompos* of Hades, leads Pandora to Epimetheus (lines 83–5):

> But when he had finished the sheer, irresistible snare,
> the Father sent the glorious Slayer of Argos to Epimetheus
> leading the gift, the swift messenger of the gods.

> αὐτὰρ ἐπεὶ δόλον αἰπὺν ἀμήχανον ἐξετέλεσσεν,
> εἰς Ἐπιμηθέα πέμπε πατὴρ κλυτὸν Ἀργεϊφόντην
> δῶρον ἄγοντα, θεῶν ταχὺν ἄγγελον·

In the *Theogony* Pandora is led out (ἐξάγειν) by Hephaistos to the gods and men (lines 585–7):

> But when he had produced the beautiful evil
>   as the price for the good,
> he led (her) out to where the other gods and men were,
> glorified in the decorations of Athena, the grey-eyed daughter
>   of a mighty father.

> αὐτὰρ ἐπεὶ δὴ τεῦξε καλὸν κακὸν ἀντ᾽ ἀγαθοῖο,
> ἐξάγαγ᾽ ἔνθά περ ἄλλοι ἔσαν θεοὶ ἠδ᾽ ἄνθρωποι,
> κόσμῳ ἀγαλλομένην γλαυκώπιδος Ὀβριμοπάτρης·

In view of the ascent clearly underlying the conveying of Pandora to Epimetheus on the pottery scenes, and implied by the other motifs of the scene, the ascent may be indicated in both these accounts by these means, by Hermes' role in *Works and Days* and by the linguistic allusion in the *Theogony*. In particular, Hermes' accompanying ascent role is familiar from the *Homeric Hymn to Demeter*, in which he leads Persephone up from the netherworld to Demeter in the upperworld (lines 335ff.). He appears to have a similar function with Pandora here.

The creation of Pandora within the earth, which seems to be implied in Hesiod's account, is consistent with another myth of Prometheus referred to in Plato's *Protagoras* 320c–322d. In this the ideas of creation being carried out beneath the surface of the earth and of conveyance to the upperworld are repeated: once there were only gods, but at the appointed time the gods fashioned man and other mortal creatures in the interior of the earth out of earth and other elements. These creatures, including man, were then brought into the light of day, emerging from the earth to Prometheus and Epimetheus, whose task it was to distribute the various qualities to them. This parallel suggests that the idea of creation beneath the earth and a following ascent is a customary feature in connection with Prometheus and Pandora.

The ascent which Pandora performs appears to concern divine figures, and it must be remembered that Pandora herself is not simply a woman, but also a goddess. Her nature as goddess is especially evident on the pottery depictions of the myth. On these she is seen rising out of the soil in the same way as the goddesses Persephone, Gaia and Aphrodite in their fertility functions. Pandora's name is an epithet of Gaia (Γῆ πάνδωρε, Hom. epigr. 7.1), as is also the name Anesidora which she receives on a fifth-century pottery depiction of the scene of her creation by Hephaistos and Athena, according with the scene as it is told by Hesiod.[25] Anesidora is also an epithet of the earth goddess Demeter in Attica.[26] The two aspects of woman and goddess may thus be presented in Hesiod's accounts, as the creation of Pandora in these is a combination of the ascent-of-the-goddess, and the creation-of-mankind traditions.[27]

The jar, which is an element of the version of *Works and Days*,

---

25 West, ed., *Hesiod Works and Days*, pp.164ff.; Kerenyi, *The Gods of the Greeks*, pl.ix.

26 Berg, *Fabula* 17 (1976) 21.

27 The view that Pandora was derived from the earth goddess was presented by various scholars earlier in this century and has been discussed since. The question is immaterial to this study. The idea of the ascent sequence is used here for a specific purpose which is consistent with the ideas usually found in such sequences. The actual fertility aspect seen with Pandora on the pottery depictions may have any number of explanations and implications, but these are probably not really relevant to Hesiod's presentation of the ascent sequence, where agricultural ideas are entirely lacking. On the discussion of Pandora and the earth goddess, see West, ed., *Hesiod Works and Days*, p.165 for a summary. On earth-goddess origins, see, for example, P. Gardner, 'A New Pandora Vase', JHS 21 (1901) 4ff.

seems to be connected with the idea of Pandora's rise from beneath the earth. In fact, it is another motif that indicates the presence of the ascent sequence here. In coming forth from within the earth, Pandora is, in effect, coming from the netherworld, and in his description of Pandora's baneful effects Hesiod seems to attribute to her hostile, netherworld characteristics. Once again, the ideas follow those seen with Inanna/Ishtar in her ascent in ID and AV.

The *pithos* is commonly understood to be a storage jar, but it is not to be interpreted in this myth as just a household storage jar from which the woman releases all the good things stored in it. Hesiod refers only briefly to the jar and its function, but it is clear that the jar held the evils and diseases which now wander voiceless among mankind (lines 94–104). The *pithos* seems to be symbolizing, on a mythological plane, the netherworld. This can be understood especially clearly by comparison with the Mesopotamian netherworld, but it also seems to be indicated clearly in the Greek material. Indeed, the jar was used in Greece in graves to hold the bones and ashes of the dead, and it may have received the connected connotation of the netherworld from this usage. In connection with this idea, the netherworld which contains the dead may be described as a jar. Tartaros seems to have this description since it is portrayed in the *Theogony* as a great gulf with the narrow opening of its gates at the top (lines 740–3).[28] In a parallel way, the Hittite netherworld is described as a jar, and this is a parallel which is of particular value here in view of the extent to which Hesiod seems to have relied on Hittite material in other aspects of the *Theogony*.[29] The diseases and evils which come out of the jar seem to be netherworld effusions, and this can be understood especially clearly in view of the Mesopotamian concept of the netherworld as the place from which demons and

28 F. Poljakov, 'The Jar and the Underworld', UF 14 (1982) 309–10, and sources in nn.1 and 2; Berg, *Fabula* 17 (1976) 15ff.; Marquardt, 'Hesiod's Ambiguous View', p.289. Other interpretations from varying points of view: John D. McLaughlin, 'Who is Hesiod's Pandora?', *Maia* 33 (1981) 17–18; Neitzel, *Hermes* 104 (1976) 387ff.; Simina Noica, 'La boîte de Pandore et "l'ambiguité" de l'elpis', *Platon* 36 (1984) 100–24; E.F. Beall, 'The Contents of Hesiod's Pandora Jar: Erga 94–8', *Hermes* 117 (1989) 227–30.

29 Poljakov, UF 14 (1982) 309–10; for a similar usage of the conception, the Hittite idea of the bronze jars beneath the earth holding Telepinu's anger, J. Harmatta, 'Zu den kleinasiatischen Beziehungen der griechischen Mythologie', AAntHung 16 (1968) 61–3.

diseases emanate. Along similar lines, demons seem to be found also in the Greek netherworld.[30] In any case, the jar seems to be symbolic of the netherworld. In accordance with this, Pandora, who apparently rises from this place in her creation, is depicted on the London amphora as emerging under Hephaistos' creative hands from within a *pithos*.

The storage jar from which Pandora lifts the lid and releases all the evils may have these ideas behind it; and the symbolism seems to indicate that the first woman was seen as the one responsible for releasing hostile evils from the netherworld on to mankind. In doing this, Pandora actually parallels Inanna, who returns from the netherworld in ID bringing back with her demons and other hostile forces which end up attacking her husband, (lines 290–305, 347–68), an event which is thematically in tune with Pandora's effect on her husband Epimetheus. In a parallel situation in the *Epic of Gilgamesh* (Tablet VI.96–100), Ishtar, like Ereshkigal in *Nergal and Ereshkigal*,[31] threatens to release the hostile netherworld inhabitants on to the earth to devour the living (AV 13–20). These parallels with Inanna are consistent with the ascent and dressing scene of Pandora which also correspond directly to features of the same Mesopotamian goddess. In any case, these may be some of the ideas which lie behind the usage of the jar and Pandora's action in releasing the evils from it to roam among mankind. There may be more to the symbolism of the jar than just this, however, as the jar is also seen to contain 'hope' or 'expectation' (*Works and Days*, 96–9). It is difficult to comprehend how Hesiod sees this as being contained in the same jar as the evils.[32]

---

30 James B. Pritchard, *Ancient and Near Eastern Texts Relating to the Old Testament*, 3rd edition, Princeton University Press, Princeton, 1969, p.436, *Ludlul Bēl Nēmeqi* III rev. 6ff.; Réné Labat *et al.*, *Les Religions du Proche-Orient asiatique*, Fayard/Denoël, Paris, 1970, pp.140ff. Cf. incantation text in W.G. Lambert, 'An Address of Marduk to the Demons', AfO 19 (1959–60) 117; and the *Myth of Erra* Tablet I.175. For demons in the underworld in Greece, see G.S. Kirk, ed., *The Bacchae of Euripides*, Cambridge University Press, Cambridge, 1979, p.37, notes to lines 120ff.

31 Sultantepe version col. v lines 9–12. For translations of the work, see Manfred Hutter, *Altorientalische Vorstellungen von der Unterwelt: Literar- und religionsgeschichtliche Überlegungen zu «Nergal und Ereškigal»*, Universitätsverlag, Freiburg, and Vandenhoeck & Ruprecht, Göttingen, 1985, pp.7–9, 20–31; Dalley, *Myths from Mesopotamia*, pp.163–81.

32 See, however, W.J. Verdenius on ἐλπίς as 'expectation': 'A "Hopeless" Line in Hesiod: *Works and Days*, 96', *Mnemosyne* 24 (1971) 225–31.

An integral part of the ascent sequence is the journey for power, and this is found here with Pandora, again with motifs which parallel those in Inanna/Ishtar's myths. The dressing motif which is found with the Mesopotamian goddess in her ascent is used here for the power of Pandora. The motif has also been seen in the ascent sequence of Apollo at his birth, to express his acquisition of power. This is discussed in the chapter on Apollo. The dressing motif is a conspicuous part of Pandora's myth in Hesiod's accounts, in which Pandora is dressed and adorned by Athena and other goddesses. It is apparent also on the pottery scenes of her rise, where she ascends fully dressed, in one scene complete with crown and flowers on her head. She is dressed in silver-shining raiment and adorned with veil, necklaces, spring flowers or crown. In nature, the dressing motif parallels the motif as it is found with Ishtar in her ascent sequence. Pandora's dressing recalls especially Ishtar's dressing and adornment on her return to the upperworld after her revival, with its emphasis on raiment and decorations (AV 118–25). One feature especially reminiscent of Ishtar's dressing scene and her progress to the upperworld is the crown (line 125). Pandora is also given this ornament, and it is obviously a special feature as it receives so much attention from Hesiod (*Theogony*, 578–84). Its position in the dressing scene is identical to that in Ishtar's dressing scene: Pandora is given the crown to complete the dressing and progress to life; likewise, in the Mesopotamian myth the goddess receives clothes and adornments, and then the crown to complete her regaining of powers and her return to the upperworld, the land of the living.[33]

The dressing motif incorporates ideas of the acquisition of power and its demonstration, and these are seen with Pandora in her dressing scene. The nature of the power acquired and expressed follows that of Inanna/Ishtar in her myths, and of Aphrodite in her birth myth and in the myth of her *affaire* with Anchises. In her birth myth, Aphrodite grows in seductive power by means of the dressing motif in a journey

---

33 In ID, Inanna's clothes are the me, 'divine powers', and her dressing and undressing symbolize the gain and loss of power. The sequence is followed by Ishtar in AV 119–25. The power of the clothes is also seen in the sacred marriage bathing-and-dressing sequences: SRT 5 lines 1–7, especially line 7. See Thorkild Jacobsen, *The Harps that Once . . .: Sumerian Poetry in Translation*, Yale University Press, New Haven and London, 1987, p.16, translation of line 7.

sequence (*Homeric Hymn VI*, 6–18). In her scenes, the nature of the power which Aphrodite displays is identical with that of Pandora here, the power of sexual attraction. Pandora's power over men is the same as that of Aphrodite in this hymn and in the myth of Aphrodite's *affaire* with Anchises, when she dresses in shining clothes and ornaments to overwhelm Anchises (*Homeric Hymn V*, 64–7, 75–91). Like Aphrodite here, Pandora is dressed in clothes and ornaments and arrives to overwhelm Epimetheus and the gods. As the poet says, she was brought forth to the amazed gods and men, glorified in the adornments given to her by Athena (*Theogony*, 585–9).

The same idea of the power of attraction represented by the clothes is seen with Ishtar. The power of Ishtar's clothes is apparent in an OB hymn in which her qualities of love, attraction and seductiveness are presented as her clothes, and express the goddess's greatness and power (lines 3–6):

> Chantez Ishtar, la plus imposante des déesses,
> que soit glorifiée la maitresse des femmes, la plus grande des Igigi.
> Elle est revêtue d'allégresse et d'amour,
> Elle est parée d'appas,[34] d'attirance et de charme.[35]

Pandora too has these powers of love, attraction and seductiveness, and they are due in part to the divine clothes with which she is dressed.

The three figures Aphrodite, Pandora and Ishtar seem to be connected in these and other ideas. Pandora closely parallels Inanna/Ishtar in her myths in the dressing motif, her powers of attraction, the idea of coming to life as part of an ascent sequence, and other ascent-sequence ideas such as the escort of the netherworld figure, the inimical ascent from the netherworld, and the releasing of nether-world evils. In the dressing motif and the ideas which underlie it, Pandora may have a connection with Aphrodite, as this goddess also figures in similar dressing sequences with the same underlying ideas.[36] Aphrodite also parallels Inanna/Ishtar in her myths, as Pandora does here. In Aphrodite's case the bathing-and-dressing

---

34 In-bi, '(sexual) attractiveness and power'.
35 Source: Marie-Joseph Seux, *Hymnes et prières aux dieux de Babylonie et d'Assyrie*, Les Éditions du Cerf, Paris, 1976, p.39.
36 See the discussion of Aphrodite's birth myth and her *affaire* with Anchises in the chapter on Aphrodite.

scenes which form the major activities of her journeys closely parallel the bathing-and-dressing scenes in the myths of Inanna/Ishtar, the Mesopotamian goddess from whom it appears that she was derived. As with the Mesopotamian goddess, the clothes of Aphrodite are used to symbolize power, specifically her powers of attractiveness and her ability to cause desire in men and gods.[37]

The light motif is an important one with Aphrodite, in connection with the demonstration of the goddess's power in the dressing scene, and it is found with Pandora in her dressing, where it similarly indicates her power of attractiveness. The light motif is used in *Homeric Hymn V* to indicate this power, for Aphrodite's clothes and ornaments shine when she travels to Ida and meets Anchises (lines 86–90, 161–3). The same motif of light is used in the dressing scene of Pandora, as her clothes also shine: Athena dresses her in silver-shining raiment (ἀργυφέη ἐσθῆτι, *Theogony*, 574). This is probably meant to be indicative of the role of the adornment in increasing the girl's beauty and attractiveness. In accordance with this, the girl is led before the gods and men glorified in the adornments and decorations given to her by Athena (*Theogony*, 586–7). These ideas expressed in the dressing and light motifs are typical of the theme of power in the journey myths of Mesopotamian deities and are found expressing the power of Greek deities in their journeys. Here in Pandora's myth, it is likewise found attached to an ascent sequence to express the power of the figure involved.

The dressing motif expressing power in the scene of creation is also found in a Mesopotamian myth. As with Pandora, the scene is a composite idea, with the creation by the god and goddess and the dressing motif added to it to present the idea of power with the created figure. The myth of the creation of the king by Enki and Mami, or Bēlet ilī as her title is in the myth, displays some very similar ideas to those seen in the creation and dressing of Pandora.[38] The same ideas as those seen in Pandora's myth are found together in the myth of the creation of the king: the preparation of the figurine, the

---

37 See the discussion of the myths in the chapter on Aphrodite.
38 Walter Burkert pointed out this parallel in 'Homerstudien und Orient', in Joachim Latacz, ed., *Zweihundert Jahre Homer-Forschung: Rückblick und Ausblick*, B.G. Teubner, Stuttgart and Leipzig, 1991, p.173. For the myth, see Werner R. Mayer, 'Ein Mythos von der Erschaffung des Menschen und des Königs', *Orientalia* 56 (1987) 55–68.

dressing, and the presentation by several gods of gifts of various characteristics and attributes. The figurine is constructed from clay and formed into a goodly shape. Anu then gives him his crown, Enlil his throne, Nergal his weapon, Ninurta his radiance, Bēlet ilī his good appearance and Nusku his wise counsel. The involvement in this scene of many gods giving their special gifts directly parallels the situation in Pandora's myth, in which many gods give their gifts to the woman.[39] As with Pandora, the king's power is expressed in this dressing motif, which elevates the king to his glorious status and authority. This motif of the king's power in the dressing is seen in the texts of the king's sacred marriage with Inanna/Ishtar. In these the king's clothes express his power. In one myth, the king is portrayed dressing in the ritual me-garment and putting on his crown.[40] The me express the idea of divine power involved. They are seen as garments displaying the power of the goddess in ID (lines 14ff.). The radiance of the king in the creation scene, when he receives the radiance of Ninurta (line 39), is especially indicative of the power which the king receives. It is the same idea as is found with Pandora in the radiance of her clothes, although in Pandora's case the motif takes the form found with Aphrodite and Inanna/Ishtar.

The comparison of the ideas in the myth of Pandora with those in the myths of the king's creation and the myth of Inanna/Ishtar in ID and AV provides a superlative attestation of the conscious creative use of these mythological ideas. It is a wonderful example, which demonstrates the clear understanding that the Greeks had of the material and the ideas involved in it. The creation scene, with the combination of the ideas of the dressing for power, is similar in the myth of the king's creation and in the Pandora myth, but the motifs in the dressing and the various ideas involved are replaced in the Pandora myth by the dressing motif and attached ideas of Inanna/Ishtar in her return from the netherworld. The Greek poet responsible may have based his ideas for Pandora's creation scene, which involves the dressing and the combination of gods who give their

39 The involvement of a number of goddesses in the creation scene is a feature of other earlier myths, for instance, *Enki and Ninmah*: see Lambert, 'The Relationship of Sumerian and Babylonian Myth', pp.130–1; on this myth, see also Kramer and Maier, *Myths of Enki*, pp.31–7, 211–15.

40 Samuel Noah Kramer, *The Sacred Marriage Rite: Aspects of Faith, Myth, and Ritual in Ancient Sumer*, Indiana University Press, Bloomington and London, 1969, p.63.

special gifts, on the myth of the king's creation or a similar myth, but it has been creatively re-formed using the ideas of Inanna/Ishtar to suit the story being told. The inclusion in the story of Pandora of the ideas of the ascent, the escort, the nature of Pandora's power, her inimical character and activities with the jar make the myth much greater in scope, profundity and application. If this myth of the king's creation had some input into the Greek myth, other features besides the addition of Inanna/Ishtar's ascent-sequence ideas have been re-formed to suit the story being told and the Greek environment. Obvious ideas which are different are the creation of the woman instead of the king, and the different gods and their gifts involved in the story. The entire myth of Pandora's creation, ascent and effects on mankind, the myth which results from the creative efforts of the poet, brings together many ideas seen in the Mesopotamian creation-of-mankind myths as well as ideas of the goddess Inanna/Ishtar as they are found in her ascent sequence in ID and AV.

THE PANDORA MYTH AND THE ATRAHASIS EPIC

Once the elements of the ascent idea have been isolated, it can be seen that the other major elements in the Pandora myths, in Hesiod and other sources, are seen in the Mesopotamian creation-of-mankind tradition, and predominantly in myths of Enki.[41] The OB *Epic of Atrahasis* is the most comprehensive work of the tradition, and it can be seen that virtually all of the main elements and issues of that major work are attested in the myths surrounding Pandora and Prometheus. The *Epic of Atrahasis*, dated at approximately 1600 BC or earlier, may be described generally as a 'history of mankind';[42] besides dealing with the origin of man, his purpose in life and various historical events, it defines mankind's established place in the universe under the gods.[43] Before effective comparisons can be made, a résumé of the

---

41 Cf. Duchemin, *Prométhée*, p.63, RHR 197 (1980) 27 and REG 88 (1975) viii–ix.
42 Anne Draffkorn Kilmer, 'The Mesopotamian Concept of Overpopulation and its Solution as reflected in the Mythology', *Orientalia* 41 (1972) 160. Also Jeffrey H. Tigay, *The Evolution of the Gilgamesh Epic*, University of Pennsylvania Press, Philadelphia, 1982, p.215.
43 William L. Moran, 'Atrahasis: The Babylonian Story of the Flood', *Biblica* 52 (1971) 58–9; W.G. Lambert and A.R. Millard, *Atra-hasis: The Babylonian Story of the Flood*, Clarendon Press, Oxford, 1969, pp.13ff.

epic is necessary at this point.[44] The text is fragmentary, as only something over 700 lines of a total of 1245 are extant, but enough survive to draw a fairly detailed outline of the story.[45]

After the universe had been created and Anu, Enlil and Enki had taken control over their respective spheres – heaven, earth, and *apsu* (the nether-sea) – the young gods (the Igigi) rebelled against their father, Enlil. The reason for the revolt was the hard toil imposed upon them by Enlil, who set them to digging canals and performing other agricultural work to obtain the daily needs of the gods. The rebellious gods chose a leader, and went to confront Enlil in his temple. The supreme god cut a poor figure when he fell into great fear at the news that the gods were at his gate, and cowered behind his minister, begging him for protection. Some time later, when the Assembly had come together to discuss the problem and the danger had passed, Enlil's desire for revenge took over, and he called for the death of the leader of the rebels. Anu and the Assembly demurred, however, and Anu even went so far as to admit that the rebel gods had a case. The Assembly was at an impasse.

It fell to the wise god, Enki, the hero of the work, to find a solution. His plan was to create mankind to take over the burden of toil and to provide sustenance for the gods, who would thereafter live at ease. The gods were delighted, and Enlil, acquiescing, commanded the creation of mankind. Enki, who was also the god of crafts, called for the mother–creatrix Mami, and the two set to work creating mankind. Clay was mixed with the flesh and blood of the rebel leader, and from this Enki modelled fourteen figurines of men and women. He gave them to Mami to bring to life by her own special talents as birth goddess and goddess of midwifery. With the assistance of fourteen 'mother-wombs' and birth goddesses, and using various customs of Mesopotamian midwifery, the figurines were brought to life. Using as part of the material the flesh and blood of the rebel deity answered the problem of life in mankind. The 'drumbeat' in living man was explained as the sign of this god's life in mankind, and the god's flesh also supplied the spirit in man.

Almost twelve hundred years passed after the creation of mankind,

44 Textual source: Lambert and Millard, *Atra-hasis, passim*; also Dalley, *Myths from Mesopotamia*, pp.1–38.
45 Moran, *Biblica* 52 (1971) 51–2; Kilmer, *Orientalia* 41 (1972) 106.

and Enlil returned to his senseless and self-interested ways. He complained that the noise caused by the vastly increased numbers of mankind was beginning to disturb his sleep, and he decided to diminish the population. His first attempt involved disease, when he ordered the god of plague to strike mankind. However, Enki was sympathetic towards mankind, and he advised King Atrahasis to tell the people to offer food sacrifices only to the god of plague. The god was shamed by all this attention, and he 'lifted his hand'.

Since his plan did not seem to be working, Enlil ordered Adad to withhold rain from mankind and other gods to create famine. Enki again intervened with the same advice to suffering mankind, and Enlil was thus thwarted again. Eventually, with the numbers still increasing, Enlil angrily realized that he was being tricked. To prevent any further tricks, he proceeded to obtain vows from all of the gods, and especially Enki, not to help mankind and not to reveal the scheme for the final solution to the problem of mankind. However, the clever god Enki again tricked Enlil by quickly finding a way round his vow. He revealed Enlil's intention of completely destroying mankind by a great flood, by speaking to Atrahasis through the wall of a reed hut – the reeds and not Enki thus transmitted the secret to the Flood hero.

Following Enki's advice, Atrahasis built a huge boat, and the flood-storm came. All of the gods, including Mami – or Bēlet ilī, 'queen of the gods', as she had been named after the creation of mankind, had agreed to the destruction of mankind – but were nevertheless upset by the actual event and, moreover, by the resultant loss of food sacrifices from mankind. They sat in the dust. Enlil received a sound scolding from Bēlet ilī, who decried his stupid and brutal act.

However, Atrahasis and his wife had survived the cataclysm, and as soon as they disembarked, the hero prudently sacrificed to the hungry and thirsty gods, who fluttered around in the smoke of the sacrifice. Enlil appeared on the scene and was enraged to discover that Enki had again tricked him. At this point, the mother goddess suggested vindictively that Enlil should not receive any of the sacrifice; and Enlil's adverse press continues when Enki himself delivers a broadside about the senselessness of the supreme god's acts and the trouble that he has caused everyone.

Enki, the god of wisdom, then devised a solution to Enlil's problem with mankind. He promised that, to prevent any further disturbance, he and Bēlet ilī would establish a new order and civilization by organizing the social world and restraining mankind's numbers by natural means.[46]

A comparison of the elements in this work with those of Pandora's myth shows the extent of the correspondence. The epic and the Pandora myth appear superficially quite different, with different story-lines, but many of the major elements are the same. In fact, virtually all of the main issues of the epic, and especially those peculiar to it in the myths about Enki, are found in the Pandora mythology:

1 rebellion against the supreme god;
2 resultant creation of mankind;
3 resultant imposition of hard toil and sacrifice;
4 repetition of the same roles: the supreme god commands creation, but does not play a part in the actual creation; the roles of craft god, clever god, and benefactor of mankind are repeated;
5 the same methods of creation used by Enki and Hephaistos: craftsman methods, modelling of figurines from clay; and the goddess in each having the same role;
6 the rebel deity punished as a result of his activities against the supreme god;
7 ideas of the soul with the rebel deity's punishment;
8 the clever god tricking the supreme god to benefit mankind;
9 the supreme god acting as the enemy of man and seeking to destroy him;
10 the supreme god strongly criticized: the story showing an antagonistic attitude to him; he is harsh, his actions are irresponsible and unjustified;
11 the Flood motif;
12 ideas of the history of mankind and the origin of races.

These elements are common to the Atrahasis epic and the Greek myth. There would probably have been more parallels to note if the Mesopotamian source were not fragmentary. A feature which demonstrates the direct correspondence between the myth in Hesiod and that of the Atrahasis epic is the omission in both sources of the agricultural aspect of the creation of mankind. This aspect is shown in other Greek sources and various Mesopotamian myths of Enki, Enlil

46 Cf. Moran, *Biblica* 52 (1971) 59 on this.

and An.[47] However, the correspondence of the Greek myth of Prometheus and Pandora with the Mesopotamian tradition as it is seen in this major source can now be studied in detail.

The character roles

The main characters of the Atrahasis epic, together with their roles, are reproduced in the story of Prometheus and Pandora. In the Atrahasis epic the three main divine protagonists are Enlil, the supreme god; Enki, here specifically the craftsman/creator, the sharp-witted god of wisdom and the benefactor of mankind; and Mami, the creatrix of mankind. In the Greek myth, Zeus plays the role of Enlil, the supreme god who is antagonistic towards men and wishes to destroy them. Zeus' intention to destroy mankind is preserved in Aeschylus and Apollodorus.[48] The same harshness and cruelty as that of Enlil is seen in Aeschylus' trilogy. The roles of Enki as craftsman/creator of mankind, rebel god, benefactor of mankind, and clever god, are shared between Hephaistos and Prometheus: Hephaistos has Enki's role of craftsman, while Prometheus performs as the rebel, the benefactor and the clever god. Like Enki, Prometheus is the friend and benefactor of mankind, the one who rebels against the supreme god and tricks him, who saves mankind from destruction at the hands of Zeus (*Prometheus Desmotes*, 246ff.), gives him civilization and teaches him his crafts (*Prometheus Desmotes*, 270, 458–86, 492–522): 'All the arts of men are from Prometheus', πᾶσαι τέχναι βροτοῖσιν ἐκ Προμηθέως (line 522). Prometheus also functions in Enki's role as creator of mankind in other Greek sources.[49] Together Hephaistos and Prometheus therefore present the aspects found with Enki in this

---

47 Greek pottery sources: see above; Mesopotamian sources: e.g., *Enki's Journey to Nippur*, *Enlil and the Pickaxe*.

48 Aeschylus, *Prometheus Desmotes*, 246ff.; Apollodorus I.46; Jacqueline Duchemin, 'La justice de Zeus et le destin d'Io. Sources proche-orientales d'un mythe éschyléen', REG 91 (1978) xxiii ff. There is a continuing controversy over the authorship of the Prometheus trilogy: see, for instance, Mark Griffith, *The Authenticity of 'Prometheus Bound'*, Cambridge University Press, Cambridge and New York, 1977; cf. M.L. West, 'The Prometheus Trilogy', JHS 99 (1979) 130ff., who says that Aeschylus is not the author; but cf. Lutz Lenz, 'Feuer in der Promethie', *Grazer Beiträge* 9 (1980) 24. The question is of little importance to this study, as the date is still some time in the fifth century.

49 Apollodorus I.45; Rudhardt, MH 35 (1978) 6; Walter Burkert, *Greek Religion*, Harvard University Press, Cambridge, (Mass.), 1985, p.171.

tradition. The connection between the two Greek gods is also seen where they were worshipped together by metalworkers and potters, in Athens and at the Academy. The two also appear together on a votive relief as elder (Prometheus) and younger.[50]

Athena plays the role of Mami, creatrix of mankind, in completing the creation. Athena's role is seen clearly in the version from the *Theogony*, but it is also apparent in *Works and Days*, where she is still the dominant figure: she does all of the dressing and adorning (line 76). The other goddesses act as her helpers in a role parallel with that of the birth goddesses who help Ninmah/Mami in the creation scenes of *Enki and Ninmah* (lines 30–6) and the *Epic of Atrahasis*.[51] The role of the helpers, the Horai and Charites, may also, of course, be part of the ascent idea and dressing motif which is involved here with the goddess in the Greek myth.

Rebellion and its results

The same motif of rebellion against the supreme god is found in both, and the rebellion has the same results: the creation of mankind and the imposition of toil and sacrifice.[52] The rebellion against the supreme god takes two forms in the Atrahasis epic: the rebellion of the younger gods, led by one figure, against the harsh rules of Enlil (Tablet I.ii.57ff.); and the rebellious activities of Enki, who tricks Enlil to aid mankind.[53] The role of Prometheus as rebel god combines the role of the rebel leader who is punished and Enki's role of wise and clever god, the one who thwarts the supreme god in his attempts to disadvantage or destroy the race of man.

In the Atrahasis epic the result of the rebellion of the gods is the creation of mankind.[54] This event is found in the *Theogony* as the creation of the first woman, as a result of Prometheus' rebellious tricks. As a consequence of the gods' revolt in the Atrahasis epic, mankind receives the lot of hard toil (Tablet I.189–91). In Hesiod, this fate is Zeus' revenge, and it comes about through the woman. This represents a different application of the same motif. However, the explanation of the source of toil is a central issue in the Atrahasis epic,

50 ibid., p.171; Noel Robertson, 'The Origin of the Panathenaea', RhM 128 (1985) 259–60.
51 Tablet I.231–60 and K 3399+3934 obv. iii lines 3–14.
52 Sacrifice as a result of rebellion: Sorel, RMM 87 (1982) 25.
53 Tablets II.9ff., III.i.1ff.; K 3399+3934 rev. iv 21–30.
54 Tablet I.189–91 and BM 78257 col. ii lines 1–12.

as it is in the recounting of the Pandora myth in *Works and Days*.

Mankind's role, in the Atrahasis epic, is to supply sacrifices of food to the gods. The way in which this element appears in the Greek tradition is that sacrifice is ordained because of Prometheus' division of the food at the feast of Mekone. Provision of sacrifice to the gods is the cause of mankind's creation in the Mesopotamian epic: man is created to supply the gods with food (Tablet I.189–97). In the Greek, sacrifice is ordained as man's role, and it appears also to be the result of the separation of man and gods, an event which occurred at Mekone.[55] The motif therefore has a different configuration and presents a different application of the concept. The idea of the sacrifices as food for the gods is suggested in Prometheus' offering of a portion of the ox to Zeus at this feast.

In Mesopotamia the gods are dependent on mankind to supply their food, and the destruction of mankind which occurs in the Atrahasis epic causes distress for the gods because of the loss of food and drink (Tablet III.iii.15ff.). In Greek myth the same ideas – of the essential nature of the sacrifice, and the threat of its loss to the gods – are seen in *Homeric Hymn II*.[56] In this hymn, Demeter threatens destruction of the human race, and Zeus fears the loss of sacrifice which would be the result. Mention of this, the loss of the sweet odour of sacrifice, in this hymn recalls the scene where the gods flutter eagerly about in the rising odour of Atrahasis' sacrifice, although it is, of course, a different situation.[57] In *Works and Days*, the idea of sacrifice as an essential element in mankind's relationship with the gods is shown when the silver race of mankind is destroyed for its impiety in not sacrificing to the gods.[58]

---

55 Sacrifice as man's role in life and as a result of the rebellion, and separation of gods and men: Sorel, RMM 87 (1982) 25. Separation of gods and men at the feast in *Theogony* 535: West, ed., *Hesiod Theogony*, pp.317–18; Kirk, *The Nature of Greek Myths*, p.228. Contrast C.W. Querbach, 'Hesiod's Myth of the Four Races', CJ 81 (1985) 10: separation is a 'hypothetical interpretation'. Instigation of sacrifice as an emblem of separation: Jenny Strauss Clay, 'The Hekate of the *Theogony*', GRBS 25 (1984) 37; also J. Rudhardt, 'Les mythes grecs relatifs à l'instauration du sacrifice: les rôles corrélatifs de Prométhée et de son fils Deucalion', MH 27 (1970) 9.

56 Sacrifice essential to the gods: Sorel, RMM 87 (1982) 26ff.

57 Cf. loss of the ascending savoury scent of burnt offerings as a threat to Zeus: Aristophanes' *Birds*, 1514–24. The 'Barbarian gods' are half-starved by the loss of sacrifice.

58 *Works and Days*, 136; see Sorel, RMM 87 (1982) 28; cf. also Querbach, CJ 81 (1985) 11.

Rebellion and trickery

In Hesiod, as in the Atrahasis epic, the clever god tricks the supreme god, to aid mankind and to thwart the supreme god's intention of destroying it. In his activities Prometheus combines Enki's function of trickster and that of the rebellious leader. Like the acts of the rebellious god and his companions, Prometheus' acts result in the creation of mankind and the imposition of hard toil for man. Like Enki's tricks, those of Prometheus are performed to aid mankind against the supreme god. The dual role of Prometheus is part of the reason for the ambivalent results of Prometheus' assistance.

While Prometheus' tricks are somewhat different from those of Enki, they have a similar role in the provision of food for mankind. Prometheus tricks Zeus and allocates food to mankind, while Enki's tricks with the gods of rain and grain have the purpose of alleviating the famine with which Enlil has smitten man to decrease his numbers (Tablet II.9ff.). The tricks that Enki worked on Enlil and the gods involved the sacrifices to the gods, and sacrifice is similarly involved in the Greek myth. The idea of the food, and the purpose of the tricks, are therefore similar, but in Hesiod the actual elements and their application are different.

Prometheus' theft of fire, his second trick, is connected with the issue of sacrifice and food, as the 'pair (sacrifice and fire) were with some few exceptions inseparable for the Greeks';[59] fire is part of the animal sacrifice which is the basis of Prometheus' first trick. In Aeschylus, fire is also seen as the basic tool of civilization, and Prometheus, by means of the gift of fire, taught mankind all the arts and craft of civilization (*Prometheus Desmotes*, 270, 458ff.).[60] This element also recalls the Atrahasis epic, in which civilization is, similarly, a gift from Enki. After the Flood Enki, the god of craft, with Mami, established and organized the new civilization.[61] The

---

59 William D. Furley, *Studies in the Use of Fire in Ancient Greek Religion*, Ayer, New Hampshire, 1981, p.i; Berg, *Fabula* 17 (1976) 15; Rudhardt, MH 27 (1970) 6; Kirk, *The Nature of Greek Myths*, p.139; Marcel Detienne, *Dionysos Slain*, Johns Hopkins University Press, Baltimore, 1979, p.57. Also on fire in the Prometheus trilogy, see Lenz, *Grazer Beiträge* 9 (1980) 26ff. Cf. also Agni in *Rig Veda* 1.1.1, as the god of fire and sacrifice.

60 See also Duchemin, RHR 189 (1976) 142–3: Prometheus teaches arts and craft. Fire as the basis of civilization: West, JHS 97 (1977) 28.

61 Lambert and Millard, *Atra-hasis*, p.13.

element of fire may also be presented here; however, this section of the Mesopotamian epic is virtually completely destroyed.[62]

Antagonism towards the supreme god

Zeus' role as antagonistic supreme god, the enemy of mankind, repeats Enlil's role in the epic. The Atrahasis epic is thoroughly antagonistic towards the supreme god, to the point of complete destruction of his character. He is portrayed as stupid, petty, cowardly, harsh and destructive towards mankind;[63] while Enki, by contrast, is elevated, and is presented as the clever and skilful god of craft and wisdom as well as the friend of mankind. Similar roles and the same contrast are found in Hesiod's account in the *Theogony*, though the Greek poet does his best to present Zeus as cleverer than Prometheus and to justify the supreme god's harsh reactions. Hesiod's treatment of this material accords with his purpose in the *Theogony*, that of presenting Zeus as the hero, as West points out.[64] While Aeschylus' purpose in the Prometheus trilogy may well be the ultimate vindication of Zeus, he does, however, portray Zeus' harshness and cruelty towards mankind and towards Prometheus in the trilogy. He seems to come to terms with the antagonistic role of Zeus in another and perhaps more successful way.[65]

The general disapprobation of Enlil is unique to this work in Mesopotamian mythology. One work in which the discrediting and disparagement of Enlil might have been expected is *Enuma Elish*, the purpose of which is to replace Enlil in supremacy with Marduk, the Babylonian god. However, Marduk's supremacy is achieved in this work by the simple expedient of omitting Enlil from most of the work, appropriating his position for Marduk, and employing other myths such as those of the warrior Ninurta to elevate the god. The reason for the antagonism towards the supreme god in the Atrahasis

62 Tablet III cols vi.43ff., vii.1ff.
63 Tablets I.352–60, II.7–21, III.iii.39–40, III.vi.5–26. Cf. Moran, *Biblica* 52 (1971) 60.
64 West, ed., *Hesiod Theogony*, p.321: that Zeus was thoroughly deceived by the trick has long been recognized. Hesiod is, typically, attempting to rescue Zeus' omniscience and prestige. Similarly, Kirk, *The Nature of Greek Myths*, p.138; also Jens-Uwe Schmidt, 'Die Einheit des Prometheus-Mythos in der "Theogonie" des Hesiod', *Hermes* 116 (1988) 130.
65 See also Jacqueline Duchemin, 'Le Zeus d'Eschyle et ses sources proche-orientales', RHR 197 (1980) 27–44.

epic lies in the cultic background of the Mesopotamian epic, which is one of the myths in which Enki is the hero. The reason is the rivalry between the cults of Enlil in Nippur and Enki in Eridu; it is part of the Mesopotamian politico-religious environment.[66] The conflict and the anti-hero aspect of the supreme god are aspects of the Mesopotamian mythology, but Greek mythology and the Greek environment do not supply any compelling reason for this role. As it is, both Hesiod and Aeschylus appear to be reconciling the Zeus of the Pandora tradition with the omnipotent and omniscient Zeus of other parts of the Greek tradition.

The rebel deity's punishment

In both the *Epic of Atrahasis* and the Greek myth, the rebel deity is punished as a result of his activities against the supreme god. In the Atrahasis epic he appears to be killed as part of the creation of mankind (Tablet I.208–30).[67] Prometheus is also punished for his rebellion. He does not die, however, as the Greeks considered their gods to be immortal, but Zeus despatches him to the netherworld, symbolic of the same end; he is chained to the Caucasus mountainside, and he is sent to Tartaros for 30,000 years.[68]

In the Mesopotamian epic, ideas of the soul and life in man's body are involved in the rebel deity's punishment. In the epic, the motif of the rebel's death is part of the creation of mankind: he is killed and his body is mixed with the clay,[69] to supply the life element in mankind, and the sign of this god's life in mankind is the 'drum', the beating heart (Tablet I.225–30).[70] The body of this god also supplies the soul in mankind, giving him his spirit (Tablet I.228–30).[71]

The motif of life and soul may be present with the rebel Prometheus' punishment on the mountain. The eagle descends during the day to eat his immortal liver, which at night grows back as much as is

---

66 Benito, '*Enki and Ninmah*', p.7.

67 Moran, *Biblica* 52 (1971) 52; Kilmer, *Orientalia* 41 (1972) 163.

68 Cf. Kirk, *The Nature of Greek Myths*, p.260: 'immortality of the Greek gods is much more emphatic than that of the Mesopotamian'.

69 William L. Moran, 'The Creation of Man in Atrahasis I, 192–248', BASOR 200 (1979) 50; Lambert and Millard, *Atra-hasis*, pp.9, 22.

70 Kilmer, *Orientalia* 41 (1972) 170.

71 Moran, BASOR 200 (1970) 53–5. Jacobsen on the beating heart: ibid., p.56; also Kilmer, *Orientalia* 41 (1972) 162–3; and Lambert and Millard, *Atra-hasis*, p.22.

eaten during the day. In Mesopotamia, the liver is the seat of the soul, the word 'liver' being used to mean 'soul'.[72] This organ may sometimes have had a similar function in Greece. In Plato's *Timaeus*, 70 a,e, for instance: the 'regions of the heart and liver are seats of the mortal soul (respectively superior and inferior), while the head harbours the immortal soul'.[73] On the other hand, the introduction of hepatoscopy to Greece may be relevant here.

The motif of the god dying to supply life in the creation of mankind is not present in the Greek creation of Pandora. Here, by contrast, the woman appears to receive life as a result of the attentions of the goddess Athena and those of her helpers, who complete Pandora's creation, and by the use of the ascent sequence, with its connotation of coming to life in the upperworld. Nevertheless, the remainder of the creation scene follows the same model. In fact, the motif of the dying god in the Atrahasis epic appears to be an addition to the creation method of the earlier *Enki and Ninmah*, which is also like that of the creation of Pandora by Hephaistos and Athena.[74]

The Flood motif and the origin of races

The motif of the Flood is important in the Atrahasis epic, and it is also found in the Greek myths surrounding Prometheus and Pandora. In the view of Kirk and other scholars, the Mesopotamian derivation of this motif is clear.[75] The connection of Prometheus and Pandora with the Flood motif has received little attention and needs to be stressed. While it is not a feature of Hesiod's stories of the creation of Pandora in *Theogony* and *Works and Days*, the Flood and other historical issues such as the origin of races are repeated in the genealogical material which forms part of Pandora's mythology. The sources of the genealogical evidence presented here are for the most part citations or quotations of Hesiod.[76]

72 Pritchard, *Ancient and Near Eastern*, p.436 n.4.
73 Silvestro Fiore, *Voices from the Clay*, University of Oklahoma Press, Norman, 1965, p.99 n.268.
74 Kilmer, *Orientalia* 41 (1972) 161, 165.
75 Kirk, *The Nature of Greek Myths*, pp.262–3; Duchemin, REG 88 (1975) ix.
76 For the sources cited here: F. Solmsen, *Hesiodi Theogonia Opera et Dies Scutum*, including R. Merkelbach and M.L. West, eds, *Fragmenta Selecta*, Clarendon Press, Oxford, 1970, pp.114–15; West, ed., *Hesiod Works and Days*, p.166; and Apollodorus I.46–8.

In the genealogies, the ideas of the history of mankind, his creation and one great flood, which are juxtaposed in the Mesopotamian epic, are presented together. In these Deucalion, the Greek Flood hero, is connected and related to Prometheus and Pandora; he is seen as the progenitor of the races. This is apparent in, for instance, Hesiod frag. 2 (Pandora and Prometheus appear here in the place of the creating deities represented in the Atrahasis epic as Enki and the mother goddess).[77] This scholium on Apollonius Rhodius 3.1086 states that Hesiod said in the *Catalogue of Women* that Deucalion was the son of Prometheus and Pandora, and that Prometheus, or Deucalion, with Pyrrha, gave birth to Hellen, the ancester of the Hellenes and of Hellas.

The same issues are involved in Apollodorus' reference to the Flood story,[78] in which Epimetheus has the role of husband of Pandora, as in *Works and Days*, a role which is given to his brother Prometheus in frag. 2. Here Epimetheus and Pandora give birth to Pyrrha, Deucalion's wife.[79] After the Flood has subsided, Deucalion and Pyrrha toss stones over their shoulders, and the stones (from the word λᾶας) become people (from λαός). This is seen also in Pindar 0. 9. 40ff. Similar to this arrangement of the elements with Epimetheus as the consort of Pandora, is the account of the scholium on *Works and Days*, 158a, according to which Deucalion and Pyrrha are the children of Epimetheus and Pandora.[80]

In another version of the genealogy, in Hesiod frag. 5, Deucalion appears as the father of Pandora. In this version, Zeus and Pandora are the parents of the brothers Graikos and Latinos, the ancestors of the Greeks and Latins. Pandora as the daughter of Deucalion in this source may be due to the subordination of the Graikos stemma to the Deucalion stemma, thus resulting in two Pandoras.[81] The presence of Zeus here and his role recall the Marduk version of the creation of mankind, where the supreme god takes over the creator role.

These sources all present the idea of Deucalion and his wife as progenitors of the races: Hellen, Graikos, Latinos; and generally, people, as in Apollodorus. In addition, in Hesiod frag. 7 Deucalion is

77 Berg, *Fabula* 17 (1976) 24.
78 Apollodorus 1.46–8. See West, ed., *Hesiod Works and Days*, p.166, for other sources.
79 Cf. scholium on Pindar 0. 9.68. For other genealogical roles of Epimetheus: West, ed., *Hesiod Theogony*, p.309.
80 West sees this as a harmonizing version: *Hesiod Works and Days*, p.166.
81 ibid.

also the ancestor of Makedon. Deucalion and his wife as progenitors is consistent with the Mesopotamian tradition: in the Atrahasis epic the Flood hero and his wife are the only survivors of the cataclysm, and as such are naturally the parents of the existing races of mankind.

The creation of mankind (represented chiefly in the divine figures involved here), the flood and the origin of races are all presented in these sources. Although the elements survive in differing arrangements in the various genealogical sources – for instance, with different figures in the same roles, such as Epimetheus, Prometheus and Zeus as the consort of Pandora – they consistently show the issues and interrelation of the figures, both divine and human, in the Mesopotamian tradition; and, for the most part, as it is presented in the *Epic of Atrahasis*.

The nature and extent of the correspondences between the Pandora/Prometheus myth and the Mesopotamian myths discussed here strongly suggest that there is a direct connection between them, and that the Greek myth is a result of influence from Mesopotamia. As required, the *Epic of Atrahasis* and other works in the Mesopotamian tradition of the early history of mankind existed down into the first millennium BC.[82] The works on Inanna/Ishtar were also extant in this period, as has been discussed at the end of the chapter on Apollo. The parallels fulfil the criteria established in the introductory chapter of this book, in that they are numerous and specific, and those concerning the creation and early history of mankind are found in a specific group of Mesopotamian myths. In addition, many of them are complex, and are central features in both the Mesopotamian and the Greek myths. The story that is told in the Greek material is obviously quite different from those of the Atrahasis epic and the related myths of Enki, but the major underlying ideas and issues, and major elements, are essentially the same. In effect, the myths surrounding Pandora and Prometheus appear to be the Greek rendition of the Mesopotamian tradition of the creation and early history of mankind, especially as it is presented in the myths of Enki, with the addition of the ascent-sequence ideas, which seem to come from Ishtar's myths. In fact, the Greek myths show intelligent and creative use of the same elements. Many of them, especially the ascent

82 Lambert and Millard, *Atra-hasis*, pp.31–9.

sequence of Pandora in Hesiod's accounts, display a clear under-standing of the ideas and purpose which are integral to them in the Mesopotamian myths. The Greek story shows many alterations and different applications of the same elements in a new story, but nothing that is not consistent with the creative use of a living tradition in a new cultural environment.

10

THE BIRTH OF ATHENA

The myth of Athena's birth is an example of extremely concentrated mythology. The complicated combination of ideas is
achieved by the use of a number of symbols and allusions. The
analysis of this myth has been left until this point in the study
because the purpose of the motifs and the underlying ideas can be
seen only with a thorough acquaintance with the way in which the
Mesopotamian ideas seem to be applied in Greek mythology. In this
myth they are combined and interwoven so that they can be
unravelled only in the light of the preceding experience with the
myths discussed above.

Despite the fact that the myth is presented only briefly in a short
Homeric hymn, a complete ascent sequence and the accompanying
idea of the journey for power can be seen clearly. In details which are
part of the birth scene of Athena in one of Pindar's Olympian odes,
another set of ideas attached to the birth of the goddess is visible. To
unravel the ideas in the myth, as they are presented in these two
sources, a thorough understanding of the creation-of-mankind myths
as seen in Hesiod and the Mesopotamian myths of Enki and Enlil,
and the knowledge of the goddess-and-consort ascent sequence of
Inanna/Ishtar are required. In the two sources, there is, therefore,
essentially the same combination of material as lies behind the
Pandora myth, but the application of the ideas is different since it is
used here for the presentation of the birth of the mighty warrior
goddess Athena.

The myth is presented in a number of sources, but the two main
ones are the *Homeric Hymn to Athena*, the twenty-eighth hymn of
the surviving corpus of Homeric hymns, and the seventh Olympian
ode of Pindar. The hymn to Athena presents only Athena's awe-
inspiring leap from Zeus' head.

Zeus gave birth to Tritogeneia from his august head. Clad in radiant golden armour, Athena leapt out of Zeus' immortal head. She sprang impetuously before him and shook her sharp spear, and awe struck the gods. Great Olympos began to quake fearfully at the might of the shining-eyed goddess, and the earth around shrieked terribly. The sea was stirred and agitated with purple waves; and brine burst forth suddenly. The radiant son of Hyperion halted his swift-footed horses, and they stood still for a long time, until the maiden Pallas Athena took the godlike armour from her immortal shoulders. And wise Zeus rejoiced.

Neither Hesiod's reference in the *Theogony* (lines 924–6) nor the Homeric hymn refers to the agency of Hephaistos, or Prometheus, in Athena's birth. However, Pindar refers to the event which precipitated Athena's birth: the axe-blow on Zeus' head by Hephaistos (Ol. 7.34–8):

> Thereupon the great king of the gods rained golden snow
>   on the city
> at the time when Athena, as a result of the skill of Hephaistos
> with a beaten brass axe, leaped up from the top of the Father's
>   head,
> shouting an exceedingly loud war cry.
> And Heaven and mother Earth trembled at her.

ἔνθα ποτὲ βρέχε θεῶν βασιλεὺς ὁ μέγας χρυσέαις
    νιφάδεσσι πόλιν
ἁνίχ᾽ Ἀφαίστου τέχναισιν
χαλκελάτῳ πελέκει πατέρος Ἀθαναία κορυφὰν κατ᾽
    ἄκραν
ἀνορούσαισ᾽ ἀλάλαξεν ὑπερμάκει βοᾷ.
Οὐρανὸς δ᾽ ἔφριξε νιν καὶ Γαῖα μάτηρ.

In Euripides' *Ion*, 452–7, the god who wields the axe is Prometheus. In his reference to the story, Apollodorus also names Prometheus in this role, but adds that some consider that it was Hephaistos (I.20): 'When it came time for the birth, Prometheus (or Hephaistos according to some) by the river Triton struck the head of Zeus with an axe and from his crown Athena sprang up, clad in her armour.'

An ascent sequence is involved in the birth scene in the Homeric hymn, and it is shown by various symbolic means. The most obvious indication of the presence of the ascent sequence here is the dressing motif found as part of the emergence. Athena comes forth fully dressed in warlike panoply, with her might conspicuously apparent. The motifs here in this sequence of events directly parallel those found with Inanna/Ishtar in her ascent sequence as she returns from the netherworld (ID 281–310, AV 118–26). Like Inanna/Ishtar in ID and AV, Athena comes forth fully dressed with her awesome power complete. As with the Mesopotamian goddess, her clothes represent her power. In Athena's case, the clothing is armour. She is dressed in full panoply in accordance with the warrior aspect which is being displayed here. Rather than wearing a crown and being decorated with jewellery as Ishtar is, she carries shield and spear, which she shakes, and a helmet covers her head. The dressing motif in an ascent has been seen with Apollo in his birth scene in the Delian section of his Homeric hymn (lines 120–2). There he is dressed as part of the sequence, in bright white clothes and a golden belt. Similarly, expressing his power in his return sequence, he wears shining immortal garments on his journey to the Assembly on Olympos (lines 182–4, 202–3). The light motif, expressing the power function of the clothes and the goddess's power in the sequence, is used here with Athena as it is with Apollo in both his sequences, the bright white garment at his birth and the shining immortal chiton of divinity in his journey to Olympos; similarly, Athena's golden panoply is radiant (παμφανόωντα, line 6). These motifs are all typical of the ascent or return sequence which the goddess is performing here for her birth.

Like Ishtar's ascent, Athena's is an ascent from the netherworld. This is indicated symbolically in the motif of Zeus' head as the place from which she emerges. The word used for Zeus' head, τὸ κάρηνον, also means 'mountain peak'. This usage can be seen, for instance, in the *Iliad*, 1.44 and 8.12, where it refers to the peaks of Olympos: Οὐλύμποιο κάρηνα, 'the pinnacles of Olympos'. In Euripides' *Ion*, 457 and in Pindar Ol. 7.36, the word κορυφή is used for Zeus' head, and this also has the meaning of 'mountain peak'.

The significance of this can be seen in view of both the Mesopotamian myth and various Greek myths. In Mesopotamia, the mountain or mountains signify the netherworld in iconography and in myth, and in the hymn to Apollo the mountain is present in the scene of the birth/ascent of Apollo from within the earth, as it is in the birth scene of Zeus Kretagenes, where the birth and ascent from within the earth are explicit.[1]

Athena's birth/ascent from the mountain closely follows the ascent of Ishtar from the netherworld as it is seen in Mesopotamian art. On seals, Ishtar is portrayed standing on the mountain or mountains which represent the netherworld. She is also shown emerging from between two mountains, representing her return from the netherworld.[2] In connection with the parallels between Athena and Ishtar in this feature of the rise from the netherworld, it is interesting to note that the bird so famous with Athena, her owl, is also found with Ishtar and seems to symbolize a netherworld aspect of the goddess. The bird is depicted with the winged nude goddess on a large-scale baked clay plaque of the OB or Isin-Larsa period.[3]

Athena's emergence has a terrifying effect on the gods, who are awestruck: Olympos shakes, the Earth shrieks terribly and the sea is agitated. Even Helios stops his horses (lines 9–16). As Pindar puts it (Ol. 7.38): 'Heaven and mother Earth trembled at her.' The ascent has the character seen with Inanna in ID when she returns in full power to terrify the gods of the land. Dumuzi, like Hephaistos on one pottery scene, flees from her.[4] Inanna has the same frightful effect in her return in the hymn in-nin šà-gur$_4$-ra, where she alarms An and the gods in the Assembly (lines 104–9). In the motifs involved, Athena's ascent is also similar to the return of the warrior god Ninurta, who likewise displays his power by his terrifying effect on the gods in *Angim*. He returns from the mountains, thundering across the land, his chariot dressed in emblems of his might and he himself radiant with power (lines 51–89). The same motifs are present

1 For the discussion of the ascent sequence in the birth of Apollo in the Delian section of the Homeric hymn and in the birth of Zeus Kretagenes, see the section on Apollo's birth in the Delian part of the hymn in the chapter on Apollo.

2 In the same way, Utu the sun rises in the morning from the mountains in the east. For a scene on a cylinder seal of Utu rising from the mountains, see Jeremy Black and Anthony Green, *Gods, Demons and Symbols of Ancient Mesopotamia: An Illustrated Dictionary*, British Museum Press, London, 1992, pp.182–3. See BM 89115 for a similar scene of a god emerging from the mountains.

3 For a depiction of the scene, see Black and Green, op. cit., frontispiece, and see caption to the frontispiece on the following page.

4 Kylix from Vulci by the painter Phrynos: London E 15, Beazley, ARV 136 no.1. For the scene, see C. Kerenyi, *Gods of the Greeks*, Thames & Hudson, New York, 1951, p.119.

with Athena, who has a similar effect on the awestruck gods. The dressing motif and the light motif are present and the noise motif is especially strong in Pindar as Athena shouts her exceedingly loud war-cry and makes Heaven and Earth tremble (Ol. 7.37–8). In the Homeric hymn, the noise appears with Earth, who shrieks (lines 10–11). The noise motif is parallel to that in Apollo's three return sequences in his hymn. In the first, the goddesses cry out at his emergence (line 119); in his return to Olympos, his lyre sounds as he journeys towards Olympos and in the Assembly, where he makes the gods dance (lines 184–206); in the third, the women and maidens of Crisa cry out in amazement and fear at his burst of light as he returns to his temple at Delphi (lines 444–7). Similarly, in the birth of Zeus Kretagenes from the mountain, the Kouretes clash their shields deafeningly. The motifs in Athena's ascent sequence are therefore typical of these ascent-and-return sequences, in which the motifs are used to express the power of the deities.

The various sources present different parts of the myth. The Homeric hymn presents only the birth/ascent sequence. Hesiod in the *Theogony* similarly refers only to this event (lines 924–5). However, Pindar and other sources include Prometheus or Hephaistos in the scene. Pindar is the first who refers to the event of Hephaistos striking Zeus' head with the bronze axe, splitting open the supreme god's head to release the goddess, who springs forth (Ol. 7.35–6).

In Pindar's account, then, creation-of-mankind ideas are added to the ascent sequence which is seen in the Homeric hymn. Athena plays an important role in these myths of the creation of mankind as they are seen in the creation of Pandora, and it is perhaps to be expected that this aspect of her mythology should be portrayed in her birth myth with the other central aspect of the goddess, her warrior aspect. The creation-of-mankind ideas are indicated here by the group of gods involved in the myth and symbolically by the axe-blow which precipitates the goddess's birth. Zeus, Athena and Prometheus or Hephaistos are seen together in this myth, and they are the major figures involved in the creation of Pandora, who also ascends from the netherworld as Athena appears to do here. In addition, Hephaistos, or Prometheus, is seen as the creator of the woman, or mankind in other sources, and it is these two gods who figure as the agent for Athena's birth.

The axe-blow as part of the creation of mankind is seen in the agricultural versions of the creation of Pandora. On a volute crater of about 440 BC, on which the figures are named, Pandora is emerging from the earth still half out of the soil with her arms raised. Epimetheus is clearly receiving her, as he stands looking down at her with one hand outstretched towards her and leaning on his pickaxe.[5] The agricultural nature of the scene suggests that the pickaxe has already been used to make a hole in the earth. On another vase this idea is seen in action. On a black-figured vase, the huge head of Pandora rises from the ground while two satyrs, fertility figures, standing on either side, strike the emerging head with mallets.[6] A scene very similar to this is presented in Sumerian myth with the birth of mankind from the earth in an agricultural manner. In *Enlil and the Pickaxe*, the god Enlil strikes the earth and in the hole created the head of mankind emerges.[7] The idea of the emerging head as it occurs with Pandora seems also to be found with Athena. On one pottery scene, her helmeted head, shield and spear emerge from the top of Zeus' head while to her right Hephaistos flees in apparent terror.[8]

The two sets of ideas, the ascent of the goddess like that of Ishtar and the birth-of-mankind ideas seem, therefore, to be brought together in this one myth. She is the terrifying war goddess like Inanna/Ishtar, but she also has a major role in the creation-of-mankind myths. In this role, she again parallels Ishtar, who is seen at the end of the second millennium BC and in the first as the creatrix of mankind when, in the SB version of the *Epic of Gilgamesh*, she takes over the role of Mami/Nintu in the OB Atrahasis epic.[9]

Both the ascent sequence and the creation-of-mankind ideas must have been instantly recognizable for a Greek audience and probably had much significance in the mythology of the goddess, bringing to mind ideas in her myths and cult which were of great importance to

5 Oxford 525 volute crater; M.L. West, ed., *Hesiod Works and Days*, Clarendon Press, Oxford, 1978, p.165; ARV 1562 no.4; for the scene, JHS 21 (1901) 3, pl.1. The find-spot of the volute crater is not recorded. According to Beazley, the painter is Alkimachos II, ARV 1562.

6 Black-figured vase, find-spot unknown. For the scene, see Kerenyi, op. cit., p.219; for the scene and comments, see Charles Lenormant and Jean J.A.M. de Witte, *Élite des Monuments céramographiques: Matériaux pour l'histoire des religions et des moeurs de l'antiquité, etc.*, tome, I Paris, 1844, pl.52. Cf. bell crater, Stockholm 6, from Magna Graeca, ARV 1053 no.40 (by Polygnotos and his group).

7 See the foregoing chapter on Pandora and Prometheus for the relevant lines of this myth.

8 Kylix from Vulci by the painter Phrynos: London E 15, Beazley, ARV 136 no.1. For the scene, see Kerenyi, op. cit., p.119.

9 *Epic of Gilgamesh*, Tablet XI.iii.116–23.

the concept and worship of the goddess. The fact that they could be presented in this highly compressed form is a clear indication that the underlying ideas, ideas which were first seen in Mesopotamia, were well understood. One reason for the symbolic reference to the creation-of-mankind ideas may have been to recall Athena's role in the creation of Pandora, the first woman, stressing her importance to the creation and continuance of the human race.

The warrior goddess and the creatrix of mankind are therefore two important aspects of Athena's mythology, and they are presented together in a concentrated way in her birth myth. Their significance is indicated in another way: they were portrayed together on the image of Athena Parthenos in the Parthenon in Athens. On the goddess's shield were seen the battle of the Amazons and the Gigantomachy, while on the pedestal was depicted a relief of the birth of Pandora.[10]

The birth myth demonstrates the use to which these complex ideas of the ascent sequence and the birth of mankind can be put. The two different sets of ideas are presented in symbolic ways and in a form which expresses concepts peculiar to this goddess, and they are combined to form a new, quite different myth. In fact, the creation-of-mankind ideas may have been added after the time of Hesiod and the composition of the Homeric hymn, since the agency of Prometheus or Hephaistos in splitting Zeus' head with the bronze axe is mentioned in neither source, and appears first in literature only in the time of Pindar and in artwork only from about 570 BC on. On the other hand, these sources refer only briefly to the myth, and the role of Hephaistos or Prometheus in it may have been assumed.

The discussion of Mesopotamian ideas in the birth myth of Athena completes the analysis of early archaic Greek myths in pursuit of parallels with Mesopotamian myths. The presentation of the motifs in this myth is mostly by means of allusion and symbol. Nevertheless, a thorough knowledge of Mesopotamian ideas and acquaintance with the way in which these seem to be applied in Greek myths – an acquaintance which has been acquired by the systematic analysis of the other myths in the long Homeric hymns and in Hesiod – makes it possible to penetrate to what seems to be the significance of the myth and to the subtle ideas which are expressed about the goddess Athena as warrior goddess and creatrix of the first woman.

10 Pausanias 1.24.7; Georg Wissowa, ed., *Paulys Realenzyklopädie der klassischen Altertumswissenschaft*, II, 2, J.B. Metzlersche Verlagsbuchhandlung, Stuttgart, 1896, p.2015.

11

CONCLUSION

The compelling conclusion which is indicated by this investigation of parallels is that extensive influence from Mesopotamia exists in these Homeric hymns and in the works of Hesiod, which generally speaking belong to the early archaic era. The influence appears to be of a fundamental nature, since the ideas and motifs are the basis for most of the events and activities of the gods in the myths. What is indicated by the study of this body of literature is that the Greeks seem to have had an intimate knowledge of many central ideas and concepts of Meso- potamian mythology and the motifs which express them. This is indicated by the parallels in the Greek myths with the specific Mesopotamian myths in this study, because these Mesopotamian myths are major features of the Mesopotamian religious mythological corpus. It is clear that the Greeks were fully cognizant of central ideas and many motifs of the two major strands seen in the Mesopotamian mythology, the goddess-and-consort strand and the heroic strand, and that they understood them. They also clearly knew at some stage the creation-of-mankind myths of the important god Enki. It is ideas and motifs of these three groups of myths that have figured so prominently in the study of parallels in the Greek hymns and in Hesiod. At the same time, it is clear that a large number of mythological, religious and cosmological ideas which are found in these Mesopotamian myths were not taken over or accepted, whether they were known to the Greeks or not. Some ideas seem to have had a large impact on Greece, while others are not found at all. In the same way, some Mesopotamian myths seem to have been particularly influential, since the parallels of idea and motif with these are numerous and often profound. In the case of other Mesopotamian myths, only a few parallels are found.

   The general picture which is painted by the way in which the parallel ideas are portrayed in the Greek myths indicates that not just the poets, but also the Greeks in general, the audience for whom these literary works were intended, must have had an intimate knowledge and appreciation of the concepts and motifs which give meaning to these myths, concepts and motifs which were seen first in the Mesopotamian myths in which they are likewise central and fundamental features. The fact that the knowledge of these ideas was widespread and thorough is indicated especially by the way in which the motifs and events are presented in the Homeric hymns to Apollo and to Athena. The highly symbolic and allusive nature of the presentation of the material in Apollo's hymn assumes the audience's intimate knowledge of these basic religious concepts and the significance of the motifs which express them. Similarly, in Athena's hymn the compressed nature of the ideas, which are likewise presented by symbol and allusion, indicates that the ideas and material were well known and accepted. It also assumes such an intimate knowledge of these that the subtle significance of the symbols and elliptical expression would be recognized instantly.

The poets obviously knew very well a whole array of concepts of the religion and mythology which the Mesopotamian myths in this study present. This is indicated especially by the fact that despite the difference in the stories and many motifs, they still faithfully express the concepts seen in the Mesopotamian myths. The differences are not a result of misunderstanding of the ideas and motifs, but the result of design, of careful creative work to express the concepts in a new framework and for a new purpose suitable to the Greek religious environment. This can be seen especially clearly in the *Homeric Hymn to Apollo*, in which the same underlying ideas as seen in the Mesopotamian myths are faithfully reproduced using material from these same sources which has been adapted to suit the cultural context and circumstances. The ideas and the significance of the motifs are understood so well that the poet assembles them all in such a way as to present a new story about Apollo without once misrepresenting the material or concepts which underlie it, as these are all seen in the Mesopotamian myths, and without confusing the issues. The story is very complex, using the journey of the goddess-and-consort strand with its ascent sequence in the Delian section, and three journey sequences of the heroic strand in the Pythian section. In all of these, the journey sequences closely follow those in the Mesopotamian myths and all the ideas which pertain to these sequences are presented in the correct sequences with the correct implications for the god and his power.

It is also clear that the myths as we have them are a result of conscious and creative remoulding of the Mesopotamian material in relatively late times. They are not a result of prehistorical adoption and gradual assimilation into the Greek tradition, with the alien aspects being slowly changed to make the myth properly Greek. What are seen in all of these early archaic works here are faithfully reproduced and clearcut Mesopotamian ideas which have merely been expressed in a new way. While the poets knew these ideas, the way in which they expressed them in their works indicates that they expected their audiences to know them as well.

The time of influence indicated by the sources is quite a long period. It ranges from at least several generations before Homer and Hesiod to the beginning of the sixth century BC, and the sources indicate that the knowledge of important Mesopotamian ideas was general and extensive in this time.

Several myths show that influence existed for quite some period before Homer and Hesiod, the earliest Greek literary sources. The myth of Demeter and Persephone was already in existence before Hesiod's *Theogony*, which makes a reference to it (lines 912–14). The myth of Aphrodite and Anchises was also known by both Homer (*Iliad*, 2.819–21) and Hesiod (*Theogony*, 1008–10). They mention these myths in passing, as though they were background knowledge, which suggests that they were already accepted and well established in the Greek tradition. Similarly, it is clear that the story of Prometheus and Pandora was an accepted part of the religious mythological tradition before it was taken up by Hesiod. In the *Theogony*, this poet tries to reconcile Zeus as he is presented in the Prometheus myth with the Zeus of other parts of the religious mythology, and he is not entirely successful. In fact, his treatment of the myth confirms that it was very well known and accepted. It seems that he cannot presume to change the tradition materially, but merely to alter its thrust as regards his hero Zeus: he tries to establish that, despite the way it appears, Zeus does know all and did foresee Prometheus' trick, and that he had good reasons for his harsh treatment of mankind. However, the original message of the myth which he tries to misrepresent is still plainly evident, although it is quite probable that he has changed aspects to emphasize the culpability of Prometheus. Incidentally, despite Hesiod's efforts, the traditional view persisted at least down to the classical era, when Aeschylus also attempted to reconcile the ideas presented about Zeus in the Prometheus myth with the omniscient and omnipotent Zeus of other parts of the mythological tradition.

Hesiod's efforts suggest that the Mesopotamian tradition was taken over, and the Prometheus and Pandora story created, at least several generations before Hesiod. In this way, the adoption would have lain beyond living memory, so that the story had become an accepted and important part of the tradition by Hesiod's day.

The early date of the influence of these myths on Hesiod's work is consistent with the succession myth in the *Theogony*. This myth appears to be assumed knowledge for Homer in view of Books 8 and 14 of the *Iliad*, which speak of the imprisonment of Kronos beneath the earth.[1] Homer composed his *Iliad* in the years between 750 and 700 BC. Hesiod's *Theogony* is generally considered to have been composed slightly after Homer, and this indicates that with the succession myth, which relates to both Mesopotamian and Hittite material, Hesiod was merely reproducing traditional material, in the same way as he was with the Prometheus and Pandora myth.

Judging by this, his work does not seem to present a new religious system, but rather a very traditional one. Similarly, it seems that he did not presume to change the material substantially, but acted mostly in the role of a compiler. In the *Theogony*, he does stress the supremacy of Zeus, and this is in concert with the succession myth, which is the backbone of the work and is about the rise of Zeus to power. In the Prometheus section, he attempts to present a unified idea of the supreme god, bringing everything into agreement with his theology. In accordance with this purpose, the alteration of the Prometheus myth to emphasize the supremacy of Zeus does not indicate the presentation of a new theological system, but merely Hesiod's desire to make the Prometheus story agree with his opinion of the authority of Zeus. The persistence of an older theogonic and theological system is indicated also by the age of the succession myth, which speaks of Zeus's rise to supremacy. Since this myth is clearly older than both Hesiod and Homer, the supremacy of Zeus is already part of the religious tradition for the poets.

Another feature of the *Theogony* speaks for the role of Hesiod as predominantly a compiler, in which function he presents material older than his own time. The episode of the birth of Zeus (lines

---

1 See G.S. Kirk, *The Iliad: A Commentary. Volume II, Books 5–8*, Cambridge University Press, Cambridge, 1990, p.3; H.S. Versnel, 'Greek Myth and Ritual: The Case of Kronos', in Jan Bremmer, ed., *Interpretations of Greek Mythology*, Croom Helm, London and Sydney, 1987, p.124.

477–500), which also shows Mesopotamian ideas, seems to be like a Homeric hymn in form, and together with all of the other episodic sections of this part of the work, the Titanomachy, the Typhonomachy and the Prometheus episode, this indicates that the poet is combining older material and ideas, in a rather brief way as it happens, to convey an overall, and probably largely traditional, picture of the origins of the present order of the divine world and the cosmos.

While the time of influence appears to be quite early in the case of the stories of Demeter and Aphrodite and Hesiod's work, the Homeric hymns in general show that the Mesopotamian ideas were well known also down to the end of the seventh century BC, during and after the period of Orientalizing art. The Homeric hymns presenting the stories of Apollo, Demeter and Persephone, Aphrodite and Athena appear to have been constructed or reconstructed in this century, and the form which the parallels take in them indicates that the ideas in the myths were well understood by the poets and by the audiences. Together with the material evidence of close contacts with the Near East, these myths indicate that widespread knowledge of important aspects of Mesopotamian cultural ideas was enjoyed in Greece at this time. The myths in this period and earlier therefore suggest widespread knowledge of Mesopotamian religious mythological culture over a period approaching at least two centuries, from before Homer and Hesiod into the completely historical period of the seventh and sixth centuries BC and possibly later.

Mesopotamian religious and mythological material could have reached Greece at earlier periods, but the influence apparent in these works seems to be a result of contacts in the period of intensive interaction in the first millennium BC, beginning in the middle of the ninth century BC. The late Mycenaean time before the end of the twelfth century BC has also been suggested by some as a time of influence, owing to the extensive contacts between Mycenaean Greece and the Near East at this time. Similarly, influence is possible during the period of limited contact after the fall of the Mycenaean cities, as recent archaeological finds indicate. There may have been much borrowing in these periods, especially in late Mycenaean times, with a profound effect on the religion and mythology which Homer and Hesiod inherited, but the parallels in the myths of this study which are known to have existed before Homer and Hesiod, namely the myths of Demeter and Persephone, Aphrodite and Anchises, and Prometheus and Pandora, seem to be due to influence in the first millennium, most probably from the ninth century on. This is indicated by the specific nature of the parallels and by the fact that the same precise relationship between many of the elements in these myths is seen in the Mesopotamian myths. It is most likely that the effects of the oral tradition over any lengthy period would have blurred them considerably, so that the ideas and motifs in the Greek myths would show scarcely any reliable parallels with those in the Mesopotamian myths. This would be the case especially with the Mycenaean material, because of the long period between the end of the Mycenaean era and the extant sources in the early archaic period.

One question which is sure to come to mind in view of all of the parallels is whether the gods to whom these ideas are attached have Mesopotamian origins. However, the parallels indicate no more than the influence of religious mythological ideas and material. A wide range of deities is involved in these myths: Zeus, Athena, Apollo, Hera, Demeter, Persephone, Hades, Aphrodite, Prometheus, Hephaistos, Leto, Artemis, Poseidon, Hermes, Themis, Earth and so forth. Clearly not all of these gods can be of Mesopotamian origin. The only deity among them whose Mesopotamian origins are supported by the parallels is Aphrodite, who has much other independent evidence for her Eastern origins. Indeed, the parallels only support her derivation and do not in themselves indicate it. The influence indicated by the parallels is, therefore, of religious and mythological concepts, not of new deities. Hephaistos and Prometheus, of course, show many parallels with Enki in the Pandora myths, but even if they could be proved from other sources to be originally Mesopotamian gods, the mythological material here does no more than show that they are functioning in the roles of Enki in a story which comes from Mesopotamia.

There was obviously a great infusion of Mesopotamian ideas in the early archaic period and for some time preceding it, as is indicated by the fact that three of the four long Homeric hymns which we have are full of Mesopotamian parallels, and the two shorter Homeric hymns discussed here also have many clear parallels. In addition, the works of Hesiod, the *Theogony* and *Works and Days*, which are central in the corpus of early archaic Greek literature and dependent on earlier material, also display numerous parallels. In effect, the stories are all based on Mesopotamian ideas. It seems as though many central religious concepts were taken over and assimilated. This no doubt changed the understanding which the Greeks had of their religion and of their deities, at least as they are presented in the religious mythological world. New ideas were taken up about the origin and history of man and about the divinities, and new stories about their gods were created, faithfully representing in them the religious ideas and sense of the material which had been taken over. So while the gods may be for the most part traditional, the ideas about them appear to have been altered or added to significantly.

While it is abundantly clear that the ideas and motifs manipulated by the poets are expressing a whole belief-system, there is much to the mythology and the significance of its motifs which cannot be penetrated by a modern scholar. In this study, the motifs and ideas have been followed from Mesopotamia to Greece, and their function and significance for the theme of the divinity's power can be understood in the Greek myths in the light of the Mesopotamian originals. They elucidate much about the Greek myths, but there is a limit to the extent to which one can probe. The usages can be seen, but it is not possible to penetrate the full distance and understand the real significance of these motifs on the level of religious or other belief. For instance, the motifs in the ascent or return sequence, noise, bathing, dressing, light, food and so forth, can be followed and their significance for the ascent sequence can be explained in the Greek myths, but their real significance, what they really conveyed to the Mesopotamian and Greek audiences – for their significance was probably taken over in their usage – is out of reach of a modern observer. Whatever may have been the significance of these indi- vidual motifs and many others, it must have been profound and powerful to cause the motifs to be faithfully reproduced time and time again in different myths – for instance, in the Mesopotamian myths of Inanna, Ninurta, Gilgamesh – and repeated in Greek myths of Apollo, Aphrodite, Pandora and Athena. Motifs and ideas like these must have been of great importance in the belief system to be reproduced again and again over two thousand years and in a new civilization. One can only try to guess at the meaning, for not once is there any explicit statement as to their real value. They were known and understood so well by the peoples who believed these religious ideas that their meaning was always assumed.

Similarly, in other ways the myths do not explain everything that appears in them. Many ideas appear to be background knowledge and are referred to only in passing, never to be explained. Ideas such as these are the dark wave which is driven by shrill winds against Delos at the birth of Apollo, and the idea of the floating island itself, for which a completely satisfying reason is never given. In some myths, details seem to assume the audience's knowledge of a clear and precise mythological timetable, where the order of events, especially in the setting-up of the cosmos and the birth of various gods during this, is plainly understood. This can be seen especially in the *Theogony*, in which so much of the myths is left to be understood by a knowledgeable audience, but it also seems to be involved in the birth of Apollo. At this stage one is conscious of the large amount of material which has not survived to our time, and realizes that there is a great deal more lying behind the mythological allusions than it is possible for an outsider to see, at least in the present state of knowledge. One is left, as it were, to stare in great frustration towards dim shapes barely perceptible in the half-light of our imperfect knowledge of the concepts of this ancient abstract world.

The analysis of the myths in this study has therefore revealed much about the relationship of Greek and Mesopotamian mythological ideas and the expression of them in the Greek material. There are many more Greek myths that could be considered, just as there are many more Mesopotamian myths that have not come into the discussion in this study. All indications point to the need to continue the pursuit of parallels between Greek and Mesopotamian myths. The key to fruitful investigation is a thorough knowledge of the ideas in the Mesopotamian myths and of the ways in which these ideas are expressed there. Added to this is the necessity of an intimate acquaintance with the application of these ideas in Greek myths, and this can only be acquired by means of the systematic analysis of the myths in the way that has been carried out in this study, in the total absence of hampering theoretical philosophical approaches. All of the myths analysed here show different applications of the ideas, but perhaps the most useful for further investigation, especially of religious mythology, is the myth of Athena's birth. This demonstrates clearly how the mythological ideas can be compressed and concentrated into one small scenario. The ideas are expressed, as though in shorthand, by symbol and allusion for an audience clearly thoroughly conversant with the underlying concepts and all of the necessary background material. This knowledge of the Greeks' application of their mythological ideas may prove to be very useful, for Greek mythology is not short of symbol and allusion.

This study has concentrated on Greek myths of approximately the early archaic times, but not all of the surviving material of this period has been analysed here. The works investigated are predominantly the Homeric hymns and parts of Hesiod's *Theogony* and *Works and Days*. There are others, among which the Homeric epics loom large.

Much comparative work has already been carried out in these with varying results, but the implications of this study suggest that there may yet be more of interest in these two great works. Although they contain religious mythology, they are, of course, works of a heroic-epic nature rather than of religious mythology as appears to be the nature of the Homeric hymns and Hesiod, so the approach to the investigation would probably need to be different. The results of recent research on the epics and other works of the early archaic period have raised many interesting possibilities, and an investigation along the lines followed in this study may have intriguing consequences. However, this is another, quite different story and it must be left to another occasion.

APPENDIX I
Ereshkigal's queenship of the netherworld

This appendix continues the discussion from footnote 13 in Chapter 2, referring to the discussion of Inanna's purpose in descending to the netherworld.

The view that Inanna seeks to acquire Ereshkigal's throne, her position of rulership of the netherworld, seems to conflict with certain other elements in *Inanna's Descent to the Netherworld*. If Inanna intended to usurp Ereshkigal's throne, then it appears that she did not intend to retain it permanently, for which she would have had to remain in the netherworld. Her instructions to Ninshubur indicate that she intended to make her way back to the upperworld: if she had not reappeared within a specified time, Ninshubur was to instigate the process which would secure her release and reappearance in the upperworld. Inanna's words indicate that if she had not reappeared she would have been subjugated, or killed (lines 43ff. and *passim*). As A.R. George translates the lines – which seem to involve the symbolism of dismantling and desecration of a statue of the goddess for the re-use of its component parts – in his article 'Observations on a Passage of "Inanna's Descent"', JCS 37 (1985) 109–13:

> O Father Enlil, let no one in the Netherworld kill
> your child!
> Let no one smelt your fine silver along with crude ore!
> Let no one cleave your fine lapis lazuli along with the
> lapidary's stones!
> Let no one cut up your boxwood along with the
> carpenter's timber!
> Let no one in the Netherworld kill the young woman Inanna!

a-[a] ^dmu-ul-líl du₅-mu-zu mu-lu kur-ra
   nam-ba-da-an-GAM-e
kù-ša₆-ga-zu sahar-kur-ra-ka nam-ba-da-ab-šár-re
za-gìn-ša₆-ga-zu za-zadim-ma-ka nam-ba-da-an-si-il-le
^{giš}taskarin-zu giš-nagar-ra-ka nam-ba-da-an-dar-dar-re
ki-sikil ^dga-[ša]-an-na kur-ra nam-ba-da-an-GAM-e

Other elements in ID also suggest that she did not want rulership – at least, not permanently. To descend to the netherworld, she had to give up her upperworld positions of en-ship and lagar-ship, and her powers in her temples, which thereafter fell into ruin. If she wants these back she will have to return, as indeed she intends. The Akkadian version also indicates the goddess's loss of powers in the upperworld: when Ishtar descended to the netherworld, the upperworld suffered a dearth of fertility. It is this dire result that her messenger uses to persuade the upperworld gods to recover her. While there may remain some question about Inanna's purpose in sitting on Ereshkigal's throne, her purpose in descent was to gain netherworld power. It seems that her action of sitting on the throne was intended to achieve this in some way. While she indeed failed initially to achieve power by this method, by the success of her second plan she did gain a victory over the netherworld – by virtue of gaining the power to rise again. Seizing Ereshkigal's throne surely could not have been the primary purpose, as she would then have failed in her descent; rather, her purpose was to gain by some means netherworld power in addition to her upperworld power, the power to overcome the finality of death which belonged to the netherworld. It should be said that no part of the plan she arranged with Ninshubur, which was to bring upperworld powers to her in the netherworld, involved the seizing of Ereshkigal's throne; nor were any of Inanna's later actions, after her return to life, directed towards the goddess's throne and position. In addition, Inanna's instructions are not, it appears, simply a device to escape her predicament once she had failed, for she thereby gains an important power of the netherworld, a power which none had gained before; and she becomes the initiator of the descent-and-return journey which had a central place in the ritual of the Sumerian religious life.

APPENDIX II
Some sources for Mesopotamian literature

Alster, Bendt, '"Ninurta and the Turtle", UET 6/1 2', JCS 24 (1972) 120–5. Sumerian text and translation.

—— 'Sumerian Love Songs', RA 79 (1985) 127–59. Sumerian texts and translations.

—— 'Incantation to Utu', *Acta Sumerologica* 13 (1991) 27–96. Sumerian text and translation.

Attinger, P., 'Enki et Ninhursaǧa', ZA 74 (1984) 1–52. Sumerian text and translation into French.

Behrens, Hermann, *Enlil und Ninlil. Ein sumerischer Mythos aus Nippur*, Biblical Institute Press, Rome, 1978. Sumerian text and translation into German.

Berlin, A., *Enmerkar and Ensuhkešdanna: A Sumerian Narrative Poem*, The University Museum, Philadelphia, 1979.

Civil, Miguel, 'Enlil and Namzitarra', AfO 25 (1974–7) 65–71. Sumerian text and translation.

—— 'Enlil and Ninlil: The Marriage of Sud', JAOS 103 (1983) 43–66. Sumerian text and translation.

Cooper, Jerrold S., *The Return of Ninurta to Nippur: an-gim dím-ma*, Analecta Orientalia 52, Biblical Institute Press, Rome, 1978. Sumerian text and translation.

—— 'A Critical Review [of Hermann Behrens, *Enlil und Ninlil*]', JCS 32 (1980) 175–88.

—— *The Curse of Agade*, Johns Hopkins University Press, Baltimore and London, 1983. Sumerian text and translation.

Dalley, Stephanie, *Myths from Mesopotamia*, Oxford University Press, Oxford, 1989. Translations of many important Akkadian texts.

Farber-Flügge, Gertrude, *Der Mythos 'Inanna und Enki' unter besonderer Berücksichtigung der Liste der me*, Studia Pohl, Series Minor 10, Biblical Institute Press, Rome, 1973. Sumerian text and German translation.

Ferrara, A.J., *Nanna-Suen's Journey to Nippur*, Studia Pohl, Series Maior 2, Biblical Institute Press, Rome, 1973. Sumerian text and translation.

Gardner, John and Maier, John, *Gilgamesh: Translated from the Sîn-leqi-unninnī Version*, Alfred A. Knopf, New York, 1984. Translation of the Akkadian epic.

Gurney, Oliver R. and Kramer, Samuel Noah, *Sumerian Literary Texts in the Ashmolean Museum*, Clarendon Press, Oxford, 1976. Sumerian texts and translations.

Hallo, William W., 'Lugalbanda Excavated', JAOS 103 (1983) 165–80. Sumerian text and translation.

Hallo, William W. and Moran, William L., 'The First Tablet of the SB Recension of the Anzu-Myth', JCS 31 (1979) 65–105. Akkadian text and translation.

Hallo, William W. and Van Dijk, J.J.A., *The Exaltation of Inanna*, Yale University Press, New Haven and London, 1968. Sumerian text and translation of nin-me-šár-ra, a hymn to Inanna.

Heimpel, W., 'The Nanshe Hymn', JCS 33 (1981) 65–139. Sumerian text and translation.

Jacobsen, Thorkild, *The Harps that Once . . .: Sumerian Poetry in Translation*, Yale University Press, New Haven and London, 1987. Many Sumerian works in translation.

Klein, Jacob, *Three Šulgi Hymns: Sumerian Royal Hymns Glorifying King Šulgi of Ur*, Bar-Ilan University Press, Ramat-Gan, 1981.

Kramer, Samuel Noah, 'The Death of Ur-Nammu and his Descent to the Netherworld', JCS 21 (1967) 110–22. Sumerian text and translation.

—— *The Sacred Marriage Rite*, Indiana University Press, Bloomington, 1969. Translations of Sumerian texts.

Labat, Réné, Caquot, André, Sznycer, Maurice and Vieyra, Maurice, eds, *Les Religions du Proche-Orient asiatique*, Fayard/Denoël, Paris, 1970. Translations into French of Babylonian, Ugaritic and Hittite works.

Lambert, Wilfred G., 'The Gula Hymn of Bulluṭsa-rabi (Tab. VIII–XXIII)', Or 36 (1967) 105–32. Akkadian text and translation.

Limet, Henri, 'Le poème épique "Innina et Ebih": une version des lignes 123 à 182', An Or 40 (1971) 11–23. Sumerian text and French translation.

Livingstone, Alasdair, *Mystical and Mythological Explanatory Works of Assyrian and Babylonian Scholars*, Clarendon Press, Oxford, 1986. Akkadian texts and translations of first-millennium BC ritual and mythological explanatory texts.

Pritchard, James B., ed., *Ancient Near Eastern Texts Relating to the Old Testament*, 3rd edition, Princeton University Press, Princeton, 1969. Translations of many Sumerian, Akkadian and Hittite texts.

Reiner, E. and Güterbock, H.G., 'The Great Prayer to Ishtar and its Two Versions from Bogazköy', JCS 21 (1967) 255–66. Akkadian text and translation.

Reisman, Daniel, 'Ninurta's Journey to Eridu', JCS 24 (1971) 3–8. Sumerian text and translation.

—— 'Iddin-Dagan's Sacred Marriage Hymn', JCS 25 (1973) 185–202. Sumerian text and translation.

Saggs, H.W.F., 'Additions to Anzu', AfO 33 (1986) 1–29. Important for the third tablet of the Anzu myth. Akkadian text and translation.

Shaffer, Aaron, *Sumerian Sources of Tablet XII of the Epic of Gilgamesh*, University Microfilms, Ann Arbor, 1963.

Sjöberg, Ake W., 'Nungal in the Ekur', AfO 24 (1973) 19–46. Sumerian text and translation.

—— 'in-nin šà-gur₄-ra: A Hymn to the Goddess Inanna by the en-Priestess Enheduanna', ZA 65 (1976) 161–253. Sumerian text and translation.

Sladek, William R., 'Inanna's Descent to the Netherworld', Ph.D diss., University Microfilms, Ann Arbor, 1974. Sumerian text and translation. Includes text and translation of the Akkadian work *Ishtar's Descent to the Netherworld*.

Van Dijk, J.J., *Lugal ud me-lám-bi nir-ğál: Le récit épique et didactique des Travaux de Ninurta, du Déluge et de la Nouvelle Création*, vols 1 and 2, E.J. Brill, Leiden, 1983. Sumerian text of *Lugale* and translation into French. Cuneiform texts: vol. 2.

Vogelzang, M.E., *Bin šar dadmē: Edition and Analysis of the Akkadian Anzu Poem*, Styx Publications, Groningen, 1988. Akkadian text and translation.

Wilcke, Claus, *Lugalbandaepos*, Otto Harrassowitz, Wiesbaden, 1969. Sumerian text and translation into German.

BIBLIOGRAPHY

Alderink, Larry J., 'Mythical and Cosmological Structure in the Homeric Hymn to Demeter', *Numen* 29 (1982) 1–16.

Aldrich, Keith, *Apollodorus: The Library of Greek Mythology*, Coronado Press, Lawrence, 1975.

Al-Fouadi, Abdul-Hadi A., '*Enki's Journey to Nippur*: The Journeys of the Gods', Ph.D diss., University Microfilms, Ann Arbor, 1969.

Allen, T.W., Halliday, W.R. and Sikes, E.E., *The Homeric Hymns*, 2nd edition, Oxford University Press, Amsterdam, 1963.

Alster, Bendt, '"Ninurta and the Turtle", UET 6/1 2', *JCS* 24 (1972) 120–5.

—— 'On the Interpretation of the Sumerian Myth "Inanna and Enki"', *ZA* 64 (1975) 20–34.

—— '"Enki and Ninhursağ", Creation of the First Woman', *UF* 10 (1978) 15–27.

—— 'Sumerian Love Songs', *RA* 79 (1985) 127–59.

—— 'Edin-na ú-sağ-ğá: Reconstruction, History, and Interpretation of a Sumerian Cultic Lament', in Karl Hecker and Walter Sommerfeld, eds, *Keilschriftliche Literaturen. Ausgewählte Vorträge der XXXII. Rencontre Assyriologique Internationale*, Münster, 8.–12.7.1985, Dietrich Reimer Verlag, Berlin, 1986, pp.19–31.

Amadasi, Maria Giulia Guzzo, 'Influence directe de la Mésopotamie sur les inscriptions en phénicien', in Hartmut Kühne, Hans-Jörg Nissen and Johannes Renger, eds, *Mesopotamien und seine Nachbarn. Politische und kulturelle Wechselbeziehungen im Alten Vorderasien vom 4. bis 1. Jahrtausend v. Chr.: 25. Rencontre Assyriologique Internationale, Berlin, 3. bis 7. Juli 1978*, Berliner Beiträge zum Vorderen Orient, Band 1, Dietrich Reimer Verlag, Berlin, 1982 pp.383–94.

Appel, W., 'Das Problem der Zerteilung des homerischen Apollonhymnus', *WZ Rostock* 34 (1985) 6–8.

—— 'Ultrum hymnus Homericus ad Apollinem unus sit in duas partes dividendus', *Meander* 40 (1985) 21–5.

Arthur, Marylin, 'Politics and Pomegranates: An Interpretation of the Homeric Hymn to Demeter', *Arethusa* 10.1 (1977) 7–47.

Attinger, P., 'Enki et Ninhursağa', *ZA* 74 (1984) 1–52.

Auffarth, Christoph, *Der drohende Untergang: 'Schöpfung' in Mythos und*

Ritual im Alten Orient und in Griechenland am Beispiel der Odyssee und des Ezechielbuches, Walter de Gruyter, Berlin and New York, 1991.

Ballabriga, Alain, 'Le dernier adversaire de Zeus: le mythe de Typhon dans l'épopée grecque archaïque', RHR 207 (1990) 3–30.

Baltes, Matthias, 'Die Kataloge im homerischen Apollonhymnus', *Philologus* 125 (1981) 25–43.

Barnett, Richard D., 'Ancient Oriental Influences on Archaic Greece', in Saul S. Weinberg, ed., *The Aegean and the Near East: Studies Presented to Hetty Goldman on the Occasion of Her Seventy-Fifth Birthday*, J.J. Augustin Publisher, Locust Valley (NY), 1956, pp.212–38.

Baumgarten, Albert I., *The Phoenician History of Philo of Byblos: A Commentary*, E.J. Brill, Leiden, 1981.

Beall, E.F., 'The Contents of Hesiod's Pandora Jar: Erga 94–8', *Hermes* 117 (1989) 227–30.

Behrens, Hermann, *Enlil und Ninlil. Ein sumerischer Mythos aus Nippur*, Studia Pohl, Series Maior 8, Rome, 1978.

Benito, Carlos, *'Enki and Ninmah* and *'Enki and the World Order'*, Ph.D diss., University Microfilms, Ann Arbor, 1969.

Berg, William, 'Eleusinian and Mediterranean Harvest Myths', *Fabula* 15 (1974) 202–11.

—— 'Pandora: Pathology of a Creation Myth', *Fabula* 17 (1976) 1–25.

Bergren, Ann L.T., 'Sacred Apostrophe: Re-Presentation and Imitation in the Homeric Hymns', *Arethusa* 15 (1982) 83–108.

—— '*The Homeric Hymn to Aphrodite*: Tradition and Rhetoric, Praise and Blame', CA 8 (1989) 1–41.

Bianchi, Ugo, 'Ο ΣΥΜΠΑΣ ΑΙΩΝ', in C.J. Bleeker, S.G.F. Brandon and M. Simon, eds, *Ex Orbe Religionum. Studia Geo Widengren*, vol. 1, E.J. Brill, Leiden, 1972 pp.277–86.

—— *The Greek Mysteries*, E.J. Brill, Leiden, 1976.

Bickerman, E.J., 'Love Story in the Homeric Hymn to Aphrodite', *Athenaeum* 54 (1976) 229–54.

Black, Jeremy, 'The Slain Heroes – Some Monsters of Ancient Mesopotamia', SMS Bulletin 15 (1988) 19–25.

Black, Jeremy and Green, Anthony, *Gods, Demons and Symbols of Ancient Mesopotamia: An Illustrated Dictionary*, British Museum Press, London, 1992.

Blaise, Fabienne, 'L'épisode de Typhée dans la *Théogonie* d'Hésiode (v. 820–85): la stabilisation du monde', REG 105 (1992) 349–70.

Bleeker, C. Jouco, 'Die aktuelle Bedeutung der antiken Religionen', in *Perennitas: Studi in onore di Angelo Brelich*, Edizioni dell'Ateneo, Rome, 1980, pp.37–49.

Blome, Peter, 'Die dunklen Jahrhunderte – aufgehellt', in Joachim Latacz, ed., *Zweihundert Jahre Homer-Forschung: Rückblick und Ausblick*, B.G. Teubner, Stuttgart and Leipzig, 1991, pp.45–60.

Boardman, John, *The Greeks Overseas*, Penguin Books, Harmondsworth, 1964.

—— 'Tarsus, Al Mina and Greek Chronology', JHS 85 (1965) 5–15.

Boedeker, Deborah D., *Aphrodite's Entry into Greek Epic*, Mnemosyne Supplement 32, E.J. Brill, Leiden, 1974.

—— 'Hecate: A Transfunctional Goddess in the *Theogony*?', TAPhA 113 (1983) 79–93.

Bonner, Campbell, 'ΚΕΣΤΟΣ ΙΜΑΣ and the Saltire of Aphrodite', AJPh 70 (1949) 1–6.

Booth, N.B., 'The Chorus of *Prometheus Pyrphoros* and Hesiod *Th.* 563', JHS 105 (1985) 149–50.

Bottéro, J., 'La création de l'homme et sa nature dans le poème d'Atrahasîs', in M.A. Dandamayev, J. Gerschevitch, H. Klengel, G. Komoróczy, M.T. Larsen and J.N. Postgate, eds, *Societies and Languages of the Ancient Near East: Studies in Honour of I.M. Diakonoff*, Aris & Phillips, Warminster, 1982, pp.24–32.

—— *Mythes et rites de Babylone*, Slatkine–Champion, Paris, 1985.

Buccellati, Georgio, 'The Descent of Inanna as a Ritual Journey to Kutha?', *Syro-Mesopotamian Studies* 4/3 (1982) 2–7.

Burkert, Walter, 'Apellai und Apollon', RhM 118 (1975) 1–21.

—— 'Rešep-Figuren, Apollon von Amyklai und die "Erfindung" des Opfers auf Cypern. Zur Religionsgeschichte der "Dunklen Jahrhunderte"', *Grazer Beiträge* 4 (1975) 51–79.

—— 'The Homeric Hymn to Demeter, Ed. by N.J. Richardson', Rezension, *Gnomon* 49 (1977) 440–6.

—— 'Kynaithos, Polycrates and the Homeric Hymn to Apollo', in G.W. Bowersock, W. Burkert and M.C.J. Putnam, eds, *Arktouros: Hellenic Studies presented to Bernard M.W. Knox on the occasion of his 65th birthday*, Walter de Gruyter, Berlin, 1979, pp.53–62.

—— *Structure and History in Greek Mythology and Ritual*, Sather Classical Lectures 47, University of California Press, Berkeley and London, 1979.

—— 'Literarische Texte und Funktionaler Mythos: Zu Ištar und Atrahasis', in Jan Assmann, Walter Burkert and Fritz Stolz, eds, *Funktionen und Leistungen des Mythos. Drei altorientalische Beispiele*, Universitätsverlag Freiburg and Vandenhoeck & Ruprecht, Göttingen, 1982, pp.63–78.

—— 'Itinerant Diviners and Magicians: A Neglected Element in Cultural Contacts', in Robin Hägg, ed., *The Greek Renaissance of the Eighth Century BC: Tradition and Innovation*, Proceedings of the Second International Symposium at the Swedish Institute in Athens, 1–5 June, 1981, P. Aström, Stockholm, 1983, pp.115–22.

—— 'Oriental Myth and Literature in the *Iliad*', in Robin Hägg, ed., *The Greek Renaissance of the Eighth Century BC: Tradition and Innovation*, Proceedings of the Second International Symposium at the Swedish Institute in Athens, 1–5 June, 1981, P. Aström, Stockholm, 1983, pp.51–60.

—— *Die orientalisierende Epoche in der griechischen Religion und Literatur*, Carl Winter Universitätsverlag, Heidelberg, 1984.

—— *Greek Religion*, Harvard University Press, Cambridge (Mass.) and London, 1985.

—— 'Oriental and Greek Mythology: The Meeting of Parallels', in Jan Bremmer, ed., *Interpretations of Greek Mythology*, Croom Helm, London and Sydney, 1987, pp.10–40.

—— 'Homerstudien und Orient', in Joachim Latacz, ed., *Zweihundert Jahre Homer-Forschung: Rückblick und Ausblick*, B.G. Teubner, Stuttgart and Leipzig, 1991, pp.155–81.

—— *The Orientalizing Revolution: Near Eastern Influence on Greek Culture in the Early Archaic Age*, Harvard University Press, Cambridge (Mass.) and London, 1992.

Caplice, R., 'É.NUN in Mesopotamian Literature', Or 42 (1973) 299–305.

Càssola, F., *Inni omerici*, Mondadori, Milan, 1975.

Cessi, Camillo, 'L'inno omerico ad Apollo', *Atti del Reale Istituto Veneto di Scienze, Lettere ed Arti* 87/2 (1927–8) 864–83.

Chadwick, John, 'The Descent of the Greek Epic', JHS 110 (1990) 174–7.

Cheyns, André, 'La structure du récit dans l'*Iliade* et l'*Hymn homérique à Déméter*', *Revue belge de philologie et d'histoire* 66 (1988) 32–67.

Clay, Jenny Strauss, 'Immortal and Ageless Forever', CJ 77 (1981–2) 112–17.

—— 'The Hekate of the *Theogony*', GRBS 25 (1984) 27–38.

—— *The Politics of Olympos: Form and Meaning in the Major Homeric Hymns*, Princeton University Press, Princeton, 1989.

Clinton, Kevin, *The Sacred Officials of the Eleusinian Mysteries*, Philadelphia, American Philosophical Society, 1974.

—— 'The Author of the Homeric *Hymn to Demeter*', OAth 16 (1986) 43–9.

Cook, J.M., *The Greeks in Ionia and the East*, Thames & Hudson, London, 1965.

Cooper, Jerrold S., *The Return of Ninurta to Nippur: an-gim dím-ma*, Analecta Orientalia 52, Biblical Institute Press, Rome, 1978.

—— 'Critical Review [a review of Hermann Behrens, *Enlil und Ninlil*, 1978]', JCS 32 (1980) 175–88.

Cowell, J.H., 'Foreign Influence on Greek Religion (to the End of the Fifth Century)', *Pegasus* 13 (1971) 8–29.

Culican, William, The *First Merchant Venturers*, Thames & Hudson, London, 1966.

Dalley, Stephanie, *Myths from Mesopotamia*, Oxford University Press, Oxford, 1989.

Deichgräber, Karl, 'Eleusinische Frömmigkeit und homerische Vorstellungswelt im homerischen Demeterhymnus', *Akademie der Wissenschaften und Literatur in Mainz, Geistes- und Sozialwissenschaftlichen Klasse* 6 (1950) 503–37.

Detienne, Marcel, *Dionysos Slain*, Johns Hopkins University Press, Baltimore, 1979.

Dirlmeier, Franz, 'Homerisches Epos und Orient', RhM 98 (1955) 18–37.

Dornseiff, Franz, 'Der homerische Aphroditehymnos', ArchRW 29 (1931) 203–4.

Drerup, Engelbert, 'Der homerische Apollonhymnos. Eine methodologische Studie', *Mnemosyne* 5 (1937) 81–134.

Duchemin, Jacqueline, *Prométhée: Histoire du mythe, de ses origines orientales à ses incarnations modernes*, Société d'édition «Les belles lettres», Paris, 1974.

—— 'Le mythe de Prométhée et ses sources orientales', REG 88 (1975) viii–x.

—— 'Le mythe du Déluge retrouvé dans des sources grecques?', RHR 189 (1976) 142–4.

—— 'La justice de Zeus et le destin d'Io. Sources proche-orientales d'un mythe éschyléen', REG 91 (1978) xxiii–xxv.

—— 'Les mythes de la Théogonie hésiodique. Origines orientales: essai d'interpretation', in Jean Hani, ed., *Problèmes du mythe et de son interprétation*, Actes du Colloque de Chantilly (24–25 avril 1976), Société d'édition «Les belles lettres», Paris, 1979, pp.51–67.

—— 'Le Zeus d'Eschyle et ses sources proche-orientales', RHR 197 (1980) 27–44.

—— 'Contribution à l'histoire des mythes grecs: les luttes primordiales dans l'*Iliade* à la lumière des sources proche-orientales', in φιλίας χάριν: *Miscellanea di studi classici in onore di Eugenio Manni*, Tomo III, Giorgio Bretschneider, Rome, 1980, pp.837–79.

Falkenstein, Adam, 'Der sumerische und der akkadische Mythos von Inannas Gang zur Unterwelt', in Erwin Gräf, ed., *Festschrift Werner Caskel. Zum siebzigsten Geburtstag 5. März 1966 gewidmet von Freunden und Schülern*, E.J. Brill, Leiden, 1968, pp.96–110.

Faraone, Christopher A., 'Hephaistos the Magician and Near Eastern Parallels for Alcinous' Watchdogs', GRBS 28 (1987) 257–80.

—— 'Aphrodite's ΚΕΣΤΟΣ and Apples for Atalanta: Aphrodisiacs in Early Greek Myth and Ritual', *Phoenix* 44 (1990) 219–43.

Farber-Flügge, Gertrude, *Der Mythos 'Inanna und Enki' unter besonderer Berücksichtigung der Liste der me*, Studia Pohl, Series Minor 10, Biblical Institute Press, Rome, 1973.

Farnell, Lewis, *The Cults of the Greek States*, vol. II, Clarendon Press, Oxford, 1896.

Ferrara, A.J., *Nanna-Suen's Journey to Nippur*, Studia Pohl, Series Maior 2, Biblical Institute Press, Rome, 1973.

Ferri, Silvio, 'L'inno omerici a Afrodite e la tribu anatolica degli Otrusi', in *Studi in onore di Luigi Castiglioni*, vol. I, G.C. Sansoni – Editore, Florence, 1960, pp.293–307.

Fiore, Silvestro, *Voices from the Clay*, University of Oklahoma Press, Norman, 1965.

Flintoff, E., 'The Date of the Prometheus Bound', *Mnemosyne* 39 (1986) 82–91.

Fontenrose, Joseph, *Python. A Study of Delphic Myth and its Origins*, University of California Press, Berkeley, 1959.

Förstel, Karl, *Untersuchungen zum homerischen Apollonhymnos*, Studien-verlag Dr N. Brockmeyer, Bochum, 1979.

Frankfort, Henri, *Kingship and the Gods*, University of Chicago Press, Chicago, 1948.

Freed, Grace and Bentman, Raymond, 'The Homeric Hymn to Aphrodite', CJ 50 (1955) 153–9.

Friedrich, Paul, *The Meaning of Aphrodite*, University of Chicago Press, Chicago, 1978.

Furley, William D., *Studies in the Use of Fire in Ancient Greek Religion*, Ayer (New Hampshire), 1981.

Gardner, John and Maier, John, *Gilgamesh: Translated from the Sîn-leqi-unninnī Version*, Alfred A. Knopf, New York, 1984.

Gardner, P., 'A New Pandora Vase', JHS 21 (1901) 1–9.

Geller, Markham J., 'Notes on Lugale', BSOAS 48 (1985) 215–23.

George, A.R., 'Observations on a Passage of "Inanna's Descent"', JCS 37/1 (1985) 109–13.

—— 'Sennacherib and the Tablet of Destinies,' *Iraq* 48 (1986) 133–46.

Giacomelli, Anne, 'Aphrodite and After', *Phoenix* 34 (1980) 1–19.

Gjerstad, E., 'The Stratification at Al-Mina (Syria) and its Chronological Evidence', *Acta Archaeologica* 45 (1974) 107–23.

Graf, Fritz, *Eleusis und die orphische Dichtung Athens in vorhellenistischer Zeit*, Walter de Gruyter, Berlin, 1974.

—— 'Religion und Mythologie im Zusammenhang mit Homer: Forschung und Ausblick', in Joachim Latacz, ed., *Zweihundert Jahre Homer-Forschung. Rückblick und Ausblick*, B.G. Teubner, Stuttgart and Leipzig, 1991, pp.331–62.

Green, M.W., *'Der Mythos "Inanna und Enki" unter besonderer Berücksichtigung der Liste der me*. By Gertrud Farbe-Flügge ...', (Rezension), JAOS 96 (1976) 283–6.

Gresseth, Gerald K., 'The Gilgamesh Epic and Homer', CJ 70/4 (1975) 1–18.

Griffith, Mark, *The Authenticity of 'Prometheus Bound'*, Cambridge University Press, Cambridge and New York, 1977.

Griffiths, J. Gwyn, *Plutarch's De Iside et Osiride*, University of Wales Press, Cardiff, 1970.

Groneberg, Brigitte, 'Die sumerisch-akkadische Inanna/Ištar: Hermaphroditos?', WO 17 (1986) 25–46.

—— 'Atramhasis, Tafel II iv-v', in D. Charpin and F. Joannès, eds, *Marchands, diplomates et empereurs: Études sur la civilisation mésopotamienne offertes à Paul Garelli*, Éditions Recherche sur les Civilisations, Paris, 1991, pp.397–410.

Gurney, Oliver R., 'The Sultantepe Tablets: the Myth of Nergal and Ereshkigal', AnSt 10 (1960) 105–31.

Güterbock, Hans Gustav, 'The Hittite Version of the Hurrian Kumarbi Myths: Oriental Forerunners of Hesiod', AJA 52 (1948) 123–34.

Hallo, William W. and Moran, William L., 'The First Tablet of the SB Recension of the Anzu-myth', JCS 31 (1979) 65–115.

Hallo, William W. and Van Dijk, J.J.A., *The Exaltation of Inanna*, Yale University Press, New Haven and London, 1968.

Hani, Jean, *La Religion égyptienne dans la pensée de Plutarque*, Société d'édition «Les belles lettres», Paris, 1976.

Harmatta, J., 'Zu den kleinasiatischen Beziehungen der griechischen Mythologie', AAntHung 16 (1968) 57–76.

Heath, Malcolm, 'The Structural Analysis of Myth [a review of R.L. Gordon, ed., *Myth, Religion and Society*, Cambridge University Press, Cambridge, 1981]', CR 33 (1983) 68–9.

Hegyi, Dolores, 'Die Griechen und der Alte Orient in 9. bis 6. Jahrhundert v. Chr.', in Hans-Jörg Nissen and Johannes Renger, eds, *Mesopotamien und seine Nachbarn. Politische und kulturelle Wechselbeziehungen im alten Vorderasien vom 4. bis 1. Jahrtausend v. Chr.*, 25e Rencontre Assyriologique Internationale (1978 Berlin), Berliner Beiträge zum Vorderen Orient, Band 1, Dietrich Reimer Verlag, Berlin, 1982, pp.531–8.

Heidel, Alexander, *The Gilgamesh Epic and Old Testament Parallels*,

University of Chicago Press, Chicago, 1949.

Heimpel, Wolfgang, 'The Nanshe Hymn', JCS 33 (1981) 65–139.

—— 'A Catalog of Near Eastern Venus Deities', *Syro-Mesopotamian Studies* 4/3 (1982) 9–22.

—— 'The Sun at Night and the Doors of Heaven in Babylonian Texts', JCS 38 (1986) 127–51.

Helck, Wolfgang, *Die Beziehungen Ägyptens und Vorderasiens zur Ägäis bis ins 7. Jahrhundert v. Chr.*, Wissenschaftliche Buchgesellschaft, Darmstadt, 1979.

Herter, Hans, 'Die Ursprünge des Aphroditecultes', in *Éléments orientaux dans la religion grecque ancienne*, Travaux du Centre d'Études Supérieures spécialisé d'histoire des religions de Strasbourg, Colloque de Strasbourg, 22–24 mai 1958, Presses Universitaires de France, Paris, 1960, pp.61–76.

—— 'Hermes. Ursprung und Wesen eines griechischen Gottes', *Rheinisches Museum für Philologie* 118 (1975) 193–241.

Heubeck, Alfred, 'Gedanken zum homerischen Apollonhymnos', in *Festschrift für Konstantinos J. Merentitis*, Athens, 1972, pp.131–46.

Hoekstra, A., *The Sub-Epic Stage of the Formulaic Tradition: Studies in the Homeric Hymns to Apollo, to Aphrodite and to Demeter*, Verhandelingen der Koninklijke Nederlandse Akademie van Wetenschappen, AFD. Letterkunde, North Holland Publishing Company, Amsterdam and London, 1969.

Hopkinson, N., 'Callimachus' *Hymn to Zeus*', CQ 34 (1984) 140–8.

Hunter, Richard, 'Apollo and the Argonauts: Two Notes on Ap. Rhod. 2, 669–719', MH 43 (1986) 50–60.

Hurwit, Jeffrey H., *The Art and Culture of Early Greece, 1100–480 BC*, Cornell University Press, Ithaca and London, 1985.

Hutter, Manfred, *Altorientalische Vorstellungen von der Unterwelt. Literar- und religionsgeschichtliche Überlegungen zu «Nergal und Ereškigal»*, Orbis Biblicus et Orientalis 63, Universitätsverlag, Freiburg, 1985.

Jacobsen, Thorkild, 'Sumerian Mythology: A Review Article', JNES 5 (1946) 128–52.

—— 'Inanna and Bilulu', JNES 12 (1953) 160–87.

—— 'The Myth of Inanna and Bilulu', in William L. Moran, ed., *Toward the Image of Tammuz and Other Essays in Mesopotamian History and Culture, Thorkild Jacobsen*, Harvard University Press, Cambridge (Mass.), 1970, pp.52–71.

—— 'Religious Drama in Ancient Mesopotamia', in Hans Goedicke and J.J.M. Roberts, eds, *Unity and Diversity: Essays in the History, Literature and Religion of the Ancient Near East*, Johns Hopkins University Press, Baltimore, 1975, pp.65–97.

—— *The Treasures of Darkness: A History of Mesopotamian Religion*, Yale University Press, New Haven and London, 1976.

—— *The Harps that Once ...: Sumerian Poetry in Translation*, Yale University Press, New Haven and London, 1987.

James, A.W., 'The Homeric Hymn to Demeter, Ed. by N.J. Richardson ...', JHS 96 (1976) 165–8.

Jameson, Michael H., 'The Homeric Hymn to Demeter', *Athenaeum* 54 (1976) 441–6.

Janko, Richard, 'The Structure of the Homeric Hymns: A Study in Genre', *Hermes* 109 (1981) 9–24.

—— *Homer, Hesiod and the Hymns: Diachronic Development in Epic Diction*, Cambridge University Press, Cambridge, 1982.

Jansen, H. Ludin, 'Die eleusinische Weihe', in C.J. Bleeker, S.G.F. Brandon and M. Simon, eds, *Ex Orbe Religionum: Studia Geo Widengren*, vol. 1, E.J. Brill, Leiden, 1971, pp.287–98.

Kamerbeek, J.C., 'Remarques sur l'*Hymne à Aphrodite*', *Mnemosyne* 20 (1967) 385–95.

Karageorgis, Vassos, *The Ancient Civilization of Cyprus*, Nagel, Geneva, 1969.

Keaney, John J., '*Hymn. Ven.* 140 and the Use of *ΆΠΟΙΝΑ*', AJPh 102 (1981) 261–4.

Kerenyi, C., *The Gods of the Greeks*, Thames & Hudson, New York, 1951.

—— *Eleusis*, Routledge & Kegan Paul, London, 1967.

Kilmer, Anne Draffkorn, 'The Mesopotamian Concept of Overpopulation and Its Solution as Reflected in the Mythology', Or 41 (1972) 160–79.

Kinnier-Wilson, J.V., *The Rebel Lands*, Cambridge University Press, Cambridge, 1979.

Kirk, G.S., 'Aetiology, Ritual, Charter: Three Equivocal Terms in the Study of Myths', YCS 22 (1972) 83–102.

—— 'Greek Mythology: Some New Perspectives', JHS 92 (1972) 74–85.

—— *The Nature of Greek Myths*, Penguin Books, Harmondsworth, 1974.

—— ed., *The Bacchae of Euripides*, Cambridge University Press, Cambridge, 1979.

—— *The Iliad: A Commentary. Volume II, Books 5–8*, Cambridge University Press, Cambridge, 1990.

Klein, Jacob, *Three Šulgi Hymns*, Bar-Ilan University, Ramat Gan, 1981.

Kolk, Dieter, *Der pythische Apollonhymnus als aitiologische Dichtung*, Beiträge zur Klassischen Philologie 6, Verlag Anton Hain, Meisenheim am Glan, 1963.

Komoróczy, G., 'The Separation of Sky and Earth', AAntHung 21 (1973) 21–45.

Kopcke, Günter, *Handel*, Archaeologia Homerica, Kapitel M, Vandenhoeck & Ruprecht, Göttingen, 1990.

Kragerud, A., 'The Concept of Creation in Enuma Elish', in C.J. Bleeker, S.G.F. Brandon and M. Simon, eds, *Ex Orbe Religionum: Studia Geo Widengren*, vol. 1, E.J. Brill, Leiden, 1971, pp.39–49.

Kramer, Samuel Noah, '"Inanna's Descent to the Netherworld" Continued and Revised', JCS 4 (1950) 199–211.

—— 'Revised Edition of "Inanna's Descent to the Netherworld"', JCS 5 (1951) 1–17.

—— *The Sumerians*, Chicago University Press, Chicago, 1963.

—— 'Dumuzi's Annual Resurrection: An Important Correction to "Inanna's Descent"', BASOR 183 (1966) 31.

—— 'The Death of Ur-Nammu and his Descent to the Netherworld', JCS 21 (1967) 110–22.

—— *The Sacred Marriage Rite: Aspects of Faith, Myth, and Ritual in Ancient Sumer*, Indiana University Press, Bloomington and London, 1969.

—— *From the Poetry of Sumer*, University of California Press, Berkeley, 1979.

Kramer, Samuel Noah and Maier, John, *Myths of Enki, The Crafty God*, Oxford University Press, New York and Oxford, 1989.

Krischer, Tilman, 'Der homerische Aphroditehymnus als poetische Konstruktion', *Hermes* 119 (1991) 254–6.

Kroll, Josef, 'Apollon zu Beginn des homerischen Hymnus', Studi Itali Filol Class 27–8 (1956) 181–91.

Kuhrt, Amélie, 'Assyrian and Babylonian Traditions in Classical Authors: A Critical Synthesis', in Hartmut Kühne, Hans-Jörg Nissen and Johannes Renger, eds, *Mesopotamien und seine Nachbarn. Politische und kulturelle Wechselbeziehungen im Alten Vorderasien vom 4. bis 1. Jahrtausend v. Chr.: 25. Rencontre Assyriologique Internationale, Berlin, 3. bis 7. Juli 1978*, Berliner Beiträge zum Vorderen Orient, Band 1, Dietrich Reimer Verlag, Berlin, 1982, pp.539–53.

Labat, René, Caquot, André, Sznycer, Maurice and Vieyra, Maurice, *Les religions du Proche-Orient asiatique*, Fayard/Denoël, Paris, 1970.

Lambert, Wilfred G., 'An Address of Marduk to the Demons', AfO 19 (1959–60) 114–19.

—— 'The Gula Hymn of Bullutsa-rabi', Or 36 (1967) 105–32.

—— 'The Historical Development of the Mesopotamian Pantheon: A Study of Sophisticated Polytheism', in Hans Goedicke and J.J.M. Roberts, eds, *Unity and Diversity: Essays in the History, Literature, and Religion of the Ancient Near East*, Johns Hopkins University Press, Baltimore, 1975, pp.191–200.

—— 'The Mesopotamian Background of the Hurrian Pantheon', RHA 36 (1978) 129–34.

—— 'Studies in Marduk', BSOAS 47 (1984) 1–9.

—— 'The Pair Lahmu-Lahamu in Cosmology', Or 54 (1985) 189–202.

—— 'Ninurta Mythology in the Babylonian Epic of Creation', in Karl Hecker and Walter Sommerfeld, eds, *Keilschriftliche Literaturen: Ausgewählte Vorträge der XXXII. Rencontre Assyriologique Internationale, Münster, 8.-12.7.1985*, Dietrich Reimer Verlag, Berlin, 1986, pp.55–60.

—— 'Another Trick of Enki?', in D. Charpin et F. Joannès, eds, *Marchands, diplomates et empereurs: Études sur la civilisation mésopotamienne offertes à Paul Garelli*, Éditions Recherche sur les Civilisations, Paris, 1991, pp.415–19.

—— 'Three New Pieces of Atra-hasis', in D. Charpin et F. Joannès, eds, *Marchands, diplomates et empereurs: Études sur la civilisation mésopotamienne offertes à Paul Garelli*, Éditions Recherche sur les Civilisations, Paris, 1991, pp.411–14.

—— 'The Relationship of Sumerian and Babylonian Myth as Seen in Accounts of Creation', in *La circulation des biens, des personnes et des idées dans le Proche-Orient ancien, XXXVIIIe R.A.I.*, Editions Recherche sur les Civilisations, Paris, 1992, pp.129–35.

Lambert, Wilfred G. and Millard, A.R., *Atra-hasis: The Babylonian Story of the Flood*, Clarendon Press, Oxford, 1969.

Lambert, Wilfred G. and Parker, Simon B., *Enuma eliš, the Babylonian Epic of Creation: The Cuneiform Text*, Blackwell, Oxford, 1974.

Lambert, Wilfred G. and Walcot, Peter, 'A New Babylonian Theogony and Hesiod', *Kadmos* 4 (1965) 64–72.

Leclerc, Christine, 'Le mythe hésiodique entre le silence et les mots', RHR 194 (1978) 3–22.

Lenz, Lutz, 'Feuer in der Promethie', *Grazer Beiträge* 9 (1980) 23–56.

—— [Review of P. Smith, *Nursling of Mortality*, Peter D. Lang, Bern, 1981], *Gymnasium* 89 (1982) 531–3.

Limet, Henri, 'Étude sémantique de ma.da, kur, kalam', RA 72 (1978) 1–12.

Lincoln, Bruce, 'The Rape of Persephone: A Greek Scenario of Women's Initiation', HThR 72 (1979) 223–35.

Linforth, Ivan M., *The Arts of Orpheus*, University of California Press, Berkeley, 1941.

Livingstone, Alasdair, *Mystical and Explanatory Works of Assyrian and Babylonian Scholars*, monograph of Ph.D thesis, Clarendon Press, Oxford, 1986.

Loucas, Ioannis, 'La déesse de la prospérité dans les mythes mésopotamien et égéen de la Descente aux Enfers', RHR 205 (1988) 227–44.

Maclennan, G.R., *Callimachus, Hymn to Zeus*, Edizioni dell'Ateneo e Bizzarri, Rome, 1977.

Mair, A.W. and Mair, G.R., *Callimachus, Lycophron, Aratus*, Heinemann, London, 1955.

Marquardt, Patricia A., 'Hesiod's Ambiguous View of Woman', CPh 77 (1982) 283–91.

Mayer, Werner R., 'Ein Mythos von der Erschaffung des Menschen und des Königs', Or 56 (1987) 55–68.

McLaughlin, John D., 'Who is Hesiod's Pandora?', *Maia* 33 (1981) 17–18.

Meltzer, Edmund S., 'Egyptian Parallels for an Incident in Hesiod's *Theogony* and an Episode in the Kumarbi Myth', JNES 33 (1974) 154–7.

Mendelsohn, Isaac, *Religions of the Ancient Near East*, New York, 1955.

Miller, Andrew M., 'The Address to the Delian Maidens in the Homeric Hymn to Apollo: Epilogue or Transition?', TAPhA 109 (1979) 173–86.

—— *From Delos to Delphi: A Literary Study of the Homeric Hymn to Apollo*, Mnemosyne Supplementum 93, E.J. Brill, Leiden, 1986.

Miller, D. Gary and Wheeler, P., 'Mother Goddess and Consort as Literary Motif Sequence in the Gilgamesh Epic', AcAn 29 (1981) 81–108.

Mondi, Robert, 'The Ascension of Zeus and the Composition of Hesiod's *Theogony*', GRBS 25 (1984) 325–44.

—— 'Greek Mythic Thought in the Light of the Near East', in Lowell Edmunds, ed., *Approaches to Greek Myth*, Johns Hopkins University Press, Baltimore and London, 1990, pp.142–98.

Moran, William L., *Toward the Image of Tammuz and Other Essays on Mesopotamian History and Culture, Thorkild Jacobsen*, Harvard University Press, Cambridge (Mass.), 1970.

—— 'Atrahasis: The Babylonian Story of the Flood', *Biblica* 52 (1971) 51–61.

—— 'The Creation of Man in Atrahasis I 192–248', BASOR 200 (1979) 48–56.

—— 'Notes on Anzu', AfO 35 (1988) 24–9.

Muhly, James D., 'Homer and the Phoenicians: The Relations between Greece and the Near East in the Late Bronze and Early Iron Ages', *Berytus* 19 (1970) 19–64.

Murray, Oswyn, *Early Greece*, The Harvester Press, Brighton, 1980.

Naddaf, Gérard, 'Hésiode, précurseur des cosmogonies grecques de type «évolutioniste»', RHR 203 (1986) 339–64.

Neitzel, Heinz, 'Pandora und das Faß', *Hermes* 104 (1976) 387–419.

Neschke-Hentschke, Ada, 'Geschichten und Geschichte', *Hermes* 111 (1983) 385–402.

Niles, J.D., 'On the Design of the *Hymn to Delian Apollo*', CJ 75 (1979) 36–9.

Nilsson, Martin P., *The Mycenaean Origin of Greek Mythology*, Sather Classical Lectures 8, University of California Press, Berkeley, 1932.

—— 'Die eleusinischen Gottheiten', *Archiv für Religionswissenschaft* 32 (1935) 79–141.

—— *Opuscula Selecta*, Lund, 1951–2.

—— *The Mycenaean Religion and its Survivals in Greek Religion*, Lund, 1968.

Noica, Simina, 'La boîte de Pandore et "l'ambiguité" de l'elpis', *Platon* 36 (1984) 100–24.

Notopoulos, James A., 'The Homeric Hymns as Oral Poetry: A Study of the Post-Homeric Oral Tradition', AJPh 83 (1962) 337–68.

Oppenheim, A. Leo, '*pul(u)h(t)u* and *melammu*', JAOS 63 (1943) 31–4.

—— *Ancient Mesopotamia*, University of Chicago Press, Chicago, 1964.

Ory, Thérèse, 'L'animal et le végétal dans l'*Hymne Homérique à Aphrodite*', LEC 52 (1984) 251–4.

Parker, Robert, 'The *Hymn to Demeter* and the *Homeric Hymns*', G&R 38 (1991) 1–17.

Patzek, Barbara, 'Mündliche Dichtung als historisches Zeugnis. Die "Homerische Frage" in heutiger Sicht', HZ 250 (1990) 529–48.

Podbielski, Henri, 'Le mythe cosmogonique dans la *Théogonie* d'Hésiode et les rites orientaux', LEC 52 (1984) 207–16.

Poljakov, F., 'The Jar and the Underworld', UF 14 (1982) 309–10.

Porter, H.N., 'Repetition in the Homeric Hymn to Aphrodite', AJPh 70 (1949) 249–72.

Powell, Marvin A., 'Aia ≈ Eos', in Hermann Behrens, Darlene Loding and Martha T. Roth, eds, *Dumu-e₂-dub-ba-a. Studies in Honor of Ake W. Sjöberg*, University Museum, Philadelphia, 1989, pp.447–55.

Pritchard, James B., ed., *Ancient Near Eastern Texts Relating to the Old Testament*, 3rd edition, Princeton University Press, Princeton, 1969.

Querbach, Carl W., 'Hesiod's Myth of the Four Races', CJ 81 (1985) 1–12.

Quirini, Bruno Zannini, 'L'aldila nelle religioni del mondo classico', in Paolo Xella, ed., *Archeologia dell'Inferno: L'aldilà nel mondo antico vicino-orientale e classico*, Essedue Edizioni, Verona, 1987, pp.263–307.

Race, William H., 'Aspects of Rhetoric and Form in Greek Hymns', GRBS 23 (1982) 5–14.

Reisman, Daniel, 'Ninurta's Journey to Eridu', JCS 24 (1971) 3–8.

—— 'Iddin-Dagan's Sacred Marriage Hymn', JCS 25 (1973) 185–202.

Richardson, Nicholas J., *The Homeric Hymn to Demeter*, Clarendon Press, Oxford, 1974.

BIBLIOGRAPHY

Riis, P.J., *Sukas I*, Copenhagen, 1970.

Ringgren, Helmer, 'Remarks on the Method of Comparative Mythology', in Hans Goedicke, ed., *Near Eastern Studies in Honor of William Foxwell Albright*, Johns Hopkins University Press, Baltimore and London, 1971, pp.407–11.

—— *Religions of the Ancient Near East*, SPCK, London, 1973.

Robertson, Martin, *A History of Greek Art*, Cambridge University Press, Cambridge, 1975.

Robertson, Noel, 'The Origin of the Panathenaea', RhM 128 (1985) 231–95.

Römer, W.H.Ph., 'Einige Überlegungen zur "Heiligen Hochzeit" nach altorientalischen Texten', in W.C. Delsman, J.T. Nelis, J.R.T.M. Peters, W.H.Ph. Römer and A.S. van der Woude, eds, *Von Kanaan bis Kerala. Festschrift für Prof. Mag. Dr Dr J.P.M. van der Ploeg O.P. zur Vollendung des siebzigsten Lebensjahres am 4. Juli 1979*, AOAT 211, Neukirchener Verlag, Neukirchen-Vluyn, 1982, pp.411–28.

Rose, H.J., 'Anchises and Aphrodite', CQ 18 (1924) 11–16.

Roux, Georges, 'Sur deux passages de l'hymne homérique à Apollon', REG 77 (1964) 1–22.

Rubin, Nancy Felson, and Deal, Harriet M., 'Some Functions of the Demophon Episode in the Homeric Hymn to Demeter', QUCC 34 (1980) 7–21.

Rudhardt, Jean, 'Les mythes grecs relatifs à l'instauration du sacrifice: les rôles corrélatifs de Prométhée et de son fils Deucalion', MH 27 (1970) 1–15.

—— 'A propos de l'hymne homérique à Déméter', MH 35 (1978) 1–17.

—— 'Pandora: Hésiode et les femmes', MH 43 (1986) 231–46.

—— 'L'hymne homérique à Aphrodite', MH 48 (1991) 8–20.

Saggs, H.W.F., 'Additions to Anzu', AfO 33 (1986) 1–29.

Said, Suzanne, 'Les combats de Zeus et le problème des interpolations dans la *Théogonie* d'Hésiode', REG 90 (1977) 183–210.

Schachter, A., '*Homeric Hymn to Apollo*, lines 231–8 (The Onchestos Episode): Another Interpretation', BICS 23 (1976) 102–13.

Schmidt, Jens-Uwe, 'Die Einheit des Prometheus-Mythos in der "Theogonie" des Hesiod', *Hermes* 116 (1988) 129–56.

Schmökel, Hartmut, *Sumer et la civilisation sumérienne*, Payot, Paris, 1964.

Schretter, Manfred K., *Alter Orient und Hellas: Fragen der Beeinflussung griechischen Gedankengutes aus altorientalischen Quellen, dargestellt an den Göttern Nergal, Rescheph, Apollon*, Institut für Sprachwissenschaft der Universität Innsbruck, H. Kowatsch, Innsbruck, 1974.

Schröder, Joachim, *Ilias und Apollonhymnos*, Verlag Anton Hain, Meisenheim am Glan, 1975.

Seaford, R., ed., *Euripides Cyclops*, Clarendon Press, Oxford, 1984.

Segal, Charles, 'The Homeric Hymn to Aphrodite: A Structuralist Approach', CW 67 (1974) 205–12.

Seux, Marie-Joseph, *Hymnes et prières aux dieux de Babylonie et d'Assyrie*, Les Éditions du Cerf, Paris, 1976.

—— 'La création du monde et de l'homme dans la littérature suméro-akkadienne', in Fabien Blanquart, ed., *La Création dans l'Orient ancien*, Congrès de l'Association Catholique Française pour l'Étude de la Bible, Lille, 1985, Les Éditions du Cerf, Paris, 1987, pp.41–78.

262

Sjöberg, Ake W., 'in-nin šà-gur₄-ra: A Hymn to the Goddess Inanna by the en-Priestess Enheduanna', ZA 65 (1976) 161–253.

Sladek, William R., 'Inanna's Descent to the Netherworld', Ph.D diss., University Microfilms, Ann Arbor, 1974.

Smith, Peter M., 'Notes on the Text of the Fifth Homeric Hymn', HSCP 83 (1979) 29–50.

—— 'Aeneiadai as Patrons of *Iliad* XX and the Homeric *Hymn to Aphrodite*', HSCP 85 (1981) 17–58.

—— *Nursling of Mortality: A Study of the Homeric Hymn to Aphrodite*, Studien zur klassischen Philologie 3, Verlag Peter D. Lang, Bern, 1981.

Snell, B. and Maehler, H., eds., *Pindar Carmina cum Fragmentis*, Part 1, B.G. Teubner, Leipzig.

Snodgrass, A.M., 'An Historical Homeric Society?', JHS 94 (1974) 114–25.

Sollberger, Edmond, 'The Rulers of Lagaš', JCS 21 (1967) 279–86.

Solmsen, Friedrich, 'Zur Theologie im großen Aphrodite-Hymnus', in Friedrich Solmsen, *Kleine Schriften*, vol. 1, Georg Olms Verlagsbuchhandlung, Hildesheim, 1968, pp.55–67.

—— *Hesiodi Theogonia Opera et Dies Scutum*, including R. Merkelbach, and M.L. West, eds, *Fragmenta Selecta*, Clarendon Press, Oxford, 1970.

—— 'The Two Near Eastern Sources of Hesiod', *Hermes* 117 (1989) 413–22.

Sorel, Reynal, 'Finalité et origine des hommes chez Hésiode', RMM 87 (1982) 24–30.

Sourvinou-Inwood, Christiane, 'The Boston Relief of Locri Epizephyrii', JHS 94–5 (1974–5) 126–37.

Sowa, Cora Angier, *Traditional Themes and the Homeric Hymns*, Bolchazy–Carducci Publishers, Chicago, 1984.

Steiner, Gerd, 'Der Gegensatz "Eigenes Land": "Ausland, Fremdland, Feindland" in den Vorstellungen des Alten Orients', in Hartmut Kühne, Hans-Jörg Nissen and Johannes Renger, eds, *Mesopotamien und seine Nachbarn. Politische und kulturelle Wechselbeziehungen im Alten Vorderasien vom 4. bis 1. Jahrtausend v. Chr.: 25. Rencontre Assyriologique Internationale, Berlin, 3. bis 7. Juli 1978*, Berliner Beiträge zum Vorderen Orient, Band 1, Dietrich Reimer Verlag, Berlin, 1982, pp.633–63.

Talon, Philippe, 'Le mythe de la Descente d'Ištar aux Enfers', *Akkadica* 59 (1988) 15–25.

Tigay, Jeffrey H., *The Evolution of the Gilgamesh Epic*, University of Pennsylvania Press, Philadelphia, 1982.

Unte, Wolfhart, *Studien zum homerischen Apollonhymnos*, doctoral diss., Philosophische Facultät der Freien Universität Berlin, A. Wasmund-Bothmann/Höpfner, Berlin, 1968.

Van der Ben, N., 'Hymn to Aphrodite 36–291. Notes on the Pars Epica of the Homeric Hymn to Aphrodite', *Mnemosyne* 39 (1986) 1–41.

Van der Valk, Marchinus, 'On Apollodori *Bibliotheca*', REG 71 (1958) 100–68.

—— 'A Few Observations on the Homeric *Hymn to Apollo*', AC 46 (1977) 441–52.

Van Dijk, J.J., 'Les contacts ethniques dans la Mésopotamie et les syncrétismes de la religion sumérienne', in Sven S. Hartman, ed., *Syncretism*, Almqvist & Wiksell, Stockholm, 1967, pp.171–206.

—— *Lugal ud me-lám-bi nir-ğál: Le récit épique et didactique des Travaux de Ninurta, du Déluge et de la Nouvelle Création*, vol. 1, E.J. Brill, Leiden, 1983.

Van Windekens, A.J., 'Réflexions sur la nature et l'origine du dieu Hermès', *Rheinisches Museum für Philologie* 104 (1961) 289–301.

Verbruggen, H., *Le Zeus crétois*, Collection d'études mythologiques X, Société d'édition «Les belles lettres», Paris, 1981.

Verdenius, W.J., 'A "Hopeless" Line in Hesiod: *Works and Days* 96', *Mnemosyne* 24 (1971) 225–31.

Versnel, H.S., 'Greek Myth and Ritual: The Case of Kronos', in Jan Bremmer, ed., *Interpretations of Greek Mythology*, Croom Helm, London and Sydney, 1987, pp.121–52.

Vogelzang, M.E., *Bin šar dadmē: Edition and Analysis of the Akkadian Anzu Poem*, Styx Publications, Groningen, 1988.

Walcot, Peter, *Hesiod and the Near East*, University of Wales Press, Cardiff, 1966.

—— 'The Homeric *Hymn to Aphrodite*: A Literary Appraisal', G&R 38 (1991) 137–55.

Walker, Christopher B.F., *Cuneiform*, British Museum Press, London, 1987.

Walton, Francis R., 'Athens, Eleusis, and the Homeric Hymn to Demeter', HThR 45 (1952) 105–14.

Wehrli, Fritz, 'Die Mysterien von Eleusis', ArchRW 31 (1934) 77–104.

West, Martin L., 'The Dictaeon Hymn to the Kouros', JHS 85 (1965) 149–59.

—— ed., *Hesiod Theogony*, Clarendon Press, Oxford, 1966.

—— 'Cynaethus' Hymn to Apollo', CQ 25 (1975) 161–70.

—— ed., *Hesiod Works and Days*, Clarendon Press, Oxford, 1978.

—— 'The Prometheus Trilogy', JHS 99 (1979) 130–48.

—— 'Hesiod's Titans', JHS 105 (1985) 174–5.

—— 'The Rise of the Greek Epic', JHS 108 (1988) 151–72.

Wilcke, Claus, 'Politische Opposition nach sumerischen Quellen', in *La Voix de l'opposition en Mesopotamie. Colloque organisé par l'Institut des Hautes Études de Belgique, 19 et 20 mars 1973*, Institut des Hautes Études de Belgique, Bruxelles, 1975, pp.37–65.

—— 'König Šulgis Himmelfahrt', in *Festschrift László Vajda*, Münchner Beiträge zur Völkerkunde, Band 1, Hirmer Verlag, Munich, 1988, pp.-245–55.

Will, Ernest, 'Le rituel des Adonies', *Syria* 52 (1975) 93–105.

Xella, Paolo, 'L'influence babylonienne à Ougarit, d'après les textes alphabétiques rituels et divinatoires', in Hartmut Kühne, Hans-Jörg Nissen and Johannes Renger, eds, *Mesopotamien und seine Nachbarn. Politische und kulturelle Wechselbeziehungen im Alten Vorderasien vom 4. bis 1. Jahrtausend v. Chr.: 25. Rencontre Assyriologique Internationale, Berlin, 3. bis 7. Juli 1978*, Berliner Beiträge zum Vorderen Orient, Band 1, Dietrich Reimer Verlag, Berlin, 1982, pp.321–38.

INDEX

radiance 53, 55, 98–9, 102, 110, 112, 174–5, 186–8, 231–3; of king 215
rape of Persephone 156
rebel 219, 221, 225; Enki 220; Prometheus 220
rebellion 219, 221, 223, 225
rebirth 80
return 36, 43, 54, 58, 62, 64, 90–3, 101, 108–9, 112, 131, 135, 243; of Apollo 107; of Damu 31; of Ninurta 108–10; of souls 85
returning child of plenty 134
Rhea 130, 180, 186–7
Richardson, Nicholas 133
rise 30, 37, 45–6; see also ascent
rite at Onchestos 107
river 29, 35, 38, 104, 106, 135; 'man-devouring' 40
River Ocean 129
Ruhnken 116
rulership 58

sacred marriage 30, 47, 91, 113, 166, 170, 176; kings perform 47
sacrifice 129, 219, 222–3
Sappho 178
Sargon 15, 45
scream 141, 145; great supernatural scream 141
sea 108–9, 112, 166–7, 190, 231
Sea 129
sea dykes 195–6
search 82, 92, 95, 131, 133, 141, 145, 150; of Isis 150
Seasons, see also Horai
separation of Heaven and Earth 166, 168, 206
serpent of Pytho 98, 103–5, 195
Seth 151
sexual encounter 39, 42
Shakan 24
Shamash 68; see also Utu
Shara 18, 23, 53
Sharur 19, 53, 65, 67, 194
shield: of Athena 236; of Kouretes 234
Shulgi 60
Sicily 191

sickle, adamantine 192
Sîn 27, 39, 40; see also Nanna-Suen
sinews 193
SIR.SIR epithet 104, 195
sister 32–4, 37, 39, 94, 131, 134, 144, 150
Sjöberg, Ake 45
Sladek, William 24, 25, 29
Slain Heroes 56, 59
Smith, P. 172
Smyrna 178
snare, Pandora 201, 208
snow, golden 231
sociological approach 10
son of Iapetos (Prometheus) 200
soul 225–6
Sowa, Cora Angier 120, 122–3
spirit, in man 217
spring 30, 130, 135
SRT 31 47
statue of the god 25; of Athena 94
stone of Kronos 186
stones become mankind 227
storm god 195
storm-chariot 194
Strabo 163
stream 98, 106, 112
strike of Demeter 150
STVC 34 51, 62, 64, 100; see also Ninurta's Journey to Eridu
Styx 78, 140
substitute 18, 21–3, 28, 38–40, 61, 80, 143–4, 152–3
substitution 22, 30, 37, 40, 86, 131, 139, 143
succession myth 2, 240
Sultantepe 51, 54
Sumer 26, 49, 52, 65–6, 80, 89, 93
Sumerian language 12–14
sun 65–6, 85, 89, 110, 120, 134
sun god 153–4; Apollo 88
sunrise 88–9
supreme god 1, 51, 56, 58, 73, 76, 90, 96, 100, 102, 111–12, 119, 155, 189, 219–20, 224, 240; antagonistic 224; rebellion against 221; Zeus 102, 155
supreme power 103, 190
Susa 52